Good Housekeeping™

BEST RECIPES

Plus kitchen tools, techniques & tips

1998

Good Housekeeping™

BEST RECIPES

Plus kitchen tools, techniques & tips

1998

Time Inc.
HOME ENTERTAINMENT

The Hearst Corporation

Good Housekeeping™ BEST RECIPES 1998

GOOD HOUSEKEEPING

Editor in Chief:	Ellen Levine
Food Director:	Susan Westmoreland
Associate Food Director:	Susan Deborah Goldsmith
Food Associates:	Lisa Brainerd, Marianne Marinelli, Lori Perlmutter, Mary Ann Svec, Lisa Troland
Nutrition Director:	Delia Hammock
Food Appliances Director:	Sharon Franke
Hearst Brand Development:	Fran Reilly

TIME INC. HOME ENTERTAINMENT

Managing Director:	David Gitow
Director, Continuities and Single Sales:	David Arfine
Director, Continuities and Retention:	Michael Barrett
Director, New Products:	Alicia Longobardo
Product Managers:	Chris Berzolla, Robert Fox, Stacy Hirschberg, Michael Holahan, Amy Jacobsson, Jennifer McLyman, Daniel Melore
Manager, Retail and New Markets:	Tom Mifsud
Associate Product Managers:	Louisa Bartle, Alison Ehrmann, Nancy London, Dawn Weland
Assistant Product Managers:	Meredith Shelley, Betty Su
Editorial Operations Manager:	John Calvano
Fulfillment Director:	Michelle Gudema
Financial Director:	Tricia Griffin
Assistant Financial Manager:	Amy Maselli
Marketing Assistant:	Sarah Holmes

CONSUMER MARKETING DIVISION

Production Director:	John E. Tighe
Book Production Manager:	Donna Miano-Ferrara
Assistant Book Production Manager:	Jessica McGrath

GOOD HOUSEKEEPING BEST RECIPES 1998
Produced by Rebus, Inc.
New York, NY

Contents

WELCOME TO GOOD HOUSEKEEPING'S annual recipe anthology, *Best Recipes 1998*. Not merely a year's worth of delicious recipes—from festive holiday food to easy weeknight dishes—*Best Recipes* is also packed with all the hints, tips, and techniques that you've come to expect from us. In the *Good Housekeeping* kitchens, we not only develop and triple-test dozens of new recipes each month, but we take our service to our readers to the next level. For example, when we developed the roast chicken recipes that appear in this volume, in addition to looking for the most interesting flavor combinations (try Apple & Thyme Chicken on page 52, or Asian Sesame Chicken on page 54), we also researched the best chickens to buy, the best roasting pans to use, and the preparation and roasting techniques that would guarantee perfect results each time.

One of the things that allows us to provide this in-depth information—and that makes us, and this book, special—is our access to all the other departments in the Good Housekeeping Institute. With the Institute's expertise, and extensive laboratory and product-testing facilities, we can do everything from testing the best knife for slicing tomatoes (see "News & Notes," page 15), to measuring the fat content of meat loaves cooked in three different styles of pans (see "Does a Drip Pan Cut the Fat?" on page 71), to settling once and for all the thorny question of when and how much to salt the pasta cooking water (see "Should You Salt the Water?" on page 106). Much of this research has been collected in the special "News & Notes" section on the following pages, where you will find nutrition and product news, as well as some of our most recent Buyer's Guides for food processors, bread machines, and toaster ovens.

We are proud of this book, and we hope that you will all derive as much satisfaction from using this collection of *Good Housekeeping* recipes and kitchen wisdom as we did in creating it for you.

Good Housekeeping's food editors pictured above (left to right): Lisa Troland, associate; Susan Westmoreland, director; Debby Goldsmith, associate director; Lisa Brainerd, associate; Marianne Marinelli, associate; Mary Ann Svec, associate. (Not pictured: Lori Perlmutter, associate.)

WHAT'S THE TOP ICE-CREAM SCOOP?

To find out which tool makes ice-cream serving easiest—and turns out showcase scoops for sugar cones or pie slices —32 GH staffers worked their way through gallons of Breyer's ice cream with 8 different types of scoops, then ranked them on their ability to dip in and release.

• The winner: Oxo's Good Grips (pictured above) with a cushioned rubber handle and a lever you press to release an evenly rounded scoop; at specialty stores. For information: 800-545-4411.

• First runner-up: Amco's gimmick-free stainless-steel scoop singled out for its "comfy contoured handle;" at specialty stores. For information: 800-621-4023.

• Second runner-up: The chunky Zerolon from Harold's Kitchen with a nonstick finish. From Fante; for information: 800-44-fante.

• For Special Occasions: Food Appliances Director Sharon Franke gave top billing to the Oxo Good Grips "beaked" scoop. Made from durable cast aluminum with a thick neck, its pointed spoon makes it simple to dish out ice cream fast—a plus at a big birthday party; at specialty stores. For information: 800-545-4411.

WHY YOU NEED MORE FOLIC ACID

Folate-enriched bread, flour, rice, pasta, and cornmeal began appearing in stores last year, thanks to a federal mandate. The essential B vitamin (also known as folic acid) will be added to certain grain products to help women of childbearing age get the 400 micrograms (mcg) recommended daily to reduce the risk of certain birth defects. (Women ages 19 to 50 get about half that amount now.) The regulation could benefit men and older women, too, since there's some evidence that adequate folate consumption may lower the risk of heart disease in certain individuals. But the fortified products alone may not be enough, because the mandate applies only to products that are enriched, which may not include your favorite brands. (Look for the word enriched on ingredient lists.) Plus, most fortified foods contain only a moderate amount of folate—about 40 to 100 mcg per serving. To make sure you meet the mark, include dark green, leafy vegetables, asparagus, legumes, fortified ready-to-eat cereals, and orange juice in your daily diet—or take a multivitamin with folic acid, or a folic acid supplement.

HONEY OF AN IDEA

Processed ham and turkey with a hint of honey are crowding the shelves in delis and supermarkets nationwide, with more than 85 varieties to choose from. But the honey adds more than country flavor: Research suggests it may also help prevent off-flavors, retain moisture, and keep bacterial levels down. This makes honey a perfect partner for low-fat meats, which typically have a shorter shelf life (and less natural flavor) than full-fat varieties. More sweet news: Honeyed meats have about the same calories as their plain counterparts.

IS "IMPROVED" SKIM REALLY BETTER?

Some people would never dream of switching to fat-free (formerly called skim) milk; they find it thin and watery, with an unappealing bluish color. But the dairy industry has been trying hard to make nonfat milk appealing, first with protein-fortified skim (nonfat milk solids are

added for a whiter color, richer taste, and a little more protein and calcium), and now with skim milk enriched with milk solids and an oat-based fat alternative called Replace. Manufactured by Golden Jersey Products, Replace contains beta glucan, a fiber shown to lower cholesterol. Plain and chocolate milks with Replace were introduced in both West and East Coast markets in late 1996.

But do the new milks, which cost up to 20 percent more than regular fat-free, deliver on taste? When *Good Housekeeping* staffers ranked protein-fortified, Replace-enriched, and regular skim milk in a blind test, regular skim was the favorite—with skim-milk fans and those who usually drink 1- or 2-percent milk. Some tasters liked the full-bodied flavor and appearance of milk with Replace, but others said it "tasted funny, not like regular milk." And many detected a powdered-milk flavor in the protein-fortified kind.

TRUTH IN MENUS

Many restaurants—from pricey bistros to pancake houses—flag certain dishes on their menus as heart-healthy, low-fat, or low-calorie. But until now, restaurants haven't been held accountable for their claims. The Food and Drug Administration changed that with a regulation that now requires restaurateurs (as of May 2, 1997) to substantiate health claims on menus. This means that if a menu calls a dish low-fat, the kitchen must have nutrition information to back it up—so don't hesitate to ask.

GREAT GRAVY: OUR FAVORITE WAY TO SKIM THE FAT

Defatting gravy or soup needn't be a chore: The Souper Strain (not shown) from East Hampton Industries is a 4-cup plastic pitcher with a special spout near the bottom, so that when you pour, the good stuff comes out and the fat layer, on top, doesn't. For skimming soups (too much for a 4-cup pitcher), the stainless-steel Strainer Ladle (pictured above) from Progressive International is easy to use; the lip is perforated on one side to collect the fat. Both are available at Lechter's and other houseware stores.

SMART SOLUTION: A GRATER THAT CATCHES THE CHEESE (pictured below)

A new dispenser makes the classic Zyliss grater even handier. It fits onto the side of the grater so that as you turn the crank, the grated cheese (or chocolate or nuts) falls into the container. With ¼-cup, ½-cup, and ounce marks, it eliminates a time-consuming step

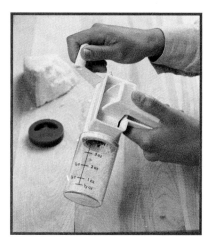

when you need to measure ingredients for a recipe. And if you want to take the shaker to the table (to sprinkle Parmesan on pizza or chocolate shavings on coffee), there is a large-holed, snap-on lid. Order the grater and/or container from Kitchen Kapers, 800-455-5567.

WILL UNFINISHED WINE KEEP?

The most common myth about wine is that it begins to "turn" soon after it's opened. We found otherwise. In a blind wine tasting, we sampled 3 bottles of identical mid-priced red Cabernet Sauvignon—one opened 48 hours before tasting, one 24 hours before, and one just before. We didn't detect any dropoff in quality at all; in fact, most of us preferred the day-old wine. The reason? According to the California-based Wine Market Council, if you drink a glassful or more from a bottle, allowing the remaining vino to stand gives it a chance to aerate, which helps release its flavors and bouquet. Store leftover wine (at the temperature it's served—white, chilled, and red, at room temperature) for up to 48 hours with the original cork.

A MILK SHAKE-UP

Have you been using 2-percent low-fat milk in your breakfast cereal or coffee because it's a skinny gulp? Think again. At 5 grams of fat per cup, the beverage doesn't comply with the current Food and Drug Administration definition of a low-fat product: 3 grams of fat or less per serving. So this milk has been renamed "reduced-fat," since it does contain 25 percent less fat than

Food Processors

Food Processors Packed with helpful features, these 6 cutting-edge machines (culled from a field of 19), are kitchen essentials. The full-size models range in price from under $100 to over $300 and have a capacity of 10 to 11 cups. The compact models hold 2 to 3 cups and are comparably priced (under $50). The models below are listed from least to most expensive.

Whether you're trying to put a family meal on the table in less than 20 minutes or prepare for a dinner party, food processors sharply reduce kitchen time. Full-size models are the most versatile; they can crumble bread, grind meat, and grate cheese. And they can hold enough liquid to make pureed soup or all the ingredients to mix and knead bread dough. But if you're just looking for a processor to do small jobs, like chop a vegetable or two, choose a compact model.

How We Chose

We had our 19 models (full-size and compact) mince garlic, chop carrots, slice pepperoni, shred cheeses, cut French fries, grind almonds, whip cream, and mix bread and pie doughs. We looked for even, consistent results without overprocessing. We also evaluated each machine for ease of use and the manuals for clarity. Our engineers verified that electrical specifications met safety standards, checked for solid construction, and measured noise levels during operation.

FULL-SIZE MODELS

BLACK & DECKER PowerPro: Compared to most models, the bowl detaches easily from the base. Has a touch-control pad and a manual that includes a quick-reference chart of techniques to use for processing everything from apples to turnips. Also offers high performance for a low price.

KRUPS MasterPro Deluxe: Great results and mix of features at a reasonable cost. Because its height is lower than most, it's ideal for storing under cabinets. Soup cooks will love its large liquid capacity, but bakers may find the whipping disc works no better than the all-purpose blade.

KITCHENAID Ultra Power: Built to last and go about its business quietly. Does double duty—a small bowl fits inside the larger one, turning it into a mini chopper.

Manual is packed with recipes. Accessory storage box included. Available in blue, white, black, or green.

CUISINART Pro Custom 11: Powerful enough to knead dough for two big loaves, yet excels at small tasks. Less noisy than most, and has an extralong warranty (5 years on the motor, 3 years on other parts). Adjustable feed tube can handle plump or slim veggies, but is complicated to use.

COMPACT MODELS

SUNBEAM Oskar: Thanks to a continuous feed chute, this model can slice or shred as much as its bigger cousins. It's a whiz at chopping and mincing, providing perfect results every time. But because it leaks when pureeing, stick to a blender for soups and sauces. Of all our picks, it's the noisiest. Capacity: 3 cups

CUISINART Mini-Prep: Also functions as a coffee or spice grinder, unlike others. This space saver is ideal for chopping just one onion or grating cheese to sprinkle on pasta. Capacity: 2½ cups

WHAT PROCESSORS CAN'T DO

If you're whipping up drinks with crushed ice or prefer soups with a supersmooth texture, use a blender. Bakers should stick to a mixer for light-textured cakes, airy whipped cream and meringues, and any large quantities of dough. And because mashed potatoes can quickly turn gluey in a processor, they're best left to a handheld masher or mixer.

whole milk (with 8.5 grams per cup). Other changes in store:

• 1-percent milk (which delivers 2.5 grams of fat per cup) may now be dubbed "light," because it has less than half the fat of whole milk.

• Skim milk can be touted as fat-free.

COLD, HARD FACTS ABOUT ICE PACKS

To find out which freezer pack is the ice queen, we tracked the performance of a milk carton filled with water and frozen, a hard pack with ice substitute (a non-toxic gel that stays frozen longer than ice), a plastic container designed to be filled with water and frozen, plain old ice cubes, and a soft pack with ice substitute —each was placed in an identical insulated cooler. What we found:

If you pack an ice chest full of food and drinks, and it remains closed until mealtime, any of the five methods keeps the contents well chilled. The choice has more to do with what you consider the most convenient option.

One exception: On a very long drive (2 hours or more), or at all-day picnics, when you'll be grabbing drinks or snacks before the main meal, packs filled with ice substitute or the milk-carton ice block are better than using a comparable amount of ice cubes or a plastic container of water, both of which melt down faster.

More Tips on the Cool Crowd:

• Packs with ice substitute can last for years if handled carefully. The possible damage: Puncture the surface, and contents will leak; set it on a hot stove, and the pack will melt. Refillable plastic containers

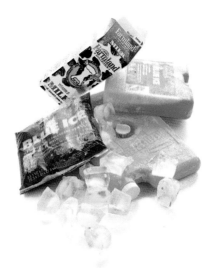

from Rubbermaid and Igloo come in 1-cup to 2.8-quart sizes.

• Prefer to make your own ice pack? Rinse and fill a milk carton with water, leaving 1-inch headroom to prevent bursting. Once frozen, tape top closed to avoid leaks.

• For optimum chilling, we suggest using 2 medium-size ice packs for a standard size cooler; 4 for a larger one.

• If you have a well-insulated ice chest, the contents should stay cool in a hot car trunk during short (1- to 2-hour) trips. For longer ones, keep the cooler up front with the air conditioning on.

THE BIG SQUEEZE: TESTING JUICE MACHINES

No matter how pricey, store-bought juice never tastes quite as good as fresh-squeezed. To find out which automatic citrus juicers deliver the biggest glassfuls with the least fuss, we ran oranges, grapefruits, and lemons through four models. To our surprise, all juicers evaluated yielded a comparable amount of juice—about ½ cup per orange, and 1 cup per grapefruit—and were comparably

priced at under $40. But each machine had distinctive features that might sway your purchase decision. The juicy scoop (listed from least to most expensive):

• Braun Citromatic Deluxe requires the least pressure to operate and has the widest cone—the best fit for a grapefruit half. But it doesn't come with a pitcher and dispenses juice straight into a glass, so it's less handy for company.

• Oster Citrus Juicer spurts juice into a glass or 14-ounce pitcher. It's tall, though; be sure you have the space for it.

• Black & Decker's Handy-Juicer features the largest pitcher—28 ounces. But it lets more pulp slip in than others.

• Krups Pressa Maxi has a cone that adjusts for more or less pulp, and a 24-ounce pitcher. It lacks a cover, though, and the cone can collect dust.

The Old-Fashioned Way

We also tested an old-fashioned juicer (pictured above) to see if there was really any reason to go modern here, and we found that a traditional hand-operated juice press yielded a bit less juice than the electrics and required more strength (evaluators' hands and wrists ached). There was a payoff, however: Juices tasted sweeter

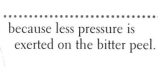

because less pressure is exerted on the bitter peel.

TASTE-TESTING CALCIUM-FORTIFIED JUICES

Ounce for ounce, orange juice with calcium contains as much of the essential bone builder as milk does, delivering about 30 percent of a woman's daily requirement per cup. But does the more nutritious juice squeeze out taste? We asked 50 *Good Housekeeping* staffers to sip regular and calcium-fortified versions of 4 brands sold in cartons: 2 from concentrate (Minute Maid and Tropicana Season's Best) and 2 not from concentrate (Tropicana Pure Premium Plus and D'Agostino, a New York brand).

The results: At least 75 percent of tasters detected subtle differences between the calcium-added and regular kind. When there was a definite preference, calcium-fortified products often came out on top; many tasters found them less acidic and sweeter. Yet in the end, most panelists reported they'd be happy with either juice. Flavor does vary among brands, so if your family doesn't like one type, try another.

NEW REASONS TO GET YOUR VITAMIN C

You probably know that citrus fruits are prime sources of vitamin C—1 orange delivers 120 percent of your daily require-

ment, a grapefruit half, 80 percent. Each also provides about 20 percent of a day's fiber quota. But that's not all these mighty fruits do. Recent research reveals they're also full of compounds (not yet found in pills) called phytochemicals that may help ward off cancer and possibly other diseases. Limonoids—phytochemicals found in citrus oil, peel, and juice—have been shown to inhibit the development of lung and skin tumors in lab animals, and stimulate the production of enzymes that can help the body fight cancer-causing agents. Flavonoids, other citrus phytochemicals, may help impede the growth of breast-cancer cells, according to studies conducted at the University of Western Ontario. Many of these plant compounds also double as antioxidants, which defuse dangerous molecules called free radicals that can damage your body's cells and tissues and may lead to cancer and cardiovascular disease.

SMART SOLUTION: BBQ TOOLS SIZED TO BE SAFE & STORABLE
(pictured at right)

When you barbecue, you want to keep a safe distance from the flames. And the long handles of Ekco's Collapsible Barbecue Tools (basting brush, fork, spatula, and tongs) extend and retract, so the 15- to 18-inch-long utensils can fit in a drawer or be used for serving or indoor cooking too. Dishwasher safe; comes as a set (fork, spatula, and tongs) and as individual tools. At mass merchandisers; call 800-367-3526 for stores near you.

FISH STORY: WHEN "WATER PACKED" IS MISLEADING

If you automatically choose tuna that's water-packed rather than oil-packed to save fat and calories, check the label next time. We found that although canned solid white tuna in oil is generally consistent—with about 3 grams of fat and 90 calories per 2-ounce serving—water-packed solid white tuna had 1, 4, or 5 fat grams and from 60 to 100 calories per serving. The numbers even differed on cans of the same brands. Why? Because of the tuna used. By federal law, only albacore can be labeled "white," but the fat and calorie content of this species varies by region and the water depth where the fish were caught. Companies are aware of these differences but since the demand for water-packed white is greater than the supply, they use both lower-fat and higher-fat albacore and change nutrition labels accordingly.

"Light" tuna, on the other hand, is made from more abundant species, and nutritional data is less varied—chunk light in water has about .5 fat gram, 60

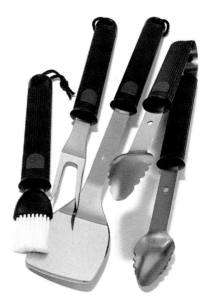

Bread Machines

With the push of a button, these 7 bread machines (chosen from a field of 20) will bake beautiful, tasty loaves— even while you sleep. They range in price from under $150 to over $200, but these are manufacturers' suggested retail prices; most stores mark them down by as much as 30 percent, so shop around. Though some machines will make small loaves (1 pound) and some large loaves (2 pounds), the majority make a standard 1½-pound loaf. (The models below are listed from least to most expensive.)

When bread machines were introduced 10 years ago, they were considered an expensive novelty. Since then, prices have fallen, and many people have come to love their convenience, with the time-consuming tasks of mixing, kneading, rising, punching, shaping, and baking all performed automatically. The machines can be programmed to bake overnight or while you're at work. The latest models make a variety of bread and offer settings for choosing crust color or speeding up the process (sometimes to a mere 2 hours). Most beep to let you know when to add extras, such as raisins, nuts, and chocolate chips, so they're evenly distributed. And you can count on the best ones, like those reviewed here, to make loaves that rise every time.

How We Chose

We examined 20 models for performance and ease of use. Using every setting, we baked white, whole wheat, raisin, and specialty breads from the manufacturers' recipes, packaged mixes, and cookbooks. Breads were tested for taste and appearance. Then our engineers checked the machines' construction, verified that electrical specifications met safety standards, and monitored interior temperatures. We also scrutinized the manuals; they provide information and recipes that can make the difference between baking success and failure.

WEST BEND: This one has few frills, but you can depend on it for good results. Includes bread mix for your first loaf. Plus, lid comes off for easy cleaning.

REGAL: Thanks to a thorough manual, easy-to-program controls, and even a free video, this model is very user-friendly. We didn't like the manufacturer's whole wheat recipes, but baked delicious loaves using cookbooks.

HITACHI: A large pan gives loaves eye-pleasing height. Plus, the manual includes lots of recipes. But forget the cake setting: You'll get better results from the oven.

BETTY CROCKER: This has the most settings, for more control. You can set the timer so it starts baking up to almost 16 hours later (about 3 hours more than other models). And unlike most, this one makes excellent quick bread. It also makes a traditional horizontal loaf instead of a tall rectangular one.

SANYO: This produces great-tasting bread from superior recipes, even on the fast setting, and doubles as a pasta maker. Not for small families—makes only extra-large loaves (in a traditional horizontal shape). Removable lid for quick cleaning.

OSTER: Thick, chewy crust is this model's specialty, thanks to a heavy aluminum pan. It has a particularly helpful instruction manual with large print. Also comes with bread mix to start you off.

PANASONIC: This was the editor's pick: Every loaf was a winner, though they take longer to bake. Kids will love the soft, fluffy sandwich slices; the loaf is horizontal. Cast-aluminum pan makes a crisp crust.

ANY WAY YOU SLICE IT

Though some new machines produce classic horizontal loaves, most bake tall rectangular ones that are unwieldy to cut unless laid on their side. Even then, you won't get familiar-looking slices with curved tops, but ones that are square and slightly smaller. Rest assured, whatever the shape, the taste remains the same.

Toss It Out or Keep It? *A Guide to Food Storage*

Just how long has that box of bread crumbs been in your pantry? Certainly months—possibly years. It looks fine—sniff—smells fine, but is it fresh enough to eat? Here, a guide to the best way to store some common pantry items and how long you can expect them to remain fresh.

PRODUCT	WHERE/HOW TO STORE	HOW LONG?	COMMENTS
All-purpose flour	unopened/opened: airtight container in cool, dry place (pantry or cupboard); refrigerator; or freezer	cool, dry place: 10 to 15 months refrigerated: 1½ to 2 years in freezer: indefinitely	Heat and moisture accelerate staleness. So, when weather is hot or humid, keep in freezer.
Whole-wheat flour	unopened/opened: airtight container in cool, dry place; refrigerator; or freezer	cool, dry place: 3 months refrigerated: 6 months in freezer: 9 months	Contains oil from bran layer that quickly becomes rancid at room temperature.
Soy sauce	unopened: room temperature opened: refrigerator	1 year	Can use for up to three years, but evaporation may darken the color and intensify the flavor.
Honey	unopened/opened: room temperature	indefinitely	If honey has crystallized, place jar in pan of simmering water, stirring, until crystals dissolve.
Hot pepper sauce	unopened/opened: room temperature; can refrigerate but not necessary	indefinitely; after 5 years color darkens	Jalapeño version has a shorter life span; keep 12 to 18 months unopened and 6 months opened.
Pancake syrup	unopened/opened: room temperature; can refrigerate but not necessary	9 months	After 9 months flavor weakens and syrup thins.
Worcestershire	unopened/opened: room temperature	12 years	Tastes better with age because liquid evaporates and flavor intensifies.
Salsa	unopened: room temperature opened: refrigerator	unopened: 1 year opened: 2 weeks	To prevent contamination, don't dip food into the jar; spoon from jar to serve.
White rice	unopened/opened: airtight container in cool, dry place or freezer	cool, dry place: indefinitely in freezer: indefinitely	Avoid bulk containers of rice, which may be contaminated.
Spices	unopened/opened: airtight container in cool, dark place red spices, poppy, and sesame seeds: refrigerate	1 year	Don't store over oven or range. Heat or long-term storage can cause loss of color and weakening of aroma, both signs of decreased potency.
Mayonnaise	unopened: cool, dark place opened: refrigerator	indefinitely but flavor will slowly diminish	In refrigerator, store on door; the oil may separate if stored in colder parts of the refrigerator.
Peanut butter	unopened/opened: cool place; can refrigerate but not necessary	1 year	Gets rancid when exposed to air or heat. To determine if it's still fresh past the expiration date, smell and taste.
Bread crumbs	unopened/opened: cool, dry place or refrigerator	cool, dry place: 3 to 6 months refrigerated: 2 years	To keep flavor fresh, refrigerate after opening.
Potatoes	cool, dark place; do not refrigerate: flavor will change	1 month	Do not store with onions; may pick up onion flavor. Don't wash before storing; dampness can cause decay. Near heat and light, potatoes turn green, develop a bitter flavor, their skins shrink, and they last only a week.
Onions	cool, dry, well-ventilated place, such as a basket, away from direct sunlight	1 to 4 weeks	Store cut onions in plastic bags in refrigerator. If an onion has a strong odor before peeling, it may have a rotten inner layer.
Vegetable oil	unopened/opened: cool, dark place or refrigerator	cool, dark place: 3 months refrigerated: 6 months	Refrigerated oil shouldn't be left out; frequent temperature changes aren't good for it.
Olive oil	unopened/opened: cool, dark place	18 months	Do not refrigerate; olive oil solidifies when cold.
Vinegar	unopened/opened: cool, dark place	unopened: indefinitely opened: 6 months	Vinegar with added ingredients such as berries and herbs should be strained into a clean bottle when vinegar level drops below ingredients.

calories per serving. Because it's in chunks—which absorb more oil—values for chunk light in oil (about 6 fat grams, 110 calories) are higher than solid tuna in oil.

CUTTING THE FAT IN CANNED FOOD
Canned favorites made with meat—including beef stew, chili, and tamales in gravy—are often packed with fat (some brands contain as much as 30 grams per cup). But our chemistry department found that by spooning off the visible excess fat before heating, you can slash fat content by 5 to 19 grams per serving—a 30- to 69-percent reduction! Better yet, we preferred the taste of the "skimmed" stew, chili, and tamales—they were less greasy, more flavorful. To trim even more fat, and calories, refrigerate the cans until cold, so the fat will be easier to remove.

TOUGH NEW TUPPERWARE
From the people who made food storage a party topic: Rock 'N Serve freezer-to-microwave containers made of Lexan—a super-strong, stain-resistant plastic—with lids that have special valves you "rock" open to safely vent steam. In assorted sizes, from a 1-cup container to a 6-piece set of various sizes. For information, call 800-858-7221.

THE BEST TOMATO SLICER
(pictured above)
The ideal knife for slicing tomatoes is so sharp it pierces the skin easily, then glides through the interior without squashing out the juices. If you don't keep a razor's edge on your regular knife blades, a serrated knife that never needs

honing is a better bet. Faced with ripe tomatoes and a few different knives, our panel of 18 Good Housekeeping food experts gave this task-specific Tomato Knife from Wüsthof high marks for feel and performance. It has a forked tip for lifting juicy slices and is handmade of high-carbon stainless steel. Designed to last; at cookware and specialty stores.

CALCIUM SUPPLEMENTS: ARE THEY DANGEROUS?
You may be wondering whether the recent scare over lead-contaminated calcium tablets applies to your brand. First, it's important to put the problem in context: Trace amounts of lead are unavoidable. They're everywhere—in the air, water, and food. The controversy is whether the federal standard—which allows 7.5 micrograms (mcg) of lead per 1,000 milligrams (mg) of calcium in supplements—is safe.

Many experts, like Robert Lindsay, M.D., Ph.D., president of the National Osteoporosis Foundation, say yes. But even though the Food and Drug Administration suggests these standards, they do not mandate them. Still, a recent study of 26 calcium supplement brands

found that all but one were within the guidelines; Source Naturals Calcium Night, made by a small California company, had almost triple the amount (20.75 mcg).

Most major brands, including Tums, Os-Cal, Caltrate, Citracal, Nature Made, and those with USP (U.S. Pharmacopoeia) on the label, meet the federal limit. And only a fraction of the lead actually reaches the bloodstream anyway, because calcium strongly inhibits lead absorption. Remember: There's a link between calcium deficiency and osteoporosis, so don't give up supplements if they help you meet your daily calcium quota (1,000 to 1,500 mg). And look for virtually lead-free brands in the future.

TIMESAVING POTS & PANS
(pictured below)
The right tools can make it much easier to get dinner on the table fast. Solutions, Revere's new line of stainless-steel cookware, streamlines meal-making with double spouts for easy draining, and strainers built into the saucepan covers so you don't need a separate colander. The saucepans are really convenient for mashed potatoes: Just cook, drain, and mash spuds all in one pot. Other features we like: heavy, perfectly flat bottoms that spread

Toaster Ovens

Toaster Ovens The newest ones are so versatile, they can work from morning (toasting the fattest bagel) till night (cooking a hearty meat loaf, baking a cake, even roasting a chicken to golden perfection). The 6 models that made the cut (from a field of 15) range in price from $60 to $160; they are listed from least to most expensive.

Toaster ovens are getting better (and sometimes bigger), crowding out other appliances for prime counter space. They're indispensable for toasting bagels, rolls, or muffins, making melted cheese sandwiches, and warming cold pizza. The best models also cook as evenly as a full-size oven, baking cookies and potatoes, and broiling burgers and chicken parts. Streamlined and self-contained, they're easier to manage and keep clean than a regular oven and won't heat up the whole kitchen. How do they toast? They take a little longer than a toaster, and the bottom of the bread, which rests on a rack, emerges with a few stripes. But our favorite brands can do 4 to 6 bread slices at a time, and reliably turn out good hot toast that's worth the wait.

How We Chose

We put 15 models to the task, toasting white bread at light, medium, and dark settings, and checking for even color, range of shades, and consistency slice after slice. We checked keep-warm settings by placing hot macaroni and cheese in the oven for one hour, and defrost settings by thawing one pound of ground beef. To monitor evenness and speed of cooking, we baked refrigerator biscuits and sugar cookies, potatoes, meat loaf, and frozen pizza, and broiled chicken breasts. In larger ovens, we baked layers cakes and roasted whole chickens. Our engineers checked that electrical specifications met safety standards and measured oven and exterior-surface temperatures on every model.

RIVAL TOASTER OVEN/BROILER: Best buy—this compact model has few frills but what it does, it does well, and it sells for a great price. We cooked a perfect meat loaf in its extra-sturdy baking pan.

BLACK & DECKER TOAST-R-OVEN/BROILER: This was the best for making toast, because it browns as quickly as a toaster and bakes evenly. It's the smallest model reviewed, with the least cooking space.

TOASTMASTER TOASTER-OVEN-BROILER: Cool to the touch—a good choice if you have small children, because unlike the other ovens here, the plastic sides and top don't heat up. It's roomy enough to bake an 8-inch round cake but can't hold a whole chicken.

MUNSEY OVEN PLUS: With its large capacity, it can accommodate a 9-inch pizza or a 4½-pound chicken. A good buy if you need a second oven. (Warning: The knobs get very hot during baking, so use a pot holder and supervise children carefully.)

KRUPS PROCHEF TOASTER/BROILER OVEN: This was the editor's pick. It has lots of user-friendly features and bakes as well as a full-size oven. With its sturdy construction, we think it's worth the money. It can hold a 9-inch cake or pie pan or a 3-pound chicken.

DELONGHI AIR STREAM CONVECTION OVEN: Here's the deluxe model—with a convection fan and 2 racks, this bakes and browns beautifully. It can make 2 sheets of cookies at once (and comes packaged with cookie sheets to fit the oven) or roast a 3½-pound chicken.

Takes longer to toast than others shown (6 minutes for 6 slices). It also has a dehydrator setting and a defrost setting.

FOR TOP PERFORMANCE

• When baking, preheat (5 to 10 minutes is enough) • Allow about 1½ inches of space between baking dishes and oven walls so air can circulate • To prevent heat loss, open the oven door as little as possible while cooking • Wipe spatters after each use so they don't bake on • Empty crumb tray regularly • Safety note: If you defrost meat or poultry in the toaster oven, be sure to cook it immediately after thawing.

heat evenly, and steam vents you can open and close. At department stores.

DAILY GRIND: PICK OF THE PEPPER MILLS

There's nothing to compare with adding fresh pepper at the table. But mills aren't cheap, and there are dozens out there, from imported wooden to battery-operated. To find the king of them all, we tried 29, from 18 manufacturers. In each, on fine, medium, and coarse settings, we ground about ½ teaspoon of pepper and then sieved it, to see if granules were uniform and whether there was a distinct difference between settings. We noted the convenience of filling and using, timed the grinding process, and had our engineers check for sound construction.

The Winner:

The sleek 10-inch Unicorn Magnum Plus was superior on every count. It has an easy-to-adjust mechanism in the base that gives the most distinct grinds, from superfine to coarsely cracked. It's fast, too, producing ½ teaspoon of pepper in 5 seconds, and the barrel holds a cup of peppercorns—twice as much as any other candidate. If you love fresh pepper, this is for you. To order, call Tom David, Inc. (800-634-8881).

Other Top Choices:

• Imperial: A close runner-up, this tall (10-inch) wooden mill is well-made and good-looking. (To adjust grind, for this and following two models, turn the finial on top.) Available in natural maple,

ebony, and walnut finishes. For a store near you, call Chef Specialties Co. (800-440-2433).

• Zassenhaus: This 7½-inch European mill is a good choice if you prefer a crank—either for old-fashioned appeal or ease. If you have arthritis, it's convenient because you can operate it with a flat palm. To order, call Penzeys, Ltd. (414-574-0277).

• Sunrise: The 5½-inch acrylic mill (pictured at left) adds a dash of cheer to the table, and a burst of flavor to food. From Olde Thompson; call 800-827-1565 for a store near you.

CHOLESTEROL WATCH: SHOULD YOU SKIP THE SHRIMP?

Shrimp are very low-fat (11 large ones, or 3.5 ounces, contain just 1 gram of fat), yet they're often omitted from heart-healthy diets because the same light bites pack a hefty 195 milligrams (mg) of cholesterol—more than twice as much as a 3-ounce hamburger, and almost two-thirds of the 300 mg daily recommended limit. But now a recent study from The Rockefeller University in New York City and the Harvard School of Public Health peels away shrimp's bad image.

For 3 weeks, a group of 18 healthy, nonsmoking adults ate a low-fat, low-cholesterol diet then switched to a diet that was almost identical (but included about 10 ounces of shrimp, or 590 mg of cholesterol, per day) for another 3 weeks. The shrimp plan did raise "bad" (LDL) cholesterol by about 7 percent—but boosted the good

kind (HDL) by around 10 percent. It even lowered triglyceride levels (also linked to heart disease risk) by 13 percent. Why? The researchers speculate that the cholesterol in shrimp may not be as easily absorbed as the kind in higher-fat foods, and that the polyunsaturated omega-3 fatty acids shrimp contains may have positive effects.

LITTLE BIG GRILL
(pictured below)

If space is an issue, consider the 48-inch tall Patio Caddie. It's neat and compact—only 22 inches in diameter—but large enough to cook 10 burgers at once. We found it cooked evenly, was sturdily constructed, and simple to clean. It comes with a small (11½-pound) propane tank, but you can substitute a standard 20-pounder. From Char-Broil; at mass merchandisers and home centers. For stores in your area, call 800-241-7548.

A GADGET THAT LENDS A HAND WHEN YOU COOK
(pictured above)
Until now, there was nowhere to put a steamy pot cover when you had to stir or turn foods except on the countertop, where it always left a puddle. To the rescue: Pan comPanion, a stainless-steel clip that fits inside a lid and has a hook for hanging the lid on the pot rim. While you stir or take a taste, the cover collects condensation, which can be emptied back into the pot instead of left on your counter. The gadget stores in the lid, so it's always there when you need it. Each set includes 5 sizes, for standard lids. From Boyajian Enterprises, Inc. To order, call Creative Solutions (800-666-6421) and ask for Department GH061.

CAN YOU WATER DOWN YOUR APPETITE?
You've heard it time and time again: Drinking lots of H2O will curb your hunger. Does it really work? "Drinking a couple of cups of water, diet soft drinks, or other calorie-free beverages with a meal may help some people eat less temporarily," says Arthur Frank, M.D., medical director of the Obesity Management Program at George Washington University. So if you're faced with, say, an all-you-can-eat buffet, your liquid-filled stomach may prevent you from stuffing yourself silly. Unfortunately, hunger can kick in later, and you could overcompensate.

If you have a snacking habit that's ruining your waistline, drinking water between meals could boost your willpower. But the best trick, says Dr. Frank, "is to do something that takes your mind off the urge to eat until it fades." The next time you're tempted to nibble, call a friend, go for a walk, or treat yourself to a bath. If all else fails, start working on your tax return—that's bound to kill your appetite.

4 PAINLESS WAYS TO IMPROVE YOUR DIET
1. If your regular cold cereal isn't high-fiber, mix it half-and-half with a bran cereal. It will still taste good, but will provide a fiber boost of up to 7 grams (28 percent of the Daily Value, which is 25 grams for adults).
2. Instead of drinking 2 cups of 2-percent milk a day, make it 1-percent (or move from 1-percent to fat-free) to save a total of 14,600 calories a year—enough for a 4-pound weight loss.
3. Pick romaine lettuce rather than iceberg for salads and sandwiches; it has twice the potassium and folate, 6 times as much vitamin C, and 8 times as much beta-carotene.

4. Pump up iron intake by cooking regularly in a cast-iron skillet or Dutch oven. Long-simmering soups, stews, and sauces tend to absorb the most iron, but even scrambling an egg in a cast-iron skillet can more than double the egg's iron content.

KEEPING CANNED FOODS SAFE
Many people assume that canned foods last forever—until one bulges, rusts, or even explodes in the cabinet. But several factors can cut shelf life short. While proper commercial canning destroys harmful bacteria, it only slows the action of naturally occurring chemical changes that can cause loss of flavor, color, texture, and nutritive value. "Over time, the food itself—especially high-acid items like tomato products, fruit, and canned fruit juice—can corrode the metal, producing a gradual buildup of gas that may cause the can to bulge or explode," says Joseph Hotchkiss, professor of food chemistry and toxicology at Cornell University in Ithaca, NY. Since high temperatures accelerate these reactions, canned goods should be kept in a clean, dry place at temperatures below 85°F.—not near your stove.

Low-acid canned foods—tuna, meat, poultry, stews, soups (except tomato), and most vegetables—keep well for 2 to 5 years; high-acid canned foods retain top quality for 12 to 18 months. To be safe, never use food from a can that's leaking, bulging, or badly dented. Without analysis, there's no way to know whether the problem is a harmless chemical reaction or a serious health threat.

APPETIZERS & SOUPS

Marinated Olives

PREP: 10 MINUTES PLUS CHILLING • COOK: 5 MINUTES

Start with olives from the supermarket deli section or a specialty store. This appetizing assortment is perfect on a dinner-party relish tray.

¼ cup extravirgin olive oil
2 teaspoons fennel seeds, crushed
4 small bay leaves
2 pounds assorted Mediterranean olives (such as Niçoise, picholine, Kalamata, and oil-cured)
6 strips (3" by 1" each) lemon peel
4 garlic cloves, crushed with side of chef's knife

1 In 1-quart saucepan, heat olive oil, fennel seeds, and bay leaves until hot but not smoking over medium heat. Remove saucepan from heat; let stand 10 minutes.

2 In large bowl, stir olive-oil mixture with olives, lemon peel, and garlic. Cover bowl with plastic wrap and refrigerate olives at least 24 hours to allow flavors to develop, stirring occasionally. (Or, in large self-sealing plastic bag, combine all ingredients, turning to coat olives well. Seal bag, pressing out as much air as possible. Place on plate; refrigerate, turning bag occasionally.)

3 Spoon olives into jars. Store in refrigerator for up to a month. Makes about 6 cups.

Each ¼ cup: About 90 calories, 0 g protein, 3 g carbohydrate, 10 g total fat (1 g saturated), 0 mg cholesterol, 700 mg sodium.

Roasted Red Pepper & Walnut Dip

PREP: 30 MINUTES PLUS COOLING • BROIL: 10 MINUTES

4 medium red peppers
½ cup walnuts
½ teaspoon ground cumin
2 slices firm white bread, torn

Left to right: Roasted Red Pepper & Walnut Dip, Omelet Española Squares (page 22)

2 tablespoons raspberry vinegar
1 tablespoon olive oil
½ teaspoon salt
⅛ teaspoon ground red pepper (cayenne)
Toasted pita triangles

1 Preheat broiler if manufacturer directs. Line broiling pan with foil. Broil peppers at closest position to source of heat, turning occasionally, 10 minutes or until charred and blistered all over. Remove from broiler. Wrap foil around peppers and allow to steam at room temperature 15 minutes or until cool enough to handle.

2 Meanwhile, turn oven control to 350°F. Spread walnuts in metal baking pan and bake 8 to 10 minutes, until toasted. In 1-quart saucepan, toast cumin over low heat 1 to 2 minutes, until very fragrant.

3 Remove peppers from foil. Peel off skin; discard skin and seeds. Cut peppers into large pieces. In food processor with knife blade attached, blend walnuts until ground. Add roasted peppers, cumin, bread, raspberry vinegar, olive oil, salt, and ground red pepper; blend until smooth. Transfer to bowl. Cover and refrigerate if not serving right away. Remove from refrigerator 30 minutes before serving. Serve with toasted pita triangles. Makes about 2 cups dip.

Each tablespoon dip: About 25 calories, 0 g protein, 2 g carbohydrate, 2 g total fat (0 g saturated), 0 mg cholesterol, 40 mg sodium.

Alaskan Salmon Spread

PREP: 30 MINUTES PLUS CHILLING
COOK: 8 TO 10 MINUTES

Fresh and smoked salmon are a winning combination in this rich and flavorful appetizer.

Salt
8 ounces skinless salmon fillet
1 medium lemon
8 ounces smoked salmon, finely chopped
½ cup margarine or butter (1 stick), softened
1 teaspoon Dijon mustard
1 teaspoon drained capers, chopped
⅛ teaspoon coarsely ground black pepper
2 tablespoons plus 1 teaspoon chopped fresh
   chives
French bread

1 Poach salmon: In 10-inch skillet, heat *4 cups water* and 1 teaspoon salt to boiling over high heat. Add salmon fillet; heat to boiling. Reduce heat to low; cover and simmer 8 to 10 minutes, until salmon flakes easily when tested with fork. With slotted pancake turner, carefully remove salmon from water; drain salmon (still on pancake turner) on paper towels. Transfer salmon to medium bowl; cool slightly.

2 Meanwhile, grate 1 teaspoon peel and squeeze 2 tablespoons juice from lemon.

3 With wooden spoon, stir and mash poached salmon almost to a smooth paste. Add smoked salmon, margarine or butter, Dijon mustard, capers, pepper, lemon peel, lemon juice, and 2 tablespoons chopped chives; blend thoroughly.

4 Spoon salmon mixture into a crock or serving bowl. Cover and refrigerate at least 2 hours. Let stand at room temperature 30 minutes before serving or until soft enough to spread. Sprinkle with remaining chopped chives and serve with sliced French bread. Makes about 2½ cups.

Each tablespoon without bread: About 35 calories, 2 g protein, 0 g carbohydrate, 3 g total fat (1 g saturated), 5 mg cholesterol, 90 mg sodium.

FOOD EDITOR'S TIP

Q. What's the difference between farm-raised and wild salmon?

A. Farm-raised (usually Atlantic) salmon, with a rich, almost buttery texture and milder flavor than its wilder sister, is mainly bred along the Northeast Coast and Chile, first in freshwater hatcheries and then in pens submerged in cold saltwater off the coastline, where the fish have a chance to swim against currents and changing tides. Since it's available all year, we generally use it in our recipes. Wild salmon, with a lean, firm texture, and a more pronounced fish flavor, comes mostly from Alaska and is available only in summer months unless purchased frozen or canned. Alaska salmon is termed "wild" because the fish swim freely in the Bering Sea, the Gulf of Alaska, and the waters of the Northern Pacific. The 5 commercially sold varieties of wild Alaska salmon are King (or Chinook), Sockeye (or Red or Blueback), Silver (or Coho), Chum, and Pink (which is primarily canned).

Omelet Española Squares

PREP: 45 MINUTES • BAKE: 15 TO 20 MINUTES

This potato omelet—called a *tortilla* in Spain—is a variation of one of the classic *tapas* (hors d'oeuvres) served there. The squares are best made a few hours ahead and served at room temperature.

2 tablespoons olive oil
1 pound all-purpose potatoes (about 2 large), diced
1 medium onion, sliced
1 medium green pepper, diced
¾ teaspoon salt
8 large eggs
¼ teaspoon coarsely ground black pepper
1 can (14½ ounces) diced tomatoes, drained
½ cup chopped pimiento-stuffed olives (salad olives)
Fresh chives for garnish

1 In nonstick 10-inch skillet with oven-safe handle (or cover handle with heavy-duty foil for baking in oven later), heat olive oil over medium heat; add potatoes, onion, green pepper, and ¼ teaspoon salt, and cook until vegetables are tender, about 20 minutes, stirring occasionally.

2 Meanwhile, preheat oven to 400°F. In medium bowl, with wire whisk or fork, beat eggs with pepper, ½ teaspoon salt, and ½ *cup water*. Stir in tomatoes and olives. Stir egg mixture into potato mixture in skillet and cook, covered, 5 minutes or until egg mixture begins to set around edge. Remove cover and place skillet in oven; bake 15 to 20 minutes, until omelet is set.

ROASTED GARLIC SPREAD

When garlic is roasted, it turns into a soft paste with a sweet and mellow flavor. Try it the classic way, spread on grilled or toasted bread. Or, do as chefs do and toss some with cooked vegetables or hot pasta; stir into soups, mashed potatoes, or rice; or spread on grilled meat, poultry, or seafood. Roasted garlic is also a good substitute for raw garlic in salad dressings, sandwich spreads, or dips.

PREP: 10 MINUTES • ROAST: 45 TO 55 MINUTES

4 whole heads garlic
2 tablespoons extravirgin olive oil
⅛ teaspoon salt
⅛ teaspoon coarsely ground black pepper
4 sprigs fresh thyme
2 sprigs fresh rosemary
2 bay leaves

1 Preheat oven to 425°F. Remove any loose papery skin from heads of garlic, leaving heads intact. Cut top from heads, just to tip of cloves (do not cut into cloves). Place heads on sheet of heavy-duty foil; drizzle with olive oil; sprinkle with salt and pepper. Top with thyme, rosemary, and bay leaves.

2 Loosely wrap foil around garlic, being careful that seam is folded to seal in oil. Roast garlic 45 to 55

minutes, until tender. Remove package from oven to plate. Open carefully and discard foil and herb sprigs. Cool slightly.

3 When garlic is cool enough to handle, separate cloves from heads and scrape or squeeze out pulp from each clove. Makes about 1¼ cups.

Each tablespoon: About 25 calories, 1 g protein, 3 g carbohydrate, 1 g total fat (0 g saturated), 0 mg cholesterol, 15 mg sodium.

3 Carefully invert omelet onto large, flat plate. Let cool before cutting into 1-inch squares. Garnish with chives. Makes about 60 hors d'oeuvres.

Each hors d'oeuvre: About 25 calories, 1 g protein, 2 g carbohydrate, 1 g total fat (0 g saturated), 28 mg cholesterol, 100 mg sodium.

Goat Cheese & Tomato Bruschetta

PREP: 15 MINUTES • GRILL: 10 MINUTES

You can make the goat-cheese mixture the day before—but bring it to room temperature before using, and assemble the bruschetta just before serving. The bread is toasted on the grill, but can just as easily be done under the broiler.

1 loaf (8 ounces) Italian bread
1 package (5½ ounces) soft mild goat cheese, such as Montrachet
1 teaspoon minced fresh oregano leaves
¼ teaspoon coarsely ground black pepper
2 ripe medium tomatoes, seeded and diced
⅛ teaspoon salt
3 tablespoons olive oil
2 teaspoons minced fresh parsley leaves
2 garlic cloves, each cut in half

1 Cut off ends from loaf of bread; reserve for making bread crumbs another day. Slice loaf diagonally into ½-inch-thick slices.

2 In small bowl, with fork, stir goat cheese, oregano, and pepper until blended. In medium bowl, stir tomatoes with salt, 1 teaspoon olive oil, and 1 teaspoon parsley.

3 Place bread slices on grill over medium heat and cook 3 to 5 minutes on each side, until lightly toasted. Rub 1 side of each toast slice with cut side of garlic. Brush with remaining olive oil.

4 Just before serving, spread goat-cheese mixture on toast slices and top with tomato mixture. Sprinkle with remaining parsley. Makes 16 bruschetta or 8 appetizer servings.

Each bruschetta: About 85 calories, 3 g protein, 7 g carbohydrate, 5 g total fat (2 g saturated), 5 mg cholesterol, 125 mg sodium.

Caponata

PREP: 30 MINUTES PLUS COOLING • COOK: 40 MINUTES

A tasty side or relish, sure to jazz up any meal. Spread the caponata on toasted slices of Italian bread for a quick bruschetta. Or, serve as a chilled vegetable accompaniment for a warm-weather dinner.

2 medium eggplants (1 pound each), cut into ¾-inch chunks
½ cup extravirgin olive oil
¼ teaspoon salt
3 small red onions, thinly sliced
4 ripe medium tomatoes (about 1½ pounds), peeled, seeded, and chopped
1 cup Mediterranean olives, pitted and chopped
3 tablespoons capers, drained
3 tablespoons golden raisins
¼ teaspoon coarsely ground black pepper
4 medium celery stalks with leaves, thinly sliced
⅓ cup red wine vinegar
2 teaspoons sugar
¼ cup loosely packed fresh Italian parsley, chopped, for garnish

1 Preheat oven to 500°F. Place eggplant on two 15½" by 10½" jelly-roll pans. Drizzle with ¼ cup olive oil and sprinkle with salt; toss to coat. Roast eggplant 10 minutes; stir, then roast 5 minutes longer or until browned.

2 Meanwhile, in 12-inch skillet, heat remaining ¼ cup olive oil over medium heat until hot but not smoking. Add onions and cook, stirring, 10 minutes or until tender but not browned. Add tomatoes, olives, capers, raisins, and pepper; reduce heat to low and simmer, covered, 15 minutes.

3 Add eggplant and celery to skillet; cook over medium heat, 8 to 10 minutes, until celery is just tender, stirring occasionally. Stir in vinegar and sugar and cook 1 minute. Cool slightly to serve at room temperature or cover and refrigerate to serve cold later. Sprinkle with chopped parsley to serve. Makes about 5 cups or 10 accompaniment servings.

Each serving: About 185 calories, 2 g protein, 16 g carbohydrate, 14 g total fat (2 g saturated), 0 mg cholesterol, 345 mg sodium.

Spicy Dallas Cheese Straws

PREP: 30 MINUTES PLUS 20 MINUTES TO THAW PASTRY
BAKE: 20 TO 22 MINUTES PER BATCH

We've seen these flaky cheese sticks at upscale gourmet shops for $12 to $15 a pound, but our recipe makes almost 1½ pounds for about $5! Best of all, these spicy twists can be made up to a week ahead and stored in an airtight container.

1 package (17¼ ounces) frozen puff-pastry
   sheets
1 tablespoon paprika
½ teaspoon dried thyme leaves
¼ to ½ teaspoon ground red pepper (cayenne)
¼ teaspoon salt
1 large egg white, slightly beaten
1 package (8 ounces) shredded sharp Cheddar
   cheese (2 cups)

1 Thaw puff pastry as label directs. Meanwhile, in small bowl, mix paprika, thyme, ground red pepper, and salt. Grease 2 large cookie sheets.

Spicy Dallas Cheese Straws

2 Unfold 1 sheet puff pastry onto lightly floured surface. With floured rolling pin, roll pastry into 14" by 14" square. Lightly brush pastry with beaten egg white. Sprinkle half of paprika mixture on pastry. Sprinkle half of cheese on half of pastry. Fold pastry over to cover cheese, forming a rectangle about 14" by 7". With rolling pin, lightly roll over pastry to seal layers. With pizza wheel or knife, cut pastry crosswise into ½-inch-wide strips.

3 Preheat oven to 375°F. Place strips, ½ inch apart, on cookie sheets, twisting each strip and pressing ends against cookie sheet to prevent strips from uncurling during baking. Bake cheese straws 20 to 22 minutes, until golden. With spatula, carefully remove straws to wire racks to cool.

4 Repeat with remaining puff pastry, egg white, paprika mixture, and cheese. Makes about 4 dozen cheese straws.

Each straw: About 75 calories, 2 g protein, 5 g carbohydrate, 6 g total fat (2 g saturated), 9 mg cholesterol, 65 mg sodium.

Tomato & Ricotta Salata Bruschetta

PREP: 20 MINUTES

Toasted country bread rubbed with garlic and topped with a mixture of tomatoes and cheese—a delicious appetizer for family or company.

8 slices (each about 4" by 3" by ½" thick)
   country-style bread, toasted and each cut in
   half
1 garlic clove, cut in half
1 pound ripe plum tomatoes (about 5 medium),
   seeded and cut into ½-inch pieces
4 ounces ricotta salata* or feta cheese, cut into
   ½-inch pieces
2 tablespoons extravirgin olive oil
1 tablespoon finely chopped red onion
1 tablespoon chopped fresh basil
2 teaspoons balsamic vinegar
¼ teaspoon salt
¼ teaspoon coarsely ground black pepper

1 Lightly rub 1 side of each piece of toast with garlic halves; discard garlic.

2 In medium bowl, gently toss plum tomatoes with remaining ingredients. If not serving right away, cover tomato mixture and let stand at room temperature for up to 2 hours.

3 Just before serving, spoon tomato mixture over garlic-rubbed side of toast slices. Makes 8 first-course servings.

*Ricotta salata is a white, firm, lightly salted cheese made from sheep's milk. Look for it in supermarkets, cheese shops, and Italian groceries.

Each serving: About 140 calories, 4 g protein, 14 g carbohydrate, 7 g total fat (3 g saturated), 13 mg cholesterol, 355 mg sodium.

Tuscan White Bean Bruschetta

PREP: 15 MINUTES • GRILL: 10 MINUTES

A first course made with slices of grilled bread and the flavors of sunny Tuscany—the perfect way to begin an outdoor dinner cooked on the grill.

1 loaf (8 ounces) Italian bread
1 can (15½ to 19 ounces) white kidney beans
    (cannellini), rinsed and drained
1 tablespoon lemon juice
1 teaspoon minced fresh sage leaves
¼ teaspoon salt
⅛ teaspoon coarsely ground black pepper
3 tablespoons olive oil
3 teaspoons minced fresh parsley leaves
2 garlic cloves, each cut in half

1 Cut off ends from loaf of bread; reserve for making bread crumbs another day. Slice loaf diagonally into ½-inch-thick slices.

2 In medium bowl, with fork, lightly mash beans with lemon juice, sage, salt, pepper, 1 tablespoon olive oil, and 2 teaspoons parsley.

3 Place bread slices on grill over medium heat and cook 3 to 5 minutes on each side, until lightly toasted. Rub 1 side of each toast slice with cut side of garlic. Brush with remaining olive oil.

4 Just before serving, top toast slices with bean mixture and sprinkle with remaining parsley. Makes 16 bruschetta or 8 appetizer servings.

Each bruschetta: About 85 calories, 3 g protein, 11 g carbohydrate, 3 g total fat (0 g saturated), 0 mg cholesterol, 175 mg sodium.

Curried Cheddar Puffs

PREP: 20 MINUTES • BAKE: 25 TO 30 MINUTES

A hot blend of curry, coriander, and cumin adds exotic flavor to these hard-to-resist morsels. Bake and freeze these up to a month ahead—so they're ready for company when you are.

2 teaspoons curry powder
½ teaspoon ground coriander
½ teaspoon ground cumin
¼ teaspoon ground red pepper (cayenne)
6 tablespoons margarine or butter (¾ stick),
    cut up
½ teaspoon salt
1 cup all-purpose flour
4 large eggs
4 ounces Cheddar cheese, shredded (1 cup)

1 Preheat oven to 400°F. Grease 2 large cookie sheets.

2 In 3-quart saucepan, heat curry powder, coriander, cumin, and ground red pepper over medium heat, stirring constantly, 1 minute or until very fragrant. Stir in margarine or butter, salt, and *1 cup water*; heat to boiling over high heat. Remove saucepan from heat and stir in flour all at once; return to medium-low heat, stirring constantly with wooden spoon, until mixture forms a ball and leaves side of pan. Remove saucepan from heat.

3 Stir in eggs, 1 at a time, beating well after each addition until batter is smooth and satiny. Stir in cheese. Spoon batter into large decorating bag fitted with large writing tip (about ½ inch diameter). Pipe batter, about 1 inch apart, onto cookie sheets, forming mounds 1 inch wide and ¾ inch high. Or, drop dough by teaspoons, forming small mounds. With fingertip dipped in water, gently smooth peaks.

4 Place cookie sheets on 2 oven racks. Bake puffs 25 to 30 minutes, until deep golden, rotating cookie sheets between upper and lower racks halfway through baking time. Remove to wire racks to cool. Repeat with remaining batter.

5 Serve puffs at room temperature or reheat to serve warm. To reheat, place puffs on cookie sheet in 400°F. oven 5 minutes. Makes about 8 dozen puffs.

Each puff: About 20 calories, 1 g protein, 1 g carbohydrate, 1 g total fat (0 g saturated), 10 mg cholesterol, 30 mg sodium.

Tortilla Spirals

Tortilla Spirals

••
PREP: 35 MINUTES PLUS CHILLING

These versatile appetizers are made with two fillings—
one with smoked salmon, the other with sun-dried
tomatoes. Prepare the tortilla spirals a day ahead and
refrigerate.

Smoked-Salmon Filling (at right)
Sun-Dried Tomato Filling (at right)
8 flour tortillas (10 inches each)

1 Prepare both fillings.

2 Spread each of the fillings evenly over 4 tortillas
(4 with salmon, 4 with tomato). Roll each tortilla up
tightly, jelly-roll fashion. Wrap each roll in plastic
wrap and refrigerate at least 4 hours or overnight,
until firm enough to slice.

3 To serve, unwrap plastic around tortilla rolls and
trim ends. Cut rolls into slightly less than ½-inch-
thick slices. Makes about 4½ dozen hors d'oeuvres.

SMOKED-SALMON FILLING: In medium bowl,
with spoon, mix *1½ packages (8 ounces each) cream
cheese, softened, ¼ pound thinly sliced smoked
salmon, chopped, 3 tablespoons capers, drained and
chopped,* and *¼ cup loosely packed fresh dill,*
chopped, until blended.

SUN-DRIED TOMATO FILLING: In medium
bowl, combine *1 package (8 ounces) cream cheese,
softened, 10 sun-dried tomato halves, packed in herb-
seasoned olive oil,* drained and chopped, *1 container
(5.2 ounces) spreadable cheese with pepper,* and *⅓
cup packed fresh basil leaves,* chopped, until blended.

Each hors d'oeuvre with salmon filling: About 85 calories, 3 g
protein, 6 g carbohydrate, 5 g total fat (3 g saturated), 15 mg
cholesterol, 155 mg sodium.

Each hors d'oeuvre with tomato filling: About 85 calories, 3 g
protein, 7 g carbohydrate, 5 g total fat (3 g saturated), 13 mg
cholesterol, 155 mg sodium.

Rustic Tomato Tart

PREP: 35 MINUTES • BAKE: 35 MINUTES

The combination of yellow and red tomatoes makes an especially attractive tart, but all red tomatoes would be just fine.

1½ cups all-purpose flour
1 teaspoon salt
4 tablespoons margarine or butter (½ stick)
¼ cup shortening
1 tablespoon olive oil
3 medium onions (about 1 pound), thinly sliced
¼ cup Kalamata olives
1 package (3½ ounces) goat cheese, crumbled
1 large yellow tomato (about 8 ounces), sliced
  ¼ inch thick
2 large red tomatoes (about 1 pound), sliced
  ¼ inch thick
½ teaspoon coarsely ground black pepper

1 Preheat oven to 425°F. In medium bowl, stir flour and ½ teaspoon salt. With pastry blender or two knives used scissor-fashion, cut in margarine or butter, and shortening until mixture resembles coarse crumbs.

2 Sprinkle 3 *to 4 tablespoons cold water*, 1 tablespoon at a time, into flour mixture, mixing lightly with a fork after each addition until dough is just moist enough to hold together.

3 On lightly floured surface, with floured rolling pin, roll dough into a 14-inch round; ease into 11" by 1¼" tart pan with removable bottom. Fold overhang in and press against side of tart pan.

4 Line tart shell with foil and fill with pie weights, uncooked rice, or dried beans. Bake tart shell 20 minutes; remove foil with pie weights. Return tart shell to oven; bake 10 minutes longer or until crust is golden.

5 While tart shell is baking, in nonstick 12-inch skillet, heat olive oil over medium heat. Add onions and ¼ teaspoon salt and cook until onions are tender and browned, stirring often, about 20 minutes. Reserve 3 or 4 Kalamata olives for garnish. Pit and slice remaining olives.

6 Turn oven control to broil. Spoon cooked onions into tart shell; top with half of goat cheese. Arrange tomato slices, alternating colors, in concentric circles over onion layer. Sprinkle with pepper and remaining ¼ teaspoon salt. Crumble remaining goat cheese over top of tart.

7 Place tart in broiler about 7 inches from source of heat. Broil tart until cheese just melts and tomatoes are heated through, about 6 to 8 minutes. Sprinkle with whole and sliced Kalamata olives to serve. Makes 12 first-course or 6 main-dish servings.

Each first-course serving: About 195 calories, 4 g protein, 19 g carbohydrate, 12 g total fat (4 g saturated), 4 mg cholesterol, 308 mg sodium.

Mexican Meatballs

PREP: 30 MINUTES • COOK: 45 MINUTES

1½ pounds ground beef
1 large egg
¾ cup plain, dried bread crumbs
½ teaspoon ground black pepper
1¼ teaspoons salt
3 garlic cloves, minced
1 can (28 ounces) tomatoes
1 chipotle chile in adobo*
2 teaspoons vegetable oil
1 small onion, minced
1 teaspoon ground cumin
1 cup chicken broth
¼ cup coarsely chopped fresh cilantro

1 In large bowl, mix ground beef, egg, bread crumbs, pepper, 1 teaspoon salt, one-third of minced garlic, and ¼ *cup water* until blended. With hands, shape meat mixture into ¾-inch meatballs.

2 In blender at low speed, blend tomatoes with their juice and chipotle chile until smooth.

3 In 5-quart Dutch oven, heat vegetable oil over medium heat. Add onion and cook 5 minutes or until tender, stirring often. Stir in cumin and remaining minced garlic; cook 30 seconds. Stir in tomato mixture, chicken broth, and ¼ teaspoon salt; heat to boiling over high heat.

4 Add raw meatballs; heat to boiling. Reduce heat to low; simmer, uncovered, 30 minutes. Place mixture in chafing dish and serve with cocktail picks. Sprinkle with cilantro. Makes 20 appetizer servings.

*Canned chipotle chiles in adobo (smoked jalapeño chiles in a vinegary marinade) are available in Hispanic markets.

Each serving: About 125 calories, 8 g protein, 5 g carbohydrate, 8 g total fat (3 g saturated), 31 mg cholesterol, 310 mg sodium.

Spicy Ground Beef Empanaditas

PREP: 1¼ HOURS • BAKE: 15 TO 17 MINUTES PER BATCH

Two-bite savory pastries stuffed with a sweet and spicy ground-beef filling called *picadillo*. Assemble them up to a month ahead and freeze. Bake according to recipe.

Flaky Turnover Pastry (at right)
2 teaspoons vegetable oil
1 small onion, finely chopped
1 large garlic clove, minced
¼ teaspoon ground cinnamon
¼ teaspoon ground red pepper (cayenne)
¼ pound ground beef
¼ teaspoon salt
1 cup canned tomatoes with juice
3 tablespoons chopped golden raisins
3 tablespoons chopped pimiento-stuffed olives
  (salad olives)
1 large egg, beaten with 2 tablespoons water,
  for glaze

1 Prepare Flaky Turnover Pastry. Wrap in plastic wrap and set aside.

2 In 10-inch skillet, heat oil over medium heat. Add onion and cook 5 minutes or until tender, stirring frequently. Stir in garlic, cinnamon, and ground red pepper; cook 30 seconds. Increase heat to medium-high; add ground beef and salt and cook 5 minutes or until beef begins to brown, stirring frequently. Stir in tomatoes with their juice, raisins, and olives, breaking up tomatoes with back of spoon; cook over high heat 7 to 10 minutes, until almost all liquid evaporates. Remove skillet from heat.

3 Divide dough into 4 equal pieces. On floured surface, with floured rolling pin, roll one-fourth of dough 1⁄16 inch thick (keep remaining dough covered with plastic wrap). With 3-inch round biscuit cutter, cut out as many rounds as possible, reserving trimmings. On half of each dough round, place 1 level measuring teaspoon filling. Brush edges of rounds with some egg mixture. Fold dough over filling. With fork, press edges together to seal. Prick tops; brush egg mixture lightly over turnovers. With pancake turner, place turnovers, about 1 inch apart, on ungreased large cookie sheet. Repeat with remaining filling and dough, rerolling trimmings. If not serving right away, cover with plastic wrap and refrigerate.

4 About 25 minutes before serving, preheat oven to 425°F. Bake turnovers 15 to 17 minutes, just until golden. Serve hot. Makes about 4½ dozen turnovers.

FLAKY TURNOVER PASTRY: In large bowl, combine 3 *cups all-purpose flour, 1½ teaspoons baking powder,* and *¾ teaspoon salt.* With pastry blender or two knives used scissor-fashion, cut in *1 cup shortening* until mixture resembles coarse crumbs. Sprinkle with about 6 *tablespoons cold water,* 1 tablespoon at a time, mixing with fork after each addition, until dough is just moist enough to hold together. Shape dough into a ball. Refrigerate pastry if not assembling turnovers right away.

Each turnover: About 70 calories, 1 g protein, 6 g carbohydrate, 5 g total fat (2 g saturated), 5 mg cholesterol, 80 mg sodium.

Greek Lemon Soup

PREP: 15 MINUTES • COOK: 35 MINUTES

Called *avgolemono* in Greek, this velvety-smooth chicken soup is thickened with eggs and rice. It's best served soon after you make it.

2 cans (13¾ to 14½ ounces each) chicken broth
1 medium skinless, boneless chicken-breast half
  (about 6 ounces)
1 small onion, peeled
2 whole cloves
1 medium carrot, peeled and cut into 2-inch
  pieces
1 medium celery stalk, cut into 2-inch pieces
⅔ cup regular long-grain rice
3 large eggs
⅓ cup fresh lemon juice (about 2 large lemons)
1 tablespoon margarine or butter
Chopped fresh chives for garnish

1 In 3-quart saucepan, heat chicken broth, chicken breast, onion studded with cloves, carrot, celery, and 2½ *cups water* to boiling over high heat. Reduce heat to low; cover and simmer 10 minutes.

2 With slotted spoon, remove chicken and vegetables from saucepan; discard vegetables. Cool chicken until easy to handle, then shred into thin strips; set aside.

Clockwise from top: Mexican Meatballs ➤
(page 27), Curried Cheddar Puffs (page 25),
Spicy Ground Beef Empanaditas

3 Add rice to simmering broth; heat to boiling over high heat. Reduce heat to low; cover and simmer 15 to 20 minutes, until rice is tender.

4 Meanwhile, in large bowl, with wire whisk, mix eggs and lemon juice until combined.

5 Slowly whisk 2 cups simmering broth into bowl with egg mixture, whisking constantly. Return broth mixture to saucepan; heat just to simmering, whisking constantly, about 5 minutes (do not boil or soup will curdle). Stir in shredded chicken and margarine or butter. Sprinkle with chopped chives if you like. Makes about 7 cups or 6 first-course servings.

Each serving: About 185 calories, 14 g protein, 18 g carbohydrate, 6 g total fat (2 g saturated), 124 mg cholesterol, 510 mg sodium.

Chesapeake Bay Crab-Stuffed Mushrooms

PREP: 45 MINUTES • BAKE: 20 MINUTES

You can assemble these hors d'oeuvres earlier in the day and refrigerate, but increase the baking time to 15 minutes covered, 10 minutes uncovered.

24 large mushrooms (2-inch diameter) with stems
3 tablespoons margarine or butter
1 small onion, finely chopped
1 large celery stalk, finely chopped
8 ounces fresh lump crabmeat
1 tablespoon all-purpose flour
½ teaspoon salt
¼ teaspoon coarsely ground black pepper
1 cup milk
2 tablespoons dry sherry
2 slices white bread, finely chopped
2 tablespoons chopped fresh parsley
Nonstick cooking spray

1 Remove stems from mushroom caps by gently wiggling and twisting stems. Chop stems.

2 If necessary, so that mushrooms stand upright without wobbling when stuffed, cut a very thin slice from rounded side of each cap. Arrange mushroom caps, cavity side up, in 15½" by 10½" jelly-roll pan.

3 In 10-inch skillet, melt margarine or butter over medium heat. Add onion, celery, and mushroom stems and cook 15 to 20 minutes, until vegetables are tender and golden, stirring occasionally.

4 Meanwhile, pick over crabmeat to remove any cartilage.

5 Increase heat to medium-high. Sprinkle flour, salt, and pepper over vegetable mixture. Cook 1 minute, stirring constantly. Gradually add milk, then sherry; heat to boiling, stirring constantly. Remove skillet from heat. Add bread crumbs, crabmeat, and 1 tablespoon chopped parsley. Stir to mix well and break up crabmeat slightly.

6 Preheat oven to 400°F. Fill mushroom cavities with crabmeat stuffing. Spray large sheet of foil with nonstick cooking spray. Place foil, greased side down, over mushrooms. Bake stuffed mushrooms 10 minutes. Remove foil and bake 10 minutes longer. Serve hot. Sprinkle with remaining chopped parsley if you like. Makes 8 first-course servings.

Each serving: About 125 calories, 9 g protein, 10 g carbohydrate, 6 g total fat (2 g saturated), 19 mg cholesterol, 550 mg sodium.

Dilled Shrimp with Cucumber Ribbons

PREP: 1¼ HOURS PLUS CHILLING
COOK: 3 TO 5 MINUTES

This festive appetizer combines the classic ingredients of salmon gravlax—dill, mustard, sugar, and salt.

1 large lemon
¼ cup olive oil
2 tablespoons chopped fresh dill
2 tablespoons sugar
2 tablespoons Dijon mustard
Salt
2 pounds large shrimp
1 bay leaf
1 teaspoon whole black peppercorns
Cucumber Salad (recipe follows)
¼ cup finely diced red pepper

1 Peel 4 strips (2½" by ½" each) from the lemon then squeeze 2 tablespoons juice. In large bowl, with wire whisk or fork, mix lemon juice, olive oil, dill, sugar, mustard, and ¼ teaspoon salt. Remove half of mustard dressing to cup; reserve.

2 Shell and devein shrimp, leaving tail part of shell on if you like. Rinse shrimp with cold running water. In 5-quart Dutch oven, heat lemon peel, bay leaf, peppercorns, 2 teaspoons salt, and 2 *quarts water* to boiling over high heat. Add shrimp; cook 3 to 5 minutes, uncovered, until shrimp turn opaque throughout. Drain shrimp well. Discard lemon peel, bay leaf, and peppercorns. Toss hot shrimp with mustard dressing in bowl; refrigerate shrimp, covered, at least 1 hour or up to 4 hours before serving.

3 Meanwhile, prepare Cucumber Salad.

4 Spoon Cucumber Salad onto 10 small plates. Arrange shrimp on top and spoon reserved mustard dressing over shrimp. Sprinkle salad with diced red pepper. Makes 10 first-course servings.

CUCUMBER SALAD: With vegetable peeler, peel *4 medium cucumbers* (about 6 ounces each). Trim ends and slice each cucumber crosswise in half. With vegetable peeler, peel long thin ribbons from cucumbers; discard seedy centers. Place cucumber ribbons in colander set over medium bowl; let drain, covered, in refrigerator up to 3 hours before serving. In small bowl, with wire whisk or fork, mix 3 *tablespoons chopped fresh dill, 1 tablespoon fresh lemon juice, 1 tablespoon sugar, 1 tablespoon mayonnaise, 1 teaspoon Dijon mustard,* and *¾ teaspoon salt.* Cover and refrigerate until ready to serve. Discard liquid in bowl under cucumbers; wipe bowl dry. Place cucumber ribbons in bowl; toss with dill dressing.

Each serving: About 160 calories, 16 g protein, 6 g carbohydrate, 8 g total fat (1 g saturated), 145 mg cholesterol, 530 mg sodium.

Bear Mountain Butternut Soup

PREP: 45 MINUTES • COOK: 20 MINUTES

Served with big, savory croutons the way they like it in New York State. To save time, you can prepare the croutons up to 2 days ahead. Store them in an airtight container.

Cinnamon Croutons (recipe follows)
1 medium leek
3 tablespoons margarine or butter
2 medium carrots, coarsely chopped
1 medium onion, coarsely chopped
1 medium butternut squash (about 2½ pounds),
   peeled and cut into 1-inch cubes

1 can (13¾ to 14½ ounces) chicken broth
½ teaspoon salt
½ cup half-and-half or light cream

1 Prepare Cinnamon Croutons.

2 Cut off root end from leek. Cut leek lengthwise in half; rinse with cold running water to remove sand. Coarsely chop white and pale-green part of leek; discard tough dark-green part.

3 In 5-quart Dutch oven or saucepot, melt margarine or butter over medium-high heat. Add carrots, onion, and leek and cook until browned, about 10 minutes, stirring occasionally. Add squash, chicken broth, salt, and 2¼ cups water; heat to boiling. Reduce heat to low; cover and simmer 15 to 20 minutes, until squash is very tender.

4 In blender (with center part of cover removed to allow steam to escape), blend squash mixture at low speed in small batches until very smooth.

5 Return squash mixture to Dutch oven; stir in half-and-half. Heat soup over medium heat until hot, stirring occasionally. Serve soup with Cinnamon Croutons. Makes about 8¾ cups or 12 first-course servings.

CINNAMON CROUTONS: Preheat oven to 400°F. Cut *4 ounces French bread* (½ loaf) into ¾-inch cubes (you should have about 4 cups). In bowl, toss 3 *tablespoons melted margarine* or butter, *¼ teaspoon ground cinnamon,* and *scant ⅛ teaspoon salt* with bread cubes. Spread bread cubes in 15½" by 10½" jelly-roll pan; bake 10 to 12 minutes, until golden.

Each serving of soup with croutons: About 150 calories, 3 g protein, 20 g carbohydrate, 7 g total fat (2 g saturated), 5 mg cholesterol, 355 mg sodium.

FOOD EDITOR'S TIP

Q. I love butternut squash, but hate peeling it. Do you have any tips?

A. After much practice (especially making our Bear Mountain Butternut Soup, at left, or Butternut-Squash Risotto with Sage, page 115), we've found that it's best to cut the squash crosswise in half, using a chef's knife, and then cut the larger bottom section vertically in half, so you can scoop out the seeds. Next, cut all of the squash into about 1- to 1½-inch-wide slices. Place each slice cut-side down on a board and use a paring knife to remove the tough skin. Other winter squashes—such as acorn and Hubbard—can be even tougher to peel and are best cut into pieces and baked with the skin on.

New Orleans Green Gumbo

PREP: 20 MINUTES • COOK: 40 MINUTES

Popular around the Mississippi Delta, this soup has a slightly thickened "gumbo" texture created by the pepper-spiked brown roux and grated potato. To cut down on last-minute preparations, wash and cut the greens a day ahead and store loosely wrapped in refrigerator.

8 slices bacon, cut into ½-inch pieces
¼ cup all-purpose flour
1 teaspoon salt
¼ teaspoon ground red pepper (cayenne)
2 cans (13¾ to 14½ ounces) chicken broth
1½ pounds fresh greens (collard or mustard, or a combination), coarse stems removed and leaves cut into ½-inch pieces
1 package (10 ounces) frozen chopped spinach, thawed
1 large (8 ounces) all-purpose potato, peeled and grated

1 In 5-quart Dutch oven, cook bacon over medium-low heat until browned. With slotted spoon, remove bacon to paper towels to drain. Reserve bacon pieces for garnish.

2 Discard all but 2 tablespoons bacon fat from Dutch oven. Stir in flour, salt, and ground red pepper and cook over medium heat until golden brown, about 5 minutes, stirring frequently.

3 Stir in chicken broth, fresh greens, spinach, potato, and 4 cups water; heat to boiling over high heat. Reduce heat to low; cover and simmer 20 to 25 minutes, until soup thickens slightly and greens are tender, stirring occasionally. Sprinkle bacon over soup to serve. Makes about 10 cups or 8 first-course servings.

Each serving: About 145 calories, 7 g protein, 14 g carbohydrate, 7 g total fat (3 g saturated), 9 mg cholesterol, 735 mg sodium.

Wisconsin Cauliflower-Cheddar Soup

PREP: 35 MINUTES • COOK: 25 MINUTES

So rich, your guests won't believe it's made with milk instead of cream. Use a blender—not a food processor—to puree the soup for an extra-smooth texture. You can make this soup a day or two ahead; reheat on low just before serving. Don't let it boil or the cheese may get stringy.

2 tablespoons margarine or butter (¼ stick)
1 medium onion, chopped
¼ cup all-purpose flour
½ teaspoon salt
2 cups milk
1 can (13¾ to 14½ ounces) chicken broth
1 head (2½ pounds) cauliflower, cut into 1-inch pieces
1 teaspoon Dijon mustard
1 package (8 ounces) shredded sharp Cheddar cheese (2 cups)

1 In 4-quart saucepan, melt margarine or butter over medium heat. Add onion and cook until golden, about 10 minutes, stirring occasionally. Stir in flour and salt; cook 2 minutes, stirring frequently.

2 Gradually stir in milk, chicken broth, and 1½ cups water; add cauliflower and heat to boiling over high heat. Reduce heat to low; cover and simmer until cauliflower is tender, about 10 minutes.

3 In blender (with center part of blender cover removed to allow steam to escape), blend cauliflower mixture at low speed in small batches until very smooth.

4 Return cauliflower mixture to saucepan; heat over medium heat until hot, stirring occasionally. Remove saucepan from heat; stir in mustard and 1½ cups cheese until melted and smooth. Garnish soup with remaining cheese to serve. Makes about 9 cups or 8 first-course servings.

Each serving: About 230 calories, 14 g carbohydrates, 13 g protein, 15 g total fat (8 g saturated), 41 mg cholesterol, 575 mg sodium.

◄ Clockwise from top left: Bear Mountain Butternut Soup (page 31), New Orleans Green Gumbo, Wisconsin Cauliflower-Cheddar Soup

Gazpacho with Cilantro Cream

PREP: 30 MINUTES PLUS 6 HOURS OR OVERNIGHT TO CHILL

Based on the popular uncooked soup from southern Spain, our chunky garden-fresh version is a welcome lunch or supper on hot days.

2 medium cucumbers (about 8 ounces each), peeled
1 medium yellow pepper
¼ small red onion
2 pounds ripe tomatoes (about 6 medium), peeled, seeded, and cut into chunks
½ to 1 small jalapeño chile, seeded
3 tablespoons fresh lime juice
2 tablespoons extravirgin olive oil
¾ plus ⅛ teaspoon salt
¼ cup light sour cream or low-fat plain yogurt
1 tablespoon milk
5 teaspoons finely chopped fresh cilantro leaves

1 Coarsely cut up half of 1 cucumber, half of the yellow pepper, and all the red onion; set aside to stir into soup later. Cut remaining cucumbers and yellow pepper into chunks.

2 In food processor with knife blade attached, blend chunks of cucumber and yellow pepper, tomatoes, jalapeño, lime juice, olive oil, and ¾ teaspoon salt until smooth. Pour into medium bowl; add cut-up cucumber, yellow pepper, and red onion. Cover and refrigerate until well chilled, at least 6 hours or overnight.

3 Meanwhile, prepare cilantro cream: In small bowl, mix sour cream, milk, 4 teaspoons chopped cilantro, and ⅛ teaspoon salt until smooth. Cover and refrigerate until ready to serve soup.

4 Serve cold soup with cilantro cream. Sprinkle with remaining chopped cilantro. Makes about 5 cups or 4 first-course servings.

Each serving with cilantro cream: About 165 calories, 4 g protein, 21 g carbohydrate, 9 g total fat (1 g saturated), 6 mg cholesterol, 505 mg sodium.

Gazpacho with Cilantro Cream

Tomato Soup

PREP: 20 MINUTES • COOK: 1 HOUR 10 MINUTES

A tasty way to use up every last ripe summer tomato when flavor will be at its peak. For a creamier version, stir in heavy or light cream or plain yogurt to taste.

1 tablespoon margarine or butter
1 medium onion, diced
1 medium celery stalk, diced
1 medium carrot, peeled and diced
1 garlic clove, crushed with garlic press
2 teaspoons fresh thyme leaves
4 pounds ripe tomatoes, cut up
1 can (13¾ to 14½ ounces) chicken broth
¾ teaspoon salt
¼ teaspoon coarsely ground black pepper
1 bay leaf
Snipped chives for garnish

1 In 5-quart Dutch oven, melt margarine over low heat. Add onion, celery, and carrot; cook 10 minutes, until tender. Stir in garlic and thyme; cook 1 minute.

2 Add tomatoes, broth, salt, pepper, bay leaf, and ½ *cup water*; heat to boiling over high heat. Reduce heat to medium-low and cook, uncovered, 45 minutes or until tomatoes are broken up and mixture has thickened slightly. Discard bay leaf.

3 In blender (with center part of cover removed),

blend tomato mixture in small batches until pureed. Pour pureed soup into large bowl after each batch.

4 Refrigerate soup to serve cold. Or reheat soup in same Dutch oven to serve hot. Sprinkle with chives to serve. Makes about 8 cups or 8 first-course servings.

Each serving: About 80 calories, 3 g protein, 13 g carbohydrate, 3 g total fat (1 g saturated), 0 mg cholesterol, 410 mg sodium.

Tuscan Pappa al Pomodoro

PREP: 35 MINUTES PLUS STANDING • COOK: 15 MINUTES

The bread acts as the thickener for this comforting Italian tomato soup. It's a cinch to prepare!

1 loaf (8 ounces) several-days-old Tuscan or
    other country-style bread
3½ pounds ripe tomatoes
4 garlic cloves, minced
1 teaspoon salt
½ cup extravirgin olive oil
½ teaspoon coarsely ground black pepper
1 can (13¾ to 14½ ounces) chicken or
    vegetable broth
⅓ cup minced fresh parsley leaves
⅓ cup thinly sliced fresh basil leaves

1 Cut bread into 1-inch cubes; place on wire racks to dry, about 1 hour.

2 Meanwhile, peel, seed, and chop tomatoes; set aside. On cutting board, with side of chef's knife, mash garlic with salt to a smooth paste.

3 In 5-quart Dutch oven, heat olive oil over low heat. Add garlic paste and cook, stirring, 2 minutes. Stir in bread cubes and pepper and cook, stirring, 2 minutes. Add tomatoes and cook, stirring, 2 minutes longer.

4 Stir in broth and 3 *cups water*; heat to boiling over high heat. Remove Dutch oven from heat; cover and let stand 1 hour for flavors to blend.

5 To serve, stir or whisk vigorously until bread is broken up and mixture is almost smooth. Serve soup warm or reheat to serve hot. Just before serving, stir in parsley and basil. Makes about 10 cups or 10 first-course servings.

Each serving: About 200 calories, 4 g protein, 19 g carbohydrate, 12 g total fat (2 g saturated), 0 mg cholesterol, 495 mg sodium.

Cranberry Bean Soup

PREP: 40 MINUTES • COOK: 45 MINUTES

A Chilean-style soup made with butternut squash, tomatoes, fresh basil, and jalapeño. Cranberry beans have large, knobby beige pods speckled with red; the beans inside are cream-colored with red streaks, and have a nutlike taste.

4 teaspoons olive oil
1 medium butternut squash (2 pounds), peeled
    and cut into ¾-inch cubes
1 medium onion, chopped
2 garlic cloves, minced
1 jalapeño chile, seeded and minced
1 teaspoon ground cumin
1 can (13¾ to 14½ ounces) chicken broth
2 medium tomatoes, diced
1½ pounds fresh cranberry beans, shelled
    (about 2 cups beans)
1 teaspoon salt
1 teaspoon sugar
1¼ cups loosely packed fresh basil leaves,
    chopped
2 cups fresh corn kernels (about 4 medium ears
    corn)

1 In 5-quart Dutch oven, heat 2 teaspoons olive oil over medium heat until hot. Add butternut squash and onion and cook, stirring occasionally, until golden, about 10 minutes. Remove squash mixture to bowl.

2 In same Dutch oven, heat remaining olive oil over medium heat; add garlic, jalapeño, and cumin and cook 1 minute, stirring. Stir in broth, tomatoes, beans, salt, sugar, squash mixture, ¼ cup chopped basil, and 2¼ *cups water*; heat to boiling over high heat. Reduce heat to low; cover and simmer 30 minutes or until beans are tender, stirring occasionally.

3 Stir in corn; heat to boiling over high heat. Reduce heat to low; cover and simmer 5 minutes longer. Stir in remaining chopped basil. Makes about 9 cups or 4 main-dish servings.

Each serving: About 360 calories, 16 g protein, 66 g carbohydrate, 7 g total fat (1 g saturated), 0 mg cholesterol, 890 mg sodium.

Borscht

PREP: 1 HOUR • COOK: 2 HOURS

1 pound boneless beef chuck, cut into ¾-inch
  pieces
2 teaspoons plus 1 tablespoon vegetable oil
1 large onion, finely chopped
2 garlic cloves, minced
1 cinnamon stick (3 inches long)
½ teaspoon ground allspice
1 can (14½ to 16 ounces) tomatoes
1 bunch beets (1 pound without tops), peeled
  and coarsely shredded
1 small bulb celeriac (about 8 ounces), peeled
  and coarsely shredded
2 cans (13¾ to 14½ ounces each) beef broth
1 bay leaf
1½ teaspoons salt
3 large carrots, peeled and cut into ½-inch
  pieces
2 medium all-purpose potatoes (12 ounces),
  peeled and cut into ½-inch pieces
2 medium parsnips, peeled and cut into ½-inch
  pieces
1 small head (1 pound) green cabbage, cut into
  quarters, with core removed, then cut into
  ½-inch pieces
¼ cup red wine vinegar
Sour cream (optional)
⅓ cup chopped fresh dill or parsley

1 Pat beef dry with paper towels. In 8-quart Dutch oven, heat 1 teaspoon oil over medium-high heat until hot. Add half of beef and cook until well browned on all sides. Transfer beef to plate. Repeat with 1 teaspoon oil and remaining beef.

2 Reduce heat to medium. In remaining 1 tablespoon oil, cook onion, stirring occasionally, 10 minutes or until very tender. Stir in garlic, cinnamon stick, and allspice; cook 30 seconds. Add tomatoes with their juice and cook 5 minutes, breaking up tomatoes with side of spoon.

3 Return beef to Dutch oven. Stir in beets, celeriac, beef broth, bay leaf, salt, and *4 cups water*; heat to boiling over high heat. Reduce heat to low; cover and simmer 1 hour.

4 Stir in carrots, potatoes, parsnips, and cabbage; heat to boiling over high heat. Reduce heat to low; cover and simmer 30 minutes or until vegetables and beef are tender. Stir in vinegar; remove from heat. Discard cinnamon stick and bay leaf.

5 Spoon borscht into bowls; top with dollops of sour cream if you like, and sprinkle with dill. Makes about 15 cups or 7 main-dish servings.

Each serving without sour cream: About 340 calories, 17 g protein, 31 g carbohydrate, 18 g total fat (6 g saturated), 47 mg cholesterol, 1085 mg sodium.

Creamy Corn Chowder

PREP: 25 MINUTES • COOK: 40 MINUTES

6 medium ears corn, husks and silk removed
4 slices bacon, cut into ½-inch pieces
1 medium red onion, finely chopped
1 jalapeño chile, seeded and minced
1 garlic clove, minced
2 tablespoons all-purpose flour
½ teaspoon salt
⅛ teaspoon ground black pepper
2 cans (13¾ to 14½ ounces each) chicken broth
2 cups half-and-half or light cream
1 pound red potatoes (6 medium), cut into
  ½-inch cubes
2 small ripe tomatoes, peeled, seeded, and diced
Thinly sliced basil leaves for garnish

1 Cut kernels from corncobs (you should have about 3 cups); reserve 3 corncobs.

2 In 5-quart Dutch oven, cook bacon over medium heat until browned. With slotted spoon, remove bacon to paper towels to drain.

3 To fat in Dutch oven, add onion and jalapeño and cook over low heat until tender but not browned, about 6 to 8 minutes, stirring. Add garlic; cook 1 minute. Stir in flour, salt, and pepper and cook, stirring, 1 minute.

4 Stir in broth, half-and-half, potatoes, and reserved corncobs; heat to boiling over high heat. Reduce heat to low; cover and simmer 10 to 15 minutes, until potatoes are fork-tender.

5 Discard cobs; stir in corn kernels and heat through. Transfer chowder to tureen; stir in tomatoes and bacon; top with basil. Makes about 9½ cups or 8 first-course or 4 main-dish servings.

Each first-course serving: About 275 calories, 9 g protein, 31 g carbohydrate, 14 g total fat (7 g saturated), 27 mg cholesterol, 570 mg sodium.

Clockwise from top right: Tomato Soup (page 34), Cranberry Bean Soup (page 35), Creamy Corn Chowder (opposite page), Tuscan Pappa al Pomodoro (page 35)

Beef & Barley Soup

PREP: 45 MINUTES • COOK: 2½ HOURS

One batch serves a party of 8. But we like to cook it over the weekend and freeze it in family-size portions for quick school-night dinners.

1 tablespoon plus 4 teaspoons vegetable oil
3 medium celery stalks, diced
1 large onion, diced
1½ pounds boneless beef chuck, cut into ½-inch pieces
½ teaspoon salt
2 cans (13¾ to 14½ ounces each) beef broth
1 can (14½ ounces) diced tomatoes
1 cup pearl barley
5 medium carrots (12 ounces), peeled and cut crosswise into ¼-inch-thick slices
5 medium parsnips (12 ounces), peeled and cut crosswise into ¼-inch-thick slices
2 medium turnips (8 ounces), peeled and diced
3 strips (3" by 1" each) orange peel
Pinch ground cloves

1 In 8-quart Dutch oven, heat 1 tablespoon vegetable oil over medium-high heat until hot. Add celery and onion and cook until tender and golden, about 10 minutes, stirring occasionally; transfer vegetables to bowl.

2 Pat beef dry with paper towels. In same Dutch oven, heat 2 teaspoons oil over high heat until hot. Add half of beef and cook until browned on all sides. Remove to plate. Repeat with remaining 2 teaspoons oil and beef.

3 Return beef to Dutch oven. Stir in salt, celery mixture, beef broth, tomatoes with their juice, and *6 cups water*; heat to boiling over high heat. Reduce heat to low; cover and simmer 1 hour.

4 Add barley, carrots, parsnips, turnips, orange peel, and cloves; heat to boiling over high heat. Reduce heat to low; cover and simmer 50 to 60 minutes, until beef, barley, and vegetables are tender. Makes about 16 cups or 8 main-dish servings.

Each serving: About 320 calories, 25 g protein, 36 g carbohydrate, 9 g total fat (3 g saturated), 41 mg cholesterol, 740 mg sodium.

Tuscan Vegetable Soup

PREP: 45 MINUTES PLUS OVERNIGHT TO SOAK BEANS
COOK: ABOUT 1½ HOURS

Healthy and hearty—dust with freshly grated Parmesan cheese.

8 ounces dry Great Northern beans (1⅓ cups)
5 medium carrots
1 jumbo onion (1 pound)
1 bay leaf
3 tablespoons olive oil
4 ounces pancetta or cooked ham, chopped
3 large celery stalks, coarsely chopped
1 fennel bulb (1 pound), trimmed and coarsely
    chopped
2 garlic cloves, finely chopped
2 cans (13¾ to 14½ ounces each) chicken broth
1 pound all-purpose potatoes (about 3 medium),
    peeled and cut into ½-inch pieces
1 medium head escarole (about 12 ounces), cut
    crosswise into ¼-inch-wide strips
½ teaspoon salt
Grated Parmesan cheese (optional)

1 Rinse beans with cold running water and discard any stones or shriveled beans. In large bowl, place beans and 8 *cups water*. Let stand at room temperature overnight. (Or, in 4-quart saucepan, heat beans and 8 *cups water* to boiling over high heat; cook 2 minutes. Remove from heat; cover and let stand 1 hour.) Drain and rinse beans.

2 Cut 1 carrot crosswise in half. Coarsely chop remaining carrots; set aside. Cut onion into 4 wedges. Leave 1 wedge whole; coarsely chop remaining wedges.

3 In 4-quart saucepan, heat beans, carrot halves, onion wedge, bay leaf, and 6 *cups water* to boiling over high heat. Reduce heat to low; cover and simmer 40 minutes to 1 hour, until beans are tender, stirring occasionally. Drain beans and vegetables, reserving 3 cups cooking liquid. Discard carrot halves and onion wedge.

4 In 5-quart saucepot or Dutch oven, heat olive oil over medium-high heat. Add pancetta, celery, fennel, coarsely chopped carrot, and coarsely chopped onion; cook 15 minutes or until vegetables begin to brown, stirring occasionally. Add garlic; cook 1 minute, stirring.

5 Stir in chicken broth, cooked beans, reserved 3 cups bean cooking liquid, potatoes, and escarole; heat to boiling over high heat. Reduce heat to low; cover and simmer 15 to 20 minutes, until all vegetables are very tender. Discard bay leaf. Stir in salt. Serve soup with grated Parmesan cheese if you like. Makes about 14 cups or 6 main-dish servings.

Each serving without Parmesan cheese: About 335 calories, 17 g protein, 48 g carbohydrate, 10 g total fat (2 g saturated), 18 mg cholesterol, 935 mg sodium.

FOOD EDITOR'S TIP

Q. What's the difference between extravirgin, virgin, regular, and light olive oil? When should I be using which?

A. Extravirgin, the highest grade and the most expensive and least acidic type, is extracted from olives in a cold-press process. Because of its superior taste (often described as intensely fruity) and aroma, it's best used at the end of cooking or just before serving to really enhance flavor. It's also wonderful in salad dressings or as a dip with country-style bread.

Virgin olive oil is produced in the same manner as extravirgin but is more acidic. It's not widely available to consumers; most of the time it's blended with other oils before bottling.

Olive oil (formerly called pure olive oil) is produced by refining and neutralizing virgin olive oil that doesn't meet International Olive Oil Council standards. The refined oil is then blended with up to 25 percent virgin or extravirgin oil to add characteristic flavor. This pale green or yellow all-purpose oil has a less pronounced flavor and aroma than extravirgin—it works well in simple dressings and sautés.

Light olive oil, which is filtered to remove some of olive oil's usual flavor, color, and fragrance, is not lower in calories or fat. But it's an excellent choice for sautéing and frying fish and other delicate foods that you don't want to overpower with a full-bodied oil. It is also interchangeable with vegetable oil in baking.

CHICKEN & TURKEY

Skillet Lemon Chicken

PREP: 15 MINUTES • COOK: ABOUT 15 MINUTES

Serve with lightly buttered bow-tie or tubetti pasta and a simple tossed green salad.

4 medium skinless, boneless chicken-breast
    halves (about 1¼ pounds)
2 tablespoons plus 1½ teaspoons all-purpose
    flour
½ teaspoon salt
1 large egg
2 teaspoons olive oil
2 tablespoons margarine or butter
3 garlic cloves, crushed with side of chef's knife
½ lemon, thinly sliced
½ cup chicken broth
¼ cup dry white wine
2 tablespoons fresh lemon juice
2 tablespoons drained capers
1 tablespoon chopped fresh parsley leaves
Lemon leaves for garnish

1 Between 2 sheets plastic wrap, with meat mallet or rolling pin, pound chicken breasts to flatten slightly. On waxed paper, mix 2 tablespoons flour with salt. In pie plate, with fork, beat egg. Coat chicken with flour mixture, then dip in egg.

2 In nonstick 12-inch skillet, heat olive oil over medium-high heat until hot. Stir in 1 tablespoon margarine or butter until melted. Add chicken; cook 5 minutes. Reduce heat to medium; turn chicken and cook about 8 to 10 minutes longer, until juices run clear when chicken is pierced with tip of knife. Transfer chicken to warm platter.

3 Add garlic and lemon slices to drippings in skillet; cook until golden. In cup, mix chicken broth, wine, lemon juice, and 1½ teaspoons flour until smooth; stir into mixture in skillet. Heat sauce to boiling; boil 1 minute. Stir in capers and remaining 1 tablespoon margarine or butter until margarine or butter melts. Discard garlic. Arrange lemon slices over and between chicken breasts. Pour sauce over chicken. Sprinkle with chopped parsley. Garnish platter with lemon leaves. Makes 4 main-dish servings.

Each serving: About 275 calories, 36 g protein, 5 g carbohydrate, 11 g total fat (2 g saturated), 136 mg cholesterol, 705 mg sodium.

Chicken Provençal

PREP: 30 MINUTES • COOK: 1 HOUR

A melt-in-your-mouth stew flavored with orange peel and fennel seed.

2 teaspoons olive oil
2 pounds skinless, boneless chicken thighs, each
    cut into quarters
¾ teaspoon salt
2 medium red peppers, cut into ¼-inch-thick
    slices
1 medium yellow pepper, cut into ¼-inch-thick
    slices
1 jumbo onion (1 pound), thinly sliced
3 garlic cloves, crushed with garlic press
1 can (28 ounces) Italian-style plum tomatoes
¼ teaspoon dried thyme leaves
¼ teaspoon fennel seeds, crushed
3 strips (3" by 1" each) orange peel
½ cup loosely packed fresh basil leaves,
    chopped

1 In nonstick 5-quart Dutch oven, heat 1 teaspoon olive oil over medium-high heat until hot. Add half of chicken and ¼ teaspoon salt and cook until lightly browned on all sides, about 10 minutes. Transfer chicken to plate. Repeat with remaining oil, chicken, and ¼ teaspoon salt.

2 In drippings in Dutch oven, cook peppers and onion with remaining ¼ teaspoon salt, stirring frequently, until tender and lightly browned, about 20 minutes. Add garlic; cook 1 minute.

3 Return chicken to Dutch oven. Add tomatoes with their juice, thyme, fennel seeds, and orange peel, stirring to break up tomatoes with spoon; heat to boiling. Reduce heat to low; cover and simmer 15 minutes or until chicken is tender.

4 Sprinkle with basil to serve. Makes 8 main-dish servings.

Each serving: About 200 calories, 25 g protein, 13 g carbohydrate, 6 g total fat (1 g saturated), 94 mg cholesterol, 460 mg sodium.

Skillet Lemon Chicken ▶

Peanut Chicken

PREP: 10 MINUTES • COOK: 10 MINUTES

"Speed is a priority. I cook all day, so I don't want to spend all night in the kitchen too," says Lisa Troland, an associate in GH's test kitchens. To that end Lisa has designed a simple weeknight meal featuring this chicken dish served with basmati rice, sautéed spinach and garlic, and fresh pineapple wedges for dessert.

1 can (14½ ounces) diced tomatoes
¼ cup packed fresh cilantro leaves
¼ cup creamy peanut butter
2 garlic cloves
½ teaspoon salt
¼ teaspoon crushed red pepper
1 teaspoon ground cumin
¼ teaspoon ground cinnamon
1 pound chicken breast tenders
1 tablespoon vegetable oil

1 Drain tomatoes and reserve juice. In blender at high speed or in food processor with knife blade attached, blend tomato juice, cilantro, peanut butter, garlic, salt, and crushed red pepper until pureed.

2 In medium bowl, mix cumin and cinnamon; stir in chicken tenders.

3 In nonstick 12-inch skillet, heat vegetable oil over

Hearty Chicken & Vegetable Stew

medium-high heat until hot. Add chicken and cook, turning once, until browned, about 5 minutes.

4 Pour peanut-butter mixture and diced tomatoes over chicken; heat to boiling. Reduce heat to low; simmer, uncovered, 5 minutes to blend flavors. Makes 4 main-dish servings.

Each serving: About 360 calories, 36 g protein, 15 g carbohydrate, 18 g total fat (3 g saturated), 118 mg cholesterol, 795 mg sodium.

Hearty Chicken & Vegetable Stew

PREP: 45 MINUTES • COOK: 1 HOUR

All you need to round out the meal is a mixed green salad and some crusty peasant bread.

2 medium leeks (about 4 ounces each)
1 fennel bulb (about 1 pound)
2 tablespoons olive oil
2 tablespoons margarine or butter (¼ stick)
1 pound skinless, boneless chicken-breast halves, cut into 1½-inch pieces
8 ounces mushrooms, thickly sliced
3 medium carrots (about 8 ounces), cut into 1-inch pieces
¾ pound red potatoes, cut into 1-inch pieces
1 bay leaf
¼ teaspoon dried tarragon leaves
½ cup dry white wine
1 can (13¾ to 14½ ounces) chicken broth
¾ cup half-and-half or light cream
3 tablespoons all-purpose flour
1 cup frozen peas, thawed
¾ teaspoon salt

1 Cut off roots and trim leaf ends of leeks; cut each leek lengthwise in half and separate leaves. Rinse well with cold running water to remove any sand. Cut leeks crosswise into ¾-inch pieces.

2 Cut root end and stalks from fennel bulb; discard. Cut bulb lengthwise into thin wedges.

3 In 5-quart Dutch oven or saucepot, heat 1 tablespoon olive oil over medium-high heat until hot. Add 1 tablespoon margarine or butter; melt. Add chicken and cook until chicken is golden and just loses its pink color throughout. With slotted spoon, remove chicken to medium bowl.

4 To drippings in Dutch oven, add mushrooms and cook until golden (do not overbrown). Remove mushrooms to bowl with chicken.

5 To Dutch oven, add remaining 1 tablespoon olive oil; heat until hot. Add remaining 1 tablespoon margarine or butter; melt. Add carrots, leeks, fennel, potatoes, bay leaf, and tarragon. Cook vegetables 10 to 15 minutes, until fennel is translucent and leeks are wilted, stirring occasionally.

6 Add wine; cook 2 minutes, stirring. Add chicken broth and ¼ *cup water*; heat to boiling over high heat. Reduce heat to low; cover and simmer 20 minutes or until vegetables are tender.

7 In cup, mix half-and-half and flour until smooth. Stir half-and-half mixture into vegetable mixture; heat to boiling over high heat. Reduce heat to medium; cook 1 minute to thicken slightly. Stir in chicken, mushrooms, peas, and salt; heat through. Discard bay leaf. Makes 4 main-dish servings.

Each serving: About 530 calories, 37 g protein, 53 g carbohydrate, 20 g total fat (5 g saturated), 85 mg cholesterol, 985 mg sodium.

Sticky Drumsticks

PREP: 20 MINUTES • BAKE: ABOUT 35 MINUTES

Have lots of napkins on hand for these delicious oven-barbecued drumsticks. These are guaranteed to be a favorite with the kids in your family, too.

½ cup apricot preserves
¼ cup teriyaki sauce
1 tablespoon dark brown sugar
1 teaspoon cornstarch
1 teaspoon cider vinegar
¼ teaspoon salt
12 medium chicken drumsticks (about 3 pounds), skin removed

1 Preheat oven to 425°F. In large bowl, with wire whisk, mix apricot preserves, teriyaki sauce, brown sugar, cornstarch, vinegar, and salt until blended. Add chicken drumsticks, tossing to coat.

2 Spoon chicken and sauce into 15½" by 10½" jelly-roll pan. Bake 15 minutes. Remove chicken from oven; with pastry brush, brush chicken with sauce in pan. Cook chicken 15 to 20 minutes longer, brushing with sauce every 5 minutes.

3 Remove chicken from oven; brush with sauce.

Allow chicken to cool on jelly-roll pan 10 minutes before serving. Place chicken in serving dish; spoon sauce in jelly-roll pan over chicken. Makes 12 main-dish servings.

Each serving: About 120 calories, 13 g protein, 12 g carbohydrate, 2 g total fat (1 g saturated), 48 mg cholesterol, 330 mg sodium.

Grilled Chicken Cutlets with Tomato-Olive Relish

PREP: 15 MINUTES • GRILL: 10 TO 12 MINUTES

Our tasty no-cook relish was inspired by Italian *puttanesca* sauce.

2 medium tomatoes, diced
¼ cup Kalamata olives, pitted and coarsely chopped
2 tablespoons minced red onion
2 tablespoons drained capers
1 teaspoon red wine vinegar
3 teaspoons olive oil
4 medium skinless, boneless chicken-breast halves (about 1 pound)
¼ teaspoon salt
¼ teaspoon coarsely ground black pepper
Kalamata olives for garnish

1 In small bowl, mix tomatoes, chopped olives, red onion, capers, vinegar, and 1 teaspoon olive oil; set aside.

2 In medium bowl, toss chicken breasts with salt, pepper, and remaining 2 teaspoons olive oil to coat.

3 Place chicken on grill over medium heat. Cook chicken 5 to 6 minutes per side or until juices run clear when thickest part is pierced with tip of knife, turning once. Serve chicken topped with relish and garnish with olives. Makes 4 main-dish servings.

Each serving: About 205 calories, 27 g protein, 4 g carbohydrate, 9 g total fat (2 g saturated), 72 mg cholesterol, 490 mg sodium.

Baby Spinach with Nectarines & Grilled Chicken

PREP: 25 MINUTES • GRILL: ABOUT 15 MINUTES

There's no waste with baby spinach—it's so tender, you can eat the stems and all.

4 medium skinless, boneless chicken-breast
   halves (about 1 pound)
1 teaspoon fresh thyme leaves
¾ teaspoon salt
½ teaspoon coarsely ground black pepper
2 tablespoons olive oil
1 tablespoon balsamic vinegar
½ teaspoon Dijon mustard
1 shallot, minced
2 large ripe nectarines, pitted and sliced
½ English (seedless) cucumber, cut lengthwise in
   half, then thinly sliced crosswise
8 ounces baby spinach
2 ounces feta cheese, crumbled

1 Rub chicken with thyme, ½ teaspoon salt, and ¼ teaspoon pepper. Place chicken on grill over medium heat. Cook chicken about 7 minutes per side or until juices run clear when thickest part is pierced with tip of knife, turning once. Transfer chicken to cutting board; cool until easy to handle.

2 Meanwhile, in large bowl, with wire whisk, mix olive oil, vinegar, mustard, shallot, ¼ teaspoon salt, and ¼ teaspoon pepper. Stir in nectarines and cucumber.

3 To serve, cut chicken into ½-inch-thick slices. Toss spinach with nectarine mixture. Arrange salad on 4 plates; top with feta and sliced chicken. Makes 4 main-dish servings.

Each serving: About 290 calories, 31 g protein, 12 g carbohydrate, 13 g total fat (4 g saturated), 85 mg cholesterol, 695 mg sodium.

Chicken Breasts in Orange Sauce

PREP: 15 MINUTES • COOK: 30 MINUTES

Use sweet seedless oranges for this flavorful entrée.

4 large navel oranges
4 medium chicken-breast halves with bones
   (about 2½ pounds), skin removed
½ teaspoon salt
½ teaspoon coarsely ground black pepper
¼ teaspoon dried thyme leaves
1 tablespoon olive oil
½ cup chicken broth
¼ cup orange marmalade
1 teaspoon cornstarch

1 With vegetable peeler, remove four 3-inch-long strips peel (about ¾ inch wide each) from 1 orange. Cut peel lengthwise into very thin slivers. Squeeze enough juice from 2 oranges to equal ⅔ cup. Cut peel and white pith from remaining 2 oranges. Cut each orange in half from stem to blossom end, then cut each half crosswise into ¼-inch-thick slices; set aside.

2 Rub chicken breasts with salt, pepper, and thyme. In nonstick 12-inch skillet, heat olive oil over medium-high heat until hot. Add chicken breasts and cook until golden, about 6 minutes, turning once. Add orange juice, orange-peel strips, and chicken broth; heat to boiling. Reduce heat to low; cover and simmer 20 minutes or until juices run clear when chicken is pierced with tip of knife.

3 In cup, mix orange marmalade and cornstarch until blended. Transfer chicken breasts to warm platter; keep warm. To same skillet, add marmalade mixture; heat to boiling. Cook, stirring constantly, 1 minute, until sauce thickens slightly. Stir in orange slices; heat through. Spoon sauce over chicken breasts on platter. Makes 4 main-dish servings.

Each serving: About 305 calories, 35 g protein, 29 g carbohydrate, 6 g total fat (1 g saturated), 82 mg cholesterol, 460 mg sodium.

◀ *Baby Spinach with Nectarines & Grilled Chicken*

Rosemary-Apricot Chicken

PREP: 20 MINUTES PLUS MARINATING
BAKE: 45 MINUTES

A crowd pleaser to dish up hot or cold and a perfect picnic dish or potluck supper offering. If you'll have access to a grill on your picnic, bake marinated chicken at home *without the glaze*, then reheat on grill, brushing with apricot mixture just before removing from flame. Bring along a variety of fully cooked sausages to put on the fire alongside chicken.

2 teaspoons salt
1 teaspoon dried rosemary leaves, crumbled
½ teaspoon ground black pepper
4 garlic cloves, crushed with garlic press
3 chickens (about 3 pounds each), each cut into
    quarters, with skin removed
½ cup apricot jam
2 tablespoons fresh lemon juice
2 teaspoons Dijon mustard

1 In cup, mix salt, rosemary, pepper, and garlic. Rub rosemary mixture over chicken quarters; cover and refrigerate in large bowl about 2 hours.

2 Preheat oven to 350°F. Place chicken quarters, skinned side up, in 2 large roasting pans (about 17" by 11½" each) or 2 jelly-roll pans (15½" by 10½" each). Bake chicken 25 minutes on 2 oven racks, rotating pans between upper and lower racks halfway through baking.

3 Meanwhile, in small bowl, with fork, mix apricot jam, lemon juice, and mustard. Brush apricot mixture over chicken; bake 20 minutes longer, rotating pans after 10 minutes or until juices run clear when thickest part of thigh is pierced with tip of knife. Serve chicken hot or cover and refrigerate to serve cold later. Makes 12 main-dish servings.

Each serving: About 275 calories, 36 g protein, 10 g carbohydrate, 9 g total fat (3 g saturated), 109 mg cholesterol, 485 mg sodium.

Rosemary-Apricot Chicken

Roast Chicken with Creamy Mushroom Sauce

PREP: 15 MINUTES • ROAST: ABOUT 1 HOUR

Perfectly cooked meat and a classic sauce you make in the same roasting pan—what could be easier?

1 whole chicken (about 3½ pounds)
½ teaspoon salt
¼ teaspoon coarsely ground black pepper
1 package (8 ounces) white mushrooms, each cut into quarters
1 package (3½ ounces) shiitake mushrooms, stemmed and each cut into quarters
1 tablespoon all-purpose flour
1¼ cups reduced-sodium chicken broth
2 tablespoons heavy or whipping cream
1 tablespoon chopped fresh parsley leaves

1 Preheat oven to 450°F. Remove giblets and neck from chicken; refrigerate for use another day. Rinse chicken with cold running water and drain well; pat dry with paper towels. Sprinkle chicken with salt and pepper.

2 With breast side up, lift wings up toward neck, then fold wing tips under back of chicken so wings stay in place. With string, tie legs together. Place chicken, breast side up, on rack in small roasting pan (about 14" by 10").

3 Roast chicken 15 minutes; add mushrooms to roasting pan, and roast chicken about 45 minutes longer. Chicken is done when temperature on meat thermometer reaches 175° to 180°F. and juices run clear when thickest part of thigh is pierced with tip of knife.

4 Place chicken on warm platter; let stand 10 minutes to allow juices to set for easier carving.

5 Meanwhile, remove rack from roasting pan. Skim and discard fat from drippings. In small bowl, with wire whisk, mix flour and ¼ cup chicken broth until smooth; stir into mushrooms in roasting pan. Heat mushroom mixture over medium heat 1 minute, stirring constantly. Slowly stir remaining 1 cup broth into roasting pan; cook, stirring constantly, until mixture boils and thickens slightly, about 5 minutes.

6 Remove pan from heat; stir in cream and parsley. Serve chicken with mushroom sauce. Remove skin from chicken before eating if you like. Makes 4 main-dish servings.

Each serving without skin: About 330 calories, 45 g protein, 6 g carbohydrate, 14 g total fat (5 g saturated), 139 mg cholesterol, 570 mg sodium.

Plum-Glazed Chicken

PREP: 10 MINUTES • ROAST: ABOUT 1 HOUR

Pop the chicken in the oven, and brush it during the last 10 minutes with a mixture of plum jam and Chinese five-spice powder.

1 whole chicken (about 3½ pounds)
¼ cup plum jam
¾ teaspoon Chinese five-spice powder
½ teaspoon salt
2 tablespoons margarine or butter (¼ stick), softened
¼ teaspoon coarsely ground black pepper

1 Preheat oven to 450°F. Remove giblets and neck from chicken; refrigerate for use another day. Rinse chicken with cold running water and drain well; pat dry with paper towels.

2 In small bowl, stir plum jam with ½ teaspoon five-spice powder and ¼ teaspoon salt. In another small bowl, stir margarine or butter with pepper, remaining ¼ teaspoon five-spice powder, and remaining ¼ teaspoon salt until blended. With fingertips, gently separate skin from meat on breast and thighs. Rub margarine mixture on meat under skin.

3 With breast side up, lift wings up toward neck, then fold wing tips under back of chicken so wings stay in place. With string, tie legs together. Place chicken, breast side up, on rack in small roasting pan (about 14" by 10").

4 Roast chicken about 1 hour, brushing occasionally with plum-jam mixture during last 10 minutes. Chicken is done when temperature on meat thermometer reaches 175° to 180°F. and juices run clear when thickest part of thigh is pierced with tip of knife.

5 Place chicken on warm platter; let stand 10 minutes to set juices for easier carving. Makes 4 main-dish servings.

Each serving with skin: About 485 calories, 44 g protein, 14 g carbohydrate, 27 g total fat (7 g saturated), 174 mg cholesterol, 470 mg sodium.

Mexico City Roast Chicken

PREP: 15 MINUTES • ROAST: ABOUT 1 HOUR

The contrast of warm spices, brown sugar, and smoky chipotle chiles in adobo* adds a delicious depth of flavor.

1 whole chicken (about 3½ pounds)
2 tablespoons chipotle chiles in adobo,* finely
    chopped
1 tablespoon brown sugar
1 tablespoon chili powder
1 tablespoon cider vinegar
1 teaspoon ground cumin
2 teaspoons tomato paste
½ teaspoon salt
⅛ teaspoon ground cinnamon
2 jumbo onions (about 12 ounces each), each
    cut into 8 wedges
2 teaspoons vegetable oil
Optional accompaniments: warm flour tortillas,
    shredded lettuce, cilantro leaves, and lime
    wedges

1 Preheat oven to 450°F. Remove giblets and neck from chicken; refrigerate for use another day. Rinse chicken with cold running water and drain well; pat dry with paper towels.

2 In small bowl, combine chipotle chiles, brown sugar, chili powder, vinegar, cumin, tomato paste, salt, and cinnamon until blended (mixture will be thick). With fingertips, gently separate skin from meat on chicken breast and thighs. Spread chipotle mixture on meat under skin.

3 With breast side up, lift wings up toward neck, then fold wing tips under back of chicken so wings stay in place. With string, tie legs together.

4 In medium roasting pan (about 15½" by 10½"), stir onions with oil and ¼ *cup water*. Place chicken, breast side up, in pan.

5 Roast chicken about 1 hour, stirring onions halfway through cooking time. Chicken is done when temperature on meat thermometer reaches 175° to 180°F. and juices run clear when thickest part of thigh is pierced with tip of knife.

6 Place chicken on warm platter; let stand 10 minutes to allow juices to set for easier carving.

7 Meanwhile, with slotted spoon, transfer onions to platter with chicken. Skim and discard fat from drippings in pan. Serve chicken with any pan juices or, slice chicken and wrap in warm tortillas with lettuce and cilantro. Serve with lime wedges. Remove skin from chicken before eating if you like. Makes 4 main-dish servings.

*Canned chipotle chiles in adobo (smoked jalapeño chiles in a vinegary marinade) are available in Hispanic markets.

Each serving without skin and accompaniments: About 385 calories, 44 g protein, 20 g carbohydrate, 14 g total fat (3 g saturated), 130 mg cholesterol, 510 mg sodium.

Peking Chicken

PREP: 20 MINUTES • ROAST: ABOUT 1 HOUR

It's glazed with a fragrant honey-soy sauce mixture near the end of roasting.

1 whole chicken (about 3½ pounds)
2 tablespoons honey
2 tablespoons soy sauce
1 tablespoon minced, peeled fresh ginger
2 garlic cloves, crushed with garlic press
1 teaspoon seasoned rice vinegar
⅛ teaspoon ground red pepper (cayenne)
1 package (10 ounces) 8-inch flour tortillas
¼ cup chicken broth
¼ cup hoisin sauce
2 green onions, each cut crosswise into thirds,
    then sliced lengthwise into thin strips

1 Preheat oven to 450°F. Remove giblets and neck from chicken; refrigerate for use another day. Rinse chicken with cold running water and drain well.

2 With breast side up, lift wings up toward neck, then fold wing tips under back of chicken so wings stay in place. With string, tie legs together.

3 Place chicken, breast side up, on rack in sink. Pour *1 quart boiling water* over chicken. Turn chicken over; pour *1 quart boiling water* over back of chicken. (This process allows fat to render easily from chicken and helps skin get crispy during roasting.)

4 Place chicken, breast side up, on rack in small roasting pan (about 14" by 10"). Roast chicken 50 minutes.

5 Meanwhile, in cup, combine honey, soy sauce, ginger, garlic, rice vinegar, and ground red pepper; set aside.

6 After chicken has roasted 50 minutes, brush with half of honey glaze; continue roasting 5 minutes. Brush with remaining glaze; roast about 5 minutes longer. Chicken is done when temperature on meat thermometer reaches 175° to 180°F. and juices run clear when thickest part of thigh is pierced with tip of knife.

7 Place chicken on warm platter; let stand 10 minutes to set juices for easier carving.

8 Meanwhile, warm tortillas as label directs. Remove rack from roasting pan. Skim and discard fat from pan. Add chicken broth and 2 *tablespoons water* to pan; heat to boiling over medium heat, stirring to loosen brown bits. Stir in hoisin sauce.

9 Remove skin from chicken if you like. Slice chicken and wrap in tortillas with hoisin-sauce mixture and green onions. Makes 4 main-dish servings.

Each serving with skin: About 680 calories, 51 g protein, 56 g carbohydrate, 27 g total fat (7 g saturated), 174 mg cholesterol, 1375 mg sodium.

Tandoori-Style Chicken

PREP: 15 MINUTES • ROAST: ABOUT 1 HOUR

A low-fat yogurt coating spiked with lime juice and spices adds zip to skinless chicken.

1 whole chicken (about 3½ pounds), skin removed
1 container (8 ounces) plain low-fat yogurt
½ small onion, chopped
1 tablespoon paprika
2 tablespoons fresh lime juice
1 tablespoon minced, peeled fresh ginger
1 teaspoon ground cumin
1 teaspoon ground coriander
¾ teaspoon salt
¼ teaspoon ground red pepper (cayenne)
Pinch ground cloves

1 Preheat oven to 450°F. Remove giblets and neck from chicken; refrigerate for use another day. Rinse chicken with cold running water and drain well; pat dry with paper towels.

2 In blender at high speed, blend all ingredients except chicken until smooth. With breast side up, lift wings up toward neck, then fold wing tips under back of chicken so wings stay in place. With string, tie legs together.

3 In large bowl, coat chicken inside and outside with yogurt mixture. Place chicken, breast side up, on rack in small roasting pan (about 14" by 10"). Brush chicken with half of yogurt mixture remaining in bowl; reserve any remaining mixture.

4 Roast chicken 30 minutes; brush with remaining yogurt mixture. Roast chicken about 30 minutes longer or until temperature on meat thermometer reaches 175° to 180°F. and juices run clear when thickest part of thigh is pierced with tip of knife.

5 Place chicken on warm platter; let stand 10 minutes to allow juices to set for easier carving. Makes 4 main-dish servings.

Each serving: About 330 calories, 45 g protein, 8 g carbohydrate, 12 g total fat (4 g saturated), 132 mg cholesterol, 565 mg sodium.

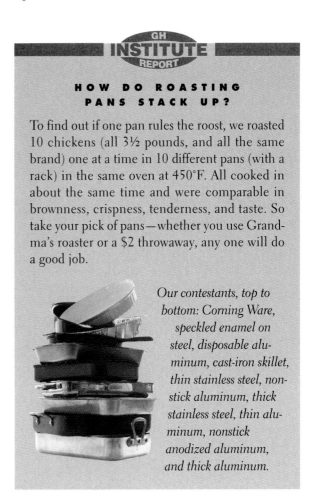

Roast Chicken with 40 Cloves of Garlic

PREP: 15 MINUTES • ROAST: ABOUT 1 HOUR

The garlic cooks in the same pan as the chicken, until the cloves are soft and golden. Some of the garlic is then mashed into the pan juices; the rest can be spread on crusty bread.

1 whole chicken (about 3½ pounds)
6 thyme sprigs
½ teaspoon salt
¼ teaspoon coarsely ground black pepper
40 garlic cloves (about 2 heads), unpeeled, with loose papery skin discarded
1 cup chicken broth

1 Preheat oven to 450°F. Remove giblets and neck from chicken; refrigerate for use another day. Rinse chicken with cold running water and drain well; pat dry with paper towels.

2 With fingertips, gently separate skin from meat on chicken breast. Place 4 thyme sprigs under skin of chicken breast. Place remaining thyme sprigs inside cavity of chicken. Sprinkle outside of chicken with salt and pepper.

3 With breast side up, lift wings up toward neck, then fold wing tips under back of chicken so wings stay in place. With string, tie legs together. Place chicken, breast side up, on rack in small roasting pan (about 14" by 10").

4 Roast chicken 30 minutes. Add garlic cloves to pan and roast about 30 minutes longer. Chicken is done when temperature on meat thermometer reaches 175° to 180°F. and juices run clear when thickest part of thigh is pierced with tip of knife.

5 Place chicken on warm platter; let stand 10 minutes to set juices for easier carving.

6 Meanwhile, remove rack from roasting pan. With slotted spoon, transfer garlic cloves to small bowl. Skim and discard fat from drippings in pan. Discard skin from 6 garlic cloves; add garlic to roasting pan with chicken broth. Heat broth mixture to boiling over medium heat, stirring to loosen brown bits and mashing garlic with spoon until well blended.

7 Serve chicken with pan juices and remaining garlic cloves. Remove skin from chicken before eating if you like. Makes 4 main-dish servings.

Each serving without skin: About 330 calories, 45 g protein, 10 g carbohydrate, 11 g total fat (3 g saturated), 129 mg cholesterol, 590 mg sodium.

Roast Chicken with Pears & Sage

PREP: 15 MINUTES • ROAST: ABOUT 1 HOUR

An easy, delicious year-round entrée. If you can't get fresh sage, used dried whole-leaf sage. Crumble the leaves that are mixed with the margarine; the leaves that go into the chicken cavity can be left whole.

1 whole chicken (about 3½ pounds)
1 teaspoon thinly sliced fresh sage leaves plus 6 sprigs
¼ teaspoon coarsely ground black pepper
2 tablespoons plus 1 teaspoon margarine or butter, softened
½ teaspoon salt
1 medium red onion, cut into ½-inch-thick slices
2 medium Bosc or Anjou pears, peeled, cored, and each cut into quarters

1 Preheat oven to 450°F. Remove giblets and neck from chicken; refrigerate for use another day. Rinse chicken with cold running water and drain well; pat dry with paper towels.

2 In small bowl, stir sliced sage, pepper, 2 tablespoons margarine or butter, and ¼ teaspoon salt. With fingertips, gently separate skin from meat on breast and thighs. Sprinkle herb mixture on meat under skin. Place sage sprigs inside cavity of chicken. Sprinkle outside of chicken with remaining ¼ teaspoon salt.

3 With breast side up, lift wings up toward neck, then fold wing tips under back of chicken so wings stay in place. With string, tie legs together.

4 In small roasting pan (about 14" by 10"), in oven, melt remaining margarine or butter. Remove pan from oven; stir in sliced onion and ¼ *cup water*. Place chicken, breast side up, on small rack in roasting pan with onion. Roast chicken and onion 30 minutes. Add pears and roast about 30 minutes longer.

Chicken is done when temperature on meat thermometer reaches 175° to 180°F. and juices run clear when thickest part of thigh is pierced with tip of knife.

5 Place chicken on warm platter; let stand 10 minutes to set juices for easier carving.

6 Meanwhile, remove rack from pan. Skim and discard fat from pear mixture. Transfer pear mixture to platter with chicken. Remove skin from chicken before eating if you like. Makes 4 main-dish servings.

Each serving without skin: About 405 calories, 42 g protein, 18 g carbohydrate, 18 g total fat (4 g saturated), 129 mg cholesterol, 480 mg sodium.

Chicken Paprikash

PREP: 15 MINUTES • ROAST: ABOUT 1 HOUR

Lots of thinly sliced onions are tossed with paprika and roasted in the pan with the chicken until they're soft and tender. Just a bit of sour cream adds a rich finish.

1 whole chicken (about 3½ pounds)
1 tablespoon margarine or butter, softened
1 garlic clove, crushed with garlic press
2 jumbo onions (about 12 ounces each), thinly sliced
1 tablespoon paprika
½ teaspoon salt
¼ cup chicken broth
2 tablespoons sour cream

1 Preheat oven to 450°F. Remove giblets and neck from chicken; refrigerate for use another day. Rinse chicken with cold running water and drain well; pat dry with paper towels.

2 In cup, mix margarine or butter with garlic. With fingertips, gently separate skin from meat on chicken breast and thighs. Spread garlic mixture on meat under skin.

3 With breast side up, lift wings up toward neck, then fold wing tips under back of chicken so wings stay in place. With string, tie legs together.

4 In small roasting pan (about 14" by 10"), stir onions with paprika, salt, and ¼ *cup water*. Place chicken, breast side up in pan.

5 Roast chicken about 1 hour, stirring onions halfway through roasting time. Chicken is done when temperature on meat thermometer reaches 175° to 180°F. and juices run clear when thickest part of thigh is pierced with tip of knife.

6 Place chicken on warm platter; let stand 10 minutes to allow juices to set for easier carving.

7 Meanwhile, skim and discard fat from onion mixture in pan. Add chicken broth to onions; heat to boiling over medium heat, stirring to loosen brown bits. Stir in sour cream. Serve chicken with onion mixture. Remove skin from chicken before eating if you like. Makes 4 main-dish servings.

Each serving without skin: About 385 calories, 44 g protein, 16 g carbohydrate, 16 g total fat (5 g saturated), 132 mg cholesterol, 485 mg sodium.

5 STEPS TO A PICTURE-PERFECT ROAST CHICKEN

1. Remove the giblets (usually packed in a paper bag) from cavity, then rinse the entire chicken under cold running water. Carefully pat dry inside and outside with paper towels.

2. Before roasting, use your fingers to remove the fatty flaps under the skin near the cavity (so there's less fat to trim later).

3. Tuck the wing tips under the chicken to secure tips and prevent them from burning, and to help steady the bird.

4. Bring the legs together and tie with kitchen string (or, in a pinch, heavy-duty thread) to secure. This helps the chicken brown evenly.

5. If using a standard meat thermometer, insert point into thickest part of thigh, next to body (be sure point touches meat, not bone). If using an instant-read thermometer, start testing after 50 minutes of roasting, placing thermometer point in thickest part of thigh. Because an instant-read thermometer isn't oven-safe, remove it if chicken needs to roast longer.

Apple & Thyme Chicken

PREP: 20 MINUTES • ROAST: ABOUT 1 HOUR

A homey favorite, with sweet roasted onion, tart green apples, and allspice.

1 whole chicken (about 3½ pounds)
1 bunch thyme
¾ teaspoon salt
¼ teaspoon coarsely ground black pepper
⅛ teaspoon ground allspice
1 jumbo onion (about 1 pound), peeled and cut into ½-inch-thick wedges
2 teaspoons olive oil
2 large Granny Smith apples, cored and each cut into quarters
2 tablespoons applejack or calvados (apple brandy)
½ cup chicken broth

1 Preheat oven to 450°F. Remove giblets and neck from chicken; refrigerate for use another day. Rinse chicken with cold running water and drain well; pat dry with paper towels.

2 Reserve 2 thyme sprigs; chop enough remaining thyme leaves to equal 1 tablespoon. With fingertips, gently separate skin from meat on chicken breast. Place 1 thyme sprig under skin of each breast half. In cup, mix chopped thyme, salt, pepper, and allspice.

3 With breast side up, lift wings up toward neck, then fold wing tips under back of chicken so wings stay in place. With string, tie legs together.

4 In medium roasting pan (about 15½" by 10½"), stir onion wedges with olive oil, chopped thyme mixture, and ¼ cup water. Push onion mixture to sides of roasting pan. Place chicken, breast side up, on small rack in center of roasting pan.

5 Roast chicken and onion wedges 40 minutes. Add apples to pan; roast about 20 minutes longer. Chicken is done when temperature on meat thermometer reaches 175° to 180°F. and juices run clear when thickest part of thigh is pierced with tip of knife.

6 Place chicken on warm platter; let stand 10 minutes to allow juices to set for easier carving.

7 Meanwhile, remove rack from roasting pan. With slotted spoon, transfer onion mixture to platter with chicken. Skim and discard fat from drippings in pan. Add applejack to pan and cook 1 minute over medium heat, stirring. Add chicken broth; heat to boiling.

Serve pan-juice mixture with chicken. Remove skin from chicken before eating if you like. Makes 4 main-dish servings.

Each serving without skin: About 420 calories, 44 g protein, 25 g carbohydrate, 15 g total fat (4 g saturated), 130 mg cholesterol, 625 mg sodium.

Roast Chicken with Herb Butter

PREP: 10 MINUTES • ROAST: ABOUT 1 HOUR

1 whole chicken (about 3½ pounds)
3 tablespoons margarine or butter, softened
2 tablespoons chopped fresh chives
1 tablespoon chopped fresh parsley leaves
¼ teaspoon salt
¼ teaspoon coarsely ground black pepper

1 Preheat oven to 450°F. Remove giblets and neck from chicken; refrigerate for use another day. Rinse chicken with cold running water and drain well; pat dry with paper towels.

2 In cup, mix margarine or butter, chives, and parsley until blended. With fingertips, gently separate skin from meat on chicken breast and thighs. Rub herb mixture on meat under skin. Sprinkle outside of chicken with salt and pepper.

3 With breast side up, lift wings up toward neck, then fold wing tips under back of chicken so wings stay in place. With string, tie legs together. Place chicken, breast side up, on rack in small roasting pan (about 14" by 10").

4 Roast chicken about 1 hour. Chicken is done when temperature on meat thermometer reaches 175° to 180°F. and juices run clear when thickest part of thigh is pierced with tip of knife.

5 Place chicken on warm platter; let stand 10 minutes to set juices for easier carving. Remove skin from chicken before eating if you like. Makes 4 main-dish servings.

Each serving without skin: About 350 calories, 42 g protein, 0 g carbohydrate, 19 g total fat (5 g saturated), 129 mg cholesterol, 370 mg sodium.

Apple & Thyme Chicken ➤

Asian Sesame Chicken

PREP: 15 MINUTES • ROAST: ABOUT 1 HOUR

Intense, exotic sesame oil, made from roasted sesame seeds, takes chicken from ordinary to out-of-this-world.

1 whole chicken (about 3½ pounds)
2 green onions, minced
1 tablespoon minced, peeled fresh ginger
1 garlic clove, minced
2 tablespoons Asian sesame oil
½ teaspoon salt
¼ teaspoon coarsely ground black pepper

1 Preheat oven to 450°F. Remove giblets and neck from chicken; refrigerate for use another day. Rinse chicken with cold running water and drain well; pat dry with paper towels.

2 In small bowl, stir green onions with ginger, garlic, and 1 tablespoon sesame oil until mixed. With fingertips, gently separate skin from meat on breast and thighs. Rub green-onion mixture on breast meat under skin.

3 With breast side up, lift wings up toward neck, then fold wing tips under back of chicken so wings stay in place. With string, tie legs together. Sprinkle chicken with salt and pepper. Place chicken, breast side up, on rack in small roasting pan (about 14" by 10").

4 Roast chicken 50 minutes. Brush with remaining 1 tablespoon sesame oil and roast about 10 minutes longer. Chicken is done when temperature on meat thermometer reaches 175° to 180°F. and juices run clear when thickest part of thigh is pierced with tip of knife.

5 Place chicken on warm platter; let stand 10 minutes to set juices for easier carving. Remove skin from chicken before eating if you like. Makes 4 main-dish servings.

Each serving without skin: About 310 calories, 42 g protein, 1 g carbohydrate, 14 g total fat (3 g saturated), 129 mg cholesterol, 390 mg sodium.

FOOD EDITOR'S TIP

Q. Sometimes, even when my roast chicken tests done, I notice pinkish juices inside the cavity. Is it still safe to eat?

A. Yes. We have seen our share of pink cavity juices over the years. The juice picks up the color of the chicken's kidneys, which are so small (each is about the size of a grape) that they're not removed along with the heart, liver, and gizzard. But there's no need to worry as long as your bird passes the traditional "done" tests: the temperature on a meat thermometer placed in the thickest part of the thigh hits 175° to 180°F., and juices run clear when the plumpest part of the thigh is pierced with a knife.

Roast Chicken with Basil Gremolata

PREP: 15 MINUTES • ROAST: ABOUT 1 HOUR

Gremolata, a flavorful Italian garnish, is usually made with garlic, lemon, and parsley; using basil makes it special.

1 whole chicken (about 3½ pounds)
10 large basil leaves
1 whole head garlic
1 lemon, cut into thin slices
½ teaspoon salt
¼ teaspoon coarsely ground black pepper
½ teaspoon finely grated lemon peel

1 Preheat oven to 450°F. Remove giblets and neck from chicken; refrigerate for use another day. Rinse chicken with cold running water and drain well; pat dry with paper towels.

2 With fingertips, gently separate skin from meat on breast. Place 2 basil leaves under the skin of each breast half. Remove 1 garlic clove from head of garlic; reserve for making gremolata. Cut head of garlic horizontally in half; place inside cavity of chicken with lemon slices. Sprinkle chicken with salt and pepper.

3 With breast side up, lift wings up toward neck, then fold wing tips under back of chicken so wings stay in place. With string, tie legs together. Place chicken, breast side up, on rack in small roasting pan (about 14" by 10").

4 Roast chicken about 1 hour. Chicken is done when temperature on meat thermometer reaches 175° to 180°F. and juices run clear when thickest part of thigh is pierced with tip of knife.

5 Meanwhile, prepare *gremolata*: Mince together grated lemon peel, reserved garlic clove, and remaining 6 basil leaves.

6 Place chicken on warm platter; let stand 10 minutes to set juices for easier carving. Remove skin from chicken before eating if you like. Sprinkle with *gremolata* to serve. Makes 4 main-dish servings.

Each serving without skin: About 275 calories, 42 g protein, 0 g carbohydrate, 11 g total fat (3 g saturated), 129 mg cholesterol, 390 mg sodium.

Roast Chicken Provençal

PREP: 20 MINUTES • ROAST: ABOUT 1 HOUR

It's cooked on a bed of red peppers and onions and seasoned with fresh basil, garlic, and olives.

1 whole chicken (about 3½ pounds)
1 head garlic, separated into cloves, unpeeled, with loose papery skin discarded
½ teaspoon salt
¼ teaspoon coarsely ground black pepper
2 medium red peppers, cut into 1½-inch-wide slices
1 jumbo onion (about 12 ounces), cut into ½-inch-wide wedges
1 teaspoon olive oil
½ cup Mediterranean olives, such as Kalamata, picholine, or Niçoise
½ cup chicken broth
2 tablespoons chopped fresh basil leaves

1 Preheat oven to 450°F. Remove giblets and neck from chicken; refrigerate for use another day. Rinse chicken with cold running water and drain well; pat dry with paper towels.

2 Place garlic cloves inside cavity of chicken. Sprinkle outside of chicken with salt and pepper.

3 With breast side up, lift wings up toward neck, then fold wing tips under back of chicken so wings stay in place. With string, tie legs together.

4 Place peppers and onion in small roasting pan (about 14" by 10"); stir in olive oil and ¼ *cup water*. Place chicken, breast side up, on vegetables.

5 Roast chicken and vegetables 45 minutes. Stir olives into vegetable mixture and roast about 15 min-

utes longer. Chicken is done when temperature on meat thermometer reaches 175° to 180°F. and juices run clear when thickest part of thigh is pierced with tip of knife.

6 Place chicken on warm platter; let stand 10 minutes to set juices for easier carving.

7 Meanwhile, with slotted spoon, transfer vegetable mixture to platter with chicken. Skim and discard fat from drippings in pan. Add chicken broth, basil, and ½ *cup water* to pan; heat to boiling over medium heat, stirring to loosen brown bits. Serve with vegetables and pan juices. Remove skin from chicken before eating if you like. Makes 4 main-dish servings.

Each serving without skin: About 405 calories, 44 g protein, 16 g carbohydrate, 18 g total fat (4 g saturated), 130 mg cholesterol, 750 mg sodium.

Tarragon Chicken

PREP: 20 MINUTES • ROAST: ABOUT 1 HOUR

Deglaze the pan with chicken broth and white wine, and spoon the juices over the tender meat.

1 whole chicken (about 3½ pounds)
2 tablespoons chopped fresh tarragon leaves
1 tablespoon margarine or butter, softened
½ teaspoon salt
¼ teaspoon coarsely ground black pepper
3 shallots, peeled
1 carrot, cut into 1-inch pieces
1 celery stalk, cut into 1-inch pieces
1 medium onion, cut into 8 wedges
1 teaspoon olive oil
¾ cup chicken broth
⅓ cup dry white wine

1 Preheat oven to 450°F. Remove giblets and neck from chicken; refrigerate for use another day. Rinse chicken with cold running water and drain well; pat dry with paper towels.

2 In cup, mix 1 tablespoon tarragon with margarine or butter until well blended. With fingertips, gently separate skin from meat on chicken breast and thighs. Rub tarragon mixture on meat under skin of chicken. Sprinkle outside of chicken with salt and pepper. Place 2 shallots inside cavity of chicken. Mince remaining shallot; set aside.

3 With breast side up, lift wings up toward neck, then fold wing tips under back of chicken so wings stay in place. With string, tie legs together.

4 In small roasting pan (about 14" by 10"), stir carrot, celery, onion, oil, and ¼ *cup water*. Push vegetables to sides of pan. Place chicken, breast side up, on small rack in center of pan.

5 Roast chicken about 1 hour. Chicken is done when temperature on meat thermometer reaches 175° to 180°F. and juices run clear when thickest part of thigh is pierced with tip of knife.

6 Place chicken on warm platter; let stand 10 minutes to set juices for easier carving.

7 Meanwhile, remove rack from roasting pan. Discard vegetables. Skim and discard all but 2 tablespoons fat from drippings in pan. Add minced shallot and cook over medium heat 2 minutes, stirring. Add broth and wine to pan; heat to boiling and cook 2 minutes longer, stirring to loosen brown bits. Stir in remaining tarragon. Serve chicken with pan juices. Remove skin from chicken before eating if you like. Makes 4 main-dish servings.

Each serving without skin: About 390 calories, 43 g protein, 3 g carbohydrate, 21 g total fat (6 g saturated), 134 mg cholesterol, 575 mg sodium.

Rolled Turkey Breast with Basil Mayonnaise

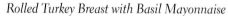

PREP: 45 MINUTES • ROAST: ABOUT 1¼ HOURS

Divide and butterfly a whole turkey breast with our simple directions. Serve hot or cold.

ROLLED TURKEY BREAST:
1 whole turkey breast with bones (about 6 pounds)
2 teaspoons salt
1 teaspoon coarsely ground black pepper
1 jar (12 ounces) roasted red peppers, drained
1½ cups loosely packed fresh basil leaves
1 tablespoon olive oil

BASIL MAYONNAISE:
2 cups loosely packed fresh basil leaves
1 cup light mayonnaise
1 cup reduced-fat sour cream
2 teaspoons fresh lemon juice
¼ teaspoon salt
Basil sprigs for garnish

Rolled Turkey Breast with Basil Mayonnaise

1 Prepare Rolled Turkey Breast: Place turkey breast on cutting board, skin side up. With sharp knife, working with 1 side of breast, starting parallel and close to large end of rib bone, cut and scrape meat away from bone and rib cage, gently pulling back meat in one piece as you cut. Repeat with remaining side of breast; discard bones and skin.

2 To butterfly breast halves: Place 1 breast half, cut side up, on cutting board. With sharp knife, starting at a long side, cut breast horizontally in half, but not all the way through, making sure that meat on other long side stays connected. Spread meat open. Place butterflied breast between 2 sheets of plastic wrap. With meat mallet or rolling pin, pound breast to about ¼-inch even thickness. Repeat with second breast half.

3 Preheat oven to 350°F. Sprinkle each breast with ½ teaspoon salt and ¼ teaspoon black pepper. Arrange red-pepper slices evenly over breasts, leaving a 2-inch border all around edges of meat; top with basil leaves. Starting at a narrow end, roll each breast with filling, jelly-roll fashion. With string, tie each rolled turkey breast at 2-inch intervals. Brush rolls with oil and sprinkle with remaining salt and pepper.

4 Place rolls, seam sides down, on rack in large roasting pan (17" by 11½"). Insert meat thermometer into center of 1 roll. Roast turkey rolls about 1 hour and 15 minutes. Turkey is done when temperature on meat thermometer reaches 160°F. Temperature will rise to 165°F. upon standing.

5 While turkey is roasting, prepare Basil Mayonnaise: In food processor with knife blade attached or in blender at medium speed, blend basil, mayonnaise, sour cream, lemon juice, and salt until sauce is creamy. Cover and refrigerate sauce until ready to use. Makes about 2 cups.

6 When turkey rolls are done, place on large platter. Let stand 10 minutes to set juices for easier carving if serving warm. If not serving right away, wrap and refrigerate turkey rolls until ready to serve.

7 To serve, remove strings. Slice turkey rolls into about ¼-inch-thick slices and serve with Basil Mayonnaise. Garnish with basil sprigs. Makes 12 main-dish servings.

Each serving of turkey: About 195 calories, 41 g protein, 2 g carbohydrate, 2 g total fat (1 g saturated), 112 mg cholesterol, 465 mg sodium.

Each tablespoon Basil Mayonnaise: About 55 calories, 1 g protein, 7 g carbohydrate, 3 g total fat (0 g saturated), 6 mg cholesterol, 245 mg sodium.

Lemon-Rosemary Roast Chicken

•••••••••••••••••••••••••••••••••••••••
PREP: 10 MINUTES • ROAST: ABOUT 1 HOUR

Scented with lemon juice and fresh rosemary, this simple dish is a good choice for beginners.

1 whole chicken (about 3½ pounds)
1 lemon, cut in half
1 bunch rosemary
¾ teaspoon salt
½ teaspoon coarsely ground black pepper
¼ cup chicken broth

1 Preheat oven to 450°F. Remove giblets and neck from chicken; refrigerate for use another day. Rinse chicken with cold running water and drain well; pat dry with paper towels.

2 Squeeze juice from lemon halves; set juice and lemon halves aside. Reserve 4 rosemary sprigs; chop enough remaining rosemary to equal 1 tablespoon. Place lemon halves and rosemary sprigs inside cavity of chicken. In cup, mix chopped rosemary with ¼ teaspoon salt and ¼ teaspoon pepper. With fingertips, gently separate skin from meat on chicken breast and thighs. Rub rosemary mixture on meat under skin. Sprinkle outside of chicken with remaining salt and pepper.

3 With breast side up, lift wings up toward neck, then fold wing tips under back of chicken so wings stay in place. With string, tie legs together. Place chicken, breast side up, on rack in small roasting pan (about 14" by 10"). Pour lemon juice over chicken.

4 Roast chicken about 1 hour. Chicken is done when temperature on meat thermometer reaches 175° to 180°F. and juices run clear when thickest part of thigh is pierced with tip of knife.

5 Place chicken on warm platter; let stand 10 minutes to set juices for easier carving.

6 Meanwhile, remove rack from roasting pan. Skim and discard fat from drippings in pan. Add chicken broth to pan drippings; heat to boiling over medium heat, stirring to loosen brown bits. Serve chicken with pan-juice mixture. Remove skin from chicken before eating if you like. Makes 4 main-dish servings.

Each serving without skin: About 280 calories, 42 g protein, 1 g carbohydrate, 11 g total fat (3 g saturated), 129 mg cholesterol, 570 mg sodium.

Roast Chicken with Orange Peel & Bay Leaves

PREP: 10 MINUTES • ROAST: ABOUT 1 HOUR

The meat is rubbed with our special orange butter, and the bay leaves are tucked under the skin before roasting.

1 whole chicken (about 3½ pounds)
2 tablespoons margarine or butter (¼ stick), softened
1½ teaspoons finely grated orange peel
¼ teaspoon coarsely ground black pepper
½ teaspoon salt
6 bay leaves

1 Preheat oven to 450°F. Remove giblets and neck from chicken; refrigerate for use another day. Rinse chicken with cold running water and drain well; pat dry with paper towels.

2 In small bowl, stir margarine or butter with orange peel, pepper, and ¼ teaspoon salt until blended. With fingertips, gently separate skin from meat on chicken breast and thighs. Rub margarine mixture on meat under skin. Place 1 bay leaf under skin of each breast half. Place remaining 4 bay leaves inside cavity of chicken. Sprinkle outside of chicken with remaining ¼ teaspoon salt.

3 With breast side up, lift wings up toward neck, then fold wing tips under back of chicken so wings stay in place. With string, tie legs together. Place chicken, breast side up, on rack in small roasting pan (about 14" by 10").

4 Roast chicken about 1 hour. Chicken is done when temperature on meat thermometer reaches 175° to 180°F. and juices run clear when thickest part of thigh is pierced with tip of knife.

5 Place chicken on warm platter; let stand 10 minutes to set juices for easier carving. Discard bay leaves. Remove skin from chicken before eating if you like. Makes 4 main-dish servings.

Each serving without skin: About 325 calories, 42 g protein, 0 g carbohydrate, 16 g total fat (4 g saturated), 129 mg cholesterol, 465 mg sodium.

Traditional Roast Turkey with Giblet Gravy

PREP: 45 MINUTES (NOT INCLUDING TIME TO PREPARE STUFFING) • ROAST: ABOUT 3¾ HOURS

Although tradition demands that the Thanksgiving bird be stuffed, we found that cooking the stuffing separately produces the juiciest meat. If you want to cook the stuffing in the bird, the stuffing temperature must reach 165°F. on a meat thermometer according to the most recent USDA food-safety guidelines.

Choice of stuffing (see pages 59 and 60)
One 14-pound fresh or frozen (thawed) ready-to-stuff turkey
1½ teaspoons salt
½ teaspoon coarsely ground black pepper
Giblet Gravy (recipe follows)
Fresh herbs for garnish

1 Prepare any of the 3 stuffings; set aside.

2 Remove giblets and neck from turkey; reserve for making Giblet Gravy. Rinse turkey with cold running water and drain well.

3 Spoon some stuffing lightly into neck cavity. Fold neck skin over stuffing; fasten neck skin to back with 1 or 2 skewers. If you like, with breast side up, lift

FOOD EDITOR'S TIP

Q. Every Thanksgiving, my gravy is lumpy. What am I doing wrong?

A. The leading cause of lumps is adding flour or cornstarch to hot pan juices; it won't completely dissolve no matter how hard you try, and your gravy won't really thicken. If you're using flour as a thickener, stir it into the fat in a saucepan and cook about 1 minute. Then, whisk in pan juices and/or other liquid and cook until gravy boils and thickens. If you're using cornstarch, whisk it with some cold water until smooth. Then, whisk the cornstarch mixture directly into the pan juices and/or other liquid and cook until the gravy boils and thickens. (The cold-water method also works with flour though we prefer the method above.) Note that cornstarch has twice the thickening power of flour.

wings toward neck, then fold them under back of turkey so they stay in place.

4 Spoon remaining stuffing lightly into body cavity. (Bake any leftover stuffing in covered small casserole during last 30 minutes of roasting time.) Close by folding skin over opening; skewer closed if necessary. Depending on brand of turkey, with string, tie legs and tail together, or push drumsticks under band of skin, or use stuffing clamp.

5 Place turkey, breast side up, on rack in large roasting pan. Rub turkey all over with salt and pepper. Cover turkey with a loose tent of foil. Insert meat thermometer through foil into thickest part of thigh next to body, being careful that pointed end of thermometer does not touch bone. Roast turkey in 325°F. oven about 3¾ hours; start checking for doneness during last hour of roasting.

6 While turkey is roasting, prepare giblets and neck to use in Giblet Gravy.

7 To brown turkey, remove foil during last hour of roasting time and baste with pan drippings occasionally. Turkey is done when thigh temperature on thermometer reaches 180° to 185°F. and drumstick feels soft when pressed with fingers protected by paper towels. (Breast temperature should be 170° to 175°F., stuffing temperature 165°F.)

8 When turkey is done, place on warm large platter; keep warm. Prepare Giblet Gravy.

9 To serve, garnish platter with fresh herbs. Serve with stuffing and gravy. Makes 14 main-dish servings.

GIBLET GRAVY: In 3-quart saucepan, heat gizzard, heart, neck, and enough *water* to cover to boiling over high heat. Reduce heat to low; cover and simmer 45 minutes. Add liver and cook 15 minutes longer. Drain, reserving broth. Pull meat from neck; discard bones. Coarsely chop neck meat and giblets. Cover and refrigerate meat and broth separately.

To make gravy, remove rack from roasting pan. Pour pan drippings through sieve into 4-cup measure or medium bowl. Add 1 cup giblet broth to roasting pan and stir until brown bits are loosened; pour into drippings in measuring cup. Let stand a few seconds until fat separates from meat juice. Spoon 2 tablespoons fat from drippings into 2-quart saucepan; skim and discard any remaining fat. Add remaining giblet broth and enough *water* to meat juice in measuring cup to equal 3 cups.

Into fat in saucepan over medium heat, stir *2 tablespoons all-purpose flour* and *½ teaspoon salt*; cook, stirring, until flour turns golden brown. Gradually stir

in meat-juice mixture and cook, stirring, until gravy boils and thickens slightly. Stir in reserved giblets and neck meat; heat through. Pour gravy into gravy boat.

Each serving of turkey without stuffing or gravy: About 445 calories, 60 g protein, 0 g carbohydrate, 21 g total fat (6 g saturated), 174 mg cholesterol, 375 mg sodium.

Each ¼ cup gravy: About 65 calories, 7 g protein, 2 g carbohydrate, 4 g total fat (1 g saturated), 63 mg cholesterol, 110 mg sodium.

Northwest Fruit Stuffing

PREP: 40 MINUTES • BAKE: 45 MINUTES

Made with tart cherries, pears, apple chunks, and raisins.

½ cup margarine or butter (1 stick)
1 large red onion, chopped
1 large fennel bulb (1¼ pounds), trimmed and diced
2 large pears, peeled, cored, and diced
1 large Granny Smith apple, peeled, cored, and diced
1½ loaves (16 ounces each) sliced firm white bread, cut into ¾-inch cubes and lightly toasted
1 cup chicken broth
⅔ cup dried tart cherries
½ cup golden raisins
⅓ cup chopped fresh parsley
2 teaspoons chopped fresh thyme leaves
1 teaspoon chopped fresh sage leaves
1 teaspoon salt
½ teaspoon coarsely ground black pepper

1 In 12-inch skillet, melt margarine or butter over medium-high heat. Add onion and fennel and cook 10 to 12 minutes, until golden, stirring occasionally. Add pears and apple and cook 5 minutes longer.

2 In large bowl, combine onion mixture with toasted bread cubes and remaining ingredients; toss to mix well. Use to stuff 12- to 16-pound turkey. Or, spoon into 13" by 9" glass baking dish; cover with foil and bake in preheated 325°F. oven 45 minutes or until heated through. Makes about 12 cups.

Each ½ cup: About 155 calories, 3 g protein, 25 g carbohydrate, 5 g total fat (1 g saturated), 0 mg cholesterol, 330 mg sodium.

Pennsylvania-Dutch Sauerkraut & Apple Stuffing

PREP: 45 MINUTES • BAKE: 45 MINUTES

A country favorite made with French bread and crushed caraway seeds.

½ cup margarine or butter (1 stick)
4 medium celery stalks, diced
1 large onion (12 ounces), diced
2 large Golden Delicious apples, peeled, cored, and diced
1 package (16 ounces) sauerkraut, rinsed and squeezed dry
1 can (13¾ to 14½ ounces) chicken broth
1½ teaspoons caraway seeds, crushed
¾ teaspoon dried thyme leaves
½ teaspoon salt
½ teaspoon coarsely ground black pepper
1½ loaves French bread (8 ounces each), cut into ½-inch cubes
¼ cup chopped fresh parsley

1 In 12-inch skillet, melt margarine or butter over medium-high heat. Add celery and onion and cook about 15 minutes or until golden, stirring occasionally. Add apples and cook 5 minutes longer. Stir in sauerkraut, broth, caraway seeds, thyme, salt, pepper, and ½ *cup water*.

2 In large bowl, combine vegetable mixture, bread cubes, and parsley; toss to mix well. Use to stuff 12- to 16-pound turkey. Or, spoon into 13" by 9" glass baking dish; cover with foil and bake in preheated 325°F. oven 45 minutes or until heated through. Makes about 11 cups.

Each ½ cup: About 100 calories, 2 g protein, 13 g carbohydrate, 5 g total fat (1 g saturated), 1 mg cholesterol, 345 mg sodium.

Albuquerque Corn-Bread Stuffing

PREP: 1 HOUR 20 MINUTES PLUS COOLING
BAKE: 45 MINUTES

This old-style stuffing starts with homemade corn bread, traditionally baked in a cast-iron skillet. Once you've made the bread, you've got the stuffing. Just crumble and drizzle with chicken broth!

2 cups yellow cornmeal
2 teaspoons baking powder
1 teaspoon baking soda
1 teaspoon salt
2 cups buttermilk
½ cup margarine or butter (1 stick), melted and cooled
1 can (14¾ ounces) cream-style corn
8 ounces shredded Monterey Jack cheese (2 cups)
2 cans (4 to 4½ ounces each) chopped mild green chiles
4 large eggs, lightly beaten
½ cup chicken broth

1 Prepare corn bread: Preheat oven to 350°F. Grease 13" by 9" metal baking pan or deep 12-inch skillet with oven-safe handle.

2 In large bowl, with spoon, mix cornmeal, baking powder, baking soda, and salt. Stir in buttermilk and remaining ingredients except chicken broth and mix until thoroughly blended. Pour batter into baking pan.

3 Bake corn bread 60 to 65 minutes, until top is browned and toothpick inserted in center comes out clean. Cool corn bread in pan on wire rack. (If not making stuffing right away, cover and reserve corn bread up to 2 days.)

4 Prepare stuffing: Into large bowl, crumble corn bread. Drizzle with chicken broth; toss to mix well. Use to stuff 12- to 16-pound turkey. Or, spoon into 13" by 9" glass baking dish; cover with foil and bake in preheated 325°F. oven 45 minutes or until heated through. Makes about 11 cups.

Each ½ cup: About 160 calories, 6 g protein, 15 g carbohydrate, 9 g total fat (3 g saturated), 49 mg cholesterol, 540 mg sodium.

MEAT

Scandinavian Beef Stew

PREP: 30 MINUTES • COOK: 2 TO 2¼ HOURS

Root vegetables and chunks of beef are cooked until tender in a spicy broth.

2 pounds boneless beef chuck, cut into 1½-inch pieces
2 tablespoons vegetable oil
1 medium onion, finely chopped
1 tablespoon ground coriander
2 teaspoons ground ginger
¼ teaspoon ground nutmeg
1 can (13¾ to 14½ ounces) beef broth
1 teaspoon salt
¼ teaspoon coarsely ground black pepper
¼ teaspoon dried thyme leaves
1 bag (16 ounces) carrots, peeled and cut into 1½-inch pieces
2 large parsnips (8 ounces), peeled and cut into 1½-inch pieces
½ small rutabaga, peeled and cut into 1-inch pieces (1½ cups)
1 pound small red potatoes, each cut in half
2 tablespoons chopped fresh parsley

1 Pat beef dry with paper towels. In 5-quart Dutch oven, heat 1 tablespoon oil over medium-high heat. Add half of beef and cook until browned on all sides. Transfer beef to plate. Repeat with remaining oil and beef.

2 Reduce heat to medium; add onion and cook 10 minutes or until tender. Stir in coriander, ginger, and nutmeg and cook 30 seconds. Add enough *water* to beef broth to equal 3 cups. Return beef to Dutch oven; stir in beef-broth mixture, salt, pepper, and thyme; heat to boiling over high heat. Reduce heat to low; cover and simmer 1 to 1¼ hours or until meat is almost fork-tender.

3 Skim fat from liquid in Dutch oven. Add carrots, parsnips, rutabaga, and potatoes; heat to boiling over high heat. Reduce heat to low; cover and simmer 30 minutes longer or until vegetables and meat are tender. Sprinkle with parsley. Makes 8 main-dish servings.

Each serving: About 420 calories, 27 g protein, 25 g carbohydrate, 24 g total fat (8 g saturated), 85 mg cholesterol, 515 mg sodium.

Spanish Beef Stew

PREP: 45 MINUTES • COOK: 3½ TO 4 HOURS

Unlike most stews, this begins with a whole piece of meat, which is shredded after cooking. Serve with fresh bread.

1 beef flank steak (1¾ pounds)
1 medium onion, coarsely chopped
1 medium carrot, coarsely chopped
1 bay leaf
2 teaspoons salt
4 teaspoons olive oil
1 large onion, sliced
1 red pepper, cut into ½-inch strips
1 yellow pepper, cut into ½-inch strips
1 green pepper, cut into ½-inch strips
3 garlic cloves, crushed with garlic press
3 serrano or jalapeño chiles, seeded and minced
¼ teaspoon ground cinnamon
1 can (14½ to 16 ounces) tomatoes
Capers for garnish

1 Cut flank steak into thirds. In 5-quart Dutch oven, heat steak, chopped onion, carrot, bay leaf, 1 teaspoon salt, and 5 *cups water* to boiling over high heat. Reduce heat to low; cover and simmer 2½ to 3 hours, until meat is very tender. Remove Dutch oven from heat and let steak stand, uncovered, 30 minutes. (Or, cover and refrigerate overnight.)

2 In 12-inch skillet, heat olive oil over medium-high heat. Add sliced onion, peppers, and remaining 1 teaspoon salt and cook, stirring often, 15 minutes or until vegetables are tender. Stir in garlic, serrano chiles, and cinnamon and cook 30 seconds. Stir in tomatoes with their juice; cook 5 minutes.

3 Remove beef to bowl; strain broth. Reserve 2 cups broth. (Reserve remaining broth for use another day.) With 2 forks, shred beef into fine strips.

4 Stir reserved broth and shredded meat into pepper mixture and simmer, uncovered, stirring occasionally, 10 minutes. Sprinkle with capers to serve. Makes 6 main-dish servings.

Each serving: About 350 calories, 38 g protein, 10 g carbohydrate, 17 g total fat (7 g saturated), 65 mg cholesterol, 720 mg sodium.

Spanish Beef Stew ▶

Chinese-Spiced Beef Stew

PREP: 30 MINUTES • COOK: 2 TO 2½ HOURS

Our new beef stew with broccoli and snow peas has a thin yet flavorful sauce accented with ginger and star anise.

2 pounds boneless beef chuck, cut into 1½-inch pieces
2 tablespoons vegetable oil
⅓ cup dry sherry
2 tablespoons sugar
3 tablespoons soy sauce
1 piece fresh ginger (3" by 1"), peeled and thinly sliced
2 garlic cloves, peeled
2 whole star anise
4 strips (3" by 1" each) orange peel
1 bunch broccoli (1½ pounds), cut into 1½" by 1" pieces
4 ounces snow peas, trimmed
1 bunch green onions, cut into 2-inch pieces

1 Pat beef dry with paper towels. In 5-quart Dutch oven, heat 1 tablespoon vegetable oil over medium-high heat until hot. Add half of beef and cook until browned on all sides. Transfer beef to plate. Repeat with remaining oil and beef.

2 Return beef to Dutch oven. Add sherry, sugar, soy sauce, ginger, garlic, star anise, orange peel, and *3 cups water*; heat to boiling over high heat. Reduce heat to low; cover and simmer 1 to 1½ hours, until meat is fork-tender.

3 With slotted spoon, transfer meat to serving bowl and keep warm. Discard star anise. Increase heat to high and boil liquid 15 minutes or until reduced to about 2 cups. Skim fat.

4 Meanwhile, in 4-quart saucepan, heat *1 inch water* to boiling over high heat. Add broccoli. Reduce heat to low; cover and simmer 5 minutes. Add snow peas and green onions and cook, covered, about 3 minutes longer or until all vegetables are tender-crisp. Drain vegetables and add to beef mixture. Pour reduced broth on top. Makes 8 main-dish servings.

Each serving: About 370 calories, 27 g protein, 12 g carbohydrate, 24 g total fat (8 g saturated), 85 mg cholesterol, 460 mg sodium.

Chili Potpie with Cheddar-Biscuit Crust

PREP: 30 MINUTES • COOK: 1¾ TO 2 HOURS

The cornmeal-Cheddar crust adds an old-fashioned crowning touch that no one can resist.

1 tablespoon plus 3 teaspoons olive oil
1 pound boneless beef chuck, cut into ½-inch pieces
1 medium onion, chopped
2 garlic cloves, minced
1 tablespoon chili powder
1 teaspoon ground coriander
½ teaspoon salt
½ teaspoon ground cumin
1 can (16 ounces) whole tomatoes in puree
1 can (4 to 4½ ounces) chopped mild green chiles
1 tablespoon dark brown sugar
1 tablespoon tomato paste
1 can (15 to 16 ounces) pink beans
¼ cup chopped fresh cilantro leaves
Cheddar-Biscuit Crust (recipe follows)
2 teaspoons milk
Green onions for garnish

1 In 5-quart Dutch oven or saucepot, heat 1 tablespoon olive oil over medium-high heat until hot. Add half the beef, and cook until browned and juices evaporate. Transfer beef to small bowl. Repeat with remaining beef and 2 teaspoons olive oil.

2 Add remaining 1 teaspoon olive oil to Dutch oven. Reduce heat to medium. Add onion and cook 10 minutes or until tender and golden. Add garlic; cook 2 minutes, stirring. Add chili powder, coriander, salt, and cumin; cook 1 minute, stirring.

3 Add tomatoes with their puree, breaking up tomatoes with side of spoon. Add chiles with their juice, brown sugar, tomato paste, beef with any accumulated juices in bowl, and *¼ cup water*; heat to boiling over high heat. Reduce heat to low; cover and simmer 30 minutes, stirring occasionally.

4 Rinse and drain beans. Add beans; heat to boiling over high heat. Reduce heat to low; cover and simmer 30 to 45 minutes longer, until beef is very tender. Stir in cilantro.

5 Preheat oven to 425°F. Meanwhile, prepare Cheddar-Biscuit Crust.

6 Spoon hot chili mixture into deep 2-quart casserole or 9-inch deep-dish pie plate. Top with biscuit crust, tucking in edge to fit. With tip of knife, cut out 5 oval openings in crust to allow steam to escape during baking. (Do not just make slits, they will close up as crust bakes.) Brush crust with milk.

7 Place sheet of foil underneath casserole; crimp foil edges to form a rim to catch any drips during baking. Bake pie 20 minutes or until crust is browned. Cool slightly. Garnish each serving with green onions if you like. Makes 6 main-dish servings.

CHEDDAR-BISCUIT CRUST: In medium bowl, mix *1 cup all-purpose flour, ⅓ cup shredded sharp Cheddar cheese, ¼ cup yellow cornmeal, 2 teaspoons baking powder,* and *½ teaspoon salt.* With pastry blender or two knives used scissor-fashion, cut in 3 *tablespoons cold margarine or butter* until mixture resembles coarse crumbs. Stir in *½ cup milk*; quickly mix just until a soft dough forms and leaves side of bowl. Turn dough onto lightly floured surface; gently knead about 5 strokes to mix thoroughly. With floured rolling pin, roll dough into a round 1 inch larger in diameter than top of casserole.

Each serving: About 515 calories, 24 g protein, 45 g carbohydrate, 27 g total fat (8 g saturated), 58 mg cholesterol, 1320 mg sodium.

Chili Potpie with Cheddar-Biscuit Crust

Beef Stir-Fry with Arugula

PREP: 10 MINUTES • COOK: 10 MINUTES

"I like to give my family a hearty dinner—and that means meat or chicken with a high-carbohydrate side dish," says Lynda Gunn of GH's test kitchens. And for a speedy weeknight meal, there's nothing like a stir-fry. To round out this meal, serve the stir-fry with rice and chilled red grapes for dessert. While the rice is cooking, rinse the arugula, then prepare the stir-fry. (If you can't find precut beef, slice a piece of round steak.)

4 teaspoons vegetable oil
1 bunch green onions, cut into 1½-inch pieces
1 package (8 ounces) sliced mushrooms
1 package (16 ounces) sliced beef for stir-fry
3 tablespoons soy sauce
3 tablespoons balsamic vinegar
2 tablespoons brown sugar
2 bunches arugula or 2 packages (8 ounces each) prewashed spinach

1 In nonstick 12-inch skillet, heat 2 teaspoons oil over medium-high heat. Add green onions and mushrooms and cook until tender and brown, about 5 minutes, stirring often. Remove to bowl.

2 In same skillet, heat 1 teaspoon oil. Add half the beef and cook, stirring constantly, until beef just loses its pink color. Remove to bowl with vegetables. Cook remaining beef as above, adding remaining 1 teaspoon oil.

3 In cup, mix soy sauce, balsamic vinegar, and brown sugar. Return beef mixture to skillet; stir in soy-sauce mixture. Cook 1 minute to heat through, stirring. Remove from heat; stir in half the arugula.

4 Spoon beef mixture over remaining arugula on platter. Makes 4 main-dish servings.

Each serving: About 260 calories, 29 g protein, 18 g carbohydrate, 15 g total fat (5 g saturated), 48 mg cholesterol, 875 mg sodium.

Spicy Tangerine Beef

PREP: 25 MINUTES • COOK: 25 MINUTES

4 tangerines or 3 medium navel oranges
3 tablespoons vegetable oil
1 boneless beef top sirloin steak (¾ pound), thinly sliced crosswise
2 tablespoons plus ½ teaspoon cornstarch
1 large bunch broccoli (1½ pounds), cut into flowerets, stems peeled and cut into ¼-inch-thick slices
3 medium green onions, cut diagonally into 2-inch pieces
1 medium red pepper, thinly sliced
3 garlic cloves, minced
1 tablespoon minced, peeled fresh ginger
3 tablespoons soy sauce
¼ teaspoon crushed red pepper

1 Cut peel and white pith from 1 tangerine or orange. Over small bowl, cut on either side of membranes to remove each segment, allowing fruit and juice to drop into bowl; set aside. From remaining fruit, with vegetable peeler, remove eight 3-inch-long strips peel (about ¾ inch wide each). With knife, remove any pith from peel. Squeeze ¾ cup juice.

2 In 12-inch skillet, heat 2 tablespoons vegetable oil over high heat until hot. Add strips of peel and cook until lightly browned, about 3 minutes. Remove peel to large bowl.

3 Meanwhile, on waxed paper, toss beef slices with 2 tablespoons cornstarch to coat evenly. Cook half of beef until crisp and lightly browned on both sides, about 5 minutes; remove to bowl with peel. Repeat with remaining 1 tablespoon vegetable oil and beef.

4 Add broccoli and *2 tablespoons water* to skillet. Reduce heat to medium; cover and cook 2 minutes. Increase heat to high. Remove cover and add green onions and red pepper; cook 2 minutes, stirring. Add garlic and ginger; cook 1 minute longer.

5 Meanwhile, in cup, stir juice, soy sauce, crushed red pepper, and remaining ½ teaspoon cornstarch until blended.

6 Add juice mixture and cook until sauce thickens slightly and boils, stirring. Return beef mixture to skillet. Add citrus segments with any juice in bowl; gently toss to combine. Makes 4 main-dish servings.

Each serving without rice: About 335 calories, 22 g protein, 24 g carbohydrate, 19 g total fat (4 g saturated), 42 mg cholesterol, 860 mg sodium.

Anise Beef Kabobs

PREP: 10 MINUTES PLUS STANDING
GRILL: 8 TO 10 MINUTES

We like to buy a sirloin steak and cut it into chunks to ensure equal-size pieces for even grilling. But, if you prefer, use precut beef cubes for kabobs, from your supermarket.

4 (8-inch) wooden skewers
2 teaspoons olive oil
1 teaspoon anise seeds or crushed fennel seeds
½ teaspoon salt
¼ teaspoon coarsely ground black pepper
Pinch crushed red pepper (optional)
1 boneless beef top sirloin steak (1 pound), 1 inch thick, cut into 1¼-inch chunks

1 Soak wooden skewers in water 15 minutes.

2 Meanwhile, in medium bowl, combine olive oil, anise seeds, salt, coarsely ground black pepper, and crushed red pepper. Add steak chunks and toss to coat; let stand 10 minutes.

3 Thread steak chunks on skewers. Place skewers on grill over medium heat; cook 8 to 10 minutes for medium-rare, turning occasionally. Makes 4 main-dish servings.

Each serving: About 185 calories, 23 g protein, 0 g carbohydrate, 10 g total fat (3 g saturated), 68 mg cholesterol, 315 mg sodium.

Beef Brisket with Fresh & Dried Mushrooms

PREP: 1½ HOURS • BAKE: 2½ HOURS

The meat is slow-simmered in a robust red-wine sauce with sliced red onions and a variety of herbs.

½ ounce sliced dried porcini mushrooms (about ½ cup)
½ pound shiitake mushrooms
½ pound small white mushrooms
¼ cup vegetable oil
1 fresh beef brisket (4 pounds), trimmed
4 medium red onions, sliced
2 garlic cloves, sliced
3 tablespoons all-purpose flour
1 can (13¾ to 14½ ounces) beef broth

Spicy Tangerine Beef

1 cup dry red wine
¼ cup brandy
4 large whole fresh sage leaves
1 bay leaf
1½ teaspoons fresh thyme leaves
½ teaspoon salt
¼ teaspoon coarsely ground black pepper
¼ cup chopped fresh parsley
Thyme sprigs for garnish

1 In small bowl, soak dried mushrooms in *¾ cup boiling water* 30 minutes. Meanwhile, cut off and discard stems from shiitake mushrooms; trim stem ends from white mushrooms. Wipe both kinds of mushrooms to remove any sand.

2 With slotted spoon, remove porcini mushrooms from soaking liquid, reserving liquid. Rinse porcini mushrooms to remove sand; chop. Strain soaking liquid through sieve lined with paper towel. Set aside.

3 In 8-quart Dutch oven, heat vegetable oil over medium-high heat. Add brisket and brown on both sides, about 10 minutes. Remove brisket and set aside. Add onions to Dutch oven and cook over medi-

um heat until they are lightly browned, about 15 minutes, stirring occasionally. Stir in garlic slices and cook 30 seconds. Stir in flour and cook until browned, about 2 minutes.

4 Preheat oven to 325°F. Return brisket to Dutch oven. Stir in chopped porcini mushrooms, mushroom liquid, whole shiitake and white mushrooms, broth, red wine, brandy, sage, bay leaf, thyme leaves, salt, pepper, and 2 tablespoons chopped parsley. Heat to boiling over high heat. Cover; place in oven and cook 2½ hours or until brisket is fork-tender.

5 Remove meat from Dutch oven to large platter; let stand 15 minutes. Skim fat from sauce in Dutch oven. Discard sage and bay leaf. Heat sauce to boiling over high heat. Reduce heat to medium-high and cook, uncovered, 15 minutes to thicken sauce slightly. Stir remaining 2 tablespoons parsley into sauce. Slice brisket across the grain. Serve brisket with sauce. Garnish with thyme sprigs. Makes 10 main-dish servings.

Each serving: About 330 calories, 34 g protein, 10 g carbohydrate, 16 g total fat (4 g saturated), 98 mg cholesterol, 320 mg sodium.

Spinach- & Mushroom-Stuffed Tenderloin

PREP: 1 HOUR • ROAST: 45 MINUTES

A real showstopper. We've dressed up this already elegant piece of meat with a melt-in-your-mouth stuffing and rich mushroom gravy. If you buy an untrimmed tenderloin, it should weigh 6 to 6½ pounds to yield 4½ pounds trimmed.

Spinach-Mushroom Stuffing (recipe follows)
2 teaspoons chopped fresh thyme leaves
1 teaspoon salt
1 teaspoon coarsely ground black pepper
1 whole beef tenderloin, trimmed (4½ pounds)
2 tablespoons margarine or butter
¼ cup plain, dried bread crumbs
2 tablespoons dry vermouth
1 can (13¾ to 14½ ounces) chicken broth
½ pound medium mushrooms, sliced
2 tablespoons all-purpose flour
Thyme sprigs for garnish

1 Prepare Spinach-Mushroom Stuffing; set aside.

2 In cup, mix thyme, salt, and pepper; rub mixture all over tenderloin. Turn thinner end under tenderloin to make meat an even thickness. With sharp knife, cut 1½-inch-deep slit in tenderloin, starting 2 inches from thicker end and ending 2 inches from thinner end.

3 Preheat oven to 425°F. Spoon Spinach-Mushroom Stuffing into slit in tenderloin. With string, tie tenderloin at 2-inch intervals to help hold its shape. Place stuffed tenderloin on rack in large roasting pan (17" by 11½"); roast tenderloin 30 minutes.

4 Meanwhile, in small saucepan, melt 1 tablespoon margarine or butter over low heat. Remove saucepan from heat; stir in bread crumbs. Set bread-crumb topping aside.

5 Remove tenderloin from oven; sprinkle bread-crumb topping over stuffing. Roast tenderloin 10 to 15 minutes longer, until bread-crumb topping is golden and meat thermometer reaches 140°F. Internal temperature of meat will rise to 145°F. (medium-rare) upon standing. Or, roast to desired doneness. Transfer tenderloin to large platter; let stand 10 minutes for easier slicing.

6 While tenderloin is standing, prepare mushroom gravy: Add vermouth and ½ cup chicken broth to drippings in roasting pan and stir over low heat until browned bits are loosened from pan. Pour drippings mixture into 4-cup measuring cup; let stand a few seconds until fat separates from meat juice. Skim fat from meat-juice mixture; add remaining chicken broth and enough *water* to equal 2½ cups; set aside.

7 In 12-inch skillet, heat remaining 1 tablespoon margarine or butter over medium-high heat. Add mushrooms and cook until golden and liquid evaporates, about 12 minutes. Stir in flour. Gradually stir meat-juice mixture into mushrooms and cook, stirring constantly, until gravy boils and thickens slightly; boil 1 minute.

8 To serve, remove string. Cut stuffed tenderloin into slices; garnish with thyme sprigs. Serve with mushroom gravy. Makes 10 main-dish servings.

SPINACH-MUSHROOM STUFFING: In 12-inch skillet, heat *4 tablespoons margarine or butter* (½ stick) over medium-high heat; add *1 pound mushrooms*, coarsely chopped, and cook until golden and liquid evaporates, 12 to 15 minutes. Stir in *2 tablespoons dry vermouth*; cook 1 minute longer. Remove skillet from heat; stir in *1 package (10 ounces) frozen chopped*

Spinach- & Mushroom-Stuffed Tenderloin with sides of Oven-Roasted Parsnips & Carrots (page 132), Peas with Greens Onions & Mint (page 132), Wild Rice Pilaf with Dried Cranberries (page 116)

spinach, thawed and squeezed dry, *2 tablespoons grated Parmesan cheese, 2 tablespoons plain dried bread crumbs, 1 teaspoon chopped fresh thyme leaves, ¼ teaspoon salt,* and *¼ teaspoon ground black pepper.*

Each serving: About 440 calories, 48 g protein, 9 g carbohydrate, 23 g total fat (7 g saturated), 108 mg cholesterol, 685 mg sodium.

Barbecued Beef Brisket

PREP: 25 MINUTES • COOK/GRILL: ABOUT 3½ HOURS

This rich barbecued brisket can be made well ahead and then finished on an outdoor grill. Slow-cook the meat on the stove top up to 2 days ahead, then glaze with sauce and grill for 20 minutes to heat through.

BRISKET:
1 fresh beef brisket (4½ pounds), trimmed
1 medium onion, cut into quarters
1 large carrot, cut into 1½-inch pieces
1 bay leaf
1 teaspoon whole black peppercorns
¼ teaspoon whole allspice

CHUNKY BBQ SAUCE:
1 tablespoon vegetable oil
1 large onion, diced
3 garlic cloves, minced
2 tablespoons minced, peeled fresh ginger
1 teaspoon ground cumin
1 can (14½ ounces) whole tomatoes in puree, chopped, with puree reserved
1 bottle (12 ounces) chili sauce
⅓ cup cider vinegar
2 tablespoons brown sugar
2 tablespoons light molasses
2 teaspoons dry mustard
1 tablespoon cornstarch

1 Prepare Brisket: In 8-quart Dutch oven, place brisket, onion, carrot, bay leaf, peppercorns, allspice, and enough *water* to cover; heat to boiling over high heat. Reduce heat to low; cover and simmer 3 hours or until meat is fork-tender.

2 Meanwhile, prepare Chunky BBQ Sauce: In 12-inch skillet, heat vegetable oil over medium heat until hot. Add diced onion and cook 10 minutes or until tender, stirring occasionally. Add garlic and ginger and cook 1 minute, stirring. Stir in cumin and cook 1 minute longer.

3 Stir in chopped tomatoes, reserved tomato puree, chili sauce, vinegar, brown sugar, molasses, and dry mustard; heat to boiling over high heat. Reduce heat to medium-high and cook, uncovered, 5 minutes, stirring occasionally.

4 In cup, with fork, mix cornstarch with *2 tablespoons water* until blended. After sauce has cooked 5 minutes, stir in cornstarch mixture and cook 1 to 2 minutes longer, until sauce boils and thickens. Cover and refrigerate sauce if not using right away. Makes about 4 cups.

5 When brisket is done, transfer to platter. If not serving right away, cover and refrigerate brisket until ready to serve.

6 To serve, prepare outdoor grill. Place brisket on grill (preferably one with a cover), over medium heat and cook 10 minutes. Turn brisket over and cook 5 minutes. Spoon 1 cup barbecue sauce on top of brisket and cook 5 minutes longer or until brisket is heated through. (Do not turn brisket after topping with sauce.) If you like, reheat remaining sauce in small saucepan on grill. Thinly slice brisket across the grain and serve with sauce. Makes 12 main-dish servings.

Each serving of brisket with sauce: About 300 calories, 31 g protein, 18 g carbohydrate, 12 g total fat (4 g saturated), 92 mg cholesterol, 200 mg sodium.

Grilled Mexican Steak

PREP: 15 MINUTES PLUS STANDING
GRILL: 10 TO 15 MINUTES

If skirt steak is difficult to find, a flank cut is a good alternative.

1 medium lime
½ cup plain low-fat yogurt
⅓ cup chopped fresh cilantro leaves
¼ cup light mayonnaise
⅛ plus ¾ teaspoon salt
3 tablespoons chili powder
1 teaspoon ground coriander
1 teaspoon ground cumin
1 beef skirt steak or flank steak (about 1¼ pounds)
1 large garlic clove, cut lengthwise in half
10 (6- to 7-inch) flour tortillas
3 cups sliced romaine lettuce

1 Grate ¼ teaspoon peel and squeeze 1 teaspoon juice from lime. In small bowl, mix lime peel and juice, yogurt, cilantro, mayonnaise, and ⅛ teaspoon salt until blended. Cover and refrigerate if not serving right away.

2 In cup, mix chili powder, coriander, cumin, and ¾ teaspoon salt. Rub steak on both sides with cut side of garlic clove. Then rub with chili-powder mixture.

3 Place steak on grill over medium heat. Grill steak 5 minutes. Turn steak over and grill 5 to 10 minutes longer, depending on thickness of steak, for medium or until of desired doneness. Transfer steak to cutting board; let stand 5 minutes to allow juices to set for easier slicing.

4 Meanwhile, wrap tortillas in foil. Heat tortillas at edge of grill over low heat until heated through.

5 To serve, thinly slice steak crosswise on the diagonal. Place sliced steak in warm tortillas with cilantro yogurt and lettuce. Makes 5 main-dish servings.

Each serving: About 450 calories, 36 g protein, 40 g carbohydrate, 16 g total fat (5 g saturated), 52 mg cholesterol, 885 mg sodium.

Heloise's Meat Loaf

PREP: 15 MINUTES • BAKE: 1¼ HOURS

Household expert and GH columnist Heloise calls this loaf Hawaii/Texas-style because her mother—the original Heloise—lived in both states and apparently combined two versions into one.

¼ cup packed brown sugar
1 teaspoon prepared mustard
Dash hot pepper sauce
¾ cup catchup
2 pounds ground beef chuck
1 large egg
⅔ cup cracker crumbs
½ cup milk
⅓ cup grated onion
¼ cup finely chopped red pepper
1 teaspoon salt
½ teaspoon dried sage leaves
½ teaspoon ground black pepper

1 Preheat oven to 350°F. If you like, for ease in removing cooked meat loaf, line metal 9" by 5" loaf pan with foil, allowing foil to extend above sides.

2 In small bowl, with spoon, mix brown sugar, mustard, hot pepper sauce, and ¼ cup catchup; set aside.

3 In large bowl, mix ground beef, egg, cracker crumbs, milk, onion, red pepper, salt, sage, black pepper, and remaining ½ cup catchup just until well combined but not overmixed.

4 Spoon meat mixture into loaf pan; press down gently. Spread catchup mixture over top of loaf. Bake meat loaf 1¼ hours. Let meat loaf stand 10 minutes in pan before removing from pan and slicing. Makes 8 main-dish servings.

Each serving: About 410 calories, 23 g protein, 22 g carbohydrate, 25 g total fat (10 g saturated), 113 mg cholesterol, 645 mg sodium.

"Susan's" Meat Loaf

PREP: 15 MINUTES • BAKE: 1 HOUR

GH Contributing Editor Dr. Joyce Brothers counts on this classic from our 1963 *Good Housekeeping Cookbook*. (The recipe dates back to our March 1948 issue; it was part of the "Susan, Our Teen-Age Cook" series, which ran for decades.) Dr. Brothers says she often serves it chilled and thinly sliced when entertaining.

2 pounds ground beef chuck
2 large eggs
2 green onions, minced
1 medium onion, minced
2 cups fresh bread crumbs
¼ cup milk
2 tablespoons prepared white horseradish
1½ teaspoons salt
1 teaspoon dry mustard
¾ cup catchup

1 Preheat oven to 400°F. In large bowl, mix ground beef, eggs, green onions, onion, bread crumbs, milk, horseradish, salt, mustard, and ¼ cup catchup just until well combined but not overmixed.

2 In 13" by 9" metal baking pan, shape meat mixture into 9" by 5" loaf; spread remaining ½ cup catchup over top of loaf. Bake meat loaf 1 hour. Let meat loaf stand 10 minutes before slicing. Makes 8 main-dish servings.

Each serving: About 305 calories, 23 g protein, 14 g carbohydrate, 17 g total fat (7 g saturated), 124 mg cholesterol, 850 mg sodium.

Lois Wyse's Meat Loaf

PREP: 25 MINUTES • BAKE: 1¼ HOURS

"If your ground beef is top quality, you can omit the crumbs," says author and longtime GH Contributing Editor Lois Wyse. In our test kitchens, where we use supermarket meat, we found the texture was too dense without the bread.

2 pounds ground beef chuck
1 cup fresh bread crumbs
½ cup milk
1½ teaspoons salt
½ teaspoon ground black pepper
¾ cup chili sauce
2 eggs, hard-cooked and shelled
1 tablespoon Worcestershire sauce

1 Preheat oven to 375°F. In large bowl, mix beef, bread crumbs, milk, salt, pepper, and ½ cup chili sauce just until well combined but not overmixed.

2 In 13" by 9" metal baking pan, shape half of meat mixture into 9" by 5" rectangle. Press whole eggs, end to end, firmly along center of meat mixture. Place remaining meat mixture on top of and around eggs, pressing firmly to form 9" by 5" loaf.

3 In cup, mix Worcestershire and remaining ¼ cup chili sauce; use to brush over loaf. Bake meat loaf 1¼ hours. Let meat loaf stand 10 minutes before slicing. Makes 8 main-dish servings.

Each serving: About 290 calories, 23 g protein, 10 g carbohydrate, 17 g total fat (7 g saturated), 125 mg cholesterol, 875 mg sodium.

GH INSTITUTE REPORT

DOES A DRIP PAN CUT THE FAT?

No better than any other method. We baked "Susan's" Meat Loaf (opposite page) in a 9" by 5" loaf pan with a drainage insert (also called a drip pan or meat loaf pan) as well as in a plain 9" by 5" loaf pan and a 13" by 9" baking pan. Our Bureau of Chemistry analyzed the loaves and found no significant difference in fat content. In fact, the drip pan affected moisture content more than fat content—the meat loaf baked in that pan lost the most liquid and was drier and less palatable than the other two.

Mushroom-Stuffed Meat Loaf

PREP: 30 MINUTES • BAKE: 1½ HOURS

Carol Wapner, associate director of the GH nutrition lab, feels that too many people think of meat loaf only as an economical meal. She loves making this for her big blended family (which includes 2 children, 5 stepchildren, and 9 grandchildren) *and* for company because of the mushroom stuffing, which adds an elegant touch. Besides, Wapner says, "I just happen to be a stuffing lover."

2 tablespoons margarine or butter (¼ stick)
1 medium onion, chopped
1 pound mushrooms, diced
¼ cup chopped fresh parsley
¼ teaspoon dried thyme leaves
4 cups fresh bread crumbs
2 tablespoons plus ½ cup chicken broth
2 pounds ground beef chuck
2 large eggs
½ cup catchup
1¼ teaspoons salt
⅛ teaspoon ground black pepper

1 In nonstick 12-inch skillet, melt margarine or butter over medium heat. Add onion and cook until golden, stirring occasionally. Increase heat to medium-high; add mushrooms and cook 5 to 8 minutes longer, until mushrooms are browned.

2 Remove skillet from heat. Stir in parsley, thyme, 3 cups bread crumbs, and 2 tablespoons chicken broth; set aside.

3 Preheat oven to 375°F. In large bowl, mix ground beef, eggs, catchup, salt, pepper, remaining 1 cup bread crumbs, and remaining ½ cup chicken broth just until well combined but not overmixed.

4 Press half the meat mixture into 9" by 5" metal loaf pan; top with all of the stuffing. Press remaining meat mixture into loaf pan over stuffing.

5 Place loaf pan on jelly-roll pan to catch any drips during baking. Bake meat loaf 1½ hours. Let meat loaf stand 10 minutes in pan.

6 Pour off fat from loaf pan. Invert meat loaf onto platter before slicing. Makes 8 main-dish servings.

Each serving: About 360 calories, 25 g protein, 19 g carbohydrate, 20 g total fat (7 g saturated), 123 mg cholesterol, 805 mg sodium.

Auntie Lynette's Meat Loaf Surprise

PREP: 30 MINUTES • BAKE: 1¼ HOURS

Stuffed with mashed potatoes and spinach, and topped with tomato sauce, this meat loaf is a favorite with Lynette Perino's four sons—as well as with her extended family, which includes *Good Housekeeping* Engineer Tony Arena and his wife, Cherilyn. If you like, serve extra tomato sauce on the side.

1½ pounds all-purpose potatoes (about 3 large), peeled and cut into 2-inch chunks
¼ cup milk
2 tablespoons margarine or butter (¼ stick)
1¼ teaspoons salt
¼ teaspoon ground black pepper
1 can (14½ ounces) diced tomatoes
2 pounds ground beef chuck
2 large eggs
¾ cup seasoned dried bread crumbs
¼ cup grated Parmesan cheese
1 garlic clove, minced
1 package (10 ounces) frozen chopped spinach, thawed and squeezed dry

1 In 3-quart saucepan, heat potatoes and enough *water* to cover to boiling over high heat. Reduce heat to low; cover and simmer 10 to 15 minutes, until potatoes are fork-tender. Drain potatoes and return to saucepan. Add milk, margarine or butter, ½ teaspoon salt, and ⅛ teaspoon pepper. With potato masher, mash potatoes until mixture is smooth; set aside.

2 Preheat oven to 350°F. In blender at high speed or in food processor with knife blade attached, blend tomatoes with their juice and ½ *cup water* until smooth.

3 In large bowl, mix ground beef, eggs, bread crumbs, grated Parmesan, garlic, ½ teaspoon salt, ⅛ teaspoon pepper, and ½ cup tomato mixture until well combined but not overmixed.

4 Onto long sheet of waxed paper (14" by 12"), pat meat mixture into 11" by 9" rectangle. Spread mashed potatoes over meat rectangle leaving a 1-inch border all around. Place spinach over potatoes; sprinkle with ¼ teaspoon salt.

5 Starting at a narrow end, roll meat with potatoes and spinach, jelly-roll fashion, lifting waxed paper and using long metal spatula to loosen meat from

waxed paper. Carefully place rolled meat loaf, seam side down, in 13" by 9" glass or ceramic baking dish.

6 Pour remaining tomato mixture over and around meat loaf. Bake meat loaf 1¼ hours. Let meat loaf stand 10 minutes before slicing. Makes 8 main-dish servings.

Each serving: About 400 calories, 28 g protein, 26 g carbohydrate, 21 g total fat (8 g saturated), 127 mg cholesterol, 1015 mg sodium.

Curried-Chutney Meat Loaf

PREP: 20 MINUTES • BAKE: 1¼ HOURS

Robyn Rowlands interned for six weeks in our test kitchens to complete her course of study for cooking school. She shared her family recipe for Indian-style meat loaf chock-full of chutney with a hint of curry.

2 pounds ground beef chuck
2 large eggs
1 large Granny Smith apple, peeled, cored, and diced
1 small onion, finely chopped
1 cup fresh bread crumbs
½ cup orange juice
2 teaspoons curry powder
1½ teaspoons salt
1 jar (8¼ ounces) mango chutney, chopped (¾ cup)

1 Preheat oven to 350°F. In large bowl, mix ground beef, eggs, apple, onion, bread crumbs, orange juice, curry powder, salt, and ½ cup chutney just until well combined but not overmixed.

2 Spoon meat mixture into 9" by 5" metal loaf pan; press down gently. Bake meat loaf 1¼ hours. Let meat loaf stand 10 minutes in pan.

3 Pour off fat from loaf pan. Invert meat loaf onto platter; spread top with remaining chutney. Makes 8 main-dish servings.

Each serving: About 335 calories, 22 g protein, 23 g carbohydrate, 17 g total fat (6 g saturated), 123 mg cholesterol, 515 mg sodium.

Auntie Lynette's Meat Loaf Surprise ▶

Adobo-Style Chili

Mexican adobo is usually a stewlike mixture cooked in a red chile sauce; this zesty pork stew gets its flavor from tomatoes and a blend of spices and herbs.

2 pounds boneless pork shoulder, cut into 1½-inch pieces
2 teaspoons vegetable oil
1 large onion, finely chopped
4 garlic cloves, crushed with garlic press
3 tablespoons chili powder
1 tablespoon ground cumin
¼ teaspoon ground cinnamon
¼ teaspoon ground red pepper (cayenne)
⅛ teaspoon ground cloves
1 can (28 ounces) Italian-style plum tomatoes
¼ cup cider vinegar
¾ teaspoon salt
½ teaspoon dried oregano leaves
1 bay leaf

2 tablespoons chopped fresh cilantro leaves
Warm corn tortillas (optional)

1 Pat pork dry with paper towels. In 5-quart Dutch oven, heat 1 teaspoon oil over medium-high heat until hot. Add half of pork and cook until browned on all sides. Transfer pork to plate. Repeat with remaining oil and pork.

2 Reduce heat to medium. Add onion and cook 10 minutes or until tender. Stir in garlic, chili powder, cumin, cinnamon, ground red pepper, and cloves; cook 1 minute. Return pork to Dutch oven. Add tomatoes with their juice, vinegar, salt, oregano, and bay leaf. Heat to boiling over high heat, breaking up tomatoes with side of spoon. Reduce heat to low; cover and simmer 2 hours or until pork is very tender.

3 Discard bay leaf. Skim fat. Sprinkle with cilantro and serve with warm tortillas if you like. Makes 8 main-dish servings.

Each serving without tortillas: About 325 calories, 30 g protein, 9 g carbohydrate, 19 g total fat (6 g saturated), 72 mg cholesterol, 475 mg sodium.

Roasted Chile & Tomatillo Stew

Sausage Calzones

PREP: 45 MINUTES • BAKE: 30 TO 35 MINUTES

These big pizza-dough turnovers are filled with sausage, onion, and three cheeses.

Calzone Dough (recipe follows)
½ pound sweet or hot Italian-sausage links,
    casings removed
1 small onion, chopped
1 container (15 ounces) part-skim ricotta cheese
½ cup shredded part-skim mozzarella cheese
⅓ cup grated Parmesan cheese
1 tablespoon cornmeal

1 Prepare Calzone Dough.

2 While dough is resting, prepare filling: In 10-inch skillet, cook sausage and onion over medium heat until browned, about 10 minutes, stirring to break up sausage. With slotted spoon, remove sausage mixture to large bowl. Stir in ricotta, mozzarella, and Parmesan until blended; set aside.

3 Preheat oven to 425°F. Sprinkle large cookie sheet with cornmeal.

4 Divide dough into 4 equal pieces. On lightly floured surface, with floured rolling pin, roll each piece of dough into a 7-inch round. Spoon about 1 cup filling onto half of each round, leaving ½-inch border. Fold other half of dough over filling and pinch edges of dough together firmly. With 4-tine fork, press edges to seal.

5 Cut three 1½-inch slits in top of each calzone to allow steam to escape during baking. Place calzones on cookie sheet on bottom rack in oven. Bake 30 to 35 minutes, until golden. Serve hot. Makes 4 main-dish servings.

CALZONE DOUGH: In 1-cup glass measuring cup, dissolve *1 package quick-rise yeast* and *1 teaspoon sugar* in *1 cup warm water* (105° to 115°F.). Let yeast mixture stand about 5 minutes, until bubbly. In large bowl, mix *2¾ cups all-purpose flour* and *1 teaspoon salt*. With wooden spoon, stir in yeast mixture and *1 tablespoon olive oil* until dough pulls away from side of bowl; add *¼ cup all-purpose flour* gradually to reduce stickiness if needed. Turn dough onto lightly floured surface and knead until smooth and elastic, about 5 to 7 minutes, adding more flour if needed. Shape dough into ball; cover and let rest 15 minutes.

Each serving: About 755 calories, 39 g protein, 84 g carbo-hydrate, 28 g total fat (13 g saturated), 85 mg cholesterol, 1320 mg sodium.

Roasted Chile & Tomatillo Stew

PREP: 1 HOUR • BAKE: 2½ TO 3 HOURS

Tomatillos, small green tomatoes with papery husks, are sold fresh or canned.

4 poblano chiles or 2 green peppers
1 bunch cilantro
3 garlic cloves, minced
1½ teaspoons salt
2 pounds boneless pork shoulder, cut into ¾-inch
    pieces
2 medium onions, finely chopped
3 serrano or jalapeño chiles, seeded and minced
1 teaspoon ground cumin
¼ teaspoon ground red pepper (cayenne)
2 pounds tomatillos, husked, rinsed, and each
    cut into quarters
1 can (15¼ to 16 ounces) whole-kernel corn,
    drained
Warm flour tortillas (optional)

1 Preheat broiler. Line broiling pan (without rack) with foil. Place poblanos or green peppers in pan and broil at closest position to source of heat, turning occasionally, until charred all over, about 15 minutes. Wrap foil around poblanos and allow to steam until cool enough to handle. Remove and discard skin and seeds; cut poblanos into 1-inch pieces.

2 Turn oven control to 325°F. Chop enough cilantro leaves and stems to measure ¼ cup; chop and reserve another ¼ cup cilantro leaves for garnish. On cutting board, mash garlic to a paste with salt. Transfer garlic mixture to heavy 5-quart Dutch oven with cilantro leaves and stems, pork, onions, serranos, cumin, and ground red pepper. Toss to combine. Cover and bake 1 hour.

3 Stir in tomatillos and roasted poblanos. Cover and bake 1½ to 2 hours, until meat is very tender. Skim fat. Stir in corn; heat through. Sprinkle with reserved cilantro and serve with tortillas. Makes 8 main-dish servings.

Each serving without tortillas: About 370 calories, 23 g protein, 20 g carbohydrate, 23 g total fat (8 g saturated), 67 mg cholesterol, 600 mg sodium.

Fennel-Orange Pork with Grilled Vegetables

PREP: 15 MINUTES • GRILL: ABOUT 10 MINUTES

Crushing the fennel seeds releases their flavor. If you don't have a mortar and pestle, place the seeds in a heavyweight plastic bag and use a rolling pin to crush them.

1 teaspoon fennel seeds
½ teaspoon dried thyme leaves
¼ teaspoon coarsely ground black pepper
¾ teaspoon salt
1 teaspoon grated orange peel
4 pork rib or loin chops, each ¾ inch thick (about 6 ounces each)
1 tablespoon olive oil
1 tablespoon balsamic vinegar
2 heads radicchio di Treviso (about 4 ounces each), each cut lengthwise in half, or 1 large round head radicchio (about 8 ounces), cut into 8 wedges
2 large heads Belgian endive (about 5 ounces each), each cut lengthwise into quarters
Orange wedges and lemon leaves for garnish

1 In mortar with pestle, crush fennel seeds with thyme, pepper, and ½ teaspoon salt. Stir orange peel into fennel-seed mixture.

2 With hand, rub both sides of pork chops with fennel-seed mixture.

3 In medium bowl, mix olive oil, balsamic vinegar, and ¼ teaspoon salt. Add radicchio and endive to bowl and gently toss to coat.

4 Place pork chops on grill over medium heat. Cook chops 5 minutes. Turn chops and add vegetables to grill. Cook pork chops and vegetables about 5 minutes or until chops have just a hint of pink color in center and vegetables are browned. Serve pork chops with grilled vegetables. Garnish with orange wedges and lemon leaves. Makes 4 main-dish servings.

Each serving: About 275 calories, 20 g protein, 6 g carbohydrate, 18 g total fat (6 g saturated), 64 mg cholesterol, 485 mg sodium.

Creamy Polenta with Sausage & Mushrooms

PREP: 25 MINUTES • COOK: 45 MINUTES

To ensure a soft consistency, prepare polenta just before serving; it will thicken upon standing.

1 pound sweet Italian-sausage links, casings removed
1 pound mushrooms, sliced
1 medium onion, chopped
2 garlic cloves, minced
¼ teaspoon coarsely ground black pepper
1 can (28 ounces) Italian-style plum tomatoes in puree
2½ cups milk
2 cups yellow cornmeal
1 can (13¾ to 14½ ounces) reduced-sodium chicken broth
⅓ cup grated Parmesan cheese
2 tablespoons chopped fresh parsley leaves for garnish

1 Heat 12-inch skillet over medium-high heat until hot. Add sausage meat and cook until browned, about 10 minutes, stirring frequently to break up sausage. With slotted spoon, remove sausage from skillet to bowl.

2 Discard all but 1 tablespoon sausage drippings from skillet. Add mushrooms, onion, garlic, and pepper; cook about 10 minutes, stirring occasionally, until liquid evaporates and vegetables are golden. Stir in tomatoes with their puree; heat to boiling over high heat, breaking up tomatoes with side of spoon. Return sausage to skillet. Reduce heat to low; cover and simmer 10 minutes.

3 Meanwhile, prepare polenta: Into 3-quart saucepan, measure milk; gradually whisk in cornmeal until smooth. In 2-quart saucepan, heat chicken broth with enough *water* to equal 5 cups to boiling over high heat. Whisk hot broth mixture into cornmeal mixture. Heat to boiling over medium-high heat and cook polenta, stirring constantly, 5 minutes or until thick. Stir in grated Parmesan. Serve polenta topped with sausage mixture. Garnish with chopped parsley. Makes 6 main-dish servings.

Each serving: About 520 calories, 24 g protein, 53 g carbohydrate, 22 g total fat (7 g saturated), 63 mg cholesterol, 1270 mg sodium.

Creamy Polenta with Sausage & Mushrooms

Spiced Pork Medallions

PREP: 8 MINUTES • COOK: 12 MINUTES

"I've always loved my mom's pork roast, but that marinates overnight," reports Lisa Brainerd, GH's cookbook editor. "This is based on the same spices." For a 20-minute weekday menu, serve the pork with Couscous with Dried Cherries (page 114), steamed green beans, and lemon sherbet.

2 pork tenderloins (about ¾ pound each)
1 teaspoon salt
½ teaspoon dried thyme leaves
½ teaspoon ground cinnamon
¼ teaspoon ground black pepper
⅛ teaspoon ground nutmeg
⅛ teaspoon ground cloves
1 tablespoon vegetable oil
¼ cup red currant jelly
⅔ cup chicken broth

1 Trim any fat and sinew from pork tenderloins. Cut each tenderloin crosswise into 4 pieces. Between 2 sheets of waxed paper, place half of pork pieces cut side up. With meat mallet or rolling pin, pound each piece of pork into a ½-inch-thick medallion. Repeat with remaining pork.

2 In medium bowl, mix salt, thyme, cinnamon, pepper, nutmeg, and cloves. Add pork medallions to spice mixture; toss to coat.

3 In 12-inch skillet, heat oil over medium-high heat until very hot. Add pork medallions; cook 5 minutes per side or until they just lose their pink color throughout.

4 Remove pork to warm platter. Stir currant jelly into drippings in skillet until melted; stir in chicken broth and heat to boiling. Spoon sauce over pork. Makes 4 main-dish servings.

Each serving: About 280 calories, 34 g protein, 14 g carbohydrate, 9 g total fat (2 g saturated), 92 mg cholesterol, 730 mg sodium.

Fresh Ham with Spiced Apple Glaze

PREP: 15 MINUTES • BAKE: ABOUT 5 HOURS

Rub our fragrant blend of cinnamon, cloves, and nutmeg on fresh ham before roasting, then brush on the glaze while the ham cooks. Serve with storebought condiments and breads.

One 15-pound whole pork leg (fresh ham)
2 teaspoons salt
2 teaspoons dried thyme leaves
2 teaspoons ground cinnamon
1 teaspoon coarsely ground black pepper
½ teaspoon ground nutmeg
½ teaspoon ground cloves
1 jar (10 ounces) apple jelly
¼ cup balsamic vinegar
Fresh thyme for garnish
Assorted mustards, relishes, and chutneys
Rye and pumpernickel breads

1 Remove skin and trim excess fat from pork leg, leaving only a thin fat covering. Place pork, fat side up, on rack in large roasting pan.

2 Preheat oven to 350°F. In small bowl, combine salt and next 5 ingredients. With hands, rub spice mixture over pork. Insert meat thermometer into center of thickest part of pork, being careful that pointed end of thermometer does not touch bone. Roast pork 3 hours. Cover pork loosely with a tent of foil. Continue roasting about 1 hour longer or until meat thermometer reaches 150°F.

3 Meanwhile, in 1-quart saucepan, heat apple jelly and balsamic vinegar over high heat to boiling; boil 2 minutes. Remove saucepan from heat; set glaze aside.

4 When pork has reached 150°F., remove foil and brush with some glaze. Continue roasting pork, brushing occasionally with remaining glaze until meat thermometer reaches 160° to 170°F., a total of about 5 hours. (Pork near bone may still be slightly pink.)

5 When pork is done, place on large platter; let stand 20 minutes for easier slicing. Garnish with fresh thyme. Serve with assorted mustards, relishes, and chutneys, and rye and pumpernickel breads. Makes 24 main-dish servings.

Each serving without condiments and breads: About 315 calories, 42 g protein, 9 g carbohydrate, 11 g total fat (4 g saturated), 98 mg cholesterol, 290 mg sodium.

Pork Steaks with Plum Glaze

PREP: 10 MINUTES • GRILL: ABOUT 6 MINUTES

Our 1973 edition of *The Good Housekeeping Cookbook* explained how to cut a pork tenderloin into 4 lean and juicy steaks—a family secret from Zoe Coulson, GH food editor from 1968 to 1975. We used the same technique here: Slice tenderloin lengthwise *almost* in half, pound, then cut into serving-size pieces. Thanks, Zoe!

1 pork tenderloin (about 1 pound)
¾ teaspoon salt
¼ teaspoon coarsely ground black pepper
½ cup plum jam or preserves
1 tablespoon brown sugar
1 tablespoon grated, peeled fresh ginger
1 tablespoon fresh lemon juice
½ teaspoon ground cinnamon
2 garlic cloves, crushed with garlic press
4 large plums (about 1 pound), each pitted and cut in half

1 Cut pork tenderloin lengthwise, almost in half, being careful not to cut all the way through. Open and spread flat. Place tenderloin between 2 sheets of plastic wrap; with meat mallet or rolling pin, pound to about ¼-inch thickness. Cut the tenderloin into 4 pieces; sprinkle with salt and pepper.

2 In small bowl, mix plum jam, brown sugar, ginger, lemon juice, cinnamon, and garlic. Brush 1 side of each pork steak and cut side of each plum half with plum-jam glaze. Place pork and plums on grill, glaze side down, over medium heat and cook 3 minutes. Brush steaks and plums with remaining glaze; turn over and cook about 3 minutes longer or until steaks are lightly browned on both sides and just lose their pink color throughout and plums are hot. Makes 4 main-dish servings.

Each serving: About 380 calories, 28 g protein, 44 g carbohydrate, 10 g total fat (3 g saturated), 71 mg cholesterol, 470 mg sodium.

Peggy Post's Meat Loaf

When Peggy Post, GH's etiquette authority, sent us her "Mom's" meat loaf, she explained that it was really a recipe from her husband's great-grandmother, Emily Post! Emily's son Edwin also included this family treasure in *The Emily Post Cookbook*, published in 1951.

3 large eggs
½ cup heavy or whipping cream
2 teaspoons dried thyme leaves
2 teaspoons salt
½ teaspoon ground black pepper
1 cup fresh bread crumbs
2 tablespoons margarine or butter (¼ stick)
½ pound chicken livers, trimmed
2 medium onions, chopped
1½ pounds ground beef chuck
½ pound ground veal
½ pound ground pork
2 tablespoons chopped celery leaves
2 green onions, chopped
4 or 5 dashes Maggi seasoning sauce or soy
   sauce
2 tablespoons spicy brown mustard
3 slices bacon

1 In medium bowl, with fork, beat eggs, heavy cream, thyme, salt, and pepper. Stir in ½ cup bread crumbs; let mixture stand 30 minutes.

2 Meanwhile, in nonstick 10-inch skillet, melt 1 tablespoon margarine or butter over medium-high heat. Add chicken livers and cook until browned on the outside but still pink on the inside, about 5 minutes, stirring frequently. Transfer chicken livers to plate; cool slightly until easy to handle. Coarsely chop livers.

3 In same skillet, melt remaining 1 tablespoon margarine or butter over medium heat. Add onions and cook until tender and lightly browned, about 15 minutes, stirring occasionally.

4 Preheat oven to 400°F. In large bowl, mix ground meats with egg mixture, chicken livers, cooked onions, celery leaves, green onions, Maggi sauce, and remaining ½ cup bread crumbs just until well combined but not overmixed.

5 In 13" by 9" metal baking pan, shape meat mixture into 10" by 5" loaf. Spread mustard over loaf; arrange bacon slices on top. Bake meat loaf 1¼ hours. Let meat loaf stand 10 minutes before slicing. Makes 10 servings.

Each serving: About 355 calories, 28 g protein, 5 g carbohydrate, 24 g total fat (10 g saturated), 243 mg cholesterol, 665 mg sodium.

FOR FOOLPROOF MEAT LOAF RESULTS

• Don't overmix or overhandle ingredients—that's the No. 1 cause of a tight, rubbery loaf. Combine ingredients with hands instead of a spoon or fork so you can feel when the texture is uniform. Dampen hands slightly when shaping loaf or patting it into pan, to keep meat from sticking.

• For slices that don't crumble, always let meat loaf stand 10 minutes after cooking. Slice with a sharp chef's or carving knife.

NOTE: We triple-tested all meat loaves to be sure they were completely cooked in the center in the times stated. To determine baking times, we cooked each until a meat thermometer inserted in center registered 155°F.; then we removed the meat loaf from the oven, and the temperature rose to 160°F. upon standing. You may want to try this test yourself, especially if using an old family recipe that says "cook until done." (If replacing all or some of the ground meat with ground poultry, which presents a possible salmonella risk, cook until thermometer reads 160°F. and let temperature rise to 165°F. before serving.)

MEAT LOAF TIME-SAVER
For faster cooking, make smaller loaves. Shape meat into 2 loaves and shave about 20 minutes off time; make 6 to 8 individual loaves and cut time in half. (Place loaves in a 13" by 9" pan or jelly-roll pan.)

Cajun Meat Loaf

PREP: 20 MINUTES • BAKE: 1¼ HOURS

"My mother didn't make meat loaf, so I never had it as a child," says GH Food Director Susan Westmoreland. "Now that I'm a mom, I find it makes a great family dinner. I came up with this gutsy version with Cajun seasonings to please my Southern husband, not realizing that my son would love it too!"

2 tablespoons margarine or butter (¼ stick)
2 medium carrots, finely chopped
1 large onion, finely chopped
1 large celery stalk, finely chopped
1 small green pepper, finely chopped
2 garlic cloves, crushed with garlic press
2 pounds ground meat for meat loaf (veal, pork, and beef)
2 large eggs
1 cup fresh bread crumbs
¼ cup milk
1 tablespoon Worcestershire sauce
2 teaspoons salt
1 teaspoon ground cumin
½ teaspoon coarsely ground black pepper
½ teaspoon dried thyme leaves
½ teaspoon ground nutmeg
½ teaspoon ground red pepper (cayenne)
½ cup plus 2 tablespoons catchup
Fresh herbs for garnish

1 In nonstick 12-inch skillet, melt margarine or butter over medium heat. Add carrots, onion, celery, and green pepper, and cook until vegetables are tender, about 15 minutes, stirring occasionally. Add garlic and cook 1 minute longer. Set aside to cool slightly.

2 Preheat oven to 375°F. In large bowl, mix ground meat, eggs, bread crumbs, milk, Worcestershire, salt, cumin, black pepper, thyme, nutmeg, ground red pepper, ½ cup catchup, and cooked vegetable mixture just until well combined but not overmixed.

3 In 13" by 9" metal baking pan, shape meat mixture into 10" by 5" loaf. Brush remaining 2 tablespoons catchup over top of loaf. Bake meat loaf 1¼ hours. Let meat loaf stand 10 minutes before slicing. Garnish with fresh herbs if you like. Makes 8 main-dish servings.

Each serving: About 340 calories, 27 g protein, 14 g carbohydrate, 19 g total fat (7 g saturated), 139 mg cholesterol, 950 mg sodium.

Jennie Panichella's Sausage & Pepper Loaf

PREP: 30 MINUTES • BAKE: 1 HOUR 10 MINUTES

Associate Food Editor Marianne Marinelli's grandma, Nana Panichella, gives her weeknight meat loaf an Italian twist by combining sausage meat with ground beef and adding sautéed peppers and onions. Then, just before the meat loaf's done, she melts shredded Fontina cheese on top.

1 tablespoon olive oil
2 medium red peppers, diced
1 large onion, diced
1 large garlic clove, crushed with garlic press
1 pound sweet Italian-sausage links, casings removed
1 pound ground beef chuck
2 large eggs
1½ cups fresh bread crumbs
⅓ cup grated Parmesan cheese
1 can (8 ounces) tomato sauce
½ teaspoon salt
½ cup shredded Fontina or mozzarella cheese (2 ounces)

1 In nonstick 12-inch skillet, heat olive oil over medium heat. Add red peppers and onion and cook until tender and lightly browned, 10 to 15 minutes, stirring occasionally. Add garlic; cook 1 minute, stirring. Set vegetables aside to cool slightly.

2 Preheat oven to 375°F. In large bowl, mix sausage meat, ground beef, eggs, bread crumbs, Parmesan, tomato sauce, salt, and cooked vegetables just until well combined but not overmixed.

3 In 13" by 9" metal baking pan, shape meat mixture into 9" by 5" loaf. Bake meat loaf 1 hour. Sprinkle Fontina cheese down center of loaf in a 2-inch-wide strip. Bake 10 minutes longer. Let meat loaf stand 10 minutes before slicing. Makes 8 main-dish servings.

Each serving: About 370 calories, 25 g protein, 10 g carbohydrate, 25 g total fat (10 g saturated), 132 mg cholesterol, 915 mg sodium.

Cajun Meat Loaf with sides of ➤
Baby Lima Beans with Onion (page 130)
and Buttered Noodles with Herbs (page 115)

Greek Meat Loaf

•••
PREP: 20 MINUTES • BAKE: 1¼ HOURS

Evdokia Koveos, born on the Greek island of Amorgos, used to tirelessly make meatballs with these ingredients. Then, she discovered how much easier it is to make meat loaf instead. She varies the herbs, depending on which are most plentiful in her backyard—sometimes oregano, more often mint, which she dries for use in winter.

1 pound ground beef chuck
1 pound ground lamb
2 large eggs
1 cup fresh bread crumbs
2 bunches green onions, minced (1 cup)
4 ounces feta cheese, finely crumbled (½ cup)
¼ cup minced fresh parsley
1 tablespoon dried mint leaves
2 tablespoons olive oil
1 tablespoon red wine vinegar
2 garlic cloves, minced
½ teaspoon salt
¼ teaspoon ground black pepper

Greek Meat Loaf

1 Preheat oven to 375°F. In large bowl, mix all ingredients just until well combined but not overmixed.

2 In 13" by 9" metal baking pan, shape meat mixture into 9" by 5" loaf. Bake meat loaf 1 hour and 15 minutes. Let meat loaf stand 10 minutes before slicing. Makes 8 main-dish servings.

Each serving: About 335 calories, 25 g protein, 5 g carbohydrate, 24 g total fat (9 g saturated), 142 mg cholesterol, 405 mg sodium.

Veal & Sage Meat Loaf

•••
PREP: 30 MINUTES • BAKE: 1¼ HOURS

If ground veal is hard to find, use all beef.

1 tablespoon olive oil
2 slices pancetta or bacon, chopped
2 medium carrots, chopped
2 medium celery stalks, chopped
1 large onion, chopped
1 large garlic clove, crushed with garlic press
1 pound ground veal
1 pound ground beef chuck
2 large eggs
1 cup jarred marinara or spaghetti sauce
1½ cups fresh bread crumbs
4 teaspoons chopped fresh sage leaves
1½ teaspoons salt
Fresh sage leaves for garnish

1 In nonstick 12-inch skillet, heat olive oil over medium heat. Add pancetta or bacon, carrots, celery, and onion and cook 10 to 15 minutes until vegetables are tender and golden. Add garlic; cook 1 minute, stirring. Set vegetable mixture aside to cool slightly.

2 Preheat oven to 375°F. In large bowl, mix ground veal, ground beef, eggs, marinara sauce, bread crumbs, sage, salt, and cooked vegetable mixture just until well combined but not overmixed.

3 In 13" by 9" metal baking pan, shape meat mixture into 9" by 5" loaf. Bake meat loaf 1¼ hours. Let meat loaf stand 10 minutes before slicing. Garnish with sage if you like. Makes 8 main-dish servings.

Each serving: About 310 calories, 24 g protein, 12 g carbohydrate, 18 g total fat (6 g saturated), 135 mg cholesterol, 775 mg sodium.

BREADS & SANDWICHES

Rosemary-Fennel Breadsticks

PREP: 40 MINUTES • BAKE: 20 MINUTES PER BATCH

Great do-ahead gifts—they keep perfectly for up to 2 weeks in an airtight container.

2 packages quick-rise yeast
2½ teaspoons salt
2 teaspoons fennel seeds, crushed
1 teaspoon dried rosemary leaves, crumbled
½ teaspoon coarsely ground black pepper
About 4¾ cups all-purpose flour
½ cup olive oil

1 In large bowl, combine yeast, salt, fennel seeds, rosemary, pepper, and 2 cups flour. With spoon, stir in *1⅓ cups very warm water* (120° to 130°F.); beat vigorously with spoon 1 minute. Stir in olive oil. Gradually stir in 2¼ cups flour.

2 Turn dough onto floured surface and knead until smooth and elastic, about 8 minutes, working in more flour (about ½ cup) while kneading. Cover dough loosely with plastic wrap; let rest 10 minutes.

3 Preheat oven to 375°F. Grease 2 large cookie sheets. Divide dough in half. Keeping remaining dough covered, cut half of dough into 32 pieces. Shape each piece into 12-inch-long rope. Place ropes on cookie sheets, about 1 inch apart.

4 Place cookie sheets on 2 oven racks and bake breadsticks 20 minutes or until golden and crisp throughout, rotating cookie sheets between upper and lower racks halfway through baking time. Remove breadsticks to wire racks to cool. Repeat with remaining dough. Makes 64 breadsticks.

Each breadstick: About 50 calories, 1 g protein, 7 g carbohydrate, 2 g total fat (0 g saturated), 0 mg cholesterol, 85 mg sodium.

Williamsburg Peppered Cornmeal Scones

PREP: 20 MINUTES • BAKE: 15 MINUTES

A nice alternative to cornbread. You can make the scones up to 2 days ahead and freeze. Reheat them, wrapped in foil, in a 350°F. oven for 20 minutes.

2¼ cups all-purpose flour
½ cup yellow cornmeal
1 tablespoon sugar
2 teaspoons baking powder
1¼ teaspoons coarsely ground black pepper
1 teaspoon salt
½ teaspoon baking soda
6 tablespoons cold margarine or butter (¾ stick)
¾ cup milk
1 large egg

1 Preheat oven to 425°F. In large bowl, combine flour, cornmeal, sugar, baking powder, black pepper, salt, and baking soda. With pastry blender or two knives used scissor-fashion, cut in margarine or butter until mixture resembles coarse crumbs.

Blueberry Hill Scones

2 In cup, mix milk and egg; stir egg mixture into flour mixture just until ingredients are blended.

3 Turn dough onto lightly floured surface. Divide dough in half. With floured hands, pat each half into a 5½-inch round. Cut each round into 6 wedges. With pancake turner, transfer wedges to ungreased large cookie sheet.

4 Bake scones 15 minutes or until lightly browned. Serve scones warm. Or, cool on wire rack; reheat if desired. Makes 12 scones.

Each scone: About 175 calories, 4 g protein, 25 g carbohydrate, 7 g total fat (2 g saturated), 20 mg cholesterol, 380 mg sodium.

Blueberry Hill Scones

PREP: 15 MINUTES • BAKE: 22 TO 25 MINUTES

If you want to make these scones with fragile berries like raspberries or blackberries, don't knead them into the dough—gently press them into the top of each dough round before cutting it into wedges and baking.

2 cups all-purpose flour
¼ cup packed brown sugar
1 tablespoon baking powder
¼ teaspoon salt
4 tablespoons cold margarine or butter (½ stick), cut up
1 cup blueberries
⅔ cup heavy or whipping cream
1 large egg
½ teaspoon finely grated lemon peel

1 Preheat oven to 375°F. In large bowl, with fork, mix flour, brown sugar, baking powder, and salt. With pastry blender or two knives used scissor-fashion, cut margarine or butter into dry ingredients until mixture resembles coarse crumbs. Add blueberries and toss to mix.

2 In small bowl, with fork, mix cream, egg, and lemon peel until blended. Slowly pour cream mixture into dry ingredients and stir with rubber spatula just until a soft dough forms.

3 With lightly floured hand, knead dough in bowl just until it comes together, about 3 to 4 times; do not overmix. Divide dough in half. On lightly floured surface, shape each half into a 6-inch round. With floured knife, cut each round into 6 wedges. Transfer wedges to ungreased large cookie sheet.

4 Bake scones 22 to 25 minutes, until golden brown. Serve warm, or cool on wire rack to serve later. Makes 12 scones.

Each scone: About 185 calories, 3 g protein, 23 g carbohydrate, 9 g total fat (4 g saturated), 36 mg cholesterol, 200 mg sodium.

Cheddar-Jalapeño Biscuits

PREP: 15 MINUTES • BAKE: ABOUT 15 MINUTES

2 cups all-purpose flour
1 tablespoon baking powder
½ teaspoon salt
½ teaspoon paprika
3 tablespoons cold margarine or butter, cut up
2 tablespoons shortening
4 ounces shredded sharp or extrasharp Cheddar cheese (1 cup)
3 tablespoons drained and chopped pickled jalapeño chiles
¾ cup milk

1 Preheat oven to 450°F. In large bowl, combine flour, baking powder, salt, and paprika. With pastry blender or two knives used scissor-fashion, cut in margarine or butter with shortening until mixture resembles coarse crumbs. Stir cheese, chiles, and milk into flour mixture just until ingredients are blended and mixture forms a soft dough that leaves side of bowl.

2 Turn dough onto lightly floured surface. With lightly floured hands, pat dough into a 10" by 4" rectangle. With floured knife, cut rectangle lengthwise in half, then cut each half crosswise into five 2-inch squares. Cut each square diagonally in half to make 20 triangles in all. Place biscuits on ungreased large cookie sheet.

3 Bake biscuits 13 to 15 minutes, until golden. Serve biscuits warm, or transfer to wire rack to cool completely. Makes 20 biscuits.

Each biscuit: About 100 calories, 3 g protein, 10 g carbohydrate, 5 g total fat (2 g saturated), 7 mg cholesterol, 200 mg sodium.

Alabama Spoon Bread with Pumpkin & Chives

PREP: 30 MINUTES • BAKE: 50 TO 55 MINUTES

This baked puddinglike side dish made with cornmeal is a cross between corn bread and a soufflé. It's usually soft enough to eat with a spoon. Although this is not a do-ahead dish, you can ease the last-minute mixing by, in advance, combining the wet ingredients as in step 1 (cover and refrigerate); then whisk together the dry ingredients as in step 2, and set aside covered.

1½ cups buttermilk
1 cup solid-pack pumpkin (not pumpkin-pie mix)
4 large eggs, separated
3 tablespoons chopped fresh chives
4 tablespoons margarine or butter (½ stick)
1½ cups yellow cornmeal
1 tablespoon brown sugar
1 teaspoon baking soda
¾ teaspoon salt
⅛ teaspoon coarsely ground black pepper

1 Preheat oven to 350°F. Lightly grease shallow 2½-quart ceramic baking dish. In medium bowl, with fork or wire whisk, mix buttermilk, pumpkin, egg yolks, and 2 tablespoons chopped chives.

2 In 4-quart saucepan, heat margarine or butter and 1½ cups water to boiling over high heat. Remove saucepan from heat. In small bowl, with wire whisk, mix cornmeal, brown sugar, baking soda, salt, and pepper. Gradually whisk cornmeal mixture into hot liquid in saucepan until blended. Then whisk in pumpkin mixture.

3 In small bowl, with mixer at high speed, beat egg whites just until stiff peaks form. Gently fold egg whites, one-third at a time, into cornmeal mixture until blended. Spoon batter into baking dish and sprinkle with remaining 1 tablespoon chives.

4 Place baking dish in roasting pan on oven rack. Pour *boiling water* into roasting pan until it reaches halfway up side of baking dish. Bake spoon bread 50 to 55 minutes until lightly browned and puffed and knife inserted 2 inches from center comes out clean. Makes 8 accompaniment servings.

Each serving: About 220 calories, 7 g protein, 27 g carbohydrate, 9 g total fat (2 g saturated), 108 mg cholesterol, 515 mg sodium.

Michigan Orange-Cranberry Bread

PREP: 20 MINUTES PLUS COOLING
BAKE: 55 TO 60 MINUTES

This delicious quick bread is made with plenty of cranberries and the essence of orange. It's not too sweet to serve with the main course (and it goes particularly well with roast turkey). Bake the bread a day ahead to allow the flavors to develop for optimum taste. Or, it can be made a month ahead and frozen.

1 large orange
2½ cups all-purpose flour
1 cup sugar
2 teaspoons baking powder
½ teaspoon baking soda
½ teaspoon salt
2 large eggs
4 tablespoons margarine or butter (½ stick), melted
2 cups cranberries, coarsely chopped
¾ cup walnuts, chopped (optional)

1 Preheat oven to 375°F. Grease 9" by 5" metal loaf pan. Grate peel from orange and squeeze ½ cup juice.

2 In large bowl, combine flour, sugar, baking powder, baking soda, and salt. In small bowl, with wire whisk or fork, beat eggs, margarine or butter, orange peel, and juice. With spoon, stir egg mixture into flour mixture until batter is just blended (batter will be stiff). Fold in cranberries, and walnuts if using.

3 Spoon batter into loaf pan. Bake 55 to 60 minutes or until toothpick inserted in center of bread comes out clean.

4 Cool bread in pan on wire rack 10 minutes; remove from pan and cool completely on wire rack. Makes 1 loaf, 12 servings.

Each serving without walnuts: About 220 calories, 4 g protein, 41 g carbohydrate, 5 g total fat (1 g saturated), 36 mg cholesterol, 265 mg sodium.

Michigan Orange-Cranberry Bread ▶

Great Plains Oatmeal-Molasses Rolls

PREP: 1 HOUR PLUS RISING • BAKE: 40 TO 45 MINUTES

Tender, moist rolls topped with oats and a butter-molasses glaze.

1 cup plus 2 tablespoons old-fashioned oats,
  uncooked
1 package active dry yeast
1 teaspoon sugar
5 tablespoons margarine or butter, slightly
  softened
⅓ cup plus 2 teaspoons light molasses
1½ teaspoons salt
About 4¼ cups all-purpose flour

1 In medium bowl, pour *1 cup boiling water* over 1 cup oats, stirring to combine. Let stand until oats absorb water, about 10 minutes.

2 Meanwhile, in small bowl, combine yeast, sugar, and ¾ *cup warm water* (105° to 115°F.). Let stand until yeast foams, about 5 minutes.

3 In large bowl, with mixer at low speed, beat 4 tablespoons margarine or butter (½ stick) until smooth; add ⅓ cup molasses, beating until combined. Beat in oat mixture, yeast mixture, and salt just until blended. Gradually beat in 2 cups flour, 1 cup at a time, just until blended. With wooden spoon, stir in 2 more cups flour. Turn dough onto lightly floured surface and knead until smooth and elastic, about 5 minutes, working in more flour (about ¼ cup) while kneading.

4 Place dough in greased bowl, turning dough to grease top. Cover and let rise in warm place (80° to 85°F.) until doubled, about 1 hour.

5 Punch down dough. On lightly floured surface, divide dough into 18 equal pieces. Shape each piece into a ball and place in greased 13" by 9" metal baking pan in 3 rows of 6 balls each. Cover and let rise in warm place until doubled, about 1 hour.

ARE YOU GETTING ENOUGH WHOLE GRAINS?

Whole grains supply a lot more than fiber. "They're important sources of antioxidants such as vitamin E and selenium, phytoestrogens, and lignans, which may play vital roles in protecting against certain types of cancer and heart disease," explains Joanne Slavin, Ph.D., R.D., professor of food science and nutrition at the University of Minnesota. They also provide more minerals (zinc, magnesium, copper, and potassium) than their enriched or nonenriched refined-grain counterparts. But most people aren't aware of humble whole grains' power: In the United States, average consumption is less than 1 serving per day—though experts recommend at least 3. Quick steps to bulk up your meals:

• Choose brown rice, whole wheat pasta, and grains such as bulgur, oatmeal, and buckwheat groats (for each, ½ cup cooked counts as 1 serving).

• Always read ingredient lists on breads, crackers, rolls, and processed cereals. To qualify as whole grain, the first words must be whole grain or whole, followed by wheat, oats, rice, or corn.

• Don't be lured by "wheat" or "grain" in the product name, or by a brown color. "Wheat" bread may be made with white flour, with a little whole grain flour buried on the ingredient list for good measure. And brown products, such as pumpernickel bread, are often made mostly from refined white flour with caramel color added.

6 Preheat oven to 350°F. Bake rolls 30 minutes or until very lightly browned.

7 Meanwhile, melt remaining 1 tablespoon margarine or butter; stir in remaining 2 teaspoons molasses.

8 After rolls have baked 30 minutes, remove from oven and brush with molasses mixture; sprinkle with remaining 2 tablespoons oats. Bake rolls 15 minutes longer or until golden. Remove rolls from pan to wire rack; cool slightly to serve warm. Or, cool completely to serve later. Reheat if desired. Makes 18 rolls.

Each roll: About 195 calories, 5 g protein, 35 g carbohydrate, 4 g total fat (1 g saturated), 0 mg cholesterol, 220 mg sodium.

4 Punch down dough. Turn dough onto lightly floured surface and cut in half. Grease large cookie sheet.

5 Shape each half of dough into a 5-inch round loaf. Place loaves on opposite corners of cookie sheet, about 2 inches from sides. Cover; let rise in warm place until doubled, about 1 hour.

6 Preheat oven to 400°F. Bake bread 20 to 25 minutes, until golden. Transfer to wire rack to cool. Makes 2 loaves, each 8 servings.

Each serving: About 185 calories, 5 g protein, 29 g carbohydrate, 7 g total fat (1 g saturated), 0 mg cholesterol, 270 mg sodium.

Walnut & Raisin Whole-Wheat Bread

PREP: 30 MINUTES PLUS RISING AND COOLING
BAKE: 20 TO 25 MINUTES

Barbara Rose, her husband, Michael, and Barbara's brother, Tom Frainier, co-owners of Semifreddi's Bakery in Emeryville, California, launched their business with a single sourdough bread recipe in 1987. But they built up a following at Bay-Area markets with loaves like this deliciously dense bread—the bakery makes 3,000 loaves of it per week.

1 package active dry yeast
1 teaspoon plus 3 tablespoons honey
2 teaspoons salt
About 3½ cups whole-wheat flour
3 tablespoons vegetable oil
¾ cup dark seedless raisins
¾ cup walnuts, chopped

1 In cup, stir yeast and 1 teaspoon honey into ½ *cup warm water* (105° to 115°F.); let stand until yeast mixture foams, about 5 minutes.

2 In large bowl, combine salt and 3 cups whole-wheat flour. With spoon, beat in yeast mixture, oil, 3 tablespoons honey, and ¾ *cup warm tap water.*

3 On floured surface, knead dough until smooth and elastic, about 10 minutes, working in raisins, walnuts, and more flour (about ½ cup). Shape into a ball; place in greased bowl, turning to grease top. Cover; let rise in warm place (80° to 85°F.) until doubled, about 1 hour.

Kansas Pecan-Topped Pumpkin Muffins

PREP: 10 MINUTES • BAKE: 25 TO 30 MINUTES

2¼ cups all-purpose flour
2½ teaspoons baking powder
2 teaspoons pumpkin-pie spice
¾ teaspoon salt
1 cup milk
¾ cup solid-pack pumpkin (not pumpkin-pie mix)
½ cup packed dark brown sugar
4 tablespoons margarine or butter (½ stick), melted
2 teaspoons vanilla extract
2 large eggs
½ cup pecans, toasted and chopped

1 Preheat oven to 400°F. Grease twelve 2½" by 1¼" muffin-pan cups.

2 In large bowl, combine flour, baking powder, pumpkin-pie spice, and salt. In medium bowl, with wire whisk, mix milk, pumpkin, brown sugar, melted margarine or butter, vanilla, and eggs until blended; stir into flour mixture until just moistened.

3 Spoon batter into muffin-pan cups. Sprinkle tops with chopped pecans. Bake 25 to 30 minutes, until toothpick inserted in center of muffin comes out clean. Immediately remove from pan; serve warm. Or, cool completely on wire rack; reheat if desired. Makes 12 muffins.

Each muffin: About 220 calories, 5 g protein, 31 g carbohydrate, 9 g total fat (2 g saturated), 38 mg cholesterol, 285 mg sodium.

Tomato Focaccia

PREP: 20 MINUTES PLUS 45 MINUTES TO RISE
BAKE: 35 TO 40 MINUTES

The dough for this popular Italian bread is "dimpled" (indented) just before baking. The dimples catch some of the olive oil drizzled on at the end for added flavor.

1 package quick-rise yeast
About 4 cups all-purpose flour
2 teaspoons salt
6 tablespoons olive oil
1 tablespoon cornmeal
1 pound ripe plum tomatoes (about 5 medium), sliced ¼ inch thick
1 tablespoon chopped fresh rosemary or
  1 teaspoon dried rosemary leaves, crushed
½ teaspoon coarsely ground black pepper

1 In large bowl, combine yeast, 1½ cups flour, and 1½ teaspoons salt.

2 In 1-quart saucepan, heat 4 tablespoons olive oil and *1⅓ cups water* over medium heat, until very warm (120° to 130°F.).

3 With mixer at low speed, beat liquid into dry ingredients just until blended. Increase speed to medium; beat 2 minutes, scraping bowl often with rubber spatula. Add ½ cup flour; beat 2 minutes. With spoon, stir in 1½ cups flour to make a soft dough.

4 On lightly floured surface, with floured hands, knead dough about 8 minutes, working in more flour (about ½ cup) while kneading. Cover dough and let rest 15 minutes.

5 Grease 15½" by 10½" jelly-roll pan; sprinkle with cornmeal. Press dough evenly into pan; cover and let rise in warm place (80° to 85°F.) until doubled, about 30 minutes.

6 Preheat oven to 400°F. Press fingers into dough almost to bottom of pan, making indentations 1 inch apart. Drizzle with 1 tablespoon olive oil. Arrange sliced tomatoes over top; sprinkle with chopped rosemary, pepper, and remaining ½ teaspoon salt.

7 Bake focaccia in top third of oven until top is lightly browned, about 35 to 40 minutes. Remove to wire rack; drizzle with remaining 1 tablespoon olive oil. Cool slightly to serve warm. Makes 12 servings.

Each serving: About 225 calories, 5 g protein, 35 g carbohydrate, 7 g total fat (1 g saturated), 0 mg cholesterol, 360 mg sodium.

Country-Style Pizzas

PREP: 45 MINUTES PLUS RISING
BAKE: 25 TO 30 MINUTES

2 cups all-purpose flour
¾ teaspoon salt
1 package quick-rise yeast
Cornmeal
1 small eggplant (¾ pound)
1 jar (6 ounces) marinated artichoke hearts
3 small tomatoes or 1 medium-size tomato, cut into thin wedges
¼ cup loosely packed basil leaves, sliced
6 ounces goat cheese such as Montrachet, broken into large chunks, or mozzarella cheese, sliced
¼ teaspoon cracked black pepper

1 In large bowl, stir flour, salt, and yeast. Stir in ¾ *cup very warm water* (120° to 130°F.), until blended and dough comes away from side of bowl. Knead dough 5 minutes.

2 Sprinkle large cookie sheet with cornmeal. Shape dough into 2 balls; place in diagonally opposite corners of cookie sheet, each about 3 inches from edges of sheet. Cover and let rest 15 minutes.

3 Preheat broiler. Cut eggplant lengthwise in half. Cut each half crosswise into ¼-inch-thick slices. Drain artichokes, reserving marinade. Cut each artichoke in half, if large.

4 In 15½" by 10½" jelly-roll pan, toss eggplant slices with 2 tablespoons artichoke marinade. Arrange eggplant in single layer. With jelly-roll pan 5 to 7 inches from source of heat, broil eggplant until tender and brown, turning slices once, 7 to 10 minutes. Remove. Turn oven control to 425°F.

5 In large bowl, toss eggplant, artichokes, tomatoes, and half of basil with remaining marinade.

6 Pat and stretch 1 ball of dough into a 10-inch round. Arrange half of eggplant mixture and half of cheese on crust, leaving 1-inch border. Bring edge of dough up; pinch to make a rim. Repeat to make a second pizza. Cover pizzas and let rise 15 minutes.

7 Bake pizzas on bottom rack in oven 25 to 30 minutes, until topping is hot and crust is browned and crisp. Sprinkle with cracked pepper and remaining basil. Makes 4 main-dish servings.

Each serving: About 380 calories, 16 g protein, 62 g carbohydrate, 8 g total fat (3 g saturated), 8 mg cholesterol, 785 mg sodium.

Fried Green-Tomato Sandwiches

PREP: 10 MINUTES • COOK: 20 MINUTES

Instead of regular mayonnaise, we blended low-fat mayo, plain yogurt, chives, and black pepper—try it on all of your favorite sandwiches.

1 package (8 ounces) sliced bacon
1 large egg white
¼ teaspoon salt
½ cup cornmeal
½ teaspoon coarsely ground black pepper
1 pound green tomatoes (3 medium), cut into
   ½-inch slices
¼ cup low-fat mayonnaise dressing
¼ cup low-fat plain yogurt
2 tablespoons chopped fresh chives
4 green-leaf lettuce leaves
8 slices firm whole-grain or white bread, toasted

1 In 12-inch skillet, cook bacon over medium heat until browned. Remove bacon to paper towels to drain.

2 Meanwhile, in pie plate, beat egg white and salt. In another pie plate or on waxed paper, combine corn-meal and ¼ teaspoon pepper. Dip tomato slices in egg-white mixture to coat both sides, then dip into cornmeal mixture to coat both sides well. Place coated slices on waxed paper.

3 In drippings in skillet, cook tomato slices, a few at a time, over medium-high heat until golden brown on both sides and heated through, about 3 minutes. Drain on paper towels.

4 In small bowl, combine mayonnaise, yogurt, chives, and ¼ teaspoon pepper.

5 Spread mayonnaise-dressing mixture on 1 side of toast slices. Arrange lettuce, tomatoes, then bacon on 4 toast slices; top with remaining toast slices, dressing-side down. Makes 4 main-dish servings.

Each serving: About 430 calories, 14 g protein, 48 g carbo-hydrate, 21 g total fat (7 g saturated), 23 mg cholesterol, 885 mg sodium.

Old-Time Tomato Sandwiches

Old-Time Tomato Sandwiches

PREP: 15 MINUTES

We love these as is, or with a few sprigs of watercress tucked inside.

1 lemon
⅓ cup mayonnaise
¼ teaspoon ground coriander
¼ teaspoon salt
¼ teaspoon coarsely ground black pepper
1 large round or oval loaf (1 pound) sourdough
   or other crusty bread
3 large ripe tomatoes, thickly sliced

1 From lemon, grate ½ teaspoon peel and squeeze 1 teaspoon juice. In small bowl, stir lemon peel and juice, mayonnaise, coriander, salt, and pepper.

2 Cut eight ½-inch-thick slices from center of bread loaf. Reserve ends for use another day. Toast bread if desired. Spread 1 side of each bread slice with may-onnaise mixture. Arrange tomato slices on 4 bread slices; top with remaining bread slices, mayonnaise side down. Cut each sandwich in half to serve. Makes 4 sandwiches.

Each sandwich: About 300 calories, 6 g protein, 35 g carbo-hydrate, 18 g total fat (3 g saturated), 7 mg cholesterol, 540 mg sodium.

Frittata Sandwiches with Peppers & Onions

PREP: 30 MINUTES • BAKE: 10 MINUTES

This hot sandwich can be wrapped in foil and carried along to serve later. For an extra-special sandwich, make this on homemade Tomato Focaccia (page 90).

2 tablespoons olive oil
2 medium onions, each cut in half and thinly sliced
4 Italian frying peppers (about 2 ounces each), thinly sliced
½ teaspoon salt
6 large eggs
¾ cup grated Parmesan cheese
¼ cup chopped fresh parsley leaves
¼ teaspoon ground black pepper
1 round or square (8-inch) focaccia bread, cut horizontally in half

1 In 12-inch skillet, heat 1 tablespoon olive oil over medium heat. Add onions and cook, stirring frequently, until tender, about 8 minutes. Add peppers; sprinkle with ¼ teaspoon salt and cook until peppers are tender, about 12 minutes longer. Keep warm.

2 Meanwhile, preheat oven to 375°F. In large bowl, with wire whisk or fork, mix eggs, Parmesan, parsley, black pepper, and remaining ¼ teaspoon salt until blended. In nonstick 10-inch skillet with oven-safe handle, heat remaining 1 tablespoon olive oil over medium heat. Pour in egg mixture and cook without stirring, 3 to 4 minutes, until frittata begins to set around the edge.

3 Place skillet in oven. Bake about 10 minutes longer or until frittata is just set and knife inserted in center comes out clean. Slide frittata onto plate.

4 Place frittata on bottom of focaccia; top with onion-pepper mixture. Replace top of focaccia. Makes 4 sandwiches.

Each sandwich: About 535 calories, 29 g protein, 49 g carbohydrate, 26 g total fat (7 g saturated), 341 mg cholesterol, 1225 mg sodium.

Tuscan Tuna on Focaccia

PREP: 15 MINUTES

This filling is equally good served in pita pockets.

1 can (16 to 19 ounces) white kidney beans (cannellini), rinsed and drained
½ cup chopped fresh basil leaves
3 tablespoons capers, chopped
2 tablespoons fresh lemon juice
2 tablespoons olive oil
½ teaspoon salt
¼ teaspoon ground black pepper
1 can (6 ounces) tuna packed in water, drained
1 bunch watercress, trimmed
1 round or square (8-inch) focaccia bread, cut horizontally in half
2 ripe tomatoes, thinly sliced

1 In large bowl, mash 1 cup kidney beans. Stir in basil, capers, lemon juice, olive oil, salt, and pepper. Add tuna, watercress, and remaining beans; toss well.

2 Spoon tuna mixture on bottom of focaccia; top with tomato slices. Replace top of focaccia. Makes 4 sandwiches.

Each sandwich: About 490 calories, 32 g protein, 65 g carbohydrate, 13 g total fat (1 g saturated), 7 mg cholesterol, 1455 mg sodium.

Greek Salad Pitas

PREP: 20 MINUTES

Hummus—the Middle Eastern spread made with mashed garbanzo beans—is fast work in a food processor or blender.

1 can (15 to 19 ounces) garbanzo beans, rinsed and drained
¼ cup plain low-fat yogurt
2 tablespoons olive oil
2 tablespoons fresh lemon juice
½ teaspoon salt
¼ teaspoon coarsely ground black pepper
¼ teaspoon ground cumin
1 garlic clove, peeled
4 whole-wheat pitas (6- to 7-inch diameter)
3 cups sliced Romaine lettuce

2 medium tomatoes, diced
1 medium cucumber, peeled and thinly sliced
2 ounces feta cheese, crumbled
2 tablespoons chopped fresh mint leaves
Fresh mint leaves for garnish

1 In food processor with knife blade attached or in blender, place beans, yogurt, oil, lemon juice, salt, pepper, cumin, and garlic; blend until smooth.

2 Cut off top third of each pita to form a pocket. Use half of bean mixture to spread inside pockets.

3 Combine lettuce, tomatoes, cucumber, feta, and chopped mint; use to fill pockets. Top with remaining bean mixture and mint leaves. Makes 4 sandwiches.

Each sandwich: About 440 calories, 17 g protein, 66 g carbohydrate, 15 g total fat (4 g saturated), 13 mg cholesterol, 1105 mg sodium.

SPREAD SHEET: 10 QUICK SANDWICH DRESSINGS

APRICOT-GINGER CREAM CHEESE: Mix *1 container (8 ounces) light cream cheese (50% less fat), ¼ cup apricot jam, and 2 teaspoons grated, peeled fresh ginger* until blended. Nice with vegetables, sliced avocado, or pork. Makes about 1 cup. [Per tablespoon: 45 calories, 3 g fat.]

NUTTY BLUE-CHEESE SPREAD: Mix *⅓ cup light cream cheese (50% less fat), 2 ounces blue cheese, 2 tablespoons chopped walnuts, and 2 tablespoons milk* until blended. Use on roast beef, steak, or burgers. Makes about ¾ cup. [Per tablespoon: 40 calories, 3 g fat.]

MEXICAN MAYO: Mix *¾ teaspoon sauce from canned chipotle chiles in adobo sauce* with ¾ cup light mayonnaise.* Dresses up pork sandwiches and BLTs. Makes about ¾ cup. [Per tablespoon: 25 calories, 1 g fat.] *Canned chipotle chiles in adobo (smoked jalapeño chiles in a vinegary marinade) are available in Hispanic markets.

CREAMY PEANUT SAUCE: Whisk *⅓ cup creamy peanut butter, ¼ cup hot tap water, 1 tablespoon reduced-sodium soy sauce, 1 tablespoon distilled white vinegar, ¾ teaspoon Asian sesame oil, 1 teaspoon grated, peeled fresh ginger,*

Creamy Peanut Sauce

and 1 small garlic clove, crushed with garlic press, until blended. Spoon over chicken, turkey, lamb, or vegetables. Makes about ⅔ cup. [Per tablespoon: 50 calories, 4 g fat.]

CUCUMBER YOGURT: Pat dry *¾ cup peeled, grated, cucumber.* Mix with *½ cup plain low-fat yogurt, 1 small garlic clove* crushed with garlic press, *½ teaspoon salt, and ⅛ teaspoon coarsely ground black pepper* until blended. Serve with smoked turkey, watercress, and tomato, or lamb. Makes about 1 cup. [Per tablespoon: 10 calories, 0 g fat.]

HORSERADISH CREAM: Mix *¼ cup reduced-fat sour cream, ¼ cup light mayonnaise, and 2 tablespoons prepared white horseradish* until blended. Add a dollop to roast beef, steak, ham, or burgers.

Makes about ½ cup. [Per tablespoon: 25 calories, 1 g fat.]

OLIVE-CAPER RELISH: Mix *½ cup finely chopped pitted Kalamata olives, 2 tablespoons drained and chopped capers, and 2 teaspoons extravirgin olive oil* until blended. Use to top grilled vegetables, chicken, or beef. Makes about ½ cup. [Per tablespoon: 35 calories, 4 g fat.]

PEACHY MUSTARD: Mix *½ cup Dijon mustard with seeds* and *¼ cup peach preserves* until blended. Spread on ham or cheese. Makes about 1 cup. [Per tablespoon: 30 calories, 1 g fat.]

ROASTED RED-PEPPER DRESSING: In blender, combine *1 jar (7 to 7½ ounces) roasted red peppers, drained, 3 tablespoons light mayonnaise, 1 teaspoon honey, and ¼ teaspoon salt* until creamy. Drizzle on seafood, turkey, grilled vegetables, or egg salad. Makes about 1 cup. [Per tablespoon: 10 calories, 0 g fat.]

SUN-DRIED TOMATO TOPPING: Mix *3 tablespoons chopped sun-dried tomatoes packed in oil and herbs, ½ cup plain low-fat yogurt, and ½ cup light mayonnaise* until pureed. Great with chicken and veggies. Makes about 1 cup. [Per tablespoon: 20 calories, 1 g fat.]

Portobello "Cheese Steaks"

PREP: 15 MINUTES • COOK: 20 MINUTES

A hearty meal served gyro-style.

2 medium portobello mushrooms (about
  4 ounces each), stems removed
2 tablespoons olive oil
2 medium yellow peppers, thinly sliced
1 jumbo sweet onion such as Vidalia or Walla
  Walla (about 12 ounces), thinly sliced
½ teaspoon salt
¼ teaspoon coarsely ground black pepper
1 tablespoon balsamic vinegar
4 pocketless pitas (7-inch diameter)
8 ounces part-skim mozzarella cheese, shredded
  (2 cups)

1 Preheat oven to 400°F. Heat nonstick 12-inch skillet over medium-high heat until hot. Brush both sides of mushrooms using 1 tablespoon olive oil. Add mushrooms to skillet and cook 5 minutes on each side or until tender and lightly browned. Transfer mushrooms to cutting board and cut into ¼-inch-thick slices; set aside.

2 In same skillet, heat remaining 1 tablespoon olive oil over medium heat until hot. Add yellow peppers, onion, salt, black pepper, and *2 tablespoons water*; cook until vegetables are tender and golden, about 15 minutes, stirring frequently. Stir in balsamic vinegar; remove skillet from heat. Gently stir in sliced portobellos.

3 Meanwhile, place pitas on large cookie sheet; sprinkle with mozzarella cheese. Heat pitas 5 minutes or until cheese melts.

4 Roll each pita into a cone; tightly wrap bottom half of each with kitchen parchment or foil to help hold its shape and prevent leakage. Fill pita cones with warm mushroom mixture. Makes 4 sandwiches.

Each sandwich: About 460 calories, 24 g protein, 52 g carbohydrate, 18 g total fat (7 g saturated), 41 mg cholesterol, 1060 mg sodium.

Panfried Steak & Onions on Grilled Bread

PREP: 40 MINUTES • COOK: 30 MINUTES

The green herb sauce is a natural with fried or grilled meat. Afghan flatbread is a good alternative to Italian-style breads.

PANFRIED STEAK & ONIONS:
2 teaspoons olive oil
1 beef flank steak (1½ pounds)
¼ teaspoon coarsely ground black pepper
¾ teaspoon salt
2 large red onions, thinly sliced

HERB SAUCE:
1 cup loosely packed fresh parsley leaves,
  chopped
1 cup loosely packed fresh cilantro leaves,
  chopped
3 tablespoons olive oil
2 tablespoons red wine vinegar
¼ teaspoon salt
¼ teaspoon coarsely ground black pepper
Pinch crushed red pepper
1 small garlic clove, crushed with garlic press

2 Italian-style grilled flatbreads (one 13½-ounce
  package), warmed, or 1 Afghan flatbread
  (16 ounces), cut crosswise in half

1 Prepare Panfried Steak & Onions: In heavy 12-inch skillet (preferably cast iron), heat olive oil over high heat until very hot. Meanwhile, sprinkle flank steak with pepper and ½ teaspoon salt.

2 Add steak to hot skillet; reduce heat to medium-high and cook 12 to 17 minutes for medium-rare (depending on thickness of meat) or until of desired doneness, turning once. Transfer steak to cutting board.

3 Reduce heat to medium. Add onions and ¼ teaspoon salt, and cook until tender and browned, 12 to 15 minutes, stirring occasionally.

4 While onions are cooking, prepare Herb Sauce: In small bowl, mix parsley, cilantro, olive oil, vinegar, salt, black pepper, crushed red pepper, and garlic; set aside.

5 To serve, thinly slice flank steak. Drizzle 1 flatbread with 2 tablespoons Herb Sauce; top with steak slices, onion slices, 2 tablespoons Herb Sauce, then remaining flatbread. Cut sandwich into 6 pieces. Pass remaining sauce to serve with sandwiches. Makes 6 sandwiches.

Each sandwich: About 490 calories, 29 g protein, 46 g carbohydrate, 20 g total fat (6 g saturated), 58 mg cholesterol, 635 mg sodium.

Goat Cheese & Red Pepper Rolls

PREP: 15 MINUTES PLUS CHILLING

These tasty spirals are even better when chilled for a couple of hours.

1 package (5½ ounces) goat cheese
1 package (3 ounces) cream cheese
½ small red onion, minced
3 tablespoons milk

¼ teaspoon coarsely ground black pepper
1 lahvash (half 14-ounce package soft Armenian flatbread)*
1 jar (12 ounces) roasted red peppers, drained
2 bunches arugula (about 4 ounces each), tough stems removed

1 In small bowl, with spoon, mix goat cheese, cream cheese, red onion, milk, and black pepper until well blended.

2 Unfold lahvash; spread with goat-cheese mixture to ½ inch from edge. Top with red peppers, then arugula. Roll lahvash jelly-roll fashion.

3 Wrap lahvash roll in plastic wrap and refrigerate 2 to 8 hours to allow bread to soften and flavor to develop.

4 To serve, trim ends, then cut lahvash roll into 1-inch-thick slices. Makes 4 main-dish servings.

*If lahvash seems dry before filling, place between dampened paper towels 10 to 15 minutes to soften.

Each serving: About 365 calories, 16 g protein, 33 g carbohydrate, 20 g total fat (13 g saturated), 55 mg cholesterol, 540 mg sodium.

Panfried Steak & Onions on Grilled Bread

Smoked Turkey & Mango Wraps

PREP: 25 MINUTES PLUS CHILLING

A sandwich of delightful counterpoints: luscious fresh mango—underscored by mango chutney—played against the rich meatiness of smoked turkey. The sandwich components are wrapped in lahvash, the soft version of Armenian cracker bread that ranges from 9 to 16 inches in diameter. Its thin texture is especially good with creamy spreads, like goat cheese or guacamole. If you can't find lahvash, divide filling ingredients among four 8- to 10-inch flour tortillas.

1 large lime
¼ cup light mayonnaise
3 tablespoons mango chutney, chopped
½ teaspoon curry powder
⅛ teaspoon paprika
1 lahvash (half 14-ounce package soft Armenian flatbread)*
1 medium cucumber, peeled and thinly sliced
8 ounces thinly sliced smoked turkey breast
1 medium mango, peeled and finely chopped
6 large green-leaf-lettuce leaves

1 Grate ¼ teaspoon peel and squeeze 1 tablespoon juice from lime. In small bowl, mix lime peel, lime juice, mayonnaise, chutney, curry, and paprika.

2 Unfold lahvash; spread with mayonnaise mixture. Top with cucumber slices, smoked turkey, chopped mango, and lettuce. Roll lahvash jelly-roll fashion.

3 Wrap lahvash roll in plastic wrap and refrigerate 2 to 4 hours to allow bread to soften and flavor to develop.

4 To serve, trim ends, then cut lahvash roll into 4 pieces. Makes 4 sandwiches.

*If lahvash seems dry before filling, place between dampened paper towels 10 to 15 minutes to soften.

Each sandwich: About 280 calories, 18 g protein, 51 g carbohydrate, 2 g total fat (0 g saturated), 23 mg cholesterol, 860 mg sodium.

Spicy Guacamole & Chicken Roll-Ups

PREP: 30 MINUTES • COOK: ABOUT 12 MINUTES

Don't miss this zesty guacamole—it's great with tortilla chips too.

2 teaspoons olive oil
4 medium skinless, boneless chicken-breast halves (about 1 pound)
½ teaspoon salt
½ teaspoon coarsely ground black pepper
2 medium avocados (about 8 ounces each), peeled and cut into small chunks
1 medium tomato, diced
¼ cup loosely packed fresh cilantro leaves, coarsely chopped
4 teaspoons fresh lime juice
2 teaspoons finely chopped red onion
1 teaspoon adobo sauce from canned chipotle chiles* or 2 tablespoons green jalapeño sauce
4 burrito-size (10-inch diameter) flour tortillas, warmed
2 cups sliced iceberg lettuce

1 In 10-inch skillet, heat olive oil over medium-high heat until hot. Add chicken and sprinkle with ¼ teaspoon salt and ¼ teaspoon pepper. Cook chicken about 12 minutes, turning once, until juices run clear when thickest part is pierced with tip of knife. Transfer chicken to plate; cool 5 minutes or until easy to handle.

2 Meanwhile, in medium bowl, with rubber spatula, gently stir avocados, tomato, cilantro, lime juice, red onion, adobo sauce, and remaining ¼ teaspoon salt and ¼ teaspoon pepper until blended.

3 Pull chicken into thin shreds. Place tortillas on work surface; spread with guacamole. Place chicken, then lettuce on top of guacamole. Roll tortillas around filling. Makes 4 sandwiches.

*Canned chipotle chiles in adobo (smoked jalapeño chiles in a vinegary marinade) are available in Hispanic markets.

Each sandwich: About 510 calories, 34 g protein, 40 g carbohydrate, 25 g total fat (4 g saturated), 72 mg cholesterol, 625 mg sodium.

◀ *Smoked Turkey & Mango Wraps*

Chicken Caesar Pockets

PREP: 20 MINUTES • COOK: ABOUT 12 MINUTES

The salad lover's favorite, nestled in a pita. Just right for supper in the backyard or at the park.

¼ teaspoon salt
2 teaspoons plus 3 tablespoons olive oil
½ teaspoon coarsely ground black pepper
4 medium skinless, boneless chicken-breast halves (about 1 pound)
3 tablespoons lemon juice
3 tablespoons light mayonnaise
1 tablespoon Dijon mustard
1 teaspoon anchovy paste
1 small garlic clove, crushed with garlic press
½ cup grated Parmesan cheese
6 pitas (6- to 7-inch diameter)
8 cups sliced Romaine lettuce (about ¾-pound head)

1 Preheat broiler. In medium bowl, mix salt, 2 teaspoons olive oil, and ¼ teaspoon pepper. Add chicken and stir to coat. Place chicken on rack in broiling pan. Place pan in broiler at closest position to source of heat; broil chicken about 12 minutes, turning once, until juices run clear when thickest part is pierced with tip of knife. Transfer chicken to cutting board; cool 5 minutes or until easy to handle.

2 Meanwhile, in large bowl, with fork, mix lemon juice, mayonnaise, mustard, anchovy paste, garlic, remaining 3 tablespoons olive oil, and ¼ teaspoon pepper until blended; stir in Parmesan cheese.

3 With sharp knife, slit top third of each pita to form an opening. Thinly slice chicken. Add lettuce and chicken slices to dressing; toss well to coat. Fill pitas with salad. Makes 6 sandwiches.

Each sandwich: About 345 calories, 17 g protein, 39 g carbohydrate, 13 g total fat (3 g saturated), 26 mg cholesterol, 770 mg sodium.

WRAP ARTISTRY

Whether you're using thin Middle Eastern lahvash or large flour tortillas, it's important to distribute the filling evenly and roll the bread tightly in a sandwich "wrap." After arranging topping on bread (it's not necessary to cover every inch), roll up bread gently but snugly, being careful not to squeeze too hard, or filling may come out ends. Trim dry ends of roll. Then, using a chef's knife, cut roll straight across or on the diagonal into pieces of desired thickness (see photo below).

Roast Beef Wraps with Horseradish Slaw

PREP: 10 MINUTES

We used deli roast beef and shredded cabbage mix for coleslaw to make these superquick.

¼ cup light mayonnaise
3 tablespoons prepared white horseradish
1 tablespoon distilled white vinegar
¼ teaspoon salt
¼ teaspoon coarsely ground black pepper
¼ teaspoon sugar
8 ounces shredded cabbage mix for coleslaw (half 16-ounce package)
4 burrito-size (10-inch diameter) flour tortillas, warmed
2 medium tomatoes, thinly sliced
8 ounces thinly sliced deli roast beef

1 In large bowl, mix mayonnaise, horseradish, vinegar, salt, pepper, and sugar. Remove half of mayonnaise mixture to cup. Toss cabbage with mayonnaise mixture in bowl.

2 With small spatula, spread some mayonnaise mixture on 1 side of each tortilla. At 1 edge of each tortilla, arrange some tomato slices, roast beef, and cabbage mixture. Roll each tortilla jelly-roll fashion. Makes 4 sandwiches.

Each sandwich: About 340 calories, 22 g protein, 43 g carbohydrate, 9 g total fat (2 g saturated), 36 mg cholesterol, 720 mg sodium.

PASTA & RICE

Penne with Yellow Peppers & Sweet Onion

PREP: 15 MINUTES • COOK: ABOUT 15 MINUTES

1 package (16 ounces) penne rigate or elbow
  twist pasta
Salt
2 tablespoons olive oil
2 medium yellow peppers, thinly sliced
1 jumbo sweet onion (12 ounces) such as Walla
  Walla or Vidalia, thinly sliced
¼ teaspoon coarsely ground black pepper
1 tablespoon balsamic vinegar
½ cup chopped fresh basil leaves

1 In large saucepot, prepare pasta in *boiling salted water* as label directs.

2 Meanwhile, in 12-inch skillet, heat olive oil over medium heat until hot. Add yellow peppers, onion, black pepper, and ½ teaspoon salt and cook until vegetables are tender and golden, about 15 minutes, stirring frequently. Remove skillet from heat; stir in balsamic vinegar and chopped basil.

3 When pasta has cooked to desired doneness, remove ½ *cup pasta cooking water*. Drain pasta and return to saucepot. Add yellow-pepper mixture and reserved pasta cooking water; toss well. Makes 4 main-dish or 8 accompaniment servings.

Each main-dish serving: About 525 calories, 16 g protein, 95 g carbohydrate, 9 g total fat (1 g saturated), 0 mg cholesterol, 455 mg sodium.

▌ FOOD EDITOR'S TIP ▐

Q. What exactly are sweet onions?

A. Sweet onions are a thin-skinned onion with a high sugar and water content. They are mellower than storage onions, because they contain fewer of the sulfuric-acid compounds that give onions their characteristic bite. Varieties include Texas Spring Sweet, Sweet Imperial, Vidalia, Walla Walla, Maui, and OSO Sweet, and can be used interchangeably (try them in Penne with Yellow Peppers & Sweet Onion, above). Store them in a single layer in a well-ventilated area; they'll last 1 to 4 weeks. If you refrigerate them, individually wrap them in paper towels or newspaper.

Radiatore with Sweet & Spicy Picadillo Sauce

PREP: 10 MINUTES • COOK: ABOUT 15 MINUTES

This popular sauce of Spanish origin is a zesty blend of ground beef, spices, raisins, and tomatoes.

1 package (16 ounces) radiatore or corkscrew
  pasta
Salt
1 teaspoon olive oil
1 small onion, finely chopped
2 garlic cloves, crushed with garlic press
¼ teaspoon ground cinnamon
⅛ to ¼ teaspoon ground red pepper (cayenne)
¾ pound ground beef
1 can (14½ ounces) whole tomatoes in puree
½ cup dark seedless raisins
¼ cup salad olives, drained, or chopped
  pimiento-stuffed olives
Chopped fresh parsley leaves for garnish

1 In large saucepot, prepare pasta in *boiling salted water* as label directs.

2 Meanwhile, in nonstick 12-inch skillet, heat olive oil over medium heat until hot. Add onion and cook 5 minutes or until tender, stirring frequently. Stir in garlic, cinnamon, and ground red pepper; cook 30 seconds. Increase heat to medium-high; add ground beef and ½ teaspoon salt and cook 5 minutes or until beef begins to brown, stirring frequently. Spoon off fat if necessary. Stir in tomatoes with their puree, raisins, and olives, breaking up tomatoes with side of spoon, and cook about 5 minutes longer or until sauce thickens slightly.

3 When pasta has cooked to desired doneness, remove *1 cup pasta cooking water*. Drain pasta and return to saucepot. Add ground-beef mixture and reserved pasta cooking water; toss well. Garnish with chopped parsley to serve. Makes 6 main-dish servings.

Each serving: About 470 calories, 20 g protein, 71 g carbohydrate, 11 g total fat (4 g saturated), 35 mg cholesterol, 775 mg sodium.

Penne with Yellow Peppers & Sweet Onion ➤

Bow Ties with a Trio of Peas

PREP: 15 MINUTES • COOK: ABOUT 15 MINUTES

Snow peas, sugar snap peas, and green peas served in a lemony broth.

1 package (16 ounces) bow-tie or corkscrew
   pasta
Salt
1 tablespoon margarine or butter
1 tablespoon olive oil
4 ounces snow peas, strings removed
4 ounces sugar snap peas, strings removed
1 garlic clove, crushed with garlic press
1 cup frozen baby peas
½ cup reduced-sodium chicken broth
¼ teaspoon coarsely ground black pepper
½ teaspoon grated lemon peel

1 In large saucepot, prepare pasta in *boiling salted water* as label directs.

2 Meanwhile, in 10-inch skillet, melt margarine or butter with olive oil over medium-high heat. Add snow peas and sugar snap peas and cook, stirring, 1 to 2 minutes, until tender-crisp. Stir in garlic and cook 30 seconds. Add peas, broth, pepper, and ¾ teaspoon salt; heat to boiling. Stir in lemon peel.

3 Drain pasta; return to saucepot. Add vegetable mixture; toss well. Makes 4 main-dish or 8 accompaniment servings.

Each main-dish serving: About 530 calories, 19 g protein, 95 g carbohydrate, 9 g total fat (1 g saturated), 0 mg cholesterol, 720 mg sodium.

Spaghetti with Cilantro Pesto

PREP: 15 MINUTES • COOK: ABOUT 15 MINUTES

This quick no-cook sauce is lighter than traditional pesto because it's made without cheese and contains less oil.

1 package (16 ounces) spaghetti or linguine
Salt
½ cup reduced-sodium chicken broth

2 tablespoons olive oil
1 tablespoon fresh lime juice
1 jalapeño chile, seeded and coarsely chopped
1 garlic clove, peeled
¼ cup pine nuts (pignoli), toasted
1½ cups packed fresh cilantro leaves with stems
   (about 2 bunches)
½ cup packed fresh parsley leaves

1 In large saucepot, prepare pasta in *boiling salted water* as label directs.

2 Meanwhile, into food processor with knife blade attached or into blender, measure chicken broth, olive oil, lime juice, jalapeño, garlic, 2 tablespoons pine nuts, and 1 teaspoon salt. Add cilantro and parsley and blend until smooth.

3 Drain pasta; return to saucepot. Add cilantro mixture; toss well. Sprinkle with remaining 2 tablespoons pine nuts to serve. Makes 4 main-dish or 8 accompaniment servings.

Each main-dish serving: About 530 calories, 18 g protein, 87 g carbohydrate, 12 g total fat (2 g saturated), 0 mg cholesterol, 755 mg sodium.

Gemelli with Ricotta & Spinach

PREP: 10 MINUTES • COOK: ABOUT 15 MINUTES

Fresh spinach is quickly sautéed with garlic and tossed in the pot with ricotta and Parmesan cheeses for a satisfying supper.

1 package (16 ounces) gemelli or corkscrew
   pasta
Salt
1 tablespoon olive oil
2 garlic cloves, crushed with side of chef's knife
2 packages (10 ounces each) prewashed
   spinach, tough stems removed
1 container (15 ounces) part-skim ricotta cheese
⅓ cup grated Parmesan cheese
¼ teaspoon coarsely ground black pepper
Shredded Parmesan cheese for garnish

1 In large saucepot, prepare pasta in *boiling salted water* as label directs.

2 Meanwhile, in 12-inch skillet, heat olive oil over medium heat until hot. Add garlic and cook 1 minute, stirring. Gradually add spinach and *2 tablespoons water*; cook, stirring often, just until spinach wilts. Remove skillet from heat.

3 When pasta has cooked to desired doneness, remove *1 cup pasta cooking water*. Drain pasta; return to saucepot. Add ricotta cheese, Parmesan cheese, pepper, ½ teaspoon salt, spinach mixture, and reserved cooking water; heat over medium heat, tossing until well blended. Garnish with shredded Parmesan cheese to serve. Makes 6 main-dish servings.

Each serving: About 445 calories, 23 g protein, 64 g carbohydrate, 11 g total fat (5 g saturated), 26 mg cholesterol, 565 mg sodium.

Wagon Wheels with Summer Squash & Mint

PREP: 15 MINUTES • COOK: ABOUT 15 MINUTES

1 package (16 ounces) wagon-wheel or bow-tie pasta
Salt
1 tablespoon margarine or butter
1 tablespoon olive oil
3 medium yellow summer squashes (about 8 ounces each), each cut lengthwise in half, then cut crosswise into ¼-inch-thick slices
3 medium zucchini (about 8 ounces each), each cut lengthwise in half, then cut crosswise into ¼-inch-thick slices
2 garlic cloves, crushed with garlic press
¼ teaspoon coarsely ground black pepper
½ cup chopped fresh mint leaves
1 cup reduced-sodium chicken broth
¼ cup grated Parmesan cheese

1 In large saucepot, prepare pasta in *boiling salted water* as label directs.

2 Meanwhile, in 12-inch skillet, heat margarine or butter with olive oil over high heat. Add yellow squash and zucchini slices, garlic, pepper, ¼ cup chopped mint, and ¾ teaspoon salt and cook until vegetables are just tender, stirring frequently, about 10 minutes.

3 Add chicken broth and Parmesan cheese to vegetable mixture; heat to boiling over high heat. Boil 1 minute.

4 Drain pasta; return to saucepot. Add vegetable mixture and remaining chopped mint; toss well. Serve with additional grated Parmesan if you like. Makes 4 main-dish or 8 accompaniment servings.

Each main-dish serving: About 565 calories, 22 g protein, 98 g carbohydrate, 11 g total fat (3 g saturated), 5 mg cholesterol, 845 mg sodium.

A PERFECT MATCH: PAIRING PASTAS & SAUCES

Not every pasta works with every topping. Fragile angel hair can absorb a creamy sauce in the time it takes to turn around and get a serving spoon, and sturdy penne overpowers a delicate seafood sauce. Here's a general guide to using the most common shapes:

• LONG [spaghetti, vermicelli, linguine, spaghettini, capellini (angel hair)]: Best with smooth tomato and oil-based sauces; these varieties don't carry a chunky topping well once you lift the fork. Save ultrathin capellini for light sauces, or use in broths.

• LONG STRAWS [perciatelli, bucatini]: Ideal for pesto, cheese, or cream sauces because the pasta gets coated inside and out.

• SHORT [farfalle (bow ties), fusilli (corkscrews), orecchiette (little ears), shells, gemelli, radiatore]: Serve with butter, cheese, tomato, meat, vegetable, and light oil-based sauces; they catch every drop.

• SHORT TUBES [penne, rigatoni, ziti]: Bite for bite, the most suitable partner for meat, vegetable, and chunky tomato sauces.

• SMALL [pastina, ditalini, orzo, stelline, tubettini, farfalline]: Use in broths or soups so you can spoon up every last morsel.

• WIDE [tagliatelle, fettuccine, pappardelle, lasagna, mafalda]: Substantial enough to support cream, cheese, and thick meat sauces.

Gnocchi with Asparagus & Mushrooms

••

PREP: 15 MINUTES • COOK: ABOUT 15 MINUTES

Make the light cream sauce in a skillet, then toss with pasta and sprinkle with Parmesan.

1 package (16 ounces) gnocchi or medium shell
   pasta
Salt
2 tablespoons margarine or butter
1 medium onion, chopped
4 ounces sliced smoked ham, cut into thin strips
1 package (8 ounces) sliced mushrooms
1 pound asparagus, trimmed and cut into 2-inch
   pieces
1 cup reduced-sodium chicken broth
½ cup heavy or whipping cream
⅛ teaspoon ground black pepper
Grated Parmesan cheese (optional)

1 In large saucepot, prepare pasta in *boiling salted water* as label directs.

2 Meanwhile, in 10-inch skillet, melt margarine or butter over medium-high heat. Add onion and ham and cook, stirring occasionally, 5 minutes or until onion is tender.

3 Add mushrooms and cook until mushrooms are tender and liquid has evaporated, about 5 minutes. Stir in asparagus, chicken broth, heavy or whipping cream, and black pepper; heat to boiling over high heat, stirring. Boil 3 to 5 minutes, until asparagus is tender.

4 Drain pasta; return to saucepot. Add mushroom mixture; toss well. Serve with Parmesan cheese if you like. Makes 6 main-dish servings.

Each serving: About 435 calories, 17 g protein, 62 g carbohydrate, 13 g total fat (6 g saturated), 38 mg cholesterol, 455 mg sodium.

Penne with Green Beans & Basil

Penne with Green Beans & Basil

•••
PREP: 15 MINUTES • COOK: ABOUT 20 MINUTES

8 ounces penne or bow-tie pasta
Salt
1 pound green beans, trimmed and halved
1 cup loosely packed fresh basil leaves
¼ cup extravirgin olive oil
½ teaspoon coarsely ground black pepper
1 medium tomato, diced
Small basil leaves for garnish

1 Prepare pasta in *boiling salted water* as label directs.

2 Meanwhile, in 12-inch skillet, heat *1 inch water* to boiling over high heat. Add beans and ½ teaspoon salt; heat to boiling. Cook, uncovered, 8 to 10 minutes, until tender-crisp. Drain. Rinse beans under cold running water to cool slightly; drain again.

3 In blender at high speed, blend basil, oil, and *1 tablespoon water* until almost smooth, stopping blender occasionally and scraping down sides with rubber spatula. Transfer basil puree to large bowl; stir in pepper and 1 teaspoon salt.

4 Drain pasta; rinse under cold running water and drain again. Toss pasta, beans, and tomato with basil puree. Garnish with basil leaves. Makes 8 cups or 4 main-dish servings.

Each serving: About 370 calories, 10 g protein, 52 g carbohydrate, 15 g total fat (2 g saturated), 0 mg cholesterol, 680 mg sodium.

Gemelli with Feta, Mint & Olives

•••
PREP: 15 MINUTES • COOK: ABOUT 15 MINUTES

Taste your olives before making this sauce—if they're very briny, you may want to omit the lemon juice.

1 package (16 ounces) gemelli or penne pasta
Salt
4 ounces feta cheese, crumbled (1 cup)
¼ cup Kalamata olives, pitted and sliced
¼ cup chopped fresh mint leaves
2 tablespoons extravirgin olive oil

1 tablespoon fresh lemon juice
⅛ teaspoon ground black pepper
1 bunch spinach (10 to 12 ounces), tough stems removed and leaves torn

1 In large saucepot, prepare pasta in *boiling salted water* as label directs.

2 Meanwhile, in medium bowl, combine feta cheese, Kalamata olives, mint, olive oil, lemon juice, and black pepper.

3 Drain pasta; return to saucepot. Add feta mixture and spinach; toss well. Makes 4 main-dish or 8 accompaniment servings.

Each main-dish serving: About 595 calories, 20 g protein, 90 g carbohydrate, 17 g total fat (6 g saturated), 25 mg cholesterol, 640 mg sodium.

Fusilli Puttanesca

•••
PREP: 15 MINUTES • COOK: ABOUT 15 MINUTES

The piquant dressing is made with shallot, red wine vinegar, capers, and a touch of lemon peel.

1 package (16 ounces) fusilli or corkscrew pasta
Salt
3 tablespoons capers, drained and chopped
3 tablespoons minced shallot
2 tablespoons red wine vinegar
1 tablespoon olive oil
½ teaspoon grated lemon peel
¼ teaspoon coarsely ground black pepper
1 can (6 ounces) light tuna in olive oil
2 medium bunches watercress, tough stems removed
½ cup loosely packed fresh basil leaves, chopped

1 In large saucepot, prepare pasta in *boiling salted water* as label directs.

2 Meanwhile, in large bowl, with fork, stir capers, shallot, red wine vinegar, olive oil, lemon peel, black pepper, and ½ teaspoon salt until well mixed. Add undrained tuna and watercress; toss well.

3 When pasta has cooked to desired doneness, remove *½ cup pasta cooking water*. Drain pasta and return to saucepot. Add tuna mixture, reserved pasta cooking water, and basil; toss well. Makes 6 main-dish servings.

Each serving: About 375 calories, 17 g protein, 58 g carbohydrate, 8 g total fat (1 g saturated), 4 mg cholesterol, 540 mg sodium.

Orecchini with Savoy Cabbage & Dill

PREP: 10 MINUTES • COOK: ABOUT 15 MINUTES

The snippets of fresh dill add wonderful flavor.

1 package (16 ounces) orecchini or small shell
   pasta
Salt
1 tablespoon margarine or butter
1 medium onion, finely chopped
1 pound savoy cabbage (about ½ medium
   head), cored and very thinly sliced, with tough
   ribs discarded
1 cup frozen baby peas
½ cup reduced-sodium chicken broth
½ cup heavy or whipping cream
¼ teaspoon coarsely ground black pepper
¼ cup chopped fresh dill
Dill sprigs for garnish

1 In large saucepot, prepare orecchini in *boiling salted water* as label directs.

2 Meanwhile, in 12-inch skillet, melt margarine or butter over medium-high heat. Add onion and cook, stirring often, 5 minutes, or until tender.

3 Add cabbage and ¾ teaspoon salt and cook until cabbage is tender-crisp, about 5 minutes, stirring often. Stir in frozen peas, chicken broth, cream, and pepper; heat to boiling. Remove skillet from heat; stir in chopped dill.

4 Drain pasta; return to saucepot. Add cabbage mixture; toss well. Garnish with dill sprigs to serve. Makes 4 main-dish or 8 accompaniment servings.

Each main-dish serving: About 615 calories, 20 g protein, 100 g carbohydrate, 16 g total fat (8 g saturated), 41 mg cholesterol, 760 mg sodium.

Creste di Gallo with Sautéed Spring Onions

PREP: 15 MINUTES • COOK: ABOUT 15 MINUTES

This intriguing pasta gets its name because it looks like a cockscomb. Our garlicky yogurt topping brings an exotic flavor to this basic dish.

1 package (16 ounces) creste di gallo or
   orecchiette pasta
Salt
2 tablespoons margarine or butter
4 bunches green onions, chopped
¼ teaspoon coarsely ground black pepper

SHOULD YOU SALT THE WATER?

It's not only a matter of cooking technique, there's a health question as well: Are you turning virtuous dried pasta—which is sodium-free—into a salt-watcher's nightmare?

To get to the bottom of this kitchen debate, we cooked 3 separate pounds of dried penne, each in 4 quarts of boiling water—the first potful had no salt; the second, 2 teaspoons; and the third, 2 tablespoons. When the pastas were al dente, we drained and tasted them. The consensus: The salt-free pasta was exceedingly bland; we longed to reach for the shaker and sprinkle away. The pasta that was cooked with 2 tablespoons salt—the amount packages recommended until recently—was a little too salty, especially since most pasta gets sauced or seasoned anyway. The penne cooked with 2 teaspoons salt— the amount we use in our test kitchens—was just right.

But we wanted to know how much sodium the pasta was actually absorbing (1 teaspoon of salt almost meets the 2400 mg daily recommended limit for sodium). So we had the Chemistry Department do a sodium analysis of all three pastas. The results: Each main-dish serving (4 ounces, cooked) absorbed 92 mg sodium when boiled with 2 teaspoons salt, and 228 mg when boiled with 2 tablespoons salt.

The surprise: Only about 10 percent of the sodium added to the water was absorbed in both cases. So in the long run, you're probably better off lightly salting the water than compensating for dull pasta by oversalting at the table.

1 cup reduced-sodium chicken broth
1 container (8 ounces) plain low-fat yogurt
1 small garlic clove, crushed with garlic press
Green onion tops for garnish

1 In large saucepot, prepare pasta in *boiling salted water* as label directs.

2 Meanwhile, in 12-inch skillet, melt margarine or butter over high heat. Add green onions, pepper, and ½ teaspoon salt and cook 2 minutes. Reduce heat to medium-high and cook until green onions are soft, 4 to 5 minutes longer. Stir in chicken broth; heat to boiling. Cover and keep warm.

3 In small bowl, mix yogurt, garlic, and ⅛ teaspoon salt until blended.

4 Drain pasta; return to saucepot. Add green-onion mixture; toss well. Serve yogurt mixture to spoon over each serving. Garnish with green onion tops. Makes 4 main-dish or 8 accompaniment servings.

Each main-dish serving: About 540 calories, 20 g protein, 96 g carbohydrate, 9 g total fat (2 g saturated), 4 mg cholesterol, 735 mg sodium.

Orecchiette with Tooomato Cream

PREP: 15 MINUTES • COOK: ABOUT 15 MINUTES

A restaurant favorite that's fast to fix at home.

1 package (16 ounces) orecchiette or bow-tie pasta
Salt
1 can (14½ to 16 ounces) tomatoes in juice, drained
½ cup heavy or whipping cream
½ cup milk
3 tablespoons vodka (optional)
4 teaspoons tomato paste
⅛ to ¼ teaspoon crushed red pepper
1 cup frozen peas, thawed
½ cup loosely packed fresh basil leaves, thinly sliced

1 In large saucepot, prepare pasta in *boiling salted water* as label directs.

2 Meanwhile, chop tomatoes. In 2-quart saucepan, heat tomatoes, cream, milk, vodka, tomato paste, crushed red pepper, and ½ teaspoon salt over medi-um-low heat just to simmering. Stir in peas and heat through.

3 Drain pasta; return to saucepot. Add tomato cream sauce; toss well. Sprinkle with basil to serve. Makes 4 main-dish or 8 accompaniment servings.

Each main-dish serving: About 590 calories, 19 g protein, 98 g carbohydrate, 15 g total fat (8 g saturated), 45 mg cholesterol, 635 mg sodium.

Penne with Salmon & Asparagus

PREP: 15 MINUTES • COOK: ABOUT 15 MINUTES

A tarragon-infused broth and sautéed shallot add zip to this classic seafood and vegetable combination.

1 package (16 ounces) penne rigate or bow-tie pasta
Salt
3 teaspoons olive oil
1 pound medium asparagus, trimmed and cut crosswise into 2-inch pieces
¼ teaspoon coarsely ground black pepper
1 large shallot, minced (about ¼ cup)
⅓ cup dry white wine
1 cup reduced-sodium chicken broth
1 piece salmon fillet (16 ounces), cut crosswise into thirds, then cut lengthwise into ¼-inch-thick slices
1 tablespoon chopped fresh tarragon leaves

1 In large saucepot, prepare pasta in *boiling salted water* as label directs.

2 Meanwhile, in 12-inch skillet, heat 2 teaspoons olive oil over medium-high heat until hot. Add asparagus, pepper, and ½ teaspoon salt, and cook 5 minutes or until asparagus is almost tender-crisp. Add shallot and remaining 1 teaspoon olive oil; cook 2 minutes longer, stirring constantly. Add wine; heat to boiling over high heat. Stir in chicken broth and heat to boiling. Place salmon slices in skillet; cover and cook until salmon turns opaque, 2 to 3 minutes. Remove skillet from heat; stir in tarragon.

3 Drain pasta; return to saucepot. Add asparagus mixture; toss well. Makes 6 main-dish servings.

Each serving: About 460 calories, 27 g protein, 59 g carbohydrate, 12 g total fat (2 g saturated), 45 mg cholesterol, 420 mg sodium.

Linguine with Scallops & Saffron

PREP: 20 MINUTES • COOK: ABOUT 15 MINUTES

We flavored the creamy sauce with orange peel and saffron threads.

1 package (16 ounces) linguine or spaghetti
Salt
3 medium leeks (about 1 pound)
2 tablespoons margarine or butter
¼ teaspoon coarsely ground black pepper
½ teaspoon grated orange peel
Large pinch saffron threads, crumbled
¼ cup dry white wine
1 bottle (8 ounces) clam juice
1 pound sea scallops, rinsed and each cut
    horizontally in half
¼ cup heavy or whipping cream
½ cup loosely packed fresh parsley leaves

1 In large saucepot, prepare pasta in *boiling salted water* as label directs.

2 Meanwhile, cut off roots and tough green tops from leeks. Cut each leek lengthwise in half, then crosswise into ½-inch-wide slices. Rinse leeks in large bowl of cold water to remove sand; drain well. (See "Food Editor's Tip," page 120.)

3 In 12-inch skillet, melt margarine or butter over medium heat. Add leeks, pepper, and ¾ teaspoon salt, and cook until leeks are soft, about 8 minutes, stirring frequently. Add orange peel and saffron and cook 2 minutes, stirring. Add wine; cook 1 minute longer. Increase heat to medium-high; add clam juice; heat to boiling. Add scallops and cook 3 to 4 minutes until opaque. Stir in cream and heat through.

4 Drain pasta; return to saucepot. Add leek mixture; toss well. Sprinkle with parsley leaves just before serving. Makes 6 main-dish servings.

Each serving: About 440 calories, 24 g protein, 66 g carbohydrate, 9 g total fat (3 g saturated), 40 mg cholesterol, 635 mg sodium.

Linguine with Asian-Style Clam Sauce

Linguine with Asian-Style Clam Sauce

PREP: 30 MINUTES • COOK: 30 MINUTES

Mussels, tiny Manila clams, or cockles would work well in this recipe too.

1 package (16 ounces) linguine or spaghetti
Salt
3 tablespoons olive oil
3 garlic cloves, crushed with side of chef's knife
1 tablespoon grated, peeled fresh ginger
¼ teaspoon crushed red pepper
3 dozen littleneck clams, scrubbed
1 bottle (8 ounces) clam juice
½ cup dry white wine
3 strips (3" by ¾" each) lemon peel, cut lengthwise into thin slivers
2 tablespoons butter or olive oil
¼ cup chopped fresh cilantro leaves

1 In saucepot, prepare linguine as label directs in *boiling salted water*. Drain linguine, reserving *¾ cup pasta cooking water*. Return linguine to saucepot.

2 Meanwhile, in nonstick 12-inch skillet, heat olive oil over medium-high heat until hot. Add garlic and cook until golden. Add ginger and crushed red pepper; cook 30 seconds, stirring. To skillet, add clams, clam juice, wine, and lemon peel; heat to boiling. Reduce heat to medium; cover and cook 10 to 15 minutes, until clams open, removing clams to bowl as they open. Discard any clams that do not open. Stir butter and reserved pasta cooking water into broth in skillet.

3 Stir sauce and cilantro into saucepot with linguine; heat to boiling over high heat. Reduce heat to low; cook 1 minute. Add clams; cover and heat through. Makes 4 main-dish servings.

Each serving: About 660 calories, 30 g protein, 90 g carbohydrate, 19 g total fat (5 g saturated), 55 mg cholesterol, 450 mg sodium.

Shells with Smoked Trout & Chives

PREP: 15 MINUTES • COOK: ABOUT 15 MINUTES

The lemony cream sauce is a delicious complement to the smoky fish. The flavors in this simple pasta dish would also work well with other smoked fish. Since the saltiness of smoked fish can vary considerably, taste first before adding salt in step 2. Although the chives are an important flavor component here, minced scallions greens are a fine substitute.

1 package (16 ounces) medium shell pasta or linguine
Salt
12 ounces green beans, trimmed
1 whole smoked trout (about 6 ounces)
½ cup half-and-half or light cream
½ teaspoon grated lemon peel
¼ teaspoon coarsely ground black pepper
4 tablespoons chopped fresh chives
Fresh chives for garnish

1 In large saucepot, prepare pasta in *boiling salted water* as label directs. If you like, cut green beans crosswise in half. After pasta has cooked 5 minutes, add green beans to pasta cooking water and continue cooking until pasta and beans are done.

2 Meanwhile, remove head, tail, skin, and bones from trout and discard. Separate flesh into 1-inch pieces. In 2-quart saucepan, heat half-and-half, lemon peel, pepper, 1 tablespoon chopped chives, and ¼ teaspoon salt over low heat to simmering. Remove saucepan from heat; cover and keep warm.

3 When pasta and beans have cooked to desired doneness, remove ½ cup *pasta cooking water*. Drain pasta and beans; return to saucepot. Add half-and-half mixture, trout, reserved pasta cooking water, and remaining 3 tablespoons chopped chives; toss well. Garnish with chives. Makes 6 main-dish servings.

Each serving: About 350 calories, 15 g protein, 62 g carbohydrate, 5 g total fat (2 g saturated), 10 mg cholesterol, 360 mg sodium.

Vermicelli with Shrimp & Broccoli

PREP: 15 MINUTES • COOK: ABOUT 15 MINUTES

1 package (16 ounces) vermicelli or thin
 spaghetti
Salt
1 tablespoon vegetable oil
1 pound medium shrimp, shelled and deveined,
 with tail part of shell left on if you like
1 tablespoon grated, peeled fresh ginger
2 garlic cloves, crushed with garlic press
¼ teaspoon crushed red pepper
2 packages (12 ounces each) broccoli flowerets
1 cup reduced-sodium chicken broth
2 tablespoons soy sauce
1 teaspoon Asian sesame oil

1 In large saucepot, prepare pasta in *boiling salted
water* as label directs.

2 Meanwhile, in 10-inch skillet, heat vegetable oil
over medium-high heat until hot. Add shrimp, ginger, garlic, and crushed red pepper. Cook, stirring, 2
minutes or just until shrimp turn opaque throughout.
Transfer shrimp to bowl.

3 Add broccoli to skillet and cook, stirring, 1 minute.
Stir in chicken broth and heat to boiling over high
heat. Cook, covered, stirring often, until broccoli is

just tender, about 3 minutes. Stir in soy sauce, sesame
oil, and shrimp; heat through.

4 Drain pasta; return to saucepot. Add shrimp mixture; toss well. Makes 6 main-dish servings.

Each serving: About 415 calories, 26 g protein, 65 g carbohydrate, 6 g total fat (1 g saturated), 95 mg cholesterol, 655
mg sodium.

Radiatore with Arugula, Tomatoes & Pancetta

PREP: 15 MINUTES • COOK: ABOUT 15 MINUTES

1 package (16 ounces) radiatore or corkscrew
 pasta
Salt
4 ounces sliced pancetta or bacon, cut into ¼-
 inch pieces
1 garlic clove, crushed with garlic press
1 container (16 ounces) cherry tomatoes, each
 cut into quarters
¼ teaspoon coarsely ground black pepper
8 ounces arugula, tough stems removed
¼ cup grated Parmesan cheese
Shredded Parmesan cheese for garnish

USING THEIR NOODLES: THE JOY OF ASIAN SOUPS

Noodle soup started out as peasant food in China;
workers visited noodle shops for filling, inexpensive
meals. Today, noodle houses are big business in
many parts of Asia. The traditional Vietnamese soup
we feature at right, called *pho* (pronounced fuh), gets
its name from the wide rice noodles it contains. But
you could substitute any of the following varieties,
available in Asian markets, specialty stores, and some
supermarkets. (All noodles are dried unless otherwise
noted.)

• BEAN THREAD (OR CELLOPHANE) NOODLES: made
from mung bean starch; they become translucent
when cooked.

• WHEAT FLOUR NOODLES: usually fresh, sometimes

dried; called *lo mein* in Chinese; somen or soba
(buckwheat) in Japanese. Somen are sometimes colored green (with green-tea powder), yellow (with
egg), or pink (with Japanese red basil oil).

• INSTANT (OR RAMEN) NOODLES: made from wheat
flour; precooked (usually fried); need just a quick
boil.

• RICE NOODLES: made from rice flour; also called
rice sticks or rice vermicelli; must soak 20 to 60 minutes before using. (Fresh noodles, *sha he fen*, are
available in flat sheets that can be cut to desired size.)

• TE'UCHI: fresh; made from wheat flour; similar to
lo mein (above), but handmade, so more expensive.

1 In large saucepot, prepare pasta in *boiling salted water* as label directs.

2 Meanwhile, in 10-inch skillet, cook pancetta over medium heat until lightly browned, stirring occasionally. (If using bacon, discard all but 1 tablespoon fat.) Add garlic; cook 30 seconds, stirring. Add tomatoes, pepper, and ½ teaspoon salt and cook 1 to 2 minutes. Remove skillet from heat; cover and keep warm.

3 Drain pasta; return to saucepot. Add pancetta mixture, arugula, and grated Parmesan cheese; toss well. Garnish with shredded Parmesan cheese. Makes 4 main-dish or 8 accompaniment servings.

Each main-dish serving: About 560 calories, 22 g protein, 93 g carbohydrate, 12 g total fat (4 g saturated), 15 mg cholesterol, 680 mg sodium.

Vietnamese Noodle Soup

PREP: 20 MINUTES • COOK: 25 MINUTES

This is typically served with thin slices of beef, but our version is made with chicken.

4 ounces flat dried rice noodles (see box at left) or linguine
4 cans (13¾ to 14½ ounces each) low-sodium chicken broth
6 sprigs basil
6 sprigs cilantro
1 teaspoon coriander seeds
1 cinnamon stick (3 inches long)
2 garlic cloves, peeled
3 green onions, thinly sliced diagonally
2 large skinless, boneless chicken-breast halves (about 1 pound), cut into thin diagonal strips
4 medium mushrooms, sliced
Fresh cilantro leaves and lime wedges (optional)
Mint sprigs for garnish

1 In large bowl, soak rice noodles in enough *warm water* to cover for 20 minutes. Drain noodles.

2 Meanwhile, in 3-quart saucepan, heat broth, basil, cilantro, coriander seeds, cinnamon stick, garlic, and one-third of green onions to boiling over high heat. Reduce heat to low; cover and simmer 10 minutes. Strain broth through sieve; discard solids and return broth to saucepan.

3 Stir chicken, mushrooms, drained noodles, and remaining green onions into broth; heat to boiling over high heat. Reduce heat to low; cover and simmer 3 minutes or until chicken loses its pink color throughout. Serve with fresh cilantro leaves and lime wedges if you like. Garnish with mint sprigs. Makes about 9 cups or 4 main-dish servings.

Each serving: About 295 calories, 32 g protein, 26 g carbohydrate, 7 g total fat (2 g saturated), 66 mg cholesterol, 145 mg sodium.

Ziti with Sausage & Zucchini

PREP: 10 MINUTES • COOK: ABOUT 15 MINUTES

1 package (16 ounces) ziti rigate or wagon-wheel pasta
Salt
¾ pound sweet Italian-sausage links, casings removed
3 medium zucchini (about 8 ounces each), each cut lengthwise in half, then cut crosswise into ¼-inch-thick slices
¼ teaspoon coarsely ground black pepper
1 can (28 ounces) whole plum tomatoes
Grated Parmesan cheese (optional)

1 In large saucepot, prepare pasta in *boiling salted water* as label directs.

2 Meanwhile, heat nonstick 12-inch skillet over medium-high heat until hot. Add sausage meat and cook until browned, about 5 minutes, stirring frequently to break up sausage. With slotted spoon, transfer sausage to bowl.

3 Discard all but 1 tablespoon sausage drippings from skillet. Add zucchini, pepper, and ¼ teaspoon salt and cook until zucchini is golden, about 5 minutes, stirring occasionally. Stir in tomatoes with their juice; heat to boiling, breaking up tomatoes with side of spoon. Return sausage to skillet. Reduce heat to low; cover and simmer about 5 minutes longer.

4 Drain pasta; return to saucepot. Add sausage mixture; toss well. Serve with grated Parmesan cheese if you like. Makes 6 main-dish servings.

Each serving: About 475 calories, 21 g protein, 66 g carbohydrate, 15 g total fat (5 g saturated), 35 mg cholesterol, 785 mg sodium.

Spaghetti with Bacon & Peas

PREP: 10 MINUTES • COOK: 10 MINUTES

"The peas cook along with the pasta, and the sauce is really easy to make with ricotta and Romano cheese," says GH Food Director Susan Westmoreland of her speedy weeknight pasta dinner. Along with the spaghetti dish, she serves a side of sliced tomatoes, and fresh figs for dessert. To optimize the time it takes to prepare the meal, put water on to boil for the pasta, and while it heats, cook the bacon and onion. Then, as the pasta cooks, slice the tomatoes.

1 pound thin spaghetti or vermicelli
Salt
4 slices bacon
1 medium onion, finely chopped
1 package (10 ounces) frozen peas
1 container (15 ounces) part-skim ricotta cheese
½ cup grated Pecorino Romano or Parmesan
   cheese
½ teaspoon salt
¼ teaspoon coarsely ground black pepper

1 In large saucepot, prepare pasta in *boiling salted water* as label directs.

2 Meanwhile, in 12-inch skillet, cook bacon over medium heat until browned. Transfer to paper towels. Pour off all but 1 tablespoon bacon fat from skillet. Add onion and cook until tender and golden, 8 to 10 minutes.

3 During last 2 minutes of pasta cooking time, add frozen peas. When pasta is cooked to desired doneness, remove *1 cup pasta cooking water*. Drain pasta and peas. Return to saucepot and toss with ricotta, Romano, salt, pepper, and reserved pasta cooking water. Crumble in bacon and toss again. Makes 4 main-dish servings.

Each serving: About 745 calories, 37 g protein, 103 g carbohydrate, 20 g total fat (10 g saturated), 54 mg cholesterol, 880 mg sodium.

Mafalda with Veal & Rosemary

PREP: 15 MINUTES • COOK: ABOUT 20 MINUTES

Any Italian cook would say "*molto bene*," or very good, after one bite.

1 package (16 ounces) mafalda or spaghetti
Salt
1 tablespoon olive oil
1 medium onion, finely chopped
1 garlic clove, minced
½ teaspoon dried rosemary leaves, crumbled
1 pound ground veal
¼ teaspoon ground black pepper
½ cup dry white wine
1 can (14½ to 16 ounces) tomatoes
1 tablespoon margarine or butter
½ cup chopped fresh Italian parsley leaves
Fresh rosemary for garnish

1 In large saucepot, prepare pasta in *boiling salted water* as label directs.

2 Meanwhile, in 12-inch skillet, heat olive oil over medium-high heat until hot. Add onion and cook until almost tender, about 3 minutes, stirring often. Stir in garlic and rosemary and cook 30 seconds.

3 Increase heat to high. Add veal, pepper, and 1 teaspoon salt and cook, stirring often, 5 to 7 minutes, until veal browns. Add wine and cook until almost evaporated, stirring to loosen brown bits. Stir in tomatoes with their juice, breaking up tomatoes with side of spoon; heat to boiling. Boil 5 minutes, stirring occasionally. Remove skillet from heat; stir in margarine or butter.

4 Drain pasta; return to saucepot. Add veal mixture and parsley; toss to coat. Garnish with fresh rosemary. Makes 6 main-dish servings.

Each serving: About 455 calories, 26 g protein, 62 g carbohydrate, 11 g total fat (3 g saturated), 62 mg cholesterol, 665 mg sodium.

◀ *Spaghetti with Bacon & Peas*

Butternut-Squash Risotto with Sage

Couscous with Dried Cherries

PREP: 2 MINUTES • COOK: 5 MINUTES

1 cup chicken broth
¼ cup dried tart cherries or raisins
1 tablespoon margarine or butter
1 cup couscous (Moroccan pasta)

In 2-quart saucepan, heat chicken broth, dried cherries, margarine or butter, and ¼ *cup water* to boiling over high heat. Stir in couscous; cover and remove saucepan from heat. Let stand 5 minutes or until ready to serve. Fluff with fork. Makes 4 accompaniment servings.

Each serving: About 230 calories, 7 g protein, 42 g carbohydrate, 4 g total fat (1 g saturated), 0 mg cholesterol, 235 mg sodium.

Rice Pilaf

PREP: 10 MINUTES • COOK: 20 MINUTES

1 cup chicken or vegetable broth
½ cup regular long-grain rice
¼ cup diced celery
¼ cup diced green pepper
1 small green onion, chopped
2 tablespoons chopped fresh parsley leaves

In 2-quart saucepan, heat broth, rice, celery, green pepper, and green onion to boiling over high heat. Reduce heat to low; cover and simmer 18 to 20 minutes, until all liquid is absorbed and rice is tender. Stir in parsley just before serving. Makes 2 accompaniment servings.

Each serving: About 200 calories, 6 g protein, 41 g carbohydrate, 1 g total fat (0 g saturated), 1 mg cholesterol, 415 mg sodium.

Butternut-Squash Risotto with Sage

PREP: 20 MINUTES • COOK: 50 MINUTES

This requires a lot of attention at the range—but it's worth it!

1 large butternut squash (2½ pounds), peeled
1 can (13¾ to 14½ ounces) chicken or
    vegetable broth
1 tablespoon margarine or butter
¼ teaspoon coarsely ground black pepper
3 tablespoons chopped fresh sage leaves
1 teaspoon salt
2 tablespoons olive oil
1 small onion, finely chopped
2 cups Arborio rice (Italian short-grain rice) or
    medium-grain rice
⅓ cup dry white wine
½ cup grated Parmesan cheese

1 Cut enough squash into ½-inch chunks to equal 3 cups. Coarsely shred enough remaining squash to equal 2 cups; set aside.

2 In 2-quart saucepan, heat broth and *4 cups water* to boiling over high heat. Reduce heat to low to maintain simmer; cover.

3 In 5-quart Dutch oven or saucepot, melt margarine or butter over medium heat. Add squash chunks, pepper, 2 tablespoons chopped sage, and ¼ teaspoon salt. Cook, covered, stirring occasionally, 10 minutes or until squash is tender. Remove squash to small bowl.

4 To same Dutch oven, add olive oil, shredded squash, onion, and remaining ¾ teaspoon salt and cook, stirring often, until vegetables are tender. Add rice and cook, stirring frequently, 2 minutes. Add wine; cook until absorbed. Add about ½ cup simmering broth to rice, stirring until liquid is absorbed.

5 Continue cooking, adding remaining broth, ½ cup at time, and stirring after each addition until all liquid is absorbed and rice is tender but still firm, about 25 minutes (risotto should have a creamy consistency). Stir in squash chunks, Parmesan, and remaining 1 tablespoon chopped sage; heat through. Makes 4 main-dish servings.

Each serving: About 700 calories, 17 g protein, 115 g carbohydrate, 14 g total fat (4 g saturated), 15 mg cholesterol, 1105 mg sodium.

Buttered Noodles with Herbs

PREP: 10 MINUTES • COOK: 15 MINUTES

A classic side dish for roast meats and poultry. Try these noodles with Apple & Thyme Chicken (page 52) or Greek Meat Loaf (page 82) and season the noodles with the same herbs that are used in the main course.

12 ounces wide egg noodles
¼ cup minced fresh parsley
2 tablespoons margarine or butter (¼ stick)
1 teaspoon minced fresh rosemary leaves
    and/or other favorite herb such as thyme,
    oregano, or sage
½ teaspoon salt
¼ teaspoon coarsely ground black pepper

1 In saucepot, prepare egg noodles as label directs in *boiling salted water*. Drain well.

2 Add parsley and remaining ingredients to saucepot, stirring until margarine melts. Return noodles to saucepot, tossing to coat well with herb mixture. Makes 6 accompaniment servings.

Each serving: About 250 calories, 8 g protein, 41 g carbohydrate, 6 g total fat (1 g saturated), 54 mg cholesterol, 240 mg sodium.

THE RIGHT WAY TO EAT RISOTTO

Italians serve this creamy rice in bowls to hold in the heat—and they eat around the perimeter (which cools off fastest) until they get to the middle. This way, every bite stays hot.

Wild Rice Pilaf with Dried Cranberries

PREP: 45 MINUTES • COOK: 40 MINUTES

Sautéed vegetables and tart fruit add flavor and color to this savory wild and white rice mix.

1 cup wild rice (about 6 ounces)
¾ cup dried cranberries
4 tablespoons margarine or butter (½ stick)
3 medium carrots, diced
1 medium celery stalk, diced
1 small fennel bulb (8 ounces), trimmed and diced
1 medium onion, diced
1½ teaspoons chopped fresh thyme leaves
2 cups regular long-grain rice
1 can (13¾ to 14½ ounces) chicken broth
¾ teaspoon salt
¼ teaspoon coarsely ground black pepper
Fresh thyme leaves for garnish

1 Rinse wild rice; drain. In 3-quart saucepan, heat wild rice and *2 cups water* to boiling over high heat. Reduce heat to low; cover and simmer 35 to 40 minutes until wild rice is tender. Stir in dried cranberries; heat 1 minute. Drain wild-rice mixture, if necessary.

2 Meanwhile, in 5-quart Dutch oven, melt margarine or butter over medium-high heat. Add carrots, celery, fennel, and onion and cook until all vegetables are tender and lightly browned, about 20 minutes, stirring occasionally. Stir in thyme; cook 1 minute. Remove vegetables to medium bowl.

3 In same 5-quart Dutch oven, heat white rice, chicken broth, and *2 cups water* to boiling over high heat. Reduce heat to low; cover and simmer 18 to 20 minutes, until rice is tender. Stir in salt, pepper, wild-rice mixture, and vegetable mixture; heat through. Spoon into serving bowl; sprinkle with thyme leaves. Makes 12 accompaniment servings.

Each serving: About 245 calories, 6 g protein, 46 g carbohydrate, 4 g total fat (1 g saturated), 0 mg cholesterol, 315 mg sodium.

Pasta & Lentils

PREP: 15 MINUTES • COOK: 45 TO 50 MINUTES

Children love the tiny macaroni in this filling pasta, lentil, and vegetable meal in a bowl.

1 ounce pancetta or cooked ham, chopped (¼ cup)
1 small onion, chopped
1 carrot, chopped
1 celery stalk, chopped
1 garlic clove, chopped
1 tablespoon olive oil
1 cup dry lentils, rinsed
¾ teaspoon salt
¼ teaspoon coarsely ground black pepper
1 cup tubetti or ditalini pasta
¼ cup chopped fresh parsley leaves

1 On cutting board, chop pancetta, onion, carrot, celery, and garlic together until very fine.

2 In 3-quart saucepan, heat olive oil over medium heat. Add chopped vegetable mixture and cook, stirring often, 10 minutes or until tender. Stir in lentils and *3 cups water*; heat to boiling over high heat. Reduce heat to low; cover and simmer 15 minutes. Stir in salt and pepper; cover and cook 15 to 20 minutes longer or until lentils are just tender.

3 Meanwhile, cook pasta as label directs in *boiling salted water*; drain. Stir pasta and parsley into lentils. Makes 4 main-dish or 8 accompaniment servings.

Each main-dish serving: About 225 calories, 11 g protein, 35 g carbohydrate, 4 g total fat (1 g saturated), 4 mg cholesterol, 535 mg sodium.

VEGETABLES

Vegetarian Bean Burritos

PREP: 10 MINUTES • COOK: 7 TO 8 MINUTES

"I love bold, assertive flavors. This is a quick version of the burritos my favorite restaurant serves," says GH test kitchen associate, Mary Ann Svec. Serve the burritos with a simple Carrot Salad (page 146) and oranges for dessert. While the tortillas heat for the burritos, make the salad. Then, slice and sauté the zucchini, and heat the beans.

4 flour tortillas (10 inches each)
2 teaspoons vegetable oil
4 medium zucchini (about 5 ounces each), each cut lengthwise in half, then sliced crosswise
¼ teaspoon salt
¼ teaspoon ground cinnamon
1 can (15 ounces) Spanish-style red kidney beans
1 can (15 to 19 ounces) black beans, rinsed and drained
½ (8-ounce) package shredded Monterey Jack cheese (1 cup)
½ cup loosely packed fresh cilantro leaves
1 jar (16 ounces) chunky-style salsa

1 Warm tortillas as label directs; keep warm.

2 In nonstick 12-inch skillet, heat oil over medium-high heat. Add zucchini, salt, and cinnamon and cook until zucchini is tender-crisp, about 5 minutes.

3 Meanwhile, in 2-quart saucepan, heat kidney beans with their sauce and black beans just to simmering over medium heat; keep warm.

4 To serve, allow each person to assemble a burrito as desired, using a warm flour tortilla, zucchini, bean mixture, cheese, and cilantro leaves. Pass salsa to serve with burritos. Makes 4 main-dish servings.

Each serving: About 550 calories, 29 g protein, 77 g carbohydrate, 17 g total fat (1 g saturated), 25 mg cholesterol, 1943 mg sodium.

Portobello Burgers

PREP: 15 MINUTES PLUS MARINATING
COOK: 16 TO 20 MINUTES

Marinate the "burgers" in a broth mixture accented with thyme before grilling, and serve on buns with a lemon and green-onion mayonnaise.

¼ cup chicken broth
2 tablespoons olive oil
2 teaspoons balsamic vinegar
1 teaspoon fresh thyme leaves
¼ teaspoon salt
¼ teaspoon coarsely ground black pepper
4 medium (about 4-inch diameter) portobello mushrooms, stems discarded
1 lemon
⅓ cup mayonnaise
1 small green onion, minced
4 large (about 4-inch diameter) buns
1 bunch arugula

1 In glass baking dish, just large enough to hold mushrooms in a single layer, mix chicken broth, olive oil, vinegar, thyme, ⅛ teaspoon salt, and ⅛ teaspoon pepper. Add mushrooms, turning to coat. Let stand 30 minutes, turning occasionally.

2 Meanwhile, from lemon, grate ½ teaspoon peel and squeeze ½ teaspoon juice. In small bowl, stir lemon peel, lemon juice, mayonnaise, green onion, remaining ⅛ teaspoon salt, and remaining ⅛ teaspoon pepper.

3 Prepare outdoor grill or heat 10-inch grill pan over medium heat until hot. Add mushrooms and cook about 8 to 10 minutes per side, turning occasionally and brushing with remaining marinade, until mushrooms are browned and cooked through.

4 Cut each bun horizontally in half. Spread cut sides of buns with mayonnaise mixture; top with arugula leaves. Place warm grilled mushrooms on bottom halves of buns; replace top half of buns to serve. Makes 4 sandwiches.

Each sandwich: About 355 calories, 6 g protein, 30 g carbohydrate, 25 g total fat (4 g saturated), 7 mg cholesterol, 585 mg sodium.

Portobello Burgers ➤

Sweet Potato Erisheri

PREP: 15 MINUTES • COOK: 30 MINUTES

This exotic dish adapted from *Good Housekeeping* Photo Editor Maya Kaimal MacMillan's book, *Curried Favors* (Abbeville Press), is a beloved classic in Kerala, South India, where her father grew up. MacMillan learned the art of Indian cooking at his side in their Boulder, Colorado, kitchen. "The first time I tasted this, it instantly became one of my favorites," says MacMillan. "The toasted coconut gives it a rich and sweet aroma." She likes to serve it with a simple cucumber and yogurt salad.

1 cup basmati rice (optional)
3 medium sweet potatoes, 2 medium yams, or 1 large butternut squash (about 2 pounds), peeled and cut into 1-inch chunks (about 4 cups)
1 teaspoon salt
¼ teaspoon ground turmeric
⅛ teaspoon ground red pepper (cayenne)
½ cup dried unsweetened coconut
1 can (15 to 19 ounces) red kidney or pinto beans, rinsed and drained
1 garlic clove, minced
¼ teaspoon ground cumin
1 green chile (jalapeño, serrano, or Thai), cut lengthwise in half and seeded
1 tablespoon vegetable oil
½ teaspoon mustard seeds
2 bay leaves
2 dried hot red chiles or ¼ teaspoon crushed red pepper

1 If you like, prepare basmati rice as label directs. Keep warm.

■ FOOD EDITOR'S TIP ■

Q. My leeks are still gritty even after rinsing. How can I get them clean?

A. Trim off roots at the base and cut off the tough leafy tops, leaving a stalk with only about an inch of green. Then, if cooking leeks whole, make a lengthwise slit from top to bottom without cutting all the way through to the other side. Rinse under cold running water, carefully separating the layers slightly until all grit is removed. If you need sliced leeks for sautéing, it's much easier to slice them first, then swish them in a bowl of cold water, changing the water if necessary. No matter how you rinse them, be sure to drain leeks well.

2 Meanwhile, in 3-quart saucepan combine sweet potatoes, salt, turmeric, ground red pepper, and *1½ cups water*; heat to boiling over high heat. Reduce heat to low; cover and simmer 8 to 10 minutes, until sweet potatoes are tender.

3 While sweet potatoes are cooking, in food processor with knife blade attached or in blender at medium speed, blend coconut until finely ground. In small skillet, cook ¼ cup coconut over medium heat, stirring constantly, until coconut turns reddish-brown and all white has disappeared; be careful not to burn coconut. Remove from heat; set aside.

4 Gently break up sweet potatoes with side of spoon or potato masher so that some chunks remain. Stir in beans, garlic, cumin, green chile, toasted coconut, and remaining coconut, and cook over medium heat 5 minutes. Remove from heat; set aside.

5 In same skillet, heat oil over medium-high heat until hot. Add mustard seeds and bay leaves; cover and cook until seeds start to pop, about 1 minute. Stir in dried red chiles. Stir spice mixture into vegetable mixture in saucepan. Discard bay leaves before eating. Serve with rice if you like. Makes 4 main-dish servings.

Each serving without rice: About 265 calories, 8 g protein, 43 g carbohydrate, 8 g total fat (3 g saturated), 0 mg cholesterol, 880 mg sodium.

Golden Leek Tart

PREP: 40 MINUTES • BAKE: ABOUT 1 HOUR

1½ cups all-purpose flour
1 teaspoon salt
¼ cup shortening
6 tablespoons cold margarine or butter
4 medium leeks (about 1¼ pounds)
1 tablespoon olive oil
¼ teaspoon coarsely ground black pepper
3 large eggs
1 cup milk
⅔ cup half-and-half or light cream

1 In medium bowl, stir flour and ½ teaspoon salt. With a pastry blender, cut in shortening with 4 tablespoons margarine or butter (½ stick) until mixture resembles coarse crumbs.

2 Sprinkle about *4 tablespoons cold water*, 1 tablespoon at a time, into flour mixture, mixing lightly with fork after each addition, until dough is just moist enough to hold together. Wrap dough with plastic wrap and refrigerate 30 minutes or until firm enough to roll.

3 Meanwhile, cut off roots from leeks. Cut leeks crosswise in half at point where light green part meets dark green top. Discard tops. Cut each leek bottom lengthwise in half, then crosswise into ½-inch-wide slices. Rinse leeks in large bowl of cold water to remove sand; repeat several times. Drain well.

4 In nonstick 12-inch skillet, heat olive oil and remaining margarine or butter over medium-high heat. Add leeks, pepper, and remaining ½ teaspoon salt, and cook 15 to 20 minutes, until leeks are tender, stirring occasionally.

5 Preheat oven to 425°F. On lightly floured surface, with floured rolling pin, roll dough into a 14-inch round. Press dough onto bottom and up side of 11" by 1" tart pan with removable bottom. Fold overhang in and press against side of tart pan to form a rim ⅛ inch above edge of pan. With fork, prick dough in 1-inch intervals to prevent puffing and shrinking during baking.

6 Line tart shell with foil and fill with pie weights. Bake 15 minutes; remove foil with weights and bake 10 minutes longer or until golden. Turn oven control to 400°F.

7 In another medium bowl, with wire whisk or fork, mix eggs, milk, and half-and-half until blended.

8 Place leeks in tart shell. Pour egg mixture over leeks. Bake 25 to 30 minutes, until filling is set and lightly browned. Serve hot or cool on rack to serve at room temperature. Makes 8 main-dish servings.

Each serving: About 325 calories, 7 g protein, 26 g carbohydrate, 22 g total fat (6 g saturated), 90 mg cholesterol, 435 mg sodium.

Vegetable Potpies with Curry Crust

PREP: 1 HOUR 15 MINUTES • BAKE: 25 MINUTES

2 teaspoons curry powder
½ teaspoon salt
1¼ cups plus 2 tablespoons all-purpose flour
2 tablespoons shortening
6 tablespoons margarine or butter (¾ stick)

1 can (13¾ to 14½ ounces) chicken or vegetable broth
3 medium carrots, peeled and cut into ½-inch slices
1 medium sweet potato, peeled and cut into 1-inch pieces
1 medium onion, diced
1 teaspoon mustard seeds
½ teaspoon ground cumin
½ teaspoon ground coriander
1 can (15 to 19 ounces) garbanzo beans, rinsed and drained
2 tablespoons mango chutney, chopped

1 In medium bowl, with fork, stir curry powder, salt, and 1¼ cups flour. With pastry blender or two knives used scissor-fashion, cut in shortening and 4 tablespoons margarine or butter (½ stick) until mixture resembles coarse crumbs. Sprinkle about 3 *tablespoons cold water*, 1 tablespoon at a time, into flour mixture, mixing lightly with fork after each addition until dough is just moist enough to hold together. Shape dough into a disk; wrap with plastic wrap and refrigerate 30 minutes or until firm enough to roll.

2 Meanwhile, in 2-quart saucepan, heat broth, carrots, and sweet potato to boiling over high heat. Reduce heat to low; cover and simmer 10 minutes or until vegetables are tender. Strain broth into 4-cup glass measuring cup or medium bowl. Transfer vegetable mixture to large bowl.

3 In same saucepan, melt 1 tablespoon margarine or butter over medium heat. Add onion and cook until tender, about 10 minutes, stirring occasionally. Stir in mustard seeds, cumin, and coriander; cook 2 minutes longer, stirring. Transfer onion mixture to bowl with vegetables.

4 Preheat oven to 425°F. In same saucepan, melt remaining 1 tablespoon margarine or butter over medium heat. Add remaining 2 tablespoons flour, and cook, whisking constantly, until golden brown, about 1 to 2 minutes. Gradually stir in reserved broth, and cook, whisking, until mixture boils and thickens slightly. Stir broth mixture, garbanzo beans, and chutney into vegetable mixture in bowl. Spoon vegetable mixture into 4 deep 1½-cup ramekins or soufflé dishes.

5 Divide dough into 4 equal pieces. On lightly floured surface, with floured rolling pin, roll 1 piece of dough ¾ inch larger in diameter than top of ramekin. With small cookie cutter or tip of knife, cut out design near center of dough to allow steam to

escape during baking. Place dough on top of ramekin, folding edge over side of ramekin and pressing
lightly to seal. Repeat with remaining dough.

6 Place filled ramekins on cookie sheet or jelly-roll
pan for easier handling and to catch any drips during
baking. Bake potpies 25 minutes or until crusts are
lightly browned and filling is hot and bubbly. Makes
4 main-dish servings.

*Each serving: About 625 calories, 15 g protein, 86 g carbo-
hydrate, 28 g total fat (7 g saturated), 0 mg cholesterol, 1170
mg sodium.*

Spanakopita

PREP: 40 MINUTES • BAKE: 35 TO 40 MINUTES

6 tablespoons margarine or butter (¾ stick)
1 jumbo onion (1 pound), diced
4 packages (10 ounces each) frozen chopped
    spinach, thawed and squeezed dry
1 package (8 ounces) feta cheese, crumbled
1 cup part-skim ricotta cheese
½ cup chopped fresh dill
¼ teaspoon salt
¼ teaspoon coarsely ground black pepper
3 large eggs
10 sheets (about 16" by 12" each) fresh or
    frozen (thawed) phyllo

1 In 12-inch skillet, melt 2 tablespoons margarine or
butter (¼ stick) over medium-high heat until hot.
Add diced onion and cook until tender and lightly
browned, about 15 minutes, stirring occasionally.

2 Transfer onion to large bowl. Stir in spinach, feta,
ricotta, dill, salt, pepper, and eggs until combined.
(You can prepare the recipe a day in advance up to
this point. If not using filling right away, cover and
refrigerate.)

3 Melt remaining 4 tablespoons margarine or butter
(½ stick). Preheat oven to 400°F. Remove phyllo
from package; keep covered with plastic wrap to prevent drying out. Lightly brush bottom and sides of
11" by 7" glass baking dish with some melted margarine or butter. On waxed paper, lightly brush 1
phyllo sheet with some melted margarine. Place
phyllo in baking dish, gently pressing phyllo against
sides of dish and allowing edges to overhang sides.
Lightly brush second sheet with some melted margarine; place over first sheet, pressing gently. Repeat
layering with 3 more phyllo sheets.

4 Spread spinach filling evenly over phyllo in baking
dish. Fold overhanging edges of phyllo over filling.
Cut remaining 5 phyllo sheets crosswise in half. On
waxed paper, lightly brush 1 phyllo sheet with some
melted margarine. Place on top of filling. Repeat
with remaining cut phyllo, brushing each sheet lightly with remaining margarine.

5 Bake Spanakopita 35 to 40 minutes, until filling is
hot in the center and top of phyllo is golden. Makes
8 main-dish servings.

*Each serving: About 355 calories, 17 g protein, 28 g carbo-
hydrate, 21 g total fat (8 g saturated), 114 mg cholesterol,
795 mg sodium.*

Green Beans with Orange & Coriander

PREP: 10 MINUTES • COOK: 10 TO 15 MINUTES

To get a head start, cook the beans a day ahead. Rinse
in cold water to stop the cooking, drain well, and
refrigerate. Add beans to the hot, spiced oil in the
skillet just before serving to heat through.

Salt
2½ pounds green beans, trimmed
2 tablespoons olive oil
1¼ teaspoons ground coriander
½ teaspoon grated orange peel
⅛ teaspoon coarsely ground black pepper
Orange-peel strips for garnish

1 In 12-inch skillet, heat *1 inch water* and 1 teaspoon
salt to boiling over high heat. Add green beans; heat
to boiling. Reduce heat to low; simmer, uncovered,
5 to 10 minutes, until beans are tender-crisp; drain.
Wipe skillet dry.

2 In same skillet, heat olive oil and coriander over
medium heat until oil is hot but not smoking. Add
green beans, grated orange peel, pepper, and ½ teaspoon salt and cook, stirring, until beans are hot,
about 5 minutes. Transfer to serving bowl. Sprinkle
with orange-peel strips to serve. Makes 10 accompaniment servings.

*Each serving: About 55 calories, 2 g protein, 8 g carbohy-
drate, 3 g total fat (0 g saturated), 0 mg cholesterol, 165 mg
sodium.*

Green Beans with Oregon Hazelnuts

PREP: 20 MINUTES • COOK: 10 MINUTES

Green beans hold well once they've been blanched, so you can prepare most of the components for this side dish ahead of time. A day ahead, toast and chop the hazelnuts and store in an airtight container. Cook the green beans until tender-crisp. Rinse with cold water to stop the cooking, then drain and store, covered, in the refrigerator. Proceed with the recipe as in step 3.

⅔ cup hazelnuts (filberts)
Salt
2 pounds green beans, trimmed
4 tablespoons margarine or butter (½ stick)
1 teaspoon grated lemon peel
¼ teaspoon ground black pepper

1 Preheat oven to 375°F. Place hazelnuts in 9" by 9" metal baking pan. Bake 10 to 15 minutes until lightly toasted. To remove skins, wrap hot hazelnuts in clean cloth towel. With hands, roll hazelnuts back and forth until skins come off. Discard skins; finely chop nuts.

2 Meanwhile, in 12-inch skillet, heat *1 inch water* and *1 teaspoon salt* to boiling over high heat. Add green beans; heat to boiling. Reduce heat to low; simmer, uncovered, 5 to 10 minutes, until beans are tender-crisp; drain. Wipe skillet dry.

3 In same skillet, melt margarine or butter over medium heat. Add hazelnuts and cook, stirring, 3 minutes or until margarine just begins to brown. Add green beans, lemon peel, pepper, and ½ teaspoon salt and cook, stirring often, for 5 minutes or until hot. Makes 8 accompaniment servings.

Each serving: About 150 calories, 3 g protein, 9 g carbohydrate, 13 g total fat (2 g saturated), 0 mg cholesterol, 250 mg sodium.

Spanakopita

Asparagus with Lemon-Caper Vinaigrette

PREP: 10 MINUTES • COOK: 5 TO 7 MINUTES

Delicious served cold or at room temperature. If you can find very small capers (they tend to be more expensive), you won't have to chop them; but the more common Spanish-style capers are quite large and need to be coarsely chopped.

3 pounds asparagus, trimmed
Salt
1 large lemon
2 tablespoons capers, drained and chopped
2 teaspoons Dijon mustard
1 teaspoon sugar
¼ teaspoon coarsely ground black pepper
3 tablespoons olive oil

1 In 12-inch skillet, heat *1 inch water* to boiling over high heat. Add asparagus and ½ teaspoon salt; heat to boiling. Reduce heat to medium-low and simmer, uncovered, 5 to 7 minutes until asparagus spears are tender-crisp; drain and rinse under cold running water to stop cooking. Drain again.

2 Meanwhile, prepare vinaigrette: With vegetable peeler, remove 3 strips of peel (about 3" by 1" each) from lemon. Slice strips lengthwise into thin slivers. Squeeze 2 tablespoons juice from lemon.

3 In small bowl, combine lemon juice with capers, mustard, sugar, pepper, and ¼ teaspoon salt. With wire whisk, slowly beat in olive oil until mixture thickens slightly.

4 Place asparagus in small deep platter. Pour vinaigrette over asparagus; toss well to coat. Sprinkle slivered lemon peel on top. Serve asparagus at room temperature or cover and refrigerate until ready to serve. Makes 10 accompaniment servings.

Each serving: About 60 calories, 2 g protein, 5 g carbohydrate, 4 g total fat (1 g saturated), 0 mg cholesterol, 170 mg sodium.

Roasted Beets & Red Onions

PREP: 20 MINUTES • ROAST: ABOUT 1½ HOURS

Roasting brings out and concentrates the natural sweetness in vegetables. Here, the beets and onions are roasted and then tossed with a simple balsamic sauce that enhances their rich flavors.

6 medium beets with tops (about 2 pounds, including tops)
3 small red onions (about 1 pound)
2 tablespoons extravirgin olive oil
⅓ cup chicken broth
¼ cup balsamic vinegar
1 teaspoon dark brown sugar
1 teaspoon fresh thyme leaves
¼ teaspoon salt
¼ teaspoon coarsely ground black pepper
Minced fresh parsley leaves for garnish

1 Trim tops from beets, leaving about 1 inch of stems attached. Scrub beets well under cold running water.

2 Preheat oven to 400°F. Place beets and unpeeled red onions in 10-inch skillet with oven-safe handle or 13" by 9" metal baking pan; drizzle with olive oil. Roast vegetables at least 1 hour and 30 minutes, depending on size of vegetables, shaking skillet occasionally, until onions are soft to the touch and beets are fork-tender. (Beets may take longer than onions to roast; remove onions as they are done and continue roasting beets.)

3 Transfer vegetables to plate; cool until easy to handle. Meanwhile, to same skillet, add broth, vinegar, brown sugar, and thyme; heat to boiling over high heat. Boil 5 to 7 minutes, stirring and scraping bottom of skillet until liquid is dark brown and syrupy and reduced to about ¼ cup; stir in salt and pepper. Remove skillet from heat.

4 Peel beets and onions. Slice beets into julienne strips and onions into thin rings; place in bowl. Pour reduced liquid over vegetables. Serve at room temperature; garnish with parsley. Makes about 4 cups or 6 accompaniment servings.

Each serving: About 120 calories, 2 g protein, 18 g carbohydrate, 5 g total fat (1 g saturated), 0 mg cholesterol, 195 mg sodium.

Braised Sweet &
Sour Red Cabbage

PREP: 20 MINUTES • COOK: 1½ HOURS

Flavored with onion, pear, apple juice, allspice, and bay leaves—a welcome winter side dish.

2 small heads red cabbage (about 2 pounds each)
3 tablespoons vegetable oil
2 medium onions, finely chopped
1 medium pear, peeled, cored, and finely chopped
1 can (13¾ to 14½ ounces) beef broth
1 cup apple juice
⅓ cup cider vinegar
¼ cup packed dark brown sugar
2 small bay leaves
¾ teaspoon salt
¼ teaspoon coarsely ground black pepper
⅛ teaspoon ground allspice

1 Cut each head of cabbage into quarters; cut out core. Thinly slice cabbage; discard tough ribs.

2 In 8-quart Dutch oven, heat vegetable oil over medium heat. Add onions and pear and cook until tender, about 10 minutes.

3 Stir in cabbage, beef broth, and remaining ingredients; heat to boiling over high heat. Reduce heat to low; cover and simmer 1 hour or until cabbage is very tender, stirring occasionally. Remove cover and cook over medium-high heat 15 minutes longer or until most of liquid evaporates, stirring occasionally. Makes 10 accompaniment servings.

Each serving: About 125 calories, 3 g protein, 21 g carbohydrate, 5 g total fat (0 g saturated), 0 mg cholesterol, 315 mg sodium.

12 WAYS TO
EAT YOUR VEGETABLES

Boost the flavor—not the fat—with these simple alternatives to classic butter, cheese, or cream sauces.

1. Make a mock hollandaise by mixing light mayonnaise with Dijon mustard, fresh lemon juice, and a pinch of ground red pepper. Drizzle the cooled sauce over steamed cauliflower or broccoli.

2. Cook minced garlic and a pinch of red pepper flakes in a teaspoon of olive oil until fragrant. Add fresh spinach or Swiss chard to pan and cook until wilted.

3. Toss chopped mixed fresh herbs (such as basil, mint, and oregano) and grated lemon zest with boiled potato halves.

4. Heat chopped fresh tomato with crushed fennel seeds in a skillet until hot. Spoon over baked or broiled eggplant slices.

5. Slice Canadian bacon (it's surprisingly low-fat) into thin strips and cook in nonstick skillet until golden. Toss with steamed collard greens or spinach.

6. Toast bread crumbs with chopped garlic in a teaspoon of olive oil. Sprinkle over steamed yellow squash with chopped parsley.

7. Chop some mango chutney and mix into carrots or cauliflower.

8. Thin orange marmalade with water and heat with ground ginger. Stir into hot green beans or broccoli.

9. When steaming bitter greens like Swiss chard, add a handful of raisins for sweetness.

10. Blend prepared horseradish, Dijon mustard, and light mayonnaise; drizzle cold over steamed green beans.

11. Whisk together seasoned rice vinegar, soy sauce, and grated fresh ginger to taste. Use as a dipping sauce for tender-crisp broccoli.

12. Dust cooked green beans with freshly grated Parmesan cheese (a little goes a long way) and cracked black pepper.

Glazed Baby Carrots

PREP: 15 MINUTES • COOK: 20 MINUTES

5 bunches baby carrots (1 pound without tops), peeled, or 1 bag (16 ounces) peeled baby carrots
Salt
2 tablespoons margarine or butter (¼ stick)
1 garlic clove, cut in half
3 tablespoons pure maple syrup or maple-flavor syrup
⅛ teaspoon coarsely ground black pepper
1 tablespoon snipped fresh chives for garnish

1 In 3-quart saucepan, heat 8 *cups water* to boiling over high heat. Add carrots and 2 teaspoons salt; heat to boiling. Reduce heat to low; cover and simmer 7 minutes or until carrots are tender. Drain well.

2 In nonstick 12-inch skillet, melt margarine or butter over medium heat. Add garlic and cook 2 minutes, stirring occasionally. With slotted spoon, remove and discard garlic. Add maple syrup, stirring to blend with melted margarine or butter.

3 Add carrots, pepper, and ¼ teaspoon salt and cook, stirring occasionally, until carrots are lightly browned, about 10 minutes. Garnish with snipped chives to serve. Makes 4 accompaniment servings.

Each serving: About 135 calories, 1 g protein, 21 g carbohydrate, 6 g total fat (1 g saturated), 0 mg cholesterol, 250 mg sodium.

Sautéed Yankee Brussels Sprouts

PREP: 25 MINUTES • COOK: 10 TO 12 MINUTES

Not everyone's favorite vegetable! But maybe this buttery version will change their minds forever. To cut down on last-minute preparations, trim and slice the sprouts early in the day and store in a plastic bag in the refrigerator until ready to sauté.

3 containers (10 ounces each) Brussels sprouts
4 tablespoons margarine or butter (½ stick)
½ teaspoon salt

1 Trim off any yellow leaves and stem from each Brussels sprout. Slice sprouts vertically very thinly.

2 In 12-inch skillet, melt margarine or butter over high heat. Add sliced sprouts; sprinkle with salt and cook, stirring, 10 to 12 minutes, until sprouts are tender-crisp and begin to brown. Makes 8 accompaniment servings.

Each serving: About 90 calories, 3 g protein, 9 g carbohydrate, 6 g total fat (1 g saturated), 0 mg cholesterol, 235 mg sodium.

Louisiana Maquechoux

PREP: 45 MINUTES • COOK: 45 MINUTES

A classic skillet side dish. When pressed for time, use 2 bags (20 ounces each) frozen whole-kernel corn, and cook only 15 minutes.

1 tablespoon vegetable oil
1 large onion, diced
1 large red pepper, diced
1 can (14½ ounces) chopped tomatoes in juice, drained
5 cups fresh corn kernels cut from cob (about 8 ears corn)
1½ teaspoons salt
½ teaspoon sugar
Pinch to ¼ teaspoon ground red pepper (cayenne)
¼ cup half-and-half or light cream
Chopped fresh parsley for garnish

1 In 12-inch skillet, heat vegetable oil until hot over medium-high heat. Add diced onion and red pepper; cook, stirring occasionally, until vegetables are tender and well browned, about 15 minutes.

2 Add drained tomatoes, corn, salt, sugar, and ground red pepper to onion mixture; heat to boiling over high heat. Reduce heat to low; cover and simmer 30 minutes, stirring occasionally.

3 Stir in half-and-half; heat through. Garnish with chopped parsley if you like. Makes 8 accompaniment servings.

Each serving: About 145 calories, 4 g protein, 29 g carbohydrate, 3 g total fat (1 g saturated), 2 mg cholesterol, 525 mg sodium.

Clockwise from top: Sautéed Yankee Brussels ▶
Sprouts, Louisiana Maquechoux, Green Beans
with Oregon Hazelnuts (page 123)

Mediterranean Grilled Eggplant & Summer Squash

PREP: 15 MINUTES • GRILL: 15 MINUTES

This recipe doubles easily—if you're feeding a crowd, grill vegetables in batches.

3 tablespoons olive oil
2 tablespoons red wine vinegar
2 teaspoons Dijon mustard
¼ teaspoon salt
¼ teaspoon coarsely ground black pepper
1 garlic clove, crushed with garlic press
1 medium zucchini (about 8 ounces), cut lengthwise into ¼-inch-thick slices
1 medium yellow squash (about 8 ounces), cut lengthwise into ¼-inch-thick slices
1 small eggplant (about 1¼ pounds), cut lengthwise into ¼-inch-thick slices
2 tablespoons chopped fresh mint leaves
1 ounce crumbled ricotta salata* or feta cheese (¼ cup)

1 Prepare vinaigrette: In small bowl, with wire whisk, mix olive oil, vinegar, mustard, salt, pepper, and garlic.

2 Brush 1 side of each vegetable slice with some vinaigrette. Place vegetables on grill over medium heat and cook, turning once and brushing with remaining vinaigrette, until vegetables are browned and tender, 10 to 15 minutes.

3 Transfer vegetables to large platter as they are done. Sprinkle with mint and ricotta salata. Makes 6 accompaniment servings.

*Ricotta salata is a white, firm, lightly salted cheese made from sheep's milk. Look for it in supermarkets, cheese shops, and Italian groceries.

Each serving: About 105 calories, 3 g protein, 9 g carbohydrate, 7 g total fat (2 g saturated), 4 mg cholesterol, 160 mg sodium.

A SHORTCUT TO PERFECT EGGPLANT

Does eggplant need to be salted and weighed down before cooking? Many old cookbooks advise using this technique to counteract bitterness—but today, food professionals are divided over its merit.

To judge, we cut 1-pound eggplants crosswise into ½-inch-thick slices, then sprinkled the first group with a teaspoon of salt, layered the slices in a colander, and weighed them down under a plate and a 35-ounce can for 30 minutes. The second group was sprinkled with salt, layered in a colander, and left for 30 minutes without a weight. And the last was neither salted nor pressed. We then cooked each sample two ways: baked, and brushed with oil and sautéed.

When our panelists put knife and fork to the eggplant in a blind taste test, they agreed unanimously that the no-salt, no-press slices—whether baked or sautéed—were tops. They held their shape, were tender but not mushy, browned nicely, and had a pleasant flavor that was neither salty nor oily. Salted slices tasted too salty; those that were salted and pressed were also misshapen.

Grilled Italian Eggplant with Mint

PREP: 10 MINUTES • COOK: 10 MINUTES

Italian eggplant is generally small, more round than oblong, and can be dark- or light-purple, white, or striped with purple.

1 ripe small tomato, seeded and chopped
2 teaspoons thinly sliced fresh mint leaves
1 teaspoon plus 2 tablespoons olive oil
¼ teaspoon salt
⅛ teaspoon ground black pepper
2 small Italian eggplants (about 6 ounces each), cut lengthwise into ½-inch-thick slices
1 bunch arugula, stems trimmed
Mint sprigs for garnish

1 In small bowl, stir tomato, sliced mint, 1 teaspoon oil, and a dash of salt and pepper. Set aside.

2 Prepare outdoor grill or heat 10-inch grill pan over medium heat until hot. Meanwhile, brush 1 side of each eggplant slice, using 1 tablespoon olive oil in total; sprinkle with the salt and pepper.

3 Add eggplant, oil side down, to grill pan, and cook 10 minutes. Brush with remaining olive oil and turn slices over. Cook eggplant 5 minutes longer or until browned and cooked through.

4 To serve, arrange arugula on platter; top with eggplant slices, then tomato mixture. Garnish with mint sprigs. Makes 4 first-course servings.

Each serving: About 100 calories, 1 g protein, 7 g carbohydrate, 8 g total fat (1 g saturated), 0 mg cholesterol, 140 mg sodium.

Idaho Creamed Pearl Onions & Peas

PREP: 30 MINUTES • COOK: 30 MINUTES

Infused with caraway for extra appeal. To shortcut last-minute preparation, cook and peel the onions and prepare the sauce a day ahead. Cover and refrigerate separately.

2 containers (10 ounces each) pearl onions
3 tablespoons margarine or butter
3 tablespoons all-purpose flour
½ teaspoon caraway seeds, crushed
½ teaspoon salt
¼ teaspoon ground black pepper
2¼ cups milk
2 packages (10 ounces each) frozen peas, thawed

1 In 10-inch skillet, heat *1 inch water* to boiling over high heat. Add onions; heat to boiling. Reduce heat to low; cover and simmer 10 to 15 minutes, until tender. Drain onions.

2 When cool enough to handle, peel onions, leaving a little of the root ends to help onions hold their shape during cooking.

3 Meanwhile, in 2-quart saucepan, melt margarine or butter over medium heat. Stir in flour, caraway seeds, salt, and pepper until blended and cook 2 minutes, stirring constantly. Gradually stir in milk and cook, stirring constantly, until sauce thickens and boils.

4 Return onions to skillet. Add peas and sauce and cook, stirring, until heated through. Makes 10 accompaniment servings.

Each serving: About 140 calories, 6 g protein, 17 g carbohydrate, 6 g total fat (2 g saturated), 7 mg cholesterol, 230 mg sodium.

Stir-Fried Greens

PREP: 15 MINUTES • COOK: ABOUT 5 MINUTES

1 tablespoon olive oil
2 garlic cloves, crushed with side of chef's knife
⅛ teaspoon crushed red pepper (optional)
1½ pounds leafy greens (such as Swiss chard, spinach, bok choy, napa cabbage, or escarole), trimmed and leaves cut up if you like
¼ teaspoon salt

1 In 12-inch skillet, heat olive oil over medium-high heat. Add garlic and cook 1 minute or until golden. Add crushed red pepper; cook 30 seconds.

2 Carefully add greens (oil in pan may splatter if greens are wet); sprinkle with salt and cook, stirring quickly and constantly, 3 to 5 minutes (depending on type of greens) or until wilted and tender. Discard garlic before serving if you like. Makes 4 accompaniment servings.

Each serving: About 60 calories, 3 g protein, 6 g carbohydrate, 4 g total fat (1 g saturated), 0 mg cholesterol, 405 mg sodium.

Sautéed Green Onions

PREP: 15 MINUTES • COOK: 10 MINUTES

1 tablespoon vegetable oil
5 bunches green onions, cut into 2-inch pieces
½ teaspoon grated lemon peel
¼ teaspoon salt
¼ teaspoon coarsely ground black pepper
2 radishes, each cut in half and thinly sliced (optional)

In 12-inch skillet, heat vegetable oil until hot over medium-high heat. Add green onions, lemon peel, salt, and pepper and cook, stirring frequently, 2 minutes. Add *½ cup water* and cook, stirring, 5 to 7 minutes longer, until green onions are tender and lightly browned and liquid evaporates. Toss with radishes if you like. Makes 4 accompaniment servings.

Each serving: About 60 calories, 2 g protein, 7 g carbohydrate, 4 g total fat (0 g saturated), 0 mg cholesterol, 140 mg sodium.

Baby Lima Beans with Onion

PREP: 15 MINUTES • COOK: 20 MINUTES

1 package (10 ounces) frozen baby lima beans
2 tablespoons olive oil
2 medium celery stalks with leaves, finely chopped
1 small red onion, finely chopped
1 large garlic clove, minced
1 tablespoon white wine vinegar
2 teaspoons minced fresh parsley
¼ teaspoon salt
⅛ teaspoon coarsely ground black pepper

1 In 10-inch skillet, prepare frozen baby lima beans as label directs. Drain lima beans well and set aside. Wipe skillet dry.

2 In same skillet, heat olive oil over medium heat. Add celery with leaves, onion, and garlic and cook 10 minutes or until vegetables are tender, stirring occasionally. Add cooked lima beans, vinegar, parsley, salt, and pepper; heat through. Makes 4 accompaniment servings.

Each serving: About 150 calories, 5 g protein, 18 g carbohydrate, 7 g total fat (1 g saturated), 0 mg cholesterol, 190 mg sodium.

Narraganset Succotash

PREP: 15 MINUTES • COOK: 5 MINUTES

Corn and lima beans topped with crumbled crisp bacon. The name *succotash* comes from a Native-American word for boiled corn. To get a head start, dice the celery and onion a day ahead; cover and refrigerate. The whole dish can be made up to 2 hours before serving.

5 slices bacon
3 medium celery stalks, cut into ¼-inch-thick slices
1 medium onion, diced
2 cans (15¼ to 16 ounces each) whole-kernel corn, drained
2 packages (10 ounces each) frozen Fordhook lima beans
½ cup chicken broth

¾ teaspoon salt
¼ teaspoon coarsely ground black pepper
2 tablespoons chopped fresh parsley

1 In 12-inch skillet, cook bacon over medium-low heat until browned. Remove bacon to paper towels to drain; crumble.

2 Discard all but 2 tablespoons bacon fat from skillet. Add celery and onion and cook over medium heat 15 minutes or until vegetables are tender and golden, stirring occasionally. Stir in corn, frozen lima beans, chicken broth, salt, and pepper; heat to boiling over high heat. Reduce heat to low; cover and simmer 5 to 10 minutes longer, until mixture is heated through. Stir in chopped parsley and sprinkle with crumbled bacon to serve. Makes 10 accompaniment servings.

Each serving: About 155 calories, 7 g protein, 24 g carbohydrate, 5 g total fat (2 g saturated), 5 mg cholesterol, 490 mg sodium.

Fast "Baked" Beans

PREP: 10 MINUTES • COOK: 12 TO 15 MINUTES

Choose a variety of canned beans and add special seasonings and molasses for homemade flavor.

2 teaspoons olive oil
1 small onion, diced
1 cup catchup
3 tablespoons light molasses
1 tablespoon Dijon mustard
½ teaspoon Worcestershire sauce
¼ teaspoon salt
Pinch ground cloves
4 cans beans (15 to 19 ounces each), such as black, kidney, white, pink, and pinto, rinsed and drained

1 In 4-quart saucepan, heat olive oil over medium-low heat until hot. Add onion and cook 5 to 8 minutes, until tender and golden.

2 Stir in catchup, molasses, mustard, Worcestershire, salt, cloves, and ½ *cup water* until blended. Increase heat to high; add beans and heat to boiling. Reduce heat to medium-low; cover and simmer 5 minutes. Makes about 6 cups or 8 accompaniment servings.

Each serving: About 320 calories, 19 g protein, 62 g carbohydrate, 2 g total fat (0 g saturated), 0 mg cholesterol, 1085 mg sodium.

Charred Peppers
with Peaches

PREP: 30 MINUTES PLUS STANDING • BROIL: 10 MINUTES

A welcome first course on its own, or on a bed of Boston or Bibb lettuce.

1 large yellow pepper
1 large red pepper
1 tablespoon olive oil
2 teaspoons fresh lemon juice
½ teaspoon ground cumin
¼ teaspoon salt
⅛ teaspoon ground red pepper (cayenne)
3 large ripe peaches

1 Preheat broiler. Line broiling pan (without rack) with foil. Cut each pepper lengthwise in half; discard stem and seeds. Arrange peppers, cut side down, in broiling pan. Place broiling pan in broiler 5 to 6 inches from source of heat and broil peppers until charred and blistered, about 8 to 10 minutes. Wrap foil around peppers and allow to steam at room temperature 15 minutes or until cool enough to handle.

2 Remove peppers from foil. Peel off skin and discard. Cut peppers lengthwise into ½-inch-wide strips. Pat dry with paper towels.

3 In bowl, stir peppers with remaining ingredients except peaches. Cover and refrigerate if not serving right away.

4 To serve, peel, pit, and slice peaches; stir into pepper mixture. Serve at room temperature. Makes about 3 cups or 4 first-course servings.

Each serving: About 100 calories, 2 g protein, 17 g carbohydrate, 4 g total fat (1 g saturated), 0 mg cholesterol, 135 mg sodium.

DO DRY BEANS NEED TO BE SOAKED?

It's common knowledge that soaking dry beans for hours before using shortens cooking time and improves texture, appearance, and even digestibility. But now some chefs are claiming soaking time can be reduced—even skipped. We tested the old-fashioned method against two shortcuts in the *Good Housekeeping* kitchens, using 3 batches of black beans and 3 of Great Northern beans, which were then cooked until tender. The results:

The winner is...overnight soaking. Grandma was right. For the best texture (not too hard or mushy) and appearance (beans held their shape, with practically no split skins), letting beans sit in a bowl of cool tap water until morning really works. Cooking time ranged from 1 hour and 10 minutes to 1 hour and 20 minutes.

Second place: no soaking. This method yielded the second most tender and shapely beans, though it required the longest cooking time (1 hour and 35 minutes). But if beans pose digestive problems for you, it's probably better to soak them and discard the water, which helps remove the complex sugars that can cause bloating and gas.

Third place: quick soaking. Bringing the beans to a boil for 2 minutes and then allowing them to soak for an hour in the same water before cooking yielded

the most broken beans but definitely the fastest cooking time (1 hour). If you're making a bean soup or chili, where perfect-looking beans don't matter, this method is fine, but we don't recommend it for a bean salad.

Note: Whichever option you choose, remember that cooking time will vary depending on the age/dryness of the beans.

Cherry Tomato Gratin

PREP: 10 MINUTES • BAKE: 20 MINUTES

¼ cup plain dried bread crumbs
¼ cup grated Parmesan cheese
1 tablespoon olive oil
¼ teaspoon coarsely ground black pepper
1 garlic clove, crushed with garlic press
2 pints red and/or yellow cherry tomatoes
2 tablespoons chopped fresh parsley

1 Preheat oven to 425°F. In small bowl, combine bread crumbs, Parmesan cheese, olive oil, pepper, and garlic.

2 Place cherry tomatoes in shallow 1½-quart casserole or 9½-inch deep-dish pie plate. Top with breadcrumb mixture; sprinkle with parsley. Bake 20 minutes or until tomatoes are heated through and crumb topping is browned. Makes 6 accompaniment servings.

Each serving: About 80 calories, 3 g protein, 9 g carbohydrate, 4 g total fat (1 g saturated), 3 mg cholesterol, 125 mg sodium.

Peas with Green Onions & Mint

PREP: 10 MINUTES • COOK: 6 MINUTES

3 tablespoons margarine or butter
1 bunch green onions, cut into ¼-inch pieces (about 1 cup)
3 packages (10 ounces each) frozen peas, thawed
¼ teaspoon coarsely ground black pepper
½ teaspoon salt
⅓ cup chopped fresh mint leaves

1 In 12-inch skillet, melt margarine or butter over medium heat. Add green onions and cook 3 minutes or until tender. Add peas, pepper, and salt and cook, stirring frequently, 3 minutes longer or until hot.

2 Remove skillet from heat; stir in mint. Makes 10 accompaniment servings.

Each serving: About 100 calories, 5 g protein, 13 g carbohydrate, 4 g total fat (1 g saturated), 0 mg cholesterol, 225 mg sodium.

Peas with Mushrooms

PREP: 10 MINUTES • COOK: 10 MINUTES

2 tablespoons margarine or butter (¼ stick)
1 package (8 ounces) small mushrooms, sliced
¼ teaspoon salt
⅛ teaspoon coarsely ground black pepper
1 package (10 ounces) frozen tiny peas, thawed
½ teaspoon chopped fresh thyme leaves

In nonstick 10-inch skillet, melt margarine or butter over medium-high heat. Add mushrooms, salt, and pepper and cook, stirring, until mushrooms are golden and liquid evaporates, about 6 minutes. Add peas and thyme and cook about 4 minutes or until hot. Makes 4 accompaniment servings.

Each serving: About 120 calories, 5 g protein, 13 g carbohydrate, 6 g total fat (1 g saturated), 0 mg cholesterol, 275 mg sodium.

Oven-Roasted Parsnips & Carrots

PREP: 15 MINUTES • COOK: 45 MINUTES

If you are planning to serve these root vegetables with roast meat or poultry, you can roast them at the same time.

2 bags parsnips (1 pound each), peeled and cut into 3-inch-long pieces
2 bags carrots (1 pound each), peeled and cut into 3-inch-long pieces
2 tablespoons olive oil
½ teaspoon salt
¼ teaspoon coarsely ground black pepper

1 Preheat oven to 425°F. If some pieces of parsnips and carrots are thick, cut lengthwise in half or into quarters. Toss vegetables in 15½" by 10½" jelly-roll pan with olive oil, salt, and pepper.

2 Roast vegetables 45 minutes or until tender and browned, tossing vegetables halfway through roasting time. Makes 10 accompaniment servings.

Each serving: About 125 calories, 2 g protein, 25 g carbohydrate, 3 g total fat (0 g saturated), 0 mg cholesterol, 145 mg sodium.

Cherry Tomato Gratin ➤

Tomato Soufflé

PREP: 50 MINUTES • BAKE: 45 MINUTES

Great tomato flavor with just the right amount of sautéed onions makes this a delicious light main dish or a perfect accompaniment to seafood, poultry, or pork.

5 tablespoons margarine or butter
1 medium onion, chopped
2 pounds ripe tomatoes (about 6 medium), peeled and diced
½ teaspoon sugar
¼ teaspoon ground black pepper
1¼ teaspoons salt
¼ cup all-purpose flour
1¼ cups milk
1 tablespoon plain dried bread crumbs
6 large eggs, separated
2 tablespoons grated Parmesan cheese

1 In 12-inch skillet, melt 1 tablespoon margarine or butter over medium heat. Add onion and cook until tender, about 10 minutes.

2 Add tomatoes with their juice, sugar, pepper, and ½ teaspoon salt. Increase heat to high and cook, stirring often, until all juices evaporate, about 15 to 20 minutes.

3 Meanwhile, in 2-quart saucepan, melt remaining 4 tablespoons margarine or butter over medium heat. Stir in flour and remaining ¾ teaspoon salt until blended; cook 1 minute. Gradually add milk and cook, stirring constantly, until mixture boils and thickens. Remove saucepan from heat; stir in tomato mixture until blended.

4 Preheat oven to 325°F. Grease 2-quart soufflé dish; sprinkle with bread crumbs.

5 In large bowl, beat egg yolks slightly; beat in a small amount of hot tomato mixture. Gradually stir yolk mixture into tomato mixture, stirring rapidly to prevent lumping. Pour mixture back into bowl.

THE QUICKEST WAY TO PEEL & SEED A TOMATO

Most of the time, you can use tomatoes without peeling or seeding—but we recommend one or both steps in certain recipes where tough skin or seeds would interfere with a smooth mouthfeel or elegant presentation. Here, how we tackle the tasks in the GH kitchens:

To peel: Cut a shallow cross at the blossom (bottom) end of each tomato. Drop tomatoes, a few at a time, into a pot of boiling water. After 15 seconds, remove and immerse immediately in a bowl of cold water to stop cooking. Gently pull the skin off with your fingers.

To seed: Cut each tomato crosswise in half. Holding one half in palm, gently squeeze over a bowl (see above), and loosen seeds from pulp with finger. If you need to save juice from tomato to use in a recipe, place a strainer in bowl before you start squeezing.

6 In small bowl, with mixer at high speed, beat egg whites until stiff peaks form. With rubber spatula, gently fold beaten egg whites, one-third at a time, into tomato mixture until blended. Pour mixture into soufflé dish. Sprinkle with Parmesan cheese. If desired, with back of spoon, make a 1-inch-deep indentation all around in soufflé mixture about 1 inch from edge of dish (the center will rise higher than the edge, creating a top-hat effect when the soufflé is done). Bake 45 minutes or until soufflé is puffy and brown and knife inserted under top hat comes out clean. Serve immediately. Makes 8 accompaniment or 4 main-dish servings.

Each accompaniment serving: About 200 calories, 8 g protein, 13 g carbohydrate, 13 g total fat (4 g saturated), 166 mg cholesterol, 540 mg sodium.

South-of-the-Border Squash Sauté

PREP: 15 MINUTES • COOK: ABOUT 10 MINUTES

The delicate flavor of yellow straight-neck or crook-neck squash with a hint of cinnamon and a light tomato-cream sauce made right in the same skillet.

1 tablespoon olive oil
4 small yellow squashes (about 6 ounces each), each cut lengthwise in half, then cut crosswise into ½-inch-thick slices
¼ teaspoon ground cinnamon
¼ teaspoon salt
⅛ teaspoon coarsely ground black pepper
1 medium tomato, diced
2 tablespoons heavy or whipping cream
⅓ cup loosely packed fresh cilantro leaves, chopped

1 In nonstick 12-inch skillet, heat olive oil over medium-high heat until hot. Add squash slices and cook 5 to 7 minutes, until lightly browned, stirring occasionally. Add cinnamon, salt, and pepper, and cook 3 minutes longer.

2 Stir in tomato; cook 1 minute. Stir in cream; cook 30 seconds. Sprinkle with cilantro to serve. Makes about 3 cups or 4 accompaniment servings.

Each serving: About 95 calories, 2 g protein, 9 g carbohydrate, 7 g total fat (2 g saturated), 10 mg cholesterol, 145 mg sodium.

Venetian-Style Zucchini

PREP: 20 MINUTES PLUS STANDING
COOK: 6 TO 8 MINUTES PER BATCH

This traditional method of preparing vegetables is called *agrodolce* (literally, "sweet and sour") in Italy. Thin zucchini slices are fried in oil, then marinated in a mint, raisin, and balsamic vinegar mixture.

3 tablespoons golden raisins
3 tablespoons balsamic vinegar
1 tablespoon minced fresh mint leaves
1 teaspoon dark brown sugar
½ teaspoon salt
⅛ teaspoon ground black pepper
1 garlic clove, peeled and cut in half
Vegetable oil for frying (at least 2 cups)
8 small zucchini (about 5 ounces each), cut crosswise into ¼-inch slices
1 tablespoon pine nuts, toasted
Mint sprigs for garnish

1 In large bowl, stir raisins, vinegar, minced mint, brown sugar, salt, pepper, and garlic; set aside.

2 In 10-inch skillet, heat ½ inch oil over medium-high heat until hot but not smoking. Add 2 cups zucchini; fry until golden, 6 to 8 minutes. With slotted spoon, remove cooked zucchini to coarse sieve set over bowl to drain. While still hot, stir zucchini into vinegar mixture.

3 Repeat with remaining zucchini in batches of 2 cups each. Let stand at room temperature at least 1 hour. Or, cover and refrigerate for up to 3 days.

4 Serve at room temperature, topped with pine nuts and mint. Makes about 3 cups or 6 accompaniment servings.

Each serving: About 140 calories, 3 g protein, 12 g carbohydrate, 10 g total fat (1 g saturated), 0 mg cholesterol, 185 mg sodium.

Bubbe's Potato Latkes

PREP: 45 MINUTES • COOK: 45 MINUTES

These crispy potato pancakes are best eaten as soon as they're fried but they can also be kept warm in a 250°F. oven for up to 30 minutes until ready to serve.

Homemade Applesauce (recipe follows)
4 large baking potatoes (about 2½ pounds)
1 medium onion
1 large egg
2 tablespoons all-purpose flour or matzoh meal
1 tablespoon minced fresh parsley or dill
1 tablespoon fresh lemon juice
½ teaspoon baking powder
½ teaspoon salt
¼ teaspoon coarsely ground black pepper
¾ cup vegetable oil for frying

1 Prepare Homemade Applesauce; cover and refrigerate until serving time.

2 Peel and finely shred potatoes and onion into colander. With hand, squeeze to press out as much liquid as possible. Place potato mixture in medium bowl; stir in egg, flour, parsley, lemon juice, baking powder, salt, and pepper.

3 Preheat oven to 250°F. Heat 3 tablespoons vegetable oil in 12-inch skillet over medium heat until hot but not smoking. Drop potato mixture by scant ¼ cups into hot skillet, cooking 5 latkes at a time. With back of spoon, flatten each latke into a 3-inch round. Cook latkes about 4 to 5 minutes, until undersides are golden. With pancake turner, turn latkes and cook 4 to 5 minutes longer, until second sides are golden brown and crisp. With slotted pancake turner, remove latkes to paper towels to drain and keep warm on cookie sheet lined with paper towels in the oven.

4 Repeat with remaining potato mixture, stirring thoroughly before frying each batch and using 3 tablespoons hot vegetable oil per batch. Serve hot with Homemade Applesauce. Makes about 20 latkes, or 10 accompaniment servings.

HOMEMADE APPLESAUCE: Cut each of *4 large Golden Delicious apples* (about 2 pounds) into eighths, but do not peel or remove core and seeds. In 3-quart saucepan, heat apples, *½ cup apple cider or apple juice*, and *1 teaspoon fresh lemon juice* to boiling over high heat. Reduce heat to low; cover and simmer 15 minutes or until very tender. Into large bowl, press apple mixture through coarse sieve or food mill to remove skin and seeds. Makes about 2 cups.

Each serving without applesauce: About 250 calories, 6 g protein, 38 g carbohydrate, 9 g total fat (1 g saturated), 43 mg cholesterol, 270 mg sodium.

Each tablespoon applesauce: About 15 calories, 0 g protein, 4 g carbohydrate, 0 g total fat, 0 mg cholesterol, 0 mg sodium.

Basil Whipped Potatoes

PREP: 20 MINUTES • COOK: 30 MINUTES

Fresh, fragrant basil and garlic give old-fashioned mashed spuds extra appeal.

2 large bunches basil
6 medium baking potatoes (3½ pounds), peeled and cut into 1-inch chunks
6 strips lemon peel (3" by ¾" each)
6 garlic cloves, peeled
Salt
4 tablespoons margarine or butter

THE LEGEND OF THE LATKE

To celebrate the hard-won freedom of the Maccabees long ago, and the hope embodied in the light that burned 8 days (when there was enough oil left for only 1 day), foods fried in oil are traditionally served as part of the Hanukkah meal. The most popular of these are latkes; other favorites include jelly doughnuts and deep-fried yeast dough dipped in honey.

Bubbe's Potato Latkes (recipe above).

2 tablespoons extravirgin olive oil
½ teaspoon coarsely ground black pepper

1 Set aside 8 large sprigs basil. Slice remaining basil leaves to equal ½ cup.

2 In 4-quart saucepan, place basil sprigs, potatoes, lemon peel, garlic, 1 teaspoon salt, and enough *water* to cover; heat to boiling over high heat. Reduce heat to low; cover and simmer 15 to 20 minutes, until potatoes are very tender.

3 Drain potatoes, reserving ¾ *cup cooking water*. Discard basil sprigs and lemon peel.

4 In large bowl, with mixer at low speed, beat potatoes with margarine, oil, pepper, and ½ teaspoon salt. Add reserved cooking water and beat until smooth. Stir in sliced basil. Makes about 6 cups or 8 accompaniment servings.

Each serving: About 220 calories, 4 g protein, 32 g carbohydrate, 9 g total fat (2 g saturated), 0 mg cholesterol, 355 mg sodium.

Mashed Potatoes with Caramelized Onions

PREP: 20 MINUTES • COOK: 30 MINUTES

3 tablespoons olive oil
3 large red onions (2 pounds), each cut in half and thinly sliced
Salt
5 medium baking potatoes (2½ pounds), peeled and cut into ½-inch pieces
⅓ cup milk
⅛ teaspoon coarsely ground black pepper

1 In nonstick 12-inch skillet, heat olive oil over medium heat. Add onions and ¼ teaspoon salt and cook, stirring occasionally, until onions are golden brown and very tender, about 30 minutes.

2 While onions are cooking, in 4-quart saucepan, heat potatoes, 1 teaspoon salt, and enough *water* to cover to boiling over high heat. Reduce heat to low; cover and simmer 8 to 10 minutes, until potatoes are tender. Drain potatoes.

3 Return potatoes to saucepan; cook over high heat, shaking pan, 30 seconds or until all liquid evaporates. Remove saucepan from heat. With potato masher, coarsely mash potatoes with milk, pepper, and ¾ tea-

spoon salt. Stir in all but 2 tablespoons onions; heat through. Spoon remaining onions on top of mashed potatoes to serve. Makes 6 accompaniment servings.

Each serving: About 250 calories, 5 g protein, 42 g carbohydrate, 8 g total fat (1 g saturated), 2 mg cholesterol, 420 mg sodium.

Chicago Mashed Potatoes with Onion & Bacon

PREP: 15 MINUTES • COOK: 25 MINUTES

A treat on Midwestern tables. This entire recipe can be made ahead and reheated in the microwave when ready to serve. Although whole milk will lend the most body and flavor here, if you're looking to trim some of the fat, we would suggest 2 percent because it's closest to whole milk's 3.25 percent fat content.

4 slices bacon, chopped
1 large onion, chopped
3 pounds all-purpose potatoes (about 9 medium), peeled and cut into 1-inch chunks
1 bay leaf
1 teaspoon salt
¼ teaspoon coarsely ground black pepper
1 cup milk, warmed

1 In 10-inch skillet, cook bacon until browned over medium-low heat. With slotted spoon, remove bacon to paper towels to drain. To bacon fat in skillet, add onion and cook over medium heat, stirring occasionally, until tender, about 15 minutes.

2 Meanwhile, in 3-quart saucepan, heat potatoes, bay leaf, and enough *water* to cover to boiling over high heat. Reduce heat to low; cover and simmer 15 minutes or until potatoes are fork-tender; drain.

3 Return potatoes to saucepan. Discard bay leaf. With potato masher, mash potatoes with salt and pepper. Gradually add milk; mash until mixture is well blended. Stir in onion and bacon. Makes 8 accompaniment servings.

Each serving: About 200 calories, 5 g protein, 28 g carbohydrate, 8 g total fat (3 g saturated), 12 mg cholesterol, 370 mg sodium.

Charleston Sweet-Potato Pancake

This side dish cooks to a rich nutty brown. Although best made just before serving, if you're pressed for time, you can make it up to 2 hours in advance and then reheat, loosely wrapped, in foil.

1 tablespoon cornstarch
½ teaspoon chopped fresh thyme leaves
½ teaspoon salt
¼ teaspoon coarsely ground black pepper
2 pounds sweet potatoes, peeled and thinly sliced
1 pound Rome Beauty apples (2 large), peeled, cored, and thinly sliced
4 tablespoons margarine or butter (½ stick)
Fresh thyme sprigs for garnish (optional)

1 In cup, mix cornstarch, thyme, salt, and pepper.

2 In large bowl, toss sweet potatoes and apples with cornstarch mixture. Then, toss with 3 tablespoons melted margarine or butter.

3 Heat nonstick 10-inch skillet until very hot over medium heat. Add remaining 1 tablespoon margarine or butter. When melted, spoon potato mixture into skillet; pat to an even thickness. Cook, covered, 18 to 20 minutes, until potatoes and apples are tender. Uncover skillet; cook 2 minutes longer.

FOOD EDITOR'S TIP

Q. What's the difference between a yam and a sweet potato?

A. Believe it or not, even though "candied yams" is such a popular dish, true yams are seldom available in this country. These large, ivory-fleshed, brown-skinned tubers are not related to sweet potatoes at all, but are a staple in the West Indies. (You can sometimes find them here in Latin-American markets.) In the United States, there are two types of sweet potato (both cultivated in the South): One is moist, sweet, and orange-fleshed; the other is drier, yellow-fleshed, and not as sweet. The orange-fleshed variety is often sold as yams. Both orange- and yellow-fleshed sweet potatoes can be used in our recipes.

4 Remove skillet from heat. Place large serving plate over top of skillet. Quickly turn skillet upside down to invert pancake. Replace any pieces on top of pancake that may have stuck to skillet. Garnish with thyme sprigs if you like. Makes 10 accompaniment servings.

Each serving: About 130 calories, 1 g protein, 21 g carbohydrate, 5 g total fat (1 g saturated), 0 mg cholesterol, 175 mg sodium.

North Carolina Brown Butter Sweet Potatoes

Just 4 ingredients! This can be made well ahead and then, just before serving, reheated either in a microwave or a double boiler.

4 pounds sweet potatoes, peeled and cut into 2-inch chunks
6 tablespoons butter (do not use margarine)
¼ cup light molasses
½ teaspoon salt

1 In 5-quart saucepot, heat sweet potatoes and enough *water* to cover to boiling over high heat. Reduce heat to low; cover and simmer 20 minutes or until sweet potatoes are fork-tender. Drain well and return sweet potatoes to saucepot.

2 Meanwhile, in 1-quart saucepan, cook butter over medium heat until browned, but not burned, 5 to 7 minutes. (Butter should be the color of maple syrup.)

3 With potato masher, mash sweet potatoes, brown butter, molasses, and salt until smooth. Makes 12 accompaniment servings.

Each serving: About 180 calories, 2 g protein, 30 g carbohydrate, 6 g total fat (4 g saturated), 15 mg cholesterol, 160 mg sodium.

SALADS

Tomato & Shrimp Salad

PREP: 45 MINUTES • COOK: ABOUT 7 MINUTES

The ideal end-of-summer meal, especially when served alfresco.

1 pound large shrimp
Salt
¾ pound green beans, each cut crosswise in half
1 pound ripe tomatoes (about 4 small), each cut into 8 wedges
1 pound Kirby cucumbers (about 4), peeled and each cut lengthwise into quarters then cut crosswise into 1-inch pieces
1 large lemon
2 tablespoons olive oil
1 tablespoon finely chopped shallot
1 tablespoon finely chopped fresh oregano leaves
1 teaspoon Dijon mustard
½ teaspoon sugar
½ teaspoon coarsely ground black pepper
4 ounces feta cheese, crumbled

1 Shell and devein shrimp, leaving tails on if you like. Rinse with running cold water. In 4-quart saucepan, heat *2 inches water* to boiling over high heat. Add shrimp and 2 teaspoons salt; cook 1 minute or until shrimp turn opaque throughout. Drain shrimp; rinse with running cold water to cool and drain again. Place shrimp in large serving bowl.

2 In 10-inch skillet, heat ¾ *inch water* to boiling over high heat. Add beans and 2 teaspoons salt; heat to boiling. Reduce heat to medium; cook, uncovered, about 5 minutes or until beans are tender-crisp. Drain beans; rinse under running cold water to cool and drain again. Place beans, tomatoes, and cucumbers in bowl with shrimp.

3 Prepare dressing: From lemon, grate ½ teaspoon peel and squeeze 3 tablespoons juice. In small bowl, with wire whisk or fork, combine lemon peel, lemon juice, olive oil, shallot, oregano, mustard, sugar, pepper, and ¾ teaspoon salt. Toss dressing with shrimp and vegetables in bowl. Sprinkle with feta cheese. Makes 4 main-dish servings.

Each serving: About 300 calories, 27 g protein, 18 g carbohydrate, 14 g total fat (5 g saturated), 205 mg cholesterol, 1105 mg sodium.

Panzanella Salad

PREP: 30 MINUTES • COOK: 15 MINUTES

This classic Mediterranean salad depends on a hearty loaf of bread that won't get mushy when mixed with moist ingredients and dressing. Our version is tossed with a homemade tomato vinaigrette for added flavor.

¼ pound pancetta or bacon, cut into ¼-inch pieces
1 tablespoon olive oil
6 ounces sourdough bread, cut into ½-inch cubes
2 tablespoons grated Parmesan cheese
¼ teaspoon ground black pepper
Tomato Vinaigrette (recipe follows)
4 bunches arugula (about 1 pound), tough stems removed
1½ pints red and/or yellow cherry tomatoes, each cut in half

1 In nonstick 12-inch skillet, cook pancetta or bacon over medium heat until lightly browned. With slotted spoon, remove pancetta to large salad bowl.

2 To drippings in skillet, add olive oil and bread cubes and cook until bread is lightly browned, about 10 minutes. Toss toasted bread cubes in bowl with pancetta, grated Parmesan, and pepper; set aside.

3 Prepare Tomato Vinaigrette.

4 Add arugula and cherry tomatoes to bread cubes in bowl; toss with Tomato Vinaigrette. Makes 6 main-dish servings.

TOMATO VINAIGRETTE: Coarsely cut up *1 small tomato*, peeled, and *1 small shallot*. In blender at medium speed, blend tomato, shallot, *2 tablespoons olive oil*, *1 tablespoon red wine vinegar*, *1 tablespoon balsamic vinegar*, *1 teaspoon sugar*, *1 teaspoon chopped fresh oregano*, *2 teaspoons Dijon mustard with seeds*, *¼ teaspoon salt*, and *¼ teaspoon ground black pepper* just until smooth. Makes about 1 cup. Store in refrigerator for up to 2 days.

Each serving: About 300 calories, 8 g protein, 25 g carbohydrate, 20 g total fat (6 g saturated), 14 mg cholesterol, 500 mg sodium.

Tomato & Shrimp Salad served with ▶
homemade Tomato Focaccia (page 90)

Warm Arugula & Mushroom Salad

PREP: 25 MINUTES • COOK: 15 MINUTES

Shaving Parmesan is easiest when the cheese is at room temperature; use a vegetable peeler to make thin pieces.

¼ cup chicken broth
2 tablespoons balsamic vinegar
2 tablespoons dry vermouth
½ teaspoon sugar
½ teaspoon salt
½ teaspoon coarsely ground black pepper
3 tablespoons olive oil
4 bunches arugula (about 12 ounces), stems trimmed
3 garlic cloves, crushed with side of chef's knife
8 ounces shiitake mushrooms, stems discarded and caps cut into quarters
8 ounces white mushrooms, sliced
1 teaspoon fresh rosemary leaves, chopped
2 ounces Parmesan-cheese shavings

1 In cup, mix chicken broth, vinegar, vermouth, sugar, salt, pepper, and 2 tablespoons olive oil. Arrange arugula on large platter; set aside.

2 In nonstick 12-inch skillet, heat remaining olive oil over medium heat. Add garlic and cook just until golden. Increase heat to medium-high. Add mushrooms and rosemary and cook 8 to 10 minutes, until mushrooms are browned and liquid evaporates; discard garlic.

3 Add chicken-broth mixture to skillet; cook 30 seconds, stirring. Immediately pour mushroom mixture over arugula. Top with Parmesan-cheese shavings. Makes 4 accompaniment servings.

Each serving: About 230 calories, 10 g protein, 14 g carbohydrate, 15 g total fat (4 g saturated), 11 mg cholesterol, 620 mg sodium.

FOOD EDITOR'S TIP

Q. What should I look for when buying Belgian endive?

A. Pay less attention to the size and shape of the head, which can vary, than to the color of this mildly bitter vegetable. It should be ivory, with pretty pastel yellow leaf tips. Also called *witloof* (white leaf), Belgian endive is cultivated in complete darkness to prevent it from turning green and very bitter; the labor-intensive growing process involves harvesting the plant, cutting off the outer leaves, and planting it again. The best heads are crisp, firmly packed, and shipped between layers of opaque waxed paper to keep out the light. At home, wrap the endive in a paper towel, place in a plastic bag, refrigerate, and use within a few days. Serve raw in salads (like the chicory and endive salad on the opposite page or our Radicchio Slaw with Toasted Walnuts, page 145), or try it braised, baked, or sautéed.

Salinas Mixed Greens with Tarragon-Vinegar Dressing

PREP: 25 MINUTES

A refreshing mix of lettuce, watercress, and green onions tossed with a fast 5-ingredient dressing. Mix the salad dressing in a small jar with a tight-fitting lid up to a week ahead and refrigerate. Rinse and spin-dry the greens a day ahead and store, refrigerated, wrapped in moist paper towels, in plastic bags.

¼ cup olive oil
2 tablespoons tarragon vinegar
½ teaspoon Dijon mustard
¼ teaspoon salt
¼ teaspoon coarsely ground black pepper
3 green onions, thinly sliced
1 head romaine lettuce, torn into bite-size pieces
1 head Boston lettuce, torn into bite-size pieces
1 bunch watercress, tough stems discarded
⅓ cup chopped fresh parsley

1 In small bowl, combine olive oil, tarragon vinegar, mustard, salt, and pepper; mix well.

2 To serve, in large salad bowl, toss green onions, romaine, Boston lettuce, watercress, and parsley with dressing until well coated. Makes 8 accompaniment servings.

Each serving: About 75 calories, 1 g protein, 2 g carbohydrate, 7 g total fat (1 g saturated), 0 mg cholesterol, 80 mg sodium.

Chicory & Endive Salad with Blue Cheese & Michigan Dried Cherries

PREP: 25 MINUTES

The sweet, tart, and bitter flavors complement one another. To cut down on last-minute preparations, wash and spin dry the chicory a day ahead. (Do not prepare the endive until ready to serve because the cut edges will turn brown.) Wrap loosely in paper towels and store in a plastic bag (or use specially designed vegetable bags with holes). Prepare the dressing in a jar and refrigerate overnight.

3 tablespoons red wine vinegar
3 tablespoons olive oil
1 tablespoon finely chopped shallot
1 teaspoon sugar
1 teaspoon Dijon mustard
½ teaspoon salt
½ teaspoon coarsely ground black pepper
2 heads chicory
2 medium heads Belgian endive (4 ounces each)
½ cup dried tart cherries
3 ounces blue cheese, crumbled

1 Prepare dressing: In medium jar with tight-fitting lid, combine vinegar, olive oil, shallot, sugar, mustard, salt and pepper; shake well.

2 Remove tender leaves from center of each head of chicory and tear into 3-inch pieces (you should have enough to equal 12 cups, lightly packed). Save outer leaves of chicory for use another day.

3 Trim tough root end from each endive. Cut each endive lengthwise in half. Place halves cut-side down and cut lengthwise into thin strips.

4 To serve, in large salad bowl, toss chicory and endive with dressing; sprinkle with dried cherries and blue cheese. Makes 12 accompaniment servings.

Each serving: About 85 calories, 3 g protein, 7 g carbohydrate, 6 g total fat (2 g saturated), 5 mg cholesterol, 250 mg sodium.

Washington State Pear & Beet Salad

PREP: 40 MINUTES PLUS STANDING
COOK: 40 TO 50 MINUTES

A delicious and vibrant way to begin any special-occasion dinner. To save time, do all the work a day ahead—cover and refrigerate the beet mixture separately from the romaine. Just remember to remove the beets from the refrigerator 1 hour before serving to bring out the best flavor.

8 medium beets (about 1½ pounds without tops)
1 medium orange
¼ cup olive oil
1 tablespoon red wine vinegar
1 teaspoon salt
½ teaspoon Dijon mustard
3 medium Bartlett pears
8 cups sliced romaine lettuce (1 small head, about ¾ pound)
Orange-peel strips for garnish

1 In 3-quart saucepan, heat beets and enough *water* to cover to boiling over high heat. Reduce heat to low; cover and simmer 30 to 35 minutes, until beets are fork-tender.

2 Meanwhile, grate ½ teaspoon peel and squeeze 2 tablespoons juice from orange. In large bowl, with wire whisk or fork, mix olive oil, vinegar, salt, mustard, orange peel, and orange juice.

3 Drain beets and rinse with cold running water to cool slightly. Peel and cut beets and pears into ¼-inch pieces.

4 To dressing in bowl, add beets and pears; toss to coat. Let mixture stand at least 1 hour to blend flavors. Just before serving, place sliced romaine on platter; top with beet mixture. Garnish with orange peel strips if you like. Makes 8 accompaniment servings.

Each serving: About 130 calories, 2 g protein, 16 g carbohydrate, 7 g total fat (1 g saturated), 0 mg cholesterol, 310 mg sodium.

Winter Salad with Ripe Pears & Toasted Pecans

PREP: 45 MINUTES

A beautiful addition to your dinner table—the combination of green and red lends a festive touch.

3 tablespoons red wine vinegar
2 teaspoons Dijon mustard
½ teaspoon salt
½ teaspoon coarsely ground black pepper
⅓ cup olive oil
3 medium, ripe pears, peeled, cored, and each cut into 16 wedges
1 wedge Parmesan cheese (about 4 ounces)

2 small heads radicchio (7 ounces each), torn into large pieces
2 small heads Belgian endive, separated into leaves
2 bunches arugula (about 4 ounces each)
½ cup toasted pecans, coarsely chopped

1 In very large bowl, with wire whisk or fork, mix vinegar, mustard, salt, and pepper. Gradually whisk in olive oil until blended. Add pear wedges; toss to coat pears with dressing.

2 With vegetable peeler, shave 1 cup loosely packed shavings from wedge of Parmesan cheese; set aside.

3 Add radicchio, endive, and arugula to bowl with pears; toss to coat evenly. Serve salad topped with Parmesan shavings and pecans. Makes 10 accompaniment servings.

Each serving: About 205 calories, 7 g protein, 14 g carbohydrate, 15 g total fat (3 g saturated), 9 mg cholesterol, 360 mg sodium.

Winter Salad with Ripe Pears & Toasted Pecans

Peaches & Greens

PREP: 25 MINUTES

A cool, refreshing alternative to classic green salads.

1 large lime
2 tablespoons honey
1 tablespoon olive oil
1 tablespoon chopped fresh mint leaves
½ teaspoon Dijon mustard
¼ teaspoon salt
¼ teaspoon coarsely ground black pepper
2 bunches watercress (each about 4 ounces), tough stems removed
6 ripe medium peaches (about 2 pounds), peeled and cut into wedges
1 medium jicama (about 1¼ pounds), peeled and cut into 1½" by ¼" sticks

1 Grate ¼ teaspoon peel from lime and squeeze 2 tablespoons juice. In small bowl, with wire whisk, mix lime peel, lime juice, honey, olive oil, mint, Dijon mustard, salt, and pepper.

2 Just before serving, in large bowl, toss watercress, peaches, and jicama with dressing. Makes 12 accompaniment servings.

Each serving: About 55 calories, 1 g protein, 11 g carbohydrate, 1 g total fat (0 g saturated), 0 mg cholesterol, 55 mg sodium.

Radicchio Slaw with Toasted Walnuts

PREP: 35 MINUTES

To keep this slaw fresh and crisp, carry the dressing separately when traveling to a picnic, and toss ingredients together just before serving.

¾ cup walnuts
1 tablespoon red wine vinegar
¾ teaspoon coarsely ground black pepper
½ teaspoon salt
3 tablespoons olive oil
2 medium heads radicchio (about 1 pound), thinly sliced
2 medium heads Belgian endive, each cut lengthwise in half, then cut lengthwise into thin strips

1 Preheat oven to 375°F. Place walnuts in 13" by 9" metal baking pan. Bake about 10 minutes or until lightly toasted; cool. Finely chop ½ cup walnuts; coarsely chop remaining walnuts.

2 In small bowl, with wire whisk, mix vinegar, black pepper, and salt. Gradually whisk in olive oil until blended.

3 Just before serving, in large bowl, toss radicchio, endive, and finely chopped walnuts with dressing. Sprinkle with coarsely chopped walnuts. Makes 10 accompaniment servings.

Each serving: About 105 calories, 2 g protein, 4 g carbohydrate, 10 g total fat (1 g saturated), 0 mg cholesterol, 120 mg sodium.

Light & Lemony Slaw

PREP: 20 MINUTES

A crisp complement to any barbecue—and much lower in fat than typical deli slaw.

2 medium lemons
½ cup light mayonnaise
¼ cup reduced-fat sour cream
1 tablespoon sugar
1 teaspoon salt
½ teaspoon coarsely ground black pepper
¼ teaspoon celery seeds
1 medium head green cabbage (about 3 pounds), thinly sliced, with tough ribs discarded
4 medium carrots, shredded

1 Grate 1 teaspoon peel from lemons and squeeze ¼ cup juice. In large bowl, with wire whisk, mix lemon peel, lemon juice, mayonnaise, sour cream, sugar, salt, pepper, and celery seeds until blended.

2 Add cabbage and carrots; toss well. Serve slaw at room temperature or cover and refrigerate until ready to serve. Makes 12 accompaniment servings.

Each serving: About 60 calories, 1 g protein, 11 g carbohydrate, 1 g total fat (0 g saturated), 2 mg cholesterol, 300 mg sodium.

Carrot & Jicama Slaw

PREP: 30 MINUTES

Jicama (pronounced *hee-kah-mah*), popular in Mexican cooking, is a bulbous root vegetable with a thin brown skin and white crunchy flesh similar to a water chestnut's. If it's not available, use 2 packages of shredded carrots.

¼ cup chopped fresh cilantro leaves or fresh
    mint leaves
¼ cup fresh lime juice (2 medium limes)
4 teaspoons honey
¼ teaspoon salt
⅛ teaspoon crushed red pepper
1 package (8 ounces) shredded carrots
1 medium jicama (about 12 ounces), peeled and
    cut into ⅛-inch-thick sticks
½ medium red pepper, cut into ⅛-inch-thick
    slices
Fresh cilantro leaves for garnish

In large bowl, with fork, mix chopped cilantro, lime juice, honey, salt, and crushed red pepper. Add carrots, jicama, and red pepper; toss. Cover and refrigerate if not serving right away. Garnish with cilantro. Makes about 5 cups or 8 accompaniment servings.

Each serving: About 45 calories, 1 g protein, 11 g carbohydrate, 0 g total fat, 0 mg cholesterol, 75 mg sodium.

Moroccan Carrot Salad

PREP: 20 MINUTES

A simple go-along dish spiced with coriander, cilantro, and cumin for a Middle Eastern twist.

1 pound (about 2 bunches) carrots, peeled and
    coarsely shredded
2 tablespoons extravirgin olive oil
2 teaspoons fresh lemon juice
¼ teaspoon ground coriander
¼ teaspoon ground cumin
¼ teaspoon salt
⅛ teaspoon ground black pepper
2 tablespoons chopped fresh cilantro leaves
Lemon slice for garnish

1 In medium bowl, stir carrots, olive oil, lemon juice, coriander, cumin, salt, and pepper. Cover and refrigerate if not serving right away.

2 To serve, stir in cilantro. Garnish with lemon slice. Makes about 2½ cups or 4 accompaniment servings.

Each serving: About 110 calories, 1 g protein, 11 g carbohydrate, 7 g total fat (1 g saturated), 0 mg cholesterol, 170 mg sodium.

Carrot Salad

PREP: 10 MINUTES

2 tablespoons fresh lime juice
1 tablespoon honey
1 tablespoon chopped fresh cilantro leaves
¼ teaspoon salt
⅛ teaspoon crushed red pepper
2 packages (8 ounces each) shredded carrots

1 In large bowl, with wire whisk or fork, mix lime juice, honey, cilantro, salt, and crushed red pepper until blended.

2 Toss carrots with lime dressing to coat. Makes 4 accompaniment servings.

Each serving: About 65 calories, 1 g protein, 17 g carbohydrate, 0 g total fat, 0 mg cholesterol, 175 mg sodium.

▌ FOOD EDITOR'S TIP ▐

Q. Is it okay to eat the wax coating on store-bought cucumbers?

A. Yes. Cucumbers, like some shiny apples and peppers, are often coated with a thin layer of edible wax to maintain freshness and prevent bruising. While the Food and Drug Administration (FDA) puts the coating in the GRAS (Generally Recognized As Safe) category, along with stabilizers like carrageenan, some consumers still worry that the wax may seal in pesticides. But the FDA's monitoring program has shown that any residue is safe. One way to be sure is to peel the cuke's tough skin—as we do in *Good Housekeeping* recipes. Or use small kirby or pickling cucumbers or English (seedless) cukes, which have lower moisture content than regular cucumbers, don't perish as quickly, and are not waxed.

Kirby Cucumber Salad

PREP: 30 MINUTES PLUS STANDING AND CHILLING

To make prep easier, start this salad a day ahead. Once done, refrigerate until ready to use. Kirby cucumbers, with their unwaxed skins, don't need to be peeled. If you can't find them, buy regular cucumbers and remove several strips of peel from each one.

4 pounds kirby cucumbers (about 16), unpeeled and thinly sliced
1 tablespoon salt
¾ cup distilled white vinegar
2 tablespoons sugar
2 tablespoons chopped fresh dill
Dill sprigs for garnish

1 In large colander set over large bowl, sprinkle cucumbers with salt; toss to mix. Let stand 30 minutes at room temperature. Discard liquid in bowl. Pat cucumbers dry with paper towels.

2 In same bowl, mix vinegar, sugar, and chopped dill. Add cucumbers and stir to coat. Cover and refrigerate at least 2 hours, stirring occasionally. Garnish with dill. Makes 12 accompaniment servings.

Each serving: About 30 calories, 1 g protein, 7 g carbohydrate, 0 g total fat, 0 mg cholesterol, 270 mg sodium.

Creamy Cucumber & Dill Salad

PREP: 15 MINUTES PLUS STANDING AND CHILLING

Great with grilled seafood.

2 English (seedless) cucumbers, unpeeled and thinly sliced
2 teaspoons salt
½ cup sour cream
2 tablespoons minced fresh dill
2 teaspoons minced fresh mint leaves
1 teaspoon distilled white vinegar
⅛ teaspoon ground black pepper

1 In large colander set over large bowl, toss cucumber slices with salt. Let stand 30 minutes at room temperature, stirring occasionally. Discard liquid in bowl. Pat cucumbers dry with paper towels.

2 In same bowl, mix sour cream, dill, mint, vinegar, and pepper. Stir in cucumbers. Cover and refrigerate at least 1 hour. Makes about 4 cups or 6 accompaniment servings.

Each serving: About 60 calories, 2 g protein, 5 g carbohydrate, 4 g total fat (3 g saturated), 9 mg cholesterol, 455 mg sodium.

Citrus Salad with Sherry Dressing

PREP: 30 MINUTES

A splash of sherry gives this crunchy, colorful salad Spanish flair; serve with grilled or broiled chicken.

2 tablespoons dry sherry
1 tablespoon red wine vinegar
1 teaspoon Dijon mustard
¼ teaspoon salt
⅛ teaspoon coarsely ground black pepper
2 tablespoons olive oil
1 large Granny Smith apple, cored and sliced paper thin
2 large navel oranges
1 large pink grapefruit
1 bunch watercress

1 In large bowl, with wire whisk or fork, beat sherry, vinegar, mustard, salt, and pepper until blended. Gradually whisk in olive oil.

2 Add apple slices to dressing in bowl and toss to coat. Cut off peel and white pith from oranges and grapefruit. Cut on either side of membranes to remove each segment from oranges and grapefruit. (If you like, squeeze juice from membranes for use another day.) Add orange and grapefruit segments to dressing; toss to coat.

3 Spread watercress on platter. Spoon fruit mixture and dressing over watercress; toss before serving. Makes 6 accompaniment or first-course servings.

Each serving: About 100 calories, 1 g protein, 14 g carbohydrate, 5 g total fat (1 g saturated), 0 mg cholesterol, 115 mg sodium.

Watermelon & Jicama Salad

Fennel Salad with Olives & Mint

····································

PREP: 20 MINUTES

Serve at lunch with bread and cheese or as a side dish.

2 medium fennel bulbs, trimmed and sliced
  lengthwise into thin strips (about 4 cups), plus
  1 tablespoon minced fennel fronds
¼ cup chopped red onion
¾ cup Mediterranean-style green olives, pitted
  and finely chopped
1 cup loosely packed fresh mint leaves, minced
3 tablespoons olive oil
3 tablespoons fresh lemon juice
2 teaspoons grated lemon peel
½ teaspoon salt
⅛ teaspoon ground black pepper

In large bowl, stir all ingredients. Cover and refriger-

ate if not serving right away. Makes about 5 cups or 6 accompaniment servings.

Each serving: About 95 calories, 1 g protein, 6 g carbohydrate, 9 g total fat (1 g saturated), 0 mg cholesterol, 460 mg sodium.

Crunchy Celery & Parsley Salad

····································

PREP: 40 MINUTES

Toss with our simple chive and shallot vinaigrette.

¼ cup olive oil
1 tablespoon white wine vinegar
1 teaspoon Dijon mustard
¼ teaspoon fennel seeds, crushed
¼ teaspoon salt
⅛ teaspoon coarsely ground black pepper

1 large shallot, minced (about ¼ cup)
1 garlic clove, minced
1 bunch flat-leaf parsley leaves (about 3 cups
    loosely packed)
1 bunch curly parsley leaves (about 3 cups
    loosely packed)
4 cups thinly sliced celery stalks with leaves
⅓ cup chopped fresh chives

1 In small bowl, with wire whisk, mix olive oil, vinegar, mustard, fennel seeds, salt, pepper, shallot, and garlic until blended.

2 In large salad bowl, toss parsley, celery, and chives with dressing. Makes 10 accompaniment servings.

Each serving: About 80 calories, 2 g protein, 6 g carbohydrate, 6 g total fat (1 g saturated), 0 mg cholesterol, 160 mg sodium.

Watermelon & Jicama Salad

PREP: 25 MINUTES PLUS CHILLING

Jicama is a slightly flattened round root vegetable with a thin brown skin and crunchy white flesh.

2 medium jicama (about 12 ounces each),
    peeled and cut into ¾-inch cubes
¼ cup fresh lime juice (about 2 limes)
½ teaspoon salt
1 piece watermelon (2½ pounds)
½ cup loosely packed fresh cilantro leaves,
    chopped
⅛ teaspoon ground red pepper (cayenne)
Lime slices for garnish

1 In large bowl, toss jicama with lime juice and salt; cover and refrigerate 30 minutes.

2 Meanwhile, cut rind from watermelon; discard rind. Cut flesh into ½-inch cubes to equal 4 cups; discard seeds.

3 To jicama, add watermelon, cilantro, and ground red pepper; toss well. Cover and refrigerate 15 minutes longer to allow flavors to blend. Garnish with lime slices. Makes about 8 cups or 12 accompaniment servings.

Each serving: About 40 calories, 1 g protein, 9 g carbohydrate, 0 g total fat, 0 mg cholesterol, 90 mg sodium.

Corn & Avocado Salad

PREP: 10 MINUTES

1 package (10 ounces) frozen whole-kernel corn,
    thawed
1 medium tomato, cut into ½-inch pieces
2 tablespoons chopped fresh cilantro leaves
2 tablespoons fresh lime juice
1 tablespoon olive oil
¼ teaspoon salt
¼ teaspoon sugar
1 medium avocado
Lettuce leaves (optional)

In medium bowl, combine all ingredients except avocado and lettuce. Just before serving, cut avocado in half; remove seed and peel. Cut avocado into ½-inch pieces; stir into corn mixture. Serve on lettuce leaves if you like. Makes 4 accompaniment servings.

Each serving: About 175 calories, 3 g protein, 20 g carbohydrate, 11 g total fat (2 g saturated), 0 mg cholesterol, 145 mg sodium.

Celery & Olive Salad

PREP: 15 MINUTES

A takeoff on the celery and olive mixture used in the famous—and beloved—New Orleans muffaletta sandwich.

1 cup drained giardiniera (Italian pickled mixed
    vegetables), coarsely chopped
6 large celery stalks with leaves, coarsely
    chopped (about 3 cups)
¼ cup pitted green olives, chopped
2 tablespoons olive oil
2 tablespoons fresh chopped Italian parsley
    leaves
1 garlic clove, minced
¼ teaspoon coarsely ground black pepper
Celery leaves for garnish

In large bowl, combine all ingredients; toss well. Cover and refrigerate if not serving right away. Garnish with celery leaves to serve. Makes about 4 cups or 6 accompaniment servings.

Each serving: About 70 calories, 1 g protein, 5 g carbohydrate, 5 g total fat (1 g saturated), 0 mg cholesterol, 565 mg sodium.

Two-Bean Salad

PREP: 15 MINUTES PLUS COOLING
COOK: ABOUT 10 MINUTES

Garden favorites tossed in a lemony dressing.

Salt
½ pound wax beans, trimmed
½ pound green beans, trimmed
1 medium lemon
1 tablespoon olive oil
⅛ teaspoon ground black pepper
⅛ teaspoon ground coriander
3 tablespoons minced fresh mint leaves

1 In 12-inch skillet, heat *1 inch water* and 1 teaspoon salt to boiling over high heat. Add beans and cook 8 to 10 minutes, until tender-crisp.

2 Meanwhile, from lemon, grate ½ teaspoon peel and squeeze 2 teaspoons juice.

3 Drain beans; transfer to bowl. Stir in olive oil, pepper, coriander, and ¼ teaspoon salt. Cool slightly.

4 Just before serving, stir in mint, lemon peel and lemon juice. Makes about 4 cups or 6 accompaniment servings.

Each serving: About 40 calories, 1 g protein, 5 g carbohydrate, 2 g total fat (0 g saturated), 0 mg cholesterol, 140 mg sodium.

Black-Eyed Pea Salad

PREP: 15 MINUTES • COOK: ABOUT 30 MINUTES

Black-eyed peas, also called cowpeas, are actually beans. Unlike most dried beans, they don't need to be soaked. Their short cooking time makes them a natural for summer salads.

1 package (16 ounces) dry black-eyed peas
⅓ cup cider vinegar
2 tablespoons olive oil
1 tablespoon cayenne pepper sauce*
2 teaspoons sugar
1½ teaspoons salt
2 medium celery stalks, diced
1 medium red onion, diced
1 package (10 ounces) frozen peas, thawed

1 Rinse black-eyed peas with cold running water and discard any stones or shriveled peas. In 8-quart Dutch oven, heat black-eyed peas and *12 cups water* to boiling over high heat. Reduce heat to low; cover and simmer 25 to 30 minutes, until peas are just tender.

2 Meanwhile, prepare dressing: In large bowl, with wire whisk or fork, mix vinegar, olive oil, pepper sauce, sugar, and salt until blended.

3 Drain black-eyed peas and rinse well. Gently toss warm black-eyed peas with dressing in bowl. Add celery, onion, and thawed peas. Serve salad at room temperature or cover and refrigerate until ready to serve. Makes 12 accompaniment servings.

*Cayenne pepper sauce is a milder variety of hot pepper sauce that adds tang and flavor, not just heat. It can be found in the condiment section of the supermarket.

Each serving: About 135 calories, 8 g protein, 21 g carbohydrate, 3 g total fat (1 g saturated), 0 mg cholesterol, 360 mg sodium.

Couscous Salad with Grapes & Thyme

PREP: 15 MINUTES • COOK: ABOUT 5 MINUTES

Green and red grapes, pine nuts, and fresh thyme liven up couscous.

1 package (10 ounces) couscous (Moroccan pasta)
1½ teaspoons fresh thyme leaves
¼ cup cider vinegar
2 tablespoons olive oil
1 teaspoon salt
1½ cups green and red seedless grapes (about ½ pound), each cut into quarters
½ cup pine nuts (pignoli), toasted
Thyme sprigs for garnish

1 Prepare couscous as label directs, but do not add salt or butter. Stir in thyme leaves with couscous.

2 In large bowl, mix vinegar, olive oil, and salt. Add grapes, pine nuts, and warm couscous; toss well to coat. Cover and refrigerate if not serving right away. Garnish with thyme sprigs to serve. Makes about 6 cups or 8 accompaniment servings.

Each serving: About 220 calories, 6 g protein, 34 g carbohydrate, 7 g total fat (1 g saturated), 0 mg cholesterol, 270 mg sodium.

Wheatberry Salad with Dried Cherries

PREP: 15 MINUTES • COOK: ABOUT 1¼ HOURS

Wheatberries, whole-wheat kernels that have not been milled or polished and have a robust, nutlike flavor, are available in healthfood stores.

2 cups wheatberries
1 large shallot, minced (about ¼ cup)
3 tablespoons fresh lemon juice
1 tablespoon Dijon mustard
1 tablespoon olive oil
2 teaspoons honey
1½ teaspoons salt
½ teaspoon coarsely ground black pepper
3 medium celery stalks, cut lengthwise in half, then cut crosswise into ¼-inch-thick slices
¾ cup dried tart cherries, chopped
½ cup chopped fresh Italian parsley leaves
Italian parsley sprigs and lettuce for garnish

Black-Eyed Pea Salad

1 In 4-quart saucepan, heat wheatberries and *8 cups water* to boiling over high heat. Reduce heat to low; cover and simmer 1½ hours or until wheatberries are just tender but still firm to the bite.

2 Meanwhile, in large bowl, with wire whisk or fork, mix shallot, lemon juice, Dijon mustard, olive oil, honey, salt, and pepper.

3 When wheatberries are cooked, drain well. Add warm wheatberries to dressing with celery, cherries, and chopped parsley; toss well. Serve salad at room temperature or cover and refrigerate until ready to serve. Garnish with parsley sprigs and lettuce. Makes 12 accompaniment servings.

Each serving: About 130 calories, 4 g protein, 26 g carbohydrate, 2 g total fat (0 g saturated), 0 mg cholesterol, 310 mg sodium.

Orzo with Sun-Dried Tomatoes

PREP: 10 MINUTES PLUS COOLING • COOK: 15 MINUTES

We used the tiny rice-shaped pasta to create an Italian summer salad.

1 package (16 ounces) orzo (rice-shaped pasta)
2 green onions, chopped
½ cup drained oil-packed sun-dried tomatoes with herbs, coarsely chopped, with 1 tablespoon oil from tomatoes reserved
2 tablespoons red wine vinegar
2 teaspoons Dijon mustard
½ teaspoon salt
¼ teaspoon coarsely ground black pepper
½ cup loosely packed fresh basil leaves, cut into thin strips

1 Prepare orzo in *boiling salted water* as label directs.

2 Meanwhile, in large bowl, combine green onions, tomatoes, reserved oil from tomatoes, vinegar, mustard, salt, and pepper.

3 Drain orzo. Add warm orzo to green-onion mixture in bowl, stirring to coat. Let orzo mixture cool slightly, then stir in basil. Cover and refrigerate if not serving right away. Makes about 7 cups or 8 accompaniment servings.

Each serving: About 240 calories, 8 g protein, 44 g carbohydrate, 4 g total fat (0 g saturated), 0 mg cholesterol, 220 mg sodium.

Red Potato Salad

PREP: 20 MINUTES PLUS COOLING
COOK: ABOUT 10 MINUTES

Extra-easy, because you don't have to peel the potatoes.

4 pounds small red potatoes, each cut into quarters (or eighths if large)
Salt
4 slices bacon
3 large shallots, chopped
⅓ cup cider vinegar
¼ cup olive oil
2 teaspoons sugar
2 teaspoons Dijon mustard
¼ teaspoon coarsely ground black pepper
2 green onions, chopped

1 In 5-quart saucepot, heat potatoes, 1 tablespoon salt, and enough *water* to cover to boiling over high heat. Reduce heat to low; cover and simmer 10 to 12 minutes, until potatoes are fork-tender.

2 Meanwhile, in 10-inch skillet, cook bacon over medium-low heat until browned. Transfer bacon to paper towels to drain. Discard all but 1 teaspoon bacon fat from skillet. Reduce heat to low. Add shallots and cook, stirring, until shallots are soft, about 5 minutes.

3 In large bowl, with wire whisk, mix shallots, vinegar, olive oil, sugar, mustard, pepper, and 1½ teaspoons salt.

4 Drain potatoes. Add hot potatoes to shallot dressing. With rubber spatula, stir gently to coat. Let potatoes cool at room temperature 30 minutes, stirring occasionally. Stir in green onions.

5 Serve salad at room temperature or cover and refrigerate until ready to serve. Sprinkle with crumbled bacon. Makes 12 accompaniment servings.

Each serving: About 170 calories, 4 g protein, 21 g carbohydrate, 6 g total fat (1 g saturated), 2 mg cholesterol, 375 mg sodium.

Basil Tabbouleh

PREP: 45 MINUTES PLUS STANDING

Raid the herb garden (or farmers' market) to make this hearty Middle Eastern salad.

¾ cup bulgur (cracked wheat)
2 ripe medium tomatoes
½ English (seedless) cucumber, unpeeled and diced
1 medium red onion, minced
1 cup loosely packed fresh Italian parsley leaves, chopped
1 cup loosely packed fresh mint leaves, chopped
¼ cup loosely packed fresh basil leaves, chopped
¼ cup extravirgin olive oil
¼ cup fresh lemon juice
1 teaspoon salt
¼ teaspoon ground allspice
⅛ teaspoon ground red pepper (cayenne)

1 In large bowl, combine bulgur with ¾ *cup boiling water*, stirring to mix. Let stand until liquid is absorbed, about 30 minutes.

2 Meanwhile, cut 2 thin wedges from 1 tomato; set aside for garnish. Discard seeds from remaining tomatoes; dice tomatoes.

3 When bulgur is ready, stir in diced tomatoes, cucumber, onion, parsley, mint, basil, olive oil, lemon juice, salt, allspice, and ground red pepper. Cover and refrigerate if not serving right away. Garnish with tomato wedges to serve. Makes about 5¼ cups or 6 accompaniment servings.

Each serving: About 170 calories, 3 g protein, 20 g carbohydrate, 10 g total fat (1 g saturated), 0 mg cholesterol, 370 mg sodium.

◄ *Red Potato Salad*

Asian Coconut Rice Salad

PREP: 15 MINUTES • COOK: ABOUT 22 MINUTES

We like this exotic salad made with regular coconut milk. But, if you prefer, use light coconut milk and save 2 grams of fat per serving.

1 tablespoon vegetable oil
2 tablespoons julienne strips peeled, fresh ginger (from about 1½" by 1" piece)
1½ cups regular long-grain rice
½ cup well-stirred canned unsweetened coconut milk (not cream of coconut)
½ teaspoon salt
¼ teaspoon hot pepper sauce
2 green onions, minced
3 tablespoons minced fresh cilantro leaves
2 tablespoons seasoned rice vinegar

1 In 2-quart saucepan, heat oil over medium-high heat until hot but not smoking. Add ginger and cook, stirring, 1 minute. Add rice and cook, stirring, 1 minute. Stir in coconut milk, salt, hot pepper sauce, and *2 cups water*; heat to boiling. Reduce heat to low; cover and simmer 18 to 20 minutes, until rice is tender and liquid is absorbed.

2 Transfer rice to bowl. Stir in green onions, cilantro, and vinegar. Cover and refrigerate if not serving the salad right away. Makes about 4 cups or 6 accompaniment servings.

Each serving: About 235 calories, 4 g protein, 41 g carbohydrate, 6 g total fat (3 g saturated), 0 mg cholesterol, 315 mg sodium.

FOOD EDITOR'S TIP

Q. What's the difference between coconut milk, cream of coconut, and coconut cream?

A. Coconut milk is made by processing equal amounts of coconut meat and water to a paste and straining out the milky liquid; light coconut milk has a higher water content, so it's lower in fat. Both types lend exotic flavor to curries and pasta dishes; look for cans in your store's ethnic food section. Cream of coconut, a sweeter, thicker version of coconut milk, contains added sugar and stabilizers. It's good in desserts and piña coladas. You'll find it where cocktail mixers are sold. Coconut cream, available in Asian and Hispanic specialty stores, is pressed and rehydrated coconut meat. It resembles vegetable shortening, and is used in some Asian and Caribbean cooking for deep-frying.

Tomato & Mint Tabbouleh

PREP: 35 MINUTES PLUS 1 HOUR TO CHILL

Serve this refreshing Middle-Eastern-style salad, made with cracked wheat, alongside grilled chicken or fish for an easy summer supper.

1½ cups bulgur (cracked wheat)
¼ cup fresh lemon juice
1 pound ripe tomatoes (about 3 medium)
1 medium cucumber (about 8 ounces)
3 green onions
¾ cup loosely packed fresh parsley leaves, chopped
½ cup loosely packed fresh mint leaves, chopped
1 tablespoon olive oil
¾ teaspoon salt
¼ teaspoon coarsely ground black pepper

1 In medium bowl, combine bulgur, lemon juice, and *1½ cups boiling water*, stirring to mix. Let stand until liquid is absorbed, about 30 minutes.

2 Meanwhile, cut tomatoes into ½-inch pieces. Peel and cut cucumber into ½-inch pieces. Chop green onions.

3 When bulgur mixture is ready, stir in remaining ingredients. Cover and refrigerate at least 1 hour or up to 24 hours to blend flavors. Makes 12 accompaniment servings.

Each serving: About 85 calories, 3 g protein, 16 g carbohydrate, 2 g total fat (0 g saturated), 0 mg cholesterol, 145 mg sodium.

LIGHT & HEALTHY

Chili Corn Chips

PREP: 5 MINUTES • BAKE: 8 TO 10 MINUTES

¼ teaspoon ground cumin
¼ teaspoon chili powder
⅛ teaspoon salt
4 low-fat corn tortillas (6 inch)
Nonstick cooking spray

1 Preheat oven to 400°F.

2 In cup, mix cumin, chili powder, and salt. Spray 1 side of each tortilla with nonstick cooking spray; sprinkle with chili-powder mixture.

3 Cut each tortilla into 8 wedges and place on ungreased large cookie sheet. Bake tortillas 8 to 10 minutes, until crisp; cool on wire rack. If not serving right away, store in tightly covered container. Makes 32 chips or 4 servings.

Each serving: About 60 calories, 2 g protein, 11 g carbohydrate, 1 g total fat (0 g saturated), 0 mg cholesterol, 110 mg sodium.

10 GUILT-FREE BEFORE-DINNER SNACKS

• Celery stuffed with nonfat bean dip

• Dried fruit (apple rings, strawberries, cherries, cranberries, apricots, or raisins)

• Fat-free cinnamon-raisin bagel chips

• Fresh tangerine or clementine sections

• Low-fat caramel or Cheddar popcorn cakes or rice cakes

• 1% or skim milk with chocolate syrup

• Pretzel sticks or whole-grain pretzels

• Red- or green-pepper strips, cucumber spears, or peeled baby carrots with salsa

• Reduced-fat mozzarella string cheese

• Toasted pita wedges with shredded reduced-fat cheese melted on top

Penne with Caramelized Onions & Radicchio

PREP: 15 MINUTES • COOK: 20 MINUTES

1 package (16 ounces) penne or ziti pasta
Salt
1 large head (8 ounces) radicchio
2 teaspoons olive oil
1 jumbo onion (1 pound), thinly sliced
1 tablespoon balsamic vinegar
¼ teaspoon coarsely ground black pepper
1 cup frozen peas, thawed
¼ cup crumbled ricotta salata or goat cheese

1 In saucepot, prepare penne as label directs in *boiling salted water*. Drain penne, reserving *¼ cup pasta cooking water*. Return penne to saucepot.

2 Meanwhile, cut radicchio lengthwise in half. Remove core, then cut crosswise into ½-inch slices. Set aside. In nonstick 12-inch skillet, heat olive oil over medium heat until hot. Add onion and cook until browned and soft, about 15 minutes, stirring occasionally. Add vinegar, pepper, and ½ teaspoon salt; cook 1 minute longer. Increase heat to medium-high; add radicchio and cook 2 to 3 minutes, until wilted.

3 Add onion mixture, peas, and reserved pasta cooking water to penne; toss to mix well. Serve sprinkled with cheese. Makes 4 main-dish servings.

Each serving: About 550 calories, 20 g protein, 104 g carbohydrate, 6 g total fat (2 g saturated), 3 mg cholesterol, 510 mg sodium.

Vegetable Lo Mein

PREP: 20 MINUTES • COOK: 20 MINUTES

1 package (16 ounces) linguine or spaghetti
⅓ cup hoisin sauce
2 tablespoons reduced-sodium soy sauce
½ teaspoon cornstarch
3 teaspoons vegetable oil
1 package (10 ounces) sliced mushrooms
1 tablespoon grated, peeled fresh ginger
1 package (10 ounces) shredded carrots

3 small zucchini (about 6 ounces each), each
  cut lengthwise in half, then cut crosswise into
  ¼-inch-thick slices
3 green onions, cut into 1-inch pieces
1 cup reduced-sodium chicken broth
2 tablespoons seasoned rice vinegar

1 Prepare linguine as label directs but do not use salt.

2 Meanwhile, in cup, stir hoisin sauce, soy sauce, and cornstarch until smooth; set aside.

3 In nonstick 12-inch skillet, heat 2 teaspoons vegetable oil over medium-high heat until hot. Add mushrooms and cook about 5 minutes or until mushrooms are golden and liquid evaporates, stirring frequently. Stir in ginger; cook 30 seconds. Remove mushroom mixture to bowl.

4 In same skillet, in remaining 1 teaspoon vegetable oil, cook carrots 2 minutes, stirring frequently. Stir in zucchini and green onions and cook about 10 minutes longer or until vegetables are tender-crisp. Stir in chicken broth, cornstarch mixture, and mushroom mixture. Heat to boiling; cook 1 minute.

5 To serve, toss linguine, cooked vegetable mixture, and rice vinegar together in large serving bowl. Makes 4 main-dish servings.

Each serving: About 570 calories, 20 g protein, 111 g carbohydrate, 7 g total fat (1 g saturated), 0 mg cholesterol, 970 mg sodium.

Moo Shu Turkey

• •
PREP: 20 MINUTES • COOK: ABOUT 15 MINUTES

The Rosemary Roast Turkey (page 158) adds an especially nice and unexpected flavor to this Asian-inspired dish. However, any leftover skinless roast turkey meat would be fine.

8 low-fat flour tortillas (6 inch)
3 tablespoons hoisin sauce
2 tablespoons soy sauce
¾ teaspoon Asian sesame oil
1 bunch green onions
3 teaspoons olive oil
1 package (8 ounces) sliced mushrooms
1 package (16 ounces) shredded cabbage mix
  for coleslaw
½ medium red pepper, thinly sliced
1 garlic clove, crushed with garlic press

2 teaspoons grated, peeled fresh ginger
12 ounces leftover skinless Rosemary Roast
  Turkey meat (page 158), pulled into shreds
  (2 cups)

1 Warm tortillas as label directs.

2 Meanwhile, in small bowl, mix hoisin sauce, soy sauce, and sesame oil until smooth; set aside. Thinly slice 3 green onions; reserve remaining green onions for garnish.

3 In nonstick 12-inch skillet, heat 1 teaspoon olive oil over medium-high heat. Add mushrooms and cook until all liquid evaporates and mushrooms are browned, about 8 minutes; remove mushrooms to bowl.

4 In same skillet, in remaining 2 teaspoons olive oil, cook cabbage mix, red pepper, and sliced green onions 3 minutes, stirring constantly. Add garlic and ginger; cook 1 minute, stirring constantly. Stir in shredded turkey, hoisin-sauce mixture, and mushrooms; heat through.

5 To serve, spoon turkey mixture onto warm tortillas and roll up. Garnish with reserved green onions. Makes 4 main-dish servings.

Each serving: About 405 calories, 35 g protein, 53 g carbohydrate, 7 g total fat (1 g saturated), 71 mg cholesterol, 1140 mg sodium.

Sautéed Turkey Cutlets with Mushroom Sauce

• •
PREP: ABOUT 15 MINUTES • COOK: ABOUT 15 MINUTES

1¼ pounds turkey cutlets
¼ teaspoon salt
¼ teaspoon coarsely ground black pepper
4 teaspoons olive oil
1 garlic clove, crushed with garlic press
1 pound mushrooms, sliced
¼ teaspoon dried thyme leaves
1 cup chicken broth
1 teaspoon cornstarch

1 Sprinkle turkey cutlets with salt and pepper. In nonstick 12-inch skillet, heat 2 teaspoons of olive oil over medium-high heat until hot. Add turkey cutlets and cook 3 to 5 minutes, turning cutlets once, until lightly browned on the outside and they just lose their pink color on the inside. Transfer cutlets to warm platter; cover and keep warm.

2 In same skillet, heat remaining 2 teaspoons olive oil over medium heat until hot. Add garlic and cook 10 seconds. Add mushrooms and thyme and cook 10 minutes longer or until mushrooms are golden and liquid evaporates. In cup, mix chicken broth and cornstarch until smooth. Add chicken-broth mixture to skillet and heat to boiling. Cook 2 minutes. Spoon sauce over cutlets. Makes 4 main-dish servings.

Each serving: About 245 calories, 37 g protein, 6 g carbohydrate, 8 g total fat (2 g saturated), 85 mg cholesterol, 420 mg sodium.

Rosemary Roast Turkey

PREP: 20 MINUTES • ROAST: 2¼ TO 2½ HOURS

Enjoy this lean meat the night you roast it. Then turn the leftovers into Moo Shu Turkey (page 157) and/or our Tex-Mex Cobb Salad (at right).

1 fresh or frozen (thawed) turkey breast (about 6½ pounds)
1½ teaspoons dried rosemary leaves, crushed
1 teaspoon salt
¾ teaspoon coarsely ground black pepper
1 cup chicken broth
Rosemary sprigs for garnish

1 Preheat oven to 350°F.

2 Rinse turkey breast with cold running water and drain well. In cup, combine rosemary, salt, and pepper. With hands, rub rosemary mixture all over turkey breast.

3 Place turkey breast in 13" by 9" roasting pan. Cover pan loosely with foil. Roast turkey breast 1½ hours.

4 Remove foil. Roast turkey breast 45 to 60 minutes longer, occasionally brushing breast with pan drippings. Start checking turkey breast for doneness during last 30 minutes of cooking. Turkey breast is done when thermometer inserted into breast (being careful that pointed end of thermometer does not touch bone) reaches 170°F.

5 When turkey breast is done, transfer to warm, large platter. Let stand 10 minutes.

6 Meanwhile, pour chicken broth into drippings in hot roasting pan, stirring to loosen brown bits from bottom of pan. Strain pan-juice mixture into small

saucepan; let stand 1 minute. Skim fat and discard. Reheat and serve pan-juice mixture with turkey. Remove skin from turkey before eating if you like. Garnish with rosemary sprigs. Makes 12 main-dish servings.

Each serving of turkey without skin and with pan juices: About 200 calories, 44 g protein, 0 g carbohydrate, 1 g total fat (0 g saturated), 120 mg cholesterol, 320 mg sodium.

Tex-Mex Cobb Salad

PREP: 30 MINUTES

Make this with the Rosemary Roast Turkey (at left) as suggested, or use any skinless roast turkey in its place.

¼ cup fresh lime juice
2 tablespoons chopped fresh cilantro leaves
4 teaspoons olive oil
1 teaspoon sugar
¼ teaspoon ground cumin
¼ teaspoon salt
¼ teaspoon coarsely ground black pepper
1 medium head romaine lettuce (about 1¼ pounds), trimmed and leaves cut into ½-inch-wide strips
1 pint cherry tomatoes, each cut into quarters
12 ounces leftover skinless Rosemary Roast Turkey meat (at left), cut into ½-inch pieces (2 cups)
1 can (15 to 19 ounces) black beans, rinsed and drained
2 small cucumbers (6 ounces each), peeled, seeded, and sliced ½ inch thick

1 Prepare dressing: In small bowl, with wire whisk, combine lime juice, cilantro, olive oil, sugar, cumin, salt, and black pepper.

2 Place lettuce in large serving bowl. Arrange tomatoes, turkey, black beans, and cucumbers in rows over lettuce to cover.

3 Just before serving, toss the salad with the dressing. Makes 4 main-dish servings.

Each serving: About 310 calories, 39 g protein, 32 g carbohydrate, 7 g total fat (1 g saturated), 71 mg cholesterol, 505 mg sodium.

Spicy Thai Chicken

••
PREP: 20 MINUTES • COOK: 10 MINUTES

Asian fish sauce (*nuoc nam*) brings a special salty undertone to Thai and Vietnamese cooking. The thin, translucent, brown liquid—extracted from salted, fermented fish—can be purchased in the Asian section of some grocery stores, but if you can't find it, increase the soy sauce to 2 tablespoons.

3 tablespoons Asian fish sauce (nuoc nam)
1 tablespoon soy sauce
1 tablespoon brown sugar
4 small skinless, boneless chicken-breast halves
    (4 ounces each), sliced crosswise into ¼-inch-
    thick slices
2 teaspoons vegetable oil
1 large onion (12 ounces), cut into ¼-inch-thick
    slices
2 red or green chiles (serrano or jalapeño),
    seeded and cut into matchstick-thin strips
2 teaspoons minced, peeled fresh ginger
2 garlic cloves, crushed with garlic press
1½ cups loosely packed fresh basil leaves
Basil sprigs for garnish

1 In medium bowl, combine fish sauce, soy sauce, and brown sugar; stir in chicken slices to coat. Let marinate 5 minutes.

2 In nonstick 12-inch skillet, heat vegetable oil over medium-high heat until very hot. Add chicken with marinade and cook, stirring occasionally, until chicken slices lose their pink color throughout, about 3 to 4 minutes. With slotted spoon, remove chicken to plate.

3 Add onion to marinade remaining in skillet and cook, stirring occasionally, until tender-crisp, about 4 minutes. Stir in chiles, ginger, and garlic; cook 1 minute longer.

4 Return chicken to skillet; heat through. Stir in basil leaves just before serving. Garnish with basil sprigs. Makes 4 main-dish servings.

Each serving: About 205 calories, 28 g protein, 14 g carbohydrate, 4 g total fat (1 g saturated), 66 mg cholesterol, 595 mg sodium.

Scrod with Tomatoes & Capers

••
PREP: 10 MINUTES • BAKE: 15 TO 20 MINUTES

4 pieces scrod fillet (6 ounces each)
¼ teaspoon coarsely ground black pepper
1 can (14½ ounces) stewed tomatoes, drained
    well
⅓ cup pitted green olives, chopped
2 tablespoons capers, drained and chopped
2 tablespoons dry vermouth or dry white wine
    (optional)
Lemon wedges

1 Preheat oven to 400°F. With tweezers, remove any small bones from scrod.

2 Place scrod in shallow 2½-quart casserole; sprinkle with pepper. Spoon tomatoes over scrod and top each piece with olives and capers. Pour vermouth over scrod if you like.

3 Bake scrod, uncovered, 15 to 20 minutes, until fish flakes easily when tested with a fork. Serve with lemon wedges to squeeze over scrod. Makes 4 main-dish servings.

Each serving: About 170 calories, 31 g protein, 5 g carbohydrate, 3 g total fat (0 g saturated), 74 mg cholesterol, 670 mg sodium.

■ FOOD EDITOR'S TIP ■

Q. What is the difference between cod and scrod?

A. Cod is a family of fish. Scrod is a small, young codfish (under 3 pounds). Sometimes, scrod is also used as a general label for other small members of the cod family, including pollack, haddock, hake, and whiting. All of these varieties—plus sea bass, halibut, and flounder—are interchangeable with cod in recipes. But remember to adjust cooking times accordingly because the smaller and thinner the fish, the faster it cooks. The general rule for any fish without sauce is 10 minutes cooking per inch of thickness.

Chili-Spiced Cod

PREP: 5 MINUTES • COOK: 10 MINUTES

This fish dish is the centerpiece of a light weeknight meal designed by Marianne Marinelli, test kitchen associate at GH. To accompany the fish, serve a simple tossed salad, flatbread crisps, and halved kiwifruit.

1 tablespoon yellow cornmeal
1 tablespoon all-purpose flour
1 tablespoon chili powder
1 teaspoon salt
4 cod fillets (about 6 ounces each)
2 tablespoons margarine or butter (¼ stick)

1 On waxed paper, combine cornmeal, flour, chili powder, and salt; use to coat cod fillets.

2 Heat nonstick 12-inch skillet until hot over medium-high heat. Add 1 tablespoon margarine or butter; let melt. Add cod fillets and cook 4 minutes. Reduce heat to medium; turn fillets. Add remaining 1 tablespoon margarine or butter and cook cod 4 to 6 minutes longer, until fish flakes easily when tested with a fork. Makes 4 main-dish servings.

Each serving: About 210 calories, 31 g protein, 4 g carbohydrate, 7 g total fat (1 g saturated), 74 mg cholesterol, 720 mg sodium.

Peruvian Fisherman's Soup

PREP: 30 MINUTES • COOK: 25 MINUTES

A true treat for seafood lovers, this is more than just a soup. It's the main course and side dish all wrapped into one wonderfully flavorful meal in a bowl.

1 tablespoon vegetable oil
1 medium onion, finely chopped
2 garlic cloves, minced
2 serrano or jalapeño chiles, seeded and minced
1 pound red potatoes, cut into ¾-inch chunks
3 bottles (8 ounces each) clam juice
¾ teaspoon salt
⅛ teaspoon dried thyme leaves
1 lime

◄ *Peruvian Fisherman's Soup*

1 pound monkfish, dark membrane removed, cut into 1-inch pieces
1 pound medium shrimp, shelled and deveined, leaving tail part of shell on if you like
¼ cup chopped fresh cilantro leaves

1 In 4-quart saucepan, heat oil over medium heat until hot. Add onion and cook, stirring often, 10 minutes or until tender. Stir in garlic and serrano chiles and cook 30 seconds. Add potatoes, clam juice, salt, thyme, and 2 *cups water*; heat to boiling over high heat. Reduce heat to medium; cook 10 minutes.

2 Cut lime in half; cut half into wedges and set aside. Add other lime half and monkfish to soup; cover and cook 5 minutes. Stir in shrimp and cook 3 to 5 minutes longer, just until shrimp turn opaque throughout.

3 Remove lime half, squeezing juice into soup. Sprinkle soup with cilantro; serve with lime wedges. Makes about 11 cups or 6 main-dish servings.

Each serving: About 215 calories, 26 g protein, 16 g carbohydrate, 5 g total fat (1 g saturated), 117 mg cholesterol, 640 mg sodium.

Cajun Shrimp

PREP: 10 MINUTES • COOK: 3 TO 4 MINUTES

1 teaspoon paprika
½ teaspoon dried thyme leaves
¼ teaspoon salt
¼ teaspoon ground red pepper
⅛ teaspoon ground nutmeg
2 teaspoons olive oil
1 garlic clove, crushed with side of chef's knife
12 extralarge shrimp (about ½ pound), shelled and deveined

1 In cup, combine paprika, thyme, salt, red pepper, and nutmeg.

2 In nonstick 10-inch skillet, heat olive oil over medium-high heat until hot. Add garlic; cook 1 minute. Discard garlic. Add spice mixture and cook 30 seconds, stirring constantly. Add shrimp, stirring to coat evenly with spices, and cook 2 to 3 minutes, until shrimp turn opaque throughout, stirring frequently. Makes 2 main-dish servings.

Each serving: About 145 calories, 19 g protein, 2 g carbohydrate, 6 g total fat (1 g saturated), 142 mg cholesterol, 405 mg sodium.

Toasted-Sesame Salmon

PREP: 10 MINUTES • COOK: 8 TO 10 MINUTES

1 egg white
3 tablespoons sesame seeds, lightly toasted
½ teaspoon salt
¼ teaspoon coarsely ground black pepper
4 pieces center-cut salmon fillet with skin (4 ounces each)
Lemon slices (optional)

1 In small bowl, lightly beat egg white with *1 tablespoon water*. On waxed paper, mix sesame seeds, salt, and pepper. Dip flesh side of each piece of salmon fillet in egg-white mixture, then dip same side in sesame-seed mixture to coat.

2 Heat nonstick 10-inch skillet over medium-high heat until hot. Add salmon fillets, sesame-seed side down, and cook 3 minutes. With pancake turner, turn salmon over and cook 5 to 7 minutes longer, until fish flakes easily when tested with a fork. Serve salmon with lemon slices if you like. Makes 4 main-dish servings.

Each serving: About 220 calories, 21 g protein, 2 g carbohydrate, 14 g total fat (3 g saturated), 54 mg cholesterol, 335 mg sodium.

Jamaican Jerk Catfish with Grilled Pineapple

PREP: 15 MINUTES • GRILL: 10 TO 12 MINUTES

Other fish fillets like sole and flounder work well with these zesty flavors too.

2 green onions, chopped
1 jalapeño chile, seeded and chopped
2 tablespoons white wine vinegar
2 tablespoons Worcestershire sauce
1 tablespoon minced, peeled fresh ginger
1 tablespoon vegetable oil
1¼ teaspoons dried thyme leaves
1 teaspoon ground allspice
¼ teaspoon salt
4 catfish fillets (about 5 ounces each)

1 small pineapple, cut lengthwise into 4 wedges
   or crosswise into ½-inch-thick slices
2 tablespoons brown sugar

1 In medium bowl, mix green onions, jalapeño chile, vinegar, Worcestershire, ginger, vegetable oil, thyme, allspice, and salt until combined. Add catfish fillets to bowl, turning to coat; let stand 5 minutes.

2 Meanwhile, rub pineapple wedges or slices with brown sugar.

3 Place pineapple and catfish fillets on grill. Spoon half of jerk mixture remaining in bowl on catfish. Cook pineapple and catfish 5 minutes. Turn over pineapple and catfish. Spoon remaining jerk mixture on fish and cook 5 to 7 minutes longer, until fish flakes easily when tested with a fork, and pineapple is golden brown. Makes 4 main-dish servings.

Each serving: About 300 calories, 22 g protein, 25 g carbohydrate, 13 g total fat (2 g saturated), 72 mg cholesterol, 305 mg sodium.

Greek Shrimp & Potatoes

PREP: 25 MINUTES • COOK: 40 MINUTES

Simple and satisfying, with garlic, canned tomatoes, fresh dill, and crumbled feta—yet only 310 calories per serving.

2 teaspoons olive oil
1 large onion, chopped
1½ pounds all-purpose potatoes, peeled and cut
   into 1-inch chunks
1 large garlic clove, crushed with garlic press
⅛ teaspoon ground red pepper (cayenne)
½ teaspoon salt
1 can (14½ ounces) diced tomatoes
1 pound large shrimp, shelled and deveined
2 tablespoons chopped fresh dill
2 ounces crumbled feta cheese (about ½ cup)

1 In nonstick 10-inch skillet, heat oil over medium heat. Add onion and cook, stirring often, about 10 minutes or until tender.

2 Add potatoes, garlic, and ground red pepper, and cook 30 seconds. Stir in salt and *1 cup water*; heat to boiling over high heat. Cover and simmer over low heat 15 minutes or until potatoes are tender.

3 Add tomatoes with their juice; heat to boiling over high heat. Cover and simmer over low heat 5 minutes. Remove cover; simmer 5 minutes longer.

4 Stir in shrimp; heat to boiling over high heat. Cover and simmer over low heat 3 to 5 minutes, until shrimp turn opaque throughout. Remove skillet from heat; stir in chopped dill and feta cheese. Spoon into bowls to serve. Makes 4 main-dish servings.

Each serving: About 310 calories, 25 g protein, 36 g carbohydrate, 7 g total fat (3 g saturated), 155 mg cholesterol, 740 mg sodium.

Thai Shrimp

PREP: 30 MINUTES • COOK: 15 MINUTES

2 medium limes
3 teaspoons vegetable oil
1 small onion, finely chopped
1 small red pepper, thinly sliced
2 teaspoons grated, peeled fresh ginger
⅛ to ¼ teaspoon ground red pepper (cayenne)
4 ounces medium mushrooms, quartered
½ teaspoon salt
1 can (13¾ to 15 ounces) light coconut milk*
1 pound large shrimp, shelled and deveined
2 ounces snow peas, cut into thin strips
⅓ cup loosely packed fresh cilantro leaves

1 With vegetable peeler, peel six 1" by ¾" strips of peel from limes, then squeeze 2 tablespoons juice. In nonstick 12-inch skillet, heat 2 teaspoons vegetable oil over medium heat until hot. Add onion and cook 5 minutes or until tender; add sliced red pepper and cook 1 minute. Stir in ginger and ground red pepper; cook 1 minute. Remove onion mixture to small bowl.

2 In same skillet, heat remaining 1 teaspoon vegetable oil over medium-high heat until hot. Add mushrooms and salt and cook until tender and lightly browned, about 3 minutes. Add coconut milk, lime peel, lime juice, and onion mixture and heat to boiling. Add shrimp and cook until shrimp turn opaque throughout. Stir in snow peas; heat through. Stir in cilantro. Makes 4 main-dish servings.

*See "Food Editor's Tip" on page 154 for an explanation of coconut milk, which is available in Asian or Hispanic grocery stores and some supermarkets.

Each serving: About 425 calories, 25 g protein, 47 g carbohydrate, 14 g total fat (6 g saturated), 142 mg cholesterol, 420 mg sodium.

Shrimp & Scallop Kabobs

PREP: 20 MINUTES • GRILL: 6 TO 8 MINUTES

1 pound large shrimp
¾ pound large sea scallops
3 tablespoons soy sauce
3 tablespoons seasoned rice vinegar
2 tablespoons grated, peeled fresh ginger
1 tablespoon brown sugar
1 tablespoon Asian sesame oil
2 garlic cloves, crushed with garlic press
1 bunch green onions, cut diagonally into
   3-inch-long pieces
12 cherry tomatoes

1 Shell and devein shrimp, leaving tail part of shell on if you like; rinse with cold running water. Rinse scallops well to remove sand from crevices. Pat shrimp and scallops dry with paper towels.

2 In large bowl, mix soy sauce, rice vinegar, ginger, brown sugar, sesame oil, and garlic; add shrimp and scallops, tossing to coat.

3 Onto 6 long metal skewers, alternately thread shrimp, scallops, green onions, and cherry tomatoes. Place skewers on grill over medium heat; cook 6 to 8 minutes, until shrimp and scallops turn opaque

throughout, turning skewers occasionally and dabbing shrimp and scallops with any remaining soy mixture halfway through cooking. Makes 6 main-dish servings.

Each serving: About 150 calories, 22 g protein, 10 g carbohydrate, 3 g total fat (0 g saturated), 119 mg cholesterol, 710 mg sodium.

Chili Scallops with Black-Bean Salsa

PREP: 15 MINUTES • COOK: 3 TO 6 MINUTES

1 can (15 to 19 ounces) black beans, rinsed and
   drained
1 can (15¼ to 16 ounces) whole-kernel corn,
   drained
¼ cup finely chopped red onion
¼ cup loosely packed fresh cilantro leaves,
   chopped
2 tablespoons fresh lime juice
½ teaspoon salt
1 pound sea scallops
1 tablespoon chili powder
1 teaspoon sugar
2 teaspoons vegetable oil
Cilantro leaves and hot red chiles for garnish
Lime wedges (optional)

1 In large bowl, mix black beans, corn, onion, chopped cilantro, lime juice, and ¼ teaspoon salt. Set black-bean salsa aside.

2 Rinse scallops with cold running water to remove sand from crevices; pat dry with paper towels. In medium bowl, mix chili powder, sugar, and remaining ¼ teaspoon salt; add scallops, tossing to coat.

3 In nonstick 12-inch skillet, heat vegetable oil over medium-high heat until very hot. Add scallops and cook 3 to 6 minutes until scallops are lightly browned on the outside and turn opaque throughout, turning once.

4 Arrange black-bean salsa and scallops on 4 dinner plates; garnish with cilantro leaves and red chiles. Serve with lime wedges if you like. Makes 4 main-dish servings.

Each serving: About 290 calories, 31 g protein, 40 g carbohydrate, 5 g total fat (1 g saturated), 38 mg cholesterol, 1005 mg sodium.

■ FOOD EDITOR'S TIP ■

Q. My market sells saffron threads, which are pretty pricey, and powdered saffron. What's the difference?

A. Saffron threads come from purple crocuses grown in Spain, Turkey, and India; they are the slender shoots (stigmas) plucked from the center of each bloom and dried. Each crocus yields only 3 stigmas, and it takes about 200,000 to make a pound of saffron—the most expensive spice in the world (up to $70 per ounce). Ground saffron is usually a blend of saffron, turmeric, and bulking agents. Because saffron threads taste better than ground saffron and a little goes a long way (our Mussels in Saffron-Tomato Broth, on opposite page, calls for a scant ½ teaspoon), it's worth using the threads. But don't add more than a recipe specifies, or the dish may have a medicinal flavor.

Mussels in Saffron-Tomato Broth

PREP: 20 MINUTES • COOK: 30 MINUTES

3 tablespoons olive oil
2 garlic cloves, crushed with side of chef's knife
1 small bay leaf
½ teaspoon loosely packed saffron threads
⅛ to ¼ teaspoon crushed red pepper
1 can (14½ ounces) diced tomatoes
1 bottle (8 ounces) clam juice
½ cup dry white wine
5 dozen medium mussels, scrubbed and beards removed
Chopped fresh parsley leaves for garnish

1 In 8-quart saucepot, heat olive oil over medium heat. Add garlic and cook until golden. Add bay leaf, saffron threads, and crushed red pepper; cook, stirring, 1 minute.

2 Add tomatoes with their liquid, clam juice, and wine; heat to boiling over high heat. Reduce heat to low; cover and simmer 20 minutes.

3 Add mussels; heat to boiling over high heat. Reduce heat to medium; cover and cook 5 minutes or until mussels open. Discard bay leaf and any mussels that do not open. Garnish with chopped parsley if you like. Makes 4 main-dish servings.

Each serving: About 220 calories, 15 g protein, 10 g carbohydrate, 13 g total fat (2 g saturated), 34 mg cholesterol, 795 mg sodium.

Honey-Soy Glazed Pork Chops

PREP: 10 MINUTES • COOK: 15 MINUTES

4 boneless pork loin chops, cut ¾ inch thick (about 4 ounces each), trimmed
¼ teaspoon coarsely ground black pepper
3 tablespoons honey
2 tablespoons soy sauce
1 tablespoon balsamic vinegar
½ teaspoon cornstarch
1 garlic clove, minced
2 green onions, sliced, for garnish

1 Sprinkle 1 side of each chop with black pepper.

2 Heat nonstick 12-inch skillet over medium-high heat until hot. Add pork chops, pepper side down, and cook about 4 minutes or until browned. Reduce heat to medium. Turn pork chops and cook 6 to 8 minutes longer, until they just lose their pink color throughout. Transfer pork chops to platter; cover with foil to keep warm.

3 Meanwhile, in cup, mix honey, soy sauce, balsamic vinegar, and cornstarch until smooth.

4 Add garlic to skillet; cook 30 seconds, stirring. Stir honey mixture into skillet (mixture will boil) and cook 1 minute, stirring. Spoon sauce over pork chops. Sprinkle with green onions for garnish if you like. Makes 4 main-dish servings.

Each serving: About 230 calories, 25 g protein, 15 g carbohydrate, 7 g total fat (3 g saturated), 61 mg cholesterol, 585 mg sodium.

BBQ Pork Sandwiches

PREP: 10 MINUTES • BROIL: 15 TO 20 MINUTES

3 tablespoons light molasses
3 tablespoons catchup
1 tablespoon Worcestershire sauce
1 teaspoon minced, peeled fresh ginger
½ teaspoon grated lemon peel
1 garlic clove, crushed with garlic press
2 whole pork tenderloins (¾ pound each)
12 small, soft dinner rolls

1 Preheat broiler. In medium bowl, combine molasses, catchup, Worcestershire, ginger, lemon peel, and garlic; add pork, turning to coat.

2 Place pork on rack in broiling pan. Spoon any remaining molasses mixture over pork tenderloins. With broiling pan 5 to 7 inches from source of heat, broil pork 15 to 20 minutes, turning pork once, until meat is browned on the outside and still slightly pink in the center (internal temperature of tenderloins should be 160°F. on meat thermometer).

3 To serve, thinly slice pork. Serve on rolls with any juices from broiling pan. Makes 6 main-dish servings.

Each serving: About 390 calories, 32 g protein, 35 g carbohydrate, 13 g total fat (4 g saturated), 70 mg cholesterol, 360 mg sodium.

Sunday Baked Ziti & Meatball Casserole

PREP: 30 MINUTES • BAKE: 25 MINUTES

This recipe was designed to use Lean Meatballs (page 168) that were made ahead and frozen. To thaw the meatballs, place frozen meatballs in refrigerator overnight. Or, unwrap the frozen meatballs and place them on a microwave-safe plate. In the microwave, cook them on Medium (50 percent power) for 2 to 4 minutes, until just thawed.

1 package (16 ounces) ziti or penne pasta
Salt
4 cups Big-Batch Tomato Sauce (page 243)
1 large egg
1 container (15 ounces) part-skim ricotta cheese
2 tablespoons grated Parmesan cheese
1 tablespoon chopped fresh parsley
¼ teaspoon coarsely ground black pepper
8 frozen Lean Meatballs (page 168), thawed and sliced
1 package (4 ounces) shredded part-skim mozzarella cheese (1 cup)

1 In saucepot, prepare pasta as label directs in *boiling salted water*; drain. Return pasta to saucepot.

2 Meanwhile, in 3-quart saucepan, heat tomato sauce, covered, until hot over medium-low heat. (If tomato sauce is frozen, add *2 tablespoons water* to saucepan to prevent scorching.) Add 3 cups sauce to pasta in saucepot; toss well. Reserve remaining 1 cup sauce.

3 In medium bowl, stir together egg, ricotta cheese, Parmesan cheese, parsley, ½ teaspoon of salt, and the pepper.

4 Preheat oven to 400°F. Into 3½- to 4-quart shallow casserole or 13" by 9" glass baking dish, spoon half the pasta mixture; top with all the sliced meatballs. Drop ricotta-cheese mixture by spoonfuls evenly over meatball layer. Spoon remaining pasta mixture over ricotta-cheese layer, then spoon remaining 1 cup sauce over pasta. Sprinkle with shredded mozzarella cheese.

5 Bake, uncovered, 25 minutes or until very hot and cheese browns slightly. Makes 8 main-dish servings.

Each serving: About 470 calories, 29 g protein, 55 g carbohydrate, 13 g total fat (5 g saturated), 79 mg cholesterol, 1040 mg sodium.

School-Night Meatball Soup

PREP: 20 MINUTES PLUS THAWING • COOK: 15 MINUTES

As with the Sunday Baked Ziti & Meatball Casserole (at left), this soup uses meatballs that are made ahead and frozen. To thaw, place in the refrigerator overnight. Or, unwrap and microwave on Medium (50 percent power) for 2 to 4 minutes, until just thawed.

½ cup regular long-grain rice
2 cans (13¾ to 14½ ounces each) chicken broth
3 medium carrots, sliced
3 medium celery stalks, sliced
5 ounces prewashed spinach (half 10-ounce bag)
8 frozen Lean Meatballs (page 168), thawed and sliced
Shredded or grated Parmesan cheese (optional)

1 In 1-quart saucepan, heat *1 cup water* to boiling over high heat. Add rice; heat to boiling. Reduce heat to low; cover and simmer 15 to 20 minutes, until water is absorbed and rice is tender.

2 Meanwhile, in 4-quart saucepan, heat chicken broth and *2 cups water* to boiling over high heat. Add carrots and celery; heat to boiling. Reduce heat to low; cover and simmer 5 to 7 minutes, until vegetables are tender.

3 Stir in spinach, rice, and sliced meatballs; heat through. Serve soup with Parmesan cheese if you like. Makes about 10 cups or 4 main-dish servings.

Each serving without Parmesan cheese: About 300 calories, 25 g protein, 30 g carbohydrate, 7 g total fat (3 g saturated), 51 mg cholesterol, 1010 mg sodium.

Clockwise from top: Big-Batch Tomato Sauce (page 243), School-Night Meatball Soup, Sunday Baked Ziti & Meatball Casserole ➤

Lean Meatballs

PREP: 25 MINUTES • BAKE: 15 TO 20 MINUTES

Great to have on hand for weeknight meals. To freeze, let cool in jelly-roll pan on wire rack. When cool, freeze in pan. Then place in large self-sealing plastic bag and freeze for up to 1 month.

3 slices firm white bread, diced
1 pound lean ground beef
1 pound lean ground turkey
2 large egg whites
⅓ cup grated Romano or Parmesan cheese
3 tablespoons grated onion
2 tablespoons minced fresh parsley
1 teaspoon salt
¼ teaspoon coarsely ground black pepper
1 garlic clove, minced

1 Preheat oven to 425°F. Line 15½" by 10½" jelly-roll pan with foil; spray with nonstick cooking spray.

2 In large bowl, combine diced bread and ⅓ *cup water*. With hand, mix until bread is evenly moistened. Add ground beef and remaining ingredients. With hand, mix until well combined.

Steak & Oven Fries

3 Shape meat mixture into twenty-four 2-inch meatballs. (For easier shaping, use slightly wet hands.) Place meatballs in jelly-roll pan and bake 15 to 20 minutes, until cooked through and lightly browned. Makes 24 meatballs.

Each meatball: About 70 calories, 9 g protein, 2 g carbohydrate, 3 g total fat (1 g saturated), 24 mg cholesterol, 140 mg sodium.

Steak & Oven Fries

PREP: 15 MINUTES • COOK: 20 TO 25 MINUTES

Oven Fries (recipe follows)
1 beef flank steak (1 pound)
¼ teaspoon coarsely ground black pepper
2 teaspoons olive oil
1 large shallot, minced (about ¼ cup)
½ cup dry red wine
½ cup chicken broth
2 tablespoons chopped fresh parsley

1 Prepare Oven Fries.

2 Meanwhile, sprinkle steak on both sides with pepper. Heat nonstick 12-inch skillet over medium-high heat until hot. Add steak and cook about 14 minutes for medium-rare or until of desired doneness, turning once. Remove steak to cutting board; keep warm.

3 To drippings in skillet, add olive oil; heat over medium heat until hot. Add shallot and cook 2 minutes or until golden, stirring occasionally. Increase heat to medium-high. Add red wine and chicken broth; heat to boiling. Cook 3 to 4 minutes. Stir in parsley.

4 To serve, holding knife almost parallel to cutting surface, thinly slice steak. Spoon red-wine sauce over steak slices and serve with Oven Fries. Makes 4 main-dish servings.

OVEN FRIES: Preheat oven to 500°F. Spray two 15½" by 10½" jelly-roll pans or 2 large cookie sheets with nonstick cooking spray. Scrub 4 *medium unpeeled baking potatoes (2 pounds)* well but do not peel. Cut each potato lengthwise in half. Holding each half flat side down, cut lengthwise into ¼-inch-thick slices, then cut each slice lengthwise into ¼-inch-wide sticks. Place potatoes in medium bowl and toss with ½ *teaspoon salt* and ¼ *teaspoon pepper*. Divide potato sticks evenly between pans. Place pans on 2 oven racks and bake potatoes 20 to 25 minutes, until tender and lightly browned, turning potatoes once with pancake turner and rotating pans between upper and lower racks halfway through baking time.

Each serving: About 390 calories, 31 g protein, 40 g carbohydrate, 11 g total fat (4 g saturated), 46 mg cholesterol, 455 mg sodium.

Creamy Low-Fat Potato Salad

PREP: 20 MINUTES • COOK: 10 TO 12 MINUTES

Using buttermilk instead of high-fat mayonnaise makes this potato salad diet-friendly—and every bite as delicious as the classic version.

2 pounds small red potatoes, cut into ¾-inch pieces
2 garlic cloves, peeled
1 small bay leaf
1 cup buttermilk
2 tablespoons olive oil
2 tablespoons tarragon vinegar
1 teaspoon Dijon mustard with seeds
1 teaspoon salt
¼ teaspoon coarsely ground black pepper
4 green onions, chopped
1 large celery stalk with leaves, chopped
¼ cup chopped fresh parsley leaves

1 In 4-quart saucepan, heat potatoes, garlic, bay leaf, and enough *water* to cover to boiling over high heat. Reduce heat to low; cover and simmer 10 to 12 minutes, until potatoes are fork-tender.

2 Meanwhile, in large bowl, with fork, blend buttermilk, olive oil, vinegar, mustard, salt, and pepper. Stir in green onions, celery, and parsley.

3 Drain potatoes; discard garlic and bay leaf. Add warm potatoes to buttermilk mixture and gently stir with rubber spatula until well coated. Cover and refrigerate if not serving right away. Makes about 7 cups or 8 accompaniment servings.

Each serving: About 130 calories, 4 g protein, 21 g carbohydrate, 4 g total fat (1 g saturated), 1 mg cholesterol, 335 mg sodium.

Skinny Mashed Potatoes & Carrots

PREP: 15 MINUTES • COOK: 15 MINUTES

1½ pounds all-purpose potatoes, peeled and cut into 2-inch pieces
1 bag (16 ounces) carrots, peeled and cut into ¼-inch-thick slices
½ cup low-fat milk (1%)
2 tablespoons olive oil
¾ teaspoon salt
¼ teaspoon coarsely ground black pepper

1 In 4-quart saucepan, heat potatoes, carrots, and enough *water* to cover to boiling over high heat. Reduce heat to low; cover and simmer 15 minutes or until potatoes and carrots are tender.

2 Drain vegetables well and return to saucepan. Cook 1 minute over medium heat, shaking pan constantly to dry out vegetables.

3 Remove saucepan from heat. Add milk, olive oil, salt, and pepper. With potato masher, mash vegetables until almost smooth; heat through. Makes 6 accompaniment servings.

Each serving: About 155 calories, 3 g protein, 25 g carbohydrate, 5 g total fat (1 g saturated), 1 mg cholesterol, 305 mg sodium.

Light Slaw

PREP: 10 MINUTES

1 bag (16 ounces) shredded cabbage mix for coleslaw
2 medium carrots, shredded
1 green onion, chopped
¼ cup seasoned rice vinegar
¼ teaspoon salt
¼ teaspoon coarsely ground black pepper

In large bowl, combine cabbage mix with remaining ingredients, tossing to mix well. If not serving right away, cover and refrigerate up to 6 hours. Toss well before serving. Makes 6 accompaniment servings.

Each serving: About 45 calories, 1 g protein, 11 g carbohydrate, 0 g total fat, 0 mg cholesterol, 380 mg sodium.

5-Minute Peach Sherbet

PREP: 5 MINUTES

Try this with strawberries, blueberries, and other frozen fruits too—or a mix. For perfect scoops, make the sherbet before dinner, freeze, and scoop at dessert time.

1 package (20 ounces) frozen sliced peaches
1 container (8 ounces) plain low-fat yogurt
1 cup confectioners' sugar
1 tablespoon fresh lemon juice
⅛ teaspoon almond extract

1 In food processor with knife blade attached, blend frozen peaches until fruit resembles finely shaved ice, stopping processor occasionally to scrape down side. If fruit is not finely shaved, dessert will not be smooth.

2 With processor running, add yogurt, confectioners' sugar, lemon juice, and almond extract, until mixture is smooth and creamy. Stop processor and scrape down sides occasionally. Serve the sherbet immediately or freeze to serve later. If refrozen, let stand at room temperature for about 30 minutes before scooping. Makes about 4 cups or 6 servings.

Each serving: About 190 calories, 3 g protein, 45 g carbohydrate, 1 g total fat (0 g saturated), 2 mg cholesterol, 35 mg sodium.

10 WAYS TO LIGHTEN UP DESSERT

You don't have to kiss your favorite recipes good-bye because they call for high-fat ingredients. Just make these easy swaps:

1. Replace the semisweet chocolate chips in treasured cookie classics with half the amount of mini semisweet chips (they'll scatter through more of the dough than big chips, but still have that authentic richness). Or try using the full amount of low-fat baking chips; the impostor effect is not quite as noticeable when the cookies are eaten warm from the oven.

2. Omit up to half the butter, margarine, or oil in cakes, muffins, or quick breads, and substitute applesauce, prune puree, or a fruit-based fat replacement (such as Lighter Bake). These switches are especially successful in coffee cakes and bar cookies.

3. Substitute plain nonfat or low-fat yogurt or reduced-fat sour cream for regular sour cream. The flavor comes very close to the original in muffins and cakes.

4. Eliminate the bottom crust in fruit pies to significantly reduce calories and fat—spoon filling into pie plate, add top crust, serve cobbler-style. (You don't even need to grease the plate—the saucy fruit will spoon right out.)

5. Cut back the amount of nuts in a recipe to a few tablespoons, finely chop, and sprinkle on top of cookies, brownies, cakes, and breads before baking—

they'll get a nice toasty flavor in the oven, and you'll see and taste them first.

6. Slip light cream cheese (Neufchâtel) into cheesecakes rather than using full-fat cheese—you'll save about 6 grams of fat and 60 calories per slice.

7. Use ¼ cup no-cholesterol egg substitute in place of each whole egg in quick breads, muffins, and cakes. Or substitute 2 whites for each egg up to 2 eggs (too many whites can make the texture a bit rubbery).

8. Count on lower-fat dairy products. Instead of whole or 2 percent milk, use 1 percent or skim. Rather than heavy cream—unless it must be whipped—pour in light cream or half-and-half (either will perform perfectly in most frostings, glazes, and doughs). If a pie or cookie calls for canned evaporated or sweetened condensed milk, get the fat-free or low-fat kind.

9. For mock whipped cream, beat evaporated skimmed milk. Chill milk, bowl, and beaters in freezer for at least 15 minutes; beat in 1 tablespoon lemon juice to stabilize the mixture, and sweeten to taste. Serve immediately, because it collapses quickly. We won't lie to you; it's no double for the real thing; but it is creamy-looking, white, and fluffy.

10. Don't grease baking pans with butter or margarine—try new nonstick pan liners, kitchen parchment, or a spritz of cooking spray.

Individual Ginger-Pear Soufflés

PREP: 45 TO 50 MINUTES • BAKE: 12 TO 15 MINUTES

Whipping up a soufflé has never been simpler—just make one of our pureed fruit bases and fold in beaten egg whites. For entertaining, prepare and refrigerate soufflé mixture in ramekins for up to 3 hours, then bake just before serving.

4 cups peeled, coarsely chopped fully ripe pears
   (5 to 6 pears)
1 tablespoon fresh lemon juice
2 teaspoons minced, peeled fresh ginger
1 tablespoon margarine or butter, melted
2 tablespoons plus ¼ cup sugar
6 large egg whites
½ teaspoon cream of tartar
1 teaspoon vanilla extract

1 In 2-quart saucepan, mix chopped pears with lemon juice and ginger. Cook over medium-high heat, covered, 15 minutes or until pears are very tender. Uncover and cook 10 to 15 minutes longer, stirring occasionally, until mixture is almost dry and reduced to about 1 cup. Transfer to blender or food processor with knife blade attached and blend until pureed. Place puree in large bowl; let cool to room temperature.

2 Meanwhile, preheat oven to 425°F. Brush six 6-ounce ramekins or custard cups with melted margarine or butter; sprinkle with 2 tablespoons sugar.

3 In large bowl, with mixer at high speed, beat egg whites and cream of tartar until whites begin to mound. Beat in vanilla. Gradually sprinkle in remaining ¼ cup sugar until sugar dissolves and whites stand in stiff peaks when beaters are lifted.

4 With rubber spatula, fold one-third of whites into pear mixture. Fold in remaining whites. Spoon mixture into ramekins. Place ramekins in jelly-roll pan for easier handling. Bake 12 to 15 minutes, until soufflés are puffed and beginning to brown. Serve immediately. Makes 6 servings.

Each serving: About 180 calories, 4 g protein, 38 g carbohydrate, 3 g total fat (0 g saturated), 0 mg cholesterol, 80 mg sodium.

BANANA SOUFFLÉS: Prepare soufflés as above, but instead of pear mixture, make banana puree: In food processor with knife blade attached, blend *3 large, very ripe bananas, 1 tablespoon fresh lemon juice,* and ¼ *teaspoon ground cinnamon* until smooth (you should have about 1 cup). Fold beaten egg whites into banana puree; spoon into ramekins and bake as above. Makes 6 servings.

Each serving: About 150 calories, 4 g protein, 30 g carbohydrate, 2 g total fat (1 g saturated), 0 mg cholesterol, 80 mg sodium.

PEACH OR APRICOT SOUFFLÉS: Prepare soufflés as above, but instead of pear mixture, make peach or apricot puree: Drain *1 can (1 pound, 13 ounces) peaches in heavy syrup* or 2 cans (16 ounces each) apricots in heavy syrup. In blender or food processor with knife blade attached, blend peaches or apricots until smooth. Transfer to 4-quart saucepan and heat to boiling over medium-high heat. Reduce heat to medium-low and cook, stirring occasionally, 15 to 20 minutes, until puree is reduced to 1 cup. Transfer fruit puree to large bowl to cool. Stir in *1 tablespoon fresh lemon juice* and ⅛ *teaspoon almond extract.* Fold beaten egg whites into fruit puree; spoon into ramekins and bake as above. Makes 6 servings.

Each serving: About 155 calories, 4 g protein, 32 g carbohydrate, 2 g total fat (0 g saturated), 0 mg cholesterol, 85 mg sodium.

Rice Pudding with Raspberry-Rhubarb Sauce

PREP: 15 MINUTES PLUS CHILLING
COOK: ABOUT 1 HOUR

You can use nonfat milk to lower the fat content even more. Pour any extra sauce over pancakes or your favorite frozen yogurt.

8 ounces rhubarb, thinly sliced (1¾ cups)
1 package (10 ounces) frozen raspberries in
   syrup, thawed
2 tablespoons plus ¼ cup sugar
4 cups low-fat (1%) milk
¼ cup regular long-grain rice
¼ teaspoon salt
1 teaspoon vanilla extract

1 Prepare raspberry-rhubarb sauce: In 3-quart saucepan, heat rhubarb and ¼ *cup water* to boiling over high heat. Reduce heat to low; simmer 5 to 10 minutes, until rhubarb is tender. Stir in raspberries in syrup and 2 tablespoons sugar. Transfer sauce to bowl; refrigerate until ready to serve.

2 Meanwhile, in 5-quart Dutch oven, heat milk, rice, salt, and remaining ¼ cup sugar to boiling over medium-high heat. Reduce heat to low and simmer, stirring occasionally, 40 to 50 minutes, until mixture is thick and rice is tender. Remove Dutch oven from heat and stir in vanilla. Transfer pudding to shallow bowl; cover surface with plastic wrap to prevent skin from forming. Refrigerate until cold, about 1½ hours.

3 Serve rice pudding with raspberry-rhubarb sauce. Makes 6 servings.

Each serving: About 205 calories, 7 g protein, 41 g carbohydrate, 2 g total fat (1 g saturated), 7 mg cholesterol, 175 mg sodium.

Lime Pavlova

New Banana Tea Bread

PREP: 15 MINUTES PLUS COOLING
BAKE: 40 TO 45 MINUTES

Enjoy a slice for dessert or to start your day off right—it also makes a great snack. For a whole-grain variation, substitute ½ cup whole-wheat flour for ½ cup of the all-purpose flour.

Nonstick cooking spray
1¾ cups all-purpose flour
½ cup sugar
1 teaspoon baking powder
½ teaspoon baking soda

½ teaspoon salt
1 cup mashed, very ripe bananas (about
   3 small)
⅓ cup fruit-based fat replacement* or
   unsweetened applesauce
2 large egg whites
1 large egg
¼ cup pecans, chopped

1 Preheat oven to 350°F. Spray 9" by 5" metal loaf pan with nonstick cooking spray.

2 In large bowl, combine flour, sugar, baking powder, baking soda, and salt.

3 In medium bowl, with fork, mix mashed bananas, fruit-based fat replacement, egg whites, and egg.

4 Stir banana mixture into flour mixture just until moistened. Spoon batter into loaf pan; sprinkle with chopped pecans.

5 Bake 40 to 45 minutes, until toothpick inserted in center of loaf comes out clean with just a few moist crumbs attached. Cool loaf in pan on wire rack 10 minutes. Remove loaf from pan; cool completely on wire rack. Makes 16 slices.

*Fruit-based fat replacements are sold in the baking section of some supermarkets and health-food stores.

Each slice: About 110 calories, 3 g protein, 22 g carbohydrate, 2 g total fat (0 g saturated), 13 mg cholesterol, 140 mg sodium.

Lime Pavlova

PREP: 30 MINUTES PLUS COOLING
BAKE: 1 HOUR 15 MINUTES PLUS DRYING IN OVEN

A crisp meringue shell with a fruit-topped cream filling, the Pavlova was created in Australia in 1926, to honor visiting world-famous Russian ballerina Anna Pavlova. The Pavlova quickly became the national dessert Down Under. The meringue can be made several days ahead and stored in an airtight container. Fill and serve on the same day.

3 large egg whites
¼ teaspoon cream of tartar
¼ teaspoon salt
1 teaspoon vanilla extract
½ cup sugar
4 to 6 limes

1 can (14 ounces) low-fat sweetened condensed
   milk
1 container (8 ounces) plain low-fat yogurt
1 envelope unflavored gelatin
5 large strawberries with leaves attached, each
   cut in half, for garnish

1 Line cookie sheet with foil. Using 9-inch round plate or cake pan as guide, with toothpick, trace a circle on foil on cookie sheet.

2 Preheat oven to 275°F. In small bowl, with mixer at high speed, beat egg whites, cream of tartar, and salt until whites begin to mound. Beating at high speed, add vanilla and gradually sprinkle in sugar, 2 tablespoons at a time, beating well after each addition, until sugar completely dissolves and whites stand in stiff, glossy peaks when beaters are lifted.

3 Spoon meringue mixture inside circle on cookie sheet. With spoon, shape and spread meringue into a "nest" with a 1½-inch-high edge.

4 Bake meringue shell 1 hour 15 minutes. Turn off oven and let meringue remain in oven 1 hour to dry out. Transfer meringue with foil to wire rack; cool completely.

5 Meanwhile, prepare filling: Finely grate 2 teaspoons peel and squeeze ½ cup juice from limes. In medium bowl, with wire whisk, mix lime juice and grated lime peel with undiluted sweetened condensed milk and yogurt until blended.

6 In 1-quart saucepan, evenly sprinkle gelatin over *¼ cup cold water*; let stand 1 minute to soften. Heat over low heat, stirring frequently, about 2 to 3 minutes, until gelatin is completely dissolved (do not boil). With wire whisk, blend gelatin into lime mixture.

7 Set bowl with lime mixture in larger bowl filled with *ice water*. With rubber spatula, stir mixture occasionally until it begins to thicken, about 20 minutes. Remove bowl with lime filling from bowl of ice water.

8 With metal spatula, carefully loosen and remove meringue from foil; discard foil. Place meringue shell on serving plate. Pour lime mixture into meringue shell; refrigerate at least 1 hour or until lime filling is firm enough to slice. Garnish with strawberry halves. Makes 10 servings.

Each serving: About 190 calories, 6 g protein, 37 g carbohydrate, 2 g total fat (1 g saturated), 7 mg cholesterol, 130 mg sodium.

PINEAPPLE PRIMER

Once you know how to select and peel a pineapple, it graduates from being an intimidating fruit to a great light dessert option. It's fat-free, and 1 cup of fresh chunks contains just 80 calories and 40 percent of your daily vitamin C requirement. Serve fresh slices on their own in a pretty glass bowl or use in our Southern-style Mint Julep Cups, at right.

Choosing a Sweetie

Once a pineapple is harvested, it won't get any sweeter. Growers don't pick pineapples until they are juicy and ripe but firm. (If picked when too ripe and soft, they could spoil before distribution.) When you shop, smell the fruit—it should have a sweet floral aroma (less pronounced when the fruit is cold). Feel it—you want one that's firm and heavy, with fresh green leaves. Don't buy a pineapple with bruises or soft spots—especially at the base. At home, refrigerate it whole or cut for 3 to 5 days; for softer, juicier fruit, store whole at room temperature for up to 5 days.

Getting Under Its Skin

1. After cutting off crown and stem ends with a sharp chef's knife, hold pineapple upright and cut skin off in long pieces, slicing from top to base.

2. To remove "eyes," lay pineapple on its side. Cut in at an angle on either side of row of eyes, inserting knife into fruit about ¼ inch, and lift out the row. Repeat at next row.

3. Cut pineapple lengthwise into quarters, slicing straight down from crown to stem end. Hold each quarter upright and cut off tough core along center edge. Then cut fruit into wedges or chunks.

Mint Julep Cups

PREP: 15 MINUTES PLUS CHILLING

1 pineapple
¼ cup chopped fresh mint leaves
¼ cup bourbon whiskey
2 tablespoons sugar
1 pint strawberries, thickly sliced

1 Prepare the pineapple as directed in "Pineapple Primer" (at left), cutting the quarters first into 1-inch slices then into 1-inch chunks.

2 In medium bowl, mix mint, bourbon, and sugar until blended. Stir in strawberry slices and pineapple chunks. Refrigerate up to 2 hours to allow flavors to blend. Makes 6 servings.

Each serving: About 105 calories, 1 g protein, 21 g carbohydrate, 1 g total fat (0 g saturated), 0 mg cholesterol, 2 mg sodium.

Rhubarb-Apple Crumble

PREP: 20 MINUTES • BAKE: 45 MINUTES

⅓ cup granulated sugar
1 tablespoon cornstarch
1¼ pounds rhubarb, cut into ½-inch pieces (about 4 cups)
3 medium Golden Delicious apples (about 1¼ pounds), peeled, cored, and cut into 1-inch pieces
½ cup packed brown sugar
2 tablespoons margarine or butter, softened
¼ teaspoon ground cinnamon
⅓ cup old-fashioned or quick-cooking oats, uncooked
¼ cup all-purpose flour

1 Preheat oven to 375°F. In large bowl, combine granulated sugar and cornstarch. Add rhubarb and apples and toss to coat. Spoon fruit mixture into 11" by 7" glass baking dish or shallow 2-quart casserole.

2 In medium bowl, with fingers, mix brown sugar, margarine or butter, and cinnamon until blended. Stir in oats and flour until evenly combined. Sprinkle oat topping evenly over fruit in baking dish.

3 Bake crumble 45 minutes or until filling is hot and bubbly and topping is browned. Serve warm. Makes 6 servings.

Each serving: About 255 calories, 3 g protein, 53 g carbohydrate, 5 g total fat (1 g saturated), 0 mg cholesterol, 60 mg sodium.

Tomato-Soup Cake

PREP: 10 MINUTES PLUS COOLING • BAKE: 30 MINUTES

Nonstick cooking spray
2 cups all-purpose flour
1 tablespoon baking powder
1½ teaspoons ground cinnamon
1 teaspoon ground ginger
1 teaspoon baking soda
½ teaspoon salt
¼ teaspoon ground nutmeg
⅛ teaspoon ground cloves
1⅓ cups sugar
4 tablespoons (½ stick) light corn-oil spread (60 to 70% fat)
1 can (10¾ ounces) condensed tomato soup
2 large egg whites
1 teaspoon vanilla extract
Confectioners' sugar for garnish

1 Preheat oven to 350°F. Spray 13" by 9" metal baking pan with nonstick cooking spray.

2 In medium bowl, combine flour, baking powder, cinnamon, ginger, baking soda, salt, nutmeg, and cloves.

3 In large bowl, with mixer at high speed, beat sugar and corn-oil spread until well mixed, about 2 minutes, constantly scraping bowl with rubber spatula.

4 Reduce speed to low; beat in undiluted tomato soup, egg whites, vanilla, and ¼ *cup water*. With mixer at low speed, gradually add flour mixture and beat until just blended.

5 Pour batter into baking pan; spread evenly. Bake cake 30 minutes or until toothpick inserted in center comes out clean. Cool cake completely in pan on rack. When cool, sprinkle lightly with confectioners' sugar. Cut cake lengthwise into 4 strips, then cut each strip crosswise into 4 pieces. Makes 16 servings.

Each serving: About 160 calories, 2 g protein, 32 g carbohydrate, 3 g total fat (1 g saturated), 0 mg cholesterol, 390 mg sodium.

Double-Chocolate Bundt Cake

PREP: 30 MINUTES PLUS COOLING • BAKE: 45 MINUTES

This will satisfy a chocolate craving with or without the glaze. If you use a dusting of confectioners' sugar instead of the glaze, you'll save 35 calories per slice.

Nonstick cooking spray
2¼ cups all-purpose flour
1½ teaspoons baking soda
½ teaspoon baking powder
½ teaspoon salt
¾ cup unsweetened cocoa
1 teaspoon instant espresso-coffee powder
2 cups sugar
⅓ cup vegetable oil
2 large egg whites
1 large egg
1 square (1 ounce) unsweetened chocolate, melted
2 teaspoons vanilla extract
½ cup buttermilk
Mocha Glaze (recipe follows)

1 Preheat oven to 350°F. Generously spray 12-cup Bundt pan with nonstick cooking spray.

2 On sheet of waxed paper, combine flour, baking soda, baking powder, and salt.

3 In 2-cup glass measuring cup, whisk cocoa and espresso-coffee powder into ¾ *cup hot tap water* until blended; set aside.

4 In large bowl, with mixer at low speed, beat sugar, oil, egg whites, and whole egg until blended. Increase speed to high; beat until creamy, about 2 minutes. Reduce speed to low; beat in cocoa mixture, melted chocolate, and vanilla. Beating at low speed, alternately add flour mixture and buttermilk, beginning and ending with flour mixture. Beat just until combined, occasionally scraping bowl with rubber spatula.

5 Pour batter into pan. Bake 45 minutes or until toothpick inserted in center of cake comes out clean. Cool cake in pan on wire rack 10 minutes. With spatula or small knife, loosen cake from edge of pan; invert onto wire rack to cool completely.

6 Prepare Mocha Glaze if you like. Pour glaze over cooled cake. Makes 20 servings.

MOCHA GLAZE: In medium bowl, dissolve ¼ *teaspoon instant espresso-coffee powder* in 2 *tablespoons hot tap water*. Stir in 3 *tablespoons unsweetened cocoa*, 3 *tablespoons dark corn syrup*, and 1 *tablespoon coffee-flavor liqueur* until blended. Then stir in 1 *cup confectioners' sugar* until smooth.

Each serving without glaze: About 185 calories, 3 g protein, 34 g carbohydrate, 5 g total fat (1 g saturated), 11 mg cholesterol, 175 mg sodium.

Each serving with glaze: About 220 calories, 3 g protein, 43 g carbohydrate, 5 g total fat (1 g saturated), 11 mg cholesterol, 175 mg sodium.

Butterscotch Blondies

PREP: 15 MINUTES PLUS COOLING
BAKE: 35 TO 40 MINUTES

These chewy treats are our test kitchen favorite—we challenge anyone to guess that they're low-fat!

Nonstick cooking spray
1 cup all-purpose flour
½ teaspoon baking powder
¼ teaspoon salt
¾ cup packed dark brown sugar
3 tablespoons margarine or butter
⅓ cup dark corn syrup
2 teaspoons vanilla extract
2 large egg whites
2 tablespoons finely chopped pecans

1 Preheat oven to 350°F. Spray 8" by 8" metal baking pan with nonstick cooking spray.

2 In medium bowl, combine flour, baking powder, and salt.

3 In large bowl, with mixer at medium speed, beat brown sugar with margarine or butter until well blended, about 2 minutes. Reduce speed to low; beat in corn syrup, vanilla, and egg whites until smooth. Beat in flour mixture just until combined.

4 Spread batter evenly in pan. Sprinkle with pecans. Bake 35 to 40 minutes, until toothpick inserted in center comes out clean and edges are lightly browned. Cool completely in pan on wire rack. When cool, cut blondies into 4 strips, then cut each strip crosswise into 4 pieces. Makes 16 blondies.

Each blondie: About 115 calories, 1 g protein, 21 g carbohydrate, 3 g total fat (0 g saturated), 0 mg cholesterol, 90 mg sodium.

Double-Chocolate Bundt Cake ➤

Midnight Fudge Brownies

PREP: 15 MINUTES PLUS COOLING
BAKE: 18 TO 22 MINUTES

Delicious, moist, *and* low-fat—a slim 100 calories and 2 grams of fat each, compared to a regular fudge brownie with 190 calories and 11 fat grams (3 grams saturated). Serve with ice-cold skim milk for a luscious treat.

Nonstick cooking spray
1 teaspoon instant espresso-coffee powder
¾ cup all-purpose flour
½ cup unsweetened cocoa
½ teaspoon baking powder
¼ teaspoon salt
3 tablespoons margarine or butter
¾ cup sugar
¼ cup dark corn syrup
1 teaspoon vanilla extract
2 large egg whites

1 Preheat oven to 350°F. Spray 8" by 8" metal baking pan with nonstick cooking spray. In cup, dissolve espresso powder in *1 teaspoon hot water*; set aside.

2 In large bowl, with wire whisk, mix flour, cocoa, baking powder, and salt.

3 In 2-quart saucepan, melt margarine or butter over low heat. Remove saucepan from heat. With same whisk, mix in sugar, corn syrup, vanilla extract, egg whites, and espresso mixture until blended. With wooden spoon, stir sugar mixture into flour mixture just until blended (do not overmix).

4 Pour batter into pan. Bake brownies 18 to 22 minutes, until toothpick inserted in center of pan comes out *almost* clean. Cool brownies in pan on wire rack at least 1 hour. When cool, cut brownies into 4 strips, then cut each strip crosswise into 4 pieces. If brownies are difficult to cut, use knife dipped in hot water and dried. Makes 16 brownies.

Each brownie: About 100 calories, 2 g protein, 19 g carbohydrate, 2 g total fat (0 g saturated), 0 mg cholesterol, 85 mg sodium.

Oatmeal-Raisin Cookies

PREP: 20 MINUTES PLUS COOLING
BAKE: 16 TO 18 MINUTES PER BATCH

You can substitute your favorite dried fruit for the raisins.

Nonstick cooking spray
½ cup (1 stick) light corn-oil spread (60 to 70% fat)
1 cup packed dark brown sugar
2 large egg whites
1 large egg
2 teaspoons vanilla extract
1¾ cups all-purpose flour
1 cup quick-cooking oats, uncooked
1 cup golden raisins
1 teaspoon baking powder
¼ teaspoon salt

1 Preheat oven to 375°F. Spray large cookie sheet with nonstick cooking spray.

2 In large bowl, with mixer at low speed, beat corn-oil spread and brown sugar until blended. Increase speed to high; beat until well combined, about 3 minutes. At low speed, add egg whites, egg, and vanilla; beat until smooth.

3 With spoon, stir in flour, oats, raisins, baking powder, and salt until combined.

4 Drop dough by heaping tablespoons, about 2 inches apart, on cookie sheet. Flatten dough into 3-inch rounds (dough will be very moist and sticky—for easier shaping, use slightly wet hands). Bake cookies 16 to 18 minutes or until golden. With pancake turner, remove cookies to wire racks to cool.

5 Repeat until all batter is used. Store cookies in tightly covered container. Makes about 2½ dozen cookies.

Each cookie: About 115 calories, 2 g protein, 21 g carbohydrate, 3 g total fat (0 g saturated), 7 mg cholesterol, 60 mg sodium.

DESSERTS

Napa Valley Poached Pears

PREP: 20 MINUTES PLUS CHILLING • COOK: 45 MINUTES

Easy and fat-free—the poaching liquid reduces to a ruby-red syrup that adds an elegant touch. Both pears and syrup can be made up to 2 days ahead.

1 bottle (750 ml) red Zinfandel wine (about 3 cups)
2 cups cranberry-juice cocktail
1¼ cups sugar
1 cinnamon stick (3 inches long)
2 whole cloves
½ teaspoon whole black peppercorns
8 medium Bosc pears with stems

1 In 5-quart Dutch oven, heat wine, cranberry juice, sugar, cinnamon stick, cloves, and peppercorns just to boiling over high heat, stirring to dissolve sugar.

2 Meanwhile, with apple corer, melon baller, or small knife, remove cores from blossom end (bottom) of pears. Peel pears but do not remove stems.

3 Place pears in wine mixture; heat to boiling. Reduce heat to low; cover and simmer 15 to 25 minutes, until pears are tender but not soft, turning pears occasionally.

4 Carefully remove pears to platter. Strain wine mixture and return it to Dutch oven. Heat wine mixture to boiling over high heat. Cook 15 to 30 minutes, uncovered, or until liquid is reduced to 1½ cups.

5 Cover pears and syrup separately and refrigerate until well chilled, at least 6 hours. To serve, spoon syrup over pears. Makes 8 servings.

Each serving: About 235 calories, 1 g protein, 63 g carbohydrate, 0 g total fat, 0 mg cholesterol, 10 mg sodium.

Quick Poached Pears with Ruby-Red Raspberry Sauce

PREP: 10 MINUTES • MICROWAVE*: 5 TO 6 MINUTES

2 medium, ripe Bosc pears
½ lemon
2 teaspoons sugar
1½ cups fresh or frozen (thawed) raspberries (reserve 10 raspberries for garnish)
⅓ cup confectioners' sugar
1 tablespoon black currant-flavor or orange-flavor liqueur
Mint sprigs for garnish

1 With apple corer, melon baller, or small knife, remove cores from blossom end (bottom) of pears. Peel pears almost to top but do not remove stems. Rub pears with lemon half; sprinkle with sugar.

2 In glass pie plate, arrange pears lying down with stems toward center; add *2 tablespoons water*. Cook, uncovered, in microwave oven on High 5 to 6 minutes, until tender, turning pears over halfway through cooking. Transfer pears, stem ends up, to 2 dessert plates; set aside until ready to serve.

3 In blender at high speed, puree raspberries. Sift confectioners' sugar through coarse sieve into small bowl. Press raspberry puree through same sieve into same bowl to remove seeds. Discard seeds. Stir liqueur into raspberry mixture.

4 To serve, spoon raspberry sauce over poached pears. Garnish with mint sprigs and reserved raspberries. Makes 2 servings.

*Recipe developed in 800-watt microwave oven.

Each serving: About 245 calories, 1 g protein, 59 g carbohydrate, 1 g total fat (0 g saturated), 0 mg cholesterol, 2 mg sodium.

Quick Poached Pears ➤
with Ruby-Red Raspberry Sauce

Summer Fruit Compote

PREP: 15 MINUTES

Refreshing and fat-free—great for Sunday brunch. Leftovers will keep in the refrigerator for up to 3 days.

1 tablespoon sugar
1 tablespoon dark Jamaican rum
1 tablespoon fresh lime juice
2 large mangoes, peeled and cut into ¾-inch
 pieces
1 pint blueberries

In medium bowl, combine sugar, rum, and lime juice. Add mangoes and blueberries; toss to coat. Cover and refrigerate if not serving right away. Makes about 4 cups or 6 servings.

Each serving: About 85 calories, 1 g protein, 21 g carbohydrate, 0 g total fat, 0 mg cholesterol, 5 mg sodium.

Island Ambrosia

PREP: 40 MINUTES • BAKE: 15 MINUTES

A light, refreshing fruit dessert. Use a vegetable peeler to get graceful, thin strips of coconut.

1 fresh coconut
1 ripe pineapple
6 large navel oranges

1 Prepare coconut: Preheat oven to 350°F. With hammer and screwdriver or large nail, puncture 2 of the 3 eyes (indentations at 1 end) of the coconut. Drain liquid. Bake coconut 15 minutes. Remove coconut from oven and wrap in kitchen towel. With hammer, hit coconut to break it into large pieces. With knife, pry coconut meat from shell. With vegetable peeler or sharp paring knife, peel brown outer skin from coconut meat. With vegetable peeler or large holes of grater, peel or grate 1 cup coconut. (Wrap and refrigerate remaining coconut up to 2 days for another use.)

2 Prepare the pineapple as directed in "Pineapple Primer" on page 174. After coring the quarters, cut them lengthwise in half; slice into chunks. Place in large bowl.

3 Prepare oranges: Cut off ends from oranges; place on a cut end on cutting board and slice off rind. Holding oranges over bowl, with paring knife, cut out sections. Squeeze juice from membranes into bowl.

4 Add shredded coconut to bowl and toss gently to combine. Makes 10 servings.

Each serving: About 120 calories, 2 g protein, 24 g carbohydrate, 3 g total fat (2 g saturated), 0 mg cholesterol, 3 mg sodium.

Fruit Salad with Vanilla-Bean Syrup

PREP: 30 MINUTES PLUS CHILLING • COOK: 10 MINUTES

Perfect alone, or with a slice of pound cake, such as Almond Pound Cake (page 212).

1 large lemon
1 vanilla bean
¾ cup sugar
3 ripe mangoes, peeled and cut into 1-inch
 chunks
2 pints strawberries, hulled and each cut in half
 or into quarters if large
1 medium honeydew melon (about 3½ pounds),
 cut into 1-inch chunks

1 With vegetable peeler, remove 1-inch-wide continuous strip of peel from lemon. Squeeze enough juice from lemon to equal ¼ cup; set aside. Cut vanilla bean lengthwise in half; spread pod open. Scrape seeds from inside of vanilla bean; reserve seeds and pod.

2 In 1-quart saucepan, heat lemon peel, vanilla-bean seeds, vanilla-bean pod, sugar, and ¾ *cup water* to boiling over high heat. Reduce heat to medium; cook, uncovered, 5 minutes or until syrup is slightly thickened. Remove vanilla-bean pod and lemon. Pour syrup into small bowl; stir in lemon juice. Cover and refrigerate syrup until chilled, about 2 hours.

3 Place fruit in large bowl; toss with syrup. Makes 12 servings.

Each serving: About 120 calories, 1 g protein, 31 g carbohydrate, 0 g total fat, 0 mg cholesterol, 10 mg sodium.

5 DESSERTS IN 5 MINUTES

Waffles & Ice Cream (right):
Lightly toast frozen Belgian waffles; top with vanilla ice cream or frozen yogurt and quick-thaw strawberries or raspberries.

Melon Cups (below):
Toss chunks of honeydew and cantaloupe with honey and freshly squeezed lime juice. Garnish with a twist of lime peel.

Grapes with Ginger Cream:
Top halved red and green seedless grapes with a dollop of regular or light sour cream and some coarsely chopped crystallized or preserved ginger.

Mini Ice-Cream Sandwiches:
Spread the flat side of chocolate or vanilla wafer cookies with a thin layer of creamy peanut butter. Sandwich a small scoop of your favorite ice cream or frozen yogurt between two peanut-butter-coated sides.

Broiled Amaretti Plums:
Put unpeeled fresh plum halves, cut side up, in ungreased broiler-safe pan. Sprinkle with crushed Amaretti (almond flavor) cookies and broil just until crumbs are lightly browned and plums are tender. Great with peaches too.

Caramel-Glazed Oranges

PREP: 30 MINUTES PLUS CHILLING • COOK: 10 MINUTES

6 large navel oranges
2 tablespoons brandy (optional)
1 small orange cut in half, for garnish
1 cup sugar

1 With vegetable peeler, remove six 3-inch-long strips peel (about ¾ inch wide each) from oranges. Cut strips lengthwise into very thin slivers.

2 Cut remaining peel and white pith from oranges. Slice oranges into ¼-inch-thick rounds and place in deep platter, overlapping slices. Sprinkle with brandy and orange peel. Garnish with orange halves.

3 In 10-inch skillet, cook sugar over medium heat until it melts and becomes deep amber in color, stirring to dissolve any lumps. Drizzle caramelized sugar over oranges. Cover and refrigerate until caramel melts, about 2 hours. Makes 6 servings.

Each serving: About 205 calories, 2 g protein, 53 g carbohydrate, 0 g total fat, 0 mg cholesterol, 2 mg sodium.

Brown-Sugar Pear Shortcakes

PREP: 45 MINUTES • BAKE: 12 TO 15 MINUTES

Flavored with a hint of cinnamon and lemon peel.

1 cup all-purpose flour
¾ cup cake flour (not self-rising)
3 tablespoons sugar
2½ teaspoons baking powder
½ teaspoon salt
9 tablespoons cold margarine or butter
⅔ cup milk
2½ pounds ripe Bosc pears (about 6 medium),
    peeled, cored, and cut lengthwise into ¾-inch
    wedges
¼ cup packed light brown sugar
¼ teaspoon ground cinnamon
2 strips (2½" by ½" each) lemon peel
1 cup heavy or whipping cream, whipped

1 Prepare biscuits: Preheat oven to 425°F. In large bowl, mix all-purpose flour, cake flour, sugar, baking powder, and salt. With pastry blender or two knives used scissor-fashion, cut in 5 tablespoons cold margarine or butter, until mixture resembles coarse crumbs. Stir in milk; quickly stir just until mixture forms a soft dough that comes together (dough will be sticky).

2 Turn dough onto floured surface; gently knead for 6 to 8 strokes to mix thoroughly. With floured hands, pat dough 1 inch thick.

3 With floured 2½-inch round biscuit cutter, cut out as many biscuits as possible. With pancake turner, place biscuits, 1 inch apart, on ungreased cookie sheet. Press trimmings together; cut as above to make 6 biscuits in all. Bake 12 to 15 minutes until golden.

4 Meanwhile, prepare pears: In nonstick 12-inch skillet, melt remaining 4 tablespoons margarine or butter over medium-high heat. Add pears and cook, uncovered, 10 to 15 minutes, until pears are brown and tender, stirring carefully with rubber spatula. Stir in brown sugar, cinnamon, lemon-peel strips, and ¼ *cup water*; cook 1 minute. Discard lemon peel.

5 To serve, with fork, split each warm biscuit horizontally in half. Spoon pear mixture onto bottom halves of biscuits; top with whipped cream, then biscuit tops. Makes 6 servings.

Each serving: About 580 calories, 6 g protein, 67 g carbohydrate, 34 g total fat (13 g saturated), 58 mg cholesterol, 590 mg sodium.

Summer Peach Cobbler

PREP: 45 MINUTES • BAKE: 45 MINUTES

Make the most of sweet, fragrant peaches with this old-fashioned finale—serve with vanilla ice cream or heavy cream.

PEACH FILLING:
16 to 18 ripe medium peaches (about 6 pounds),
    peeled and sliced (about 13 cups)
⅔ cup granulated sugar
½ cup packed dark brown sugar
¼ cup cornstarch
¼ cup fresh lemon juice

LEMON BISCUITS:
2 cups all-purpose flour
2½ teaspoons baking powder
1 teaspoon grated lemon peel
¼ teaspoon salt
½ cup plus 1 teaspoon granulated sugar
4 tablespoons cold margarine or butter (½ stick),
    cut up
⅔ cup plus 1 tablespoon half-and-half or light
    cream

1 Prepare Peach Filling: Preheat oven to 425°F. In 8-quart Dutch oven, combine peaches, granulated sugar, brown sugar, cornstarch, and lemon juice. Heat to boiling over medium heat, stirring occasionally; boil 1 minute. Spoon hot peach mixture into 13" by 9" glass baking dish. Place sheet of foil under baking dish and crimp edges to catch any drips during baking. Bake 10 minutes.

2 Meanwhile, prepare Lemon Biscuits: In medium bowl, combine flour, baking powder, lemon peel, salt, and ½ cup granulated sugar. With pastry blender or two knives used scissor-fashion, cut in margarine or butter until mixture resembles coarse crumbs. Stir ⅔ cup half-and-half into flour mixture just until ingredients are blended and mixture forms soft dough that leaves side of bowl.

◄ *Brown-Sugar Pear Shortcakes*

3 Turn dough onto lightly floured surface. With lightly floured hands, pat dough into a 10" by 6" rectangle. With floured knife, cut rectangle lengthwise in half, then cut each half crosswise into 6 pieces.

4 Remove baking dish from oven. Place biscuits on top of hot fruit filling. Brush biscuits with remaining 1 tablespoon half-and-half and sprinkle with remaining 1 teaspoon granulated sugar. Return cobbler to oven and bake 35 minutes longer or until filling is hot and bubbly and biscuits are golden brown. Cool cobbler on wire rack about 1 hour to serve warm or cool completely to serve cold later. Reheat if desired. Makes 12 servings.

Each serving: About 330 calories, 4 g protein, 69 g carbohydrate, 6 g total fat (2 g saturated), 5 mg cholesterol, 180 mg sodium.

Dried Apricot, Prune & Cherry Compote

PREP: 10 MINUTES PLUS COOLING • COOK: 8 MINUTES

Sweet fruit steeped in a lemon- and cinnamon-spiced apple-cider syrup—tastes great alone or with poundcake, shortbread, or butter cookies.

4 cups apple cider or apple juice
1 cup dried apricots (8 ounces), each cut into 3 strips
¼ cup packed light brown sugar
3 strips (3" by 1" each) lemon peel
1 cinnamon stick (3 inches)
1 cup pitted prunes (8 ounces), each cut in half
½ cup dried tart cherries (4 ounces)
½ teaspoon vanilla extract

1 In 3-quart saucepan, heat apple cider, apricots, brown sugar, lemon peel, and cinnamon stick to boiling over high heat. Reduce heat to low; simmer, uncovered, 5 minutes.

2 Spoon mixture into large bowl; stir in prunes, dried cherries, and vanilla. Serve at room temperature or cover and refrigerate. Store in refrigerator for up to 1 week. Makes 10 servings.

Each serving: About 175 calories, 2 g protein, 46 g carbohydrate, 1 g total fat (0 g saturated), 0 mg cholesterol, 7 mg sodium.

Blueberry-Lemon Tiramisù

PREP: 50 MINUTES PLUS CHILLING

A fruit-based summer alternative to traditional tiramisù—if you like, use about 1½ cups store-bought lemon curd instead of making your own.

LEMON CURD:
2 large lemons
3 large egg yolks
2 large eggs
⅓ cup sugar
6 tablespoons margarine or butter (¾ stick)

BLUEBERRY SAUCE:
6 cups blueberries
1 to 1½ cups confectioners' sugar, depending on sweetness of berries
2 to 4 teaspoons fresh lemon or lime juice, or to taste

1 large lemon
¼ cup sugar
1 package (7 ounces) Italian-style ladyfingers (*savoiardi*)
8 ounces mascarpone cheese
½ cup heavy or whipping cream

1 Prepare Lemon Curd: From 2 lemons, finely grate 1 tablespoon peel and squeeze ⅓ cup juice. In heavy 2-quart saucepan, with wire whisk, beat peel, juice, yolks, eggs, and sugar just until mixed. Add margarine and cook over low heat, stirring constantly, until mixture coats the back of a spoon (do not boil or mixture will curdle). Pour Lemon Curd through sieve into bowl; cover surface directly with plastic wrap and refrigerate until cool, about 45 minutes.

2 Meanwhile, make the Blueberry Sauce: In 2-quart saucepan, cook blueberries with 1 cup confectioners' sugar and *6 tablespoons water* over medium heat, stirring occasionally, until sauce is slightly thickened, about 5 to 8 minutes. Remove saucepan from heat; stir in 2 teaspoons lemon or lime juice. Taste and adjust sugar and juice; cool to room temperature.

3 With vegetable peeler, remove 3 strips peel (about 3" by ¾" each) from lemon. In small saucepan, heat lemon-peel strips, ¼ cup sugar, and ¼ *cup water* over medium heat until mixture boils and sugar dissolves, stirring occasionally. Pour sugar syrup into small bowl; cool to room temperature.

WHAT'S IN A NAME?

Old-fashioned cobblers, crisps, pandowdies, and other fruit desserts are popping up on menus everywhere. To brush up on your after-dinner vocabulary:

- **Brown Betty:** a layered mixture of buttered bread crumbs, fruit, and spices, covered and baked until tender. (See our version, below.)

- **Buckle:** a coffee cake with berries in the batter and a crumbly topping. (Sometimes, the batter is poured over the fruit and baked.)

- **Cobbler:** a deep-dish fruit dessert (in a casserole) topped with a thick layer of biscuit dough, or with individual pieces ("cobbles") of dough; can also have a bottom crust. (See Summer Peach Cobbler, page 185.)

- **Crisp:** fruit covered with a rich crumb topping (homemade, or bread, cookie, or cracker crumbs blended with butter, sugar, and sometimes nuts) and baked until topping is browned and fruit is bubbly.

- **Crumble:** British cousin to the crisp, but with oats and brown sugar added to the topping.

- **Grunt (or slump):** similar to the cobbler, except the fruit is usually simmered on the stove in a saucepan, not baked. The dough is dropped on top, where it steams to a dumpling consistency. (The word grunt comes from the sound the fruit makes as it bubbles and stews.)

- **Pandowdy:** a deep dish of sliced fruit covered with tender pastry. Before the crust is baked completely, it's cut into pieces and pressed back into the fruit to absorb the juices. The name is sometimes traced to the dessert's plain ("dowdy") appearance.

- **Shortcake:** "short" (rich) biscuit sliced in half and filled with sweetened fruit and whipped cream. Strawberries are the traditional filling, but other fruits work beautifully (see our Brown-Sugar Pear Shortcakes, page 185).

---

4 Line bottom of 13" by 9" glass baking dish with ladyfingers. Discard peel from syrup. Brush ladyfingers with syrup. Spread sauce over ladyfingers.

5 In large bowl, with wire whisk, mix Lemon Curd, mascarpone, and cream until smooth; spoon evenly over sauce and spread to cover top. Cover and refrigerate at least 6 hours or overnight. Makes 12 servings.

Each serving: About 380 calories, 5 g protein, 49 g carbohydrate, 21 g total fat (9 g saturated), 133 mg cholesterol, 130 mg sodium.

Apple Brown Betty

PREP: 35 MINUTES • BAKE: 50 MINUTES

We like this served with heavy cream to pour on top.

8 slices firm white bread, torn into ½-inch pieces
½ cup margarine or butter (1 stick), melted
1 teaspoon ground cinnamon
2½ pounds Granny Smith apples (about
    6 medium), peeled, cored, and thinly sliced
⅔ cup packed light brown sugar
2 tablespoons fresh lemon juice

1 teaspoon vanilla extract
¼ teaspoon ground nutmeg

1 Preheat oven to 400°F. In 15½" by 10½" jelly-roll pan, bake bread pieces until very lightly toasted, about 12 to 15 minutes, stirring occasionally. Grease shallow 2-quart ceramic or glass baking dish.

2 In medium bowl, combine melted margarine or butter and ½ teaspoon ground cinnamon. Add toasted bread; toss gently until evenly moistened.

3 In large bowl, toss sliced apples, brown sugar, lemon juice, vanilla, ground nutmeg, and remaining ½ teaspoon ground cinnamon.

4 Place ½ cup bread pieces in baking dish. Top with half the apple mixture, then 1 cup bread pieces. Place remaining apple mixture on top; sprinkle with remaining bread pieces, leaving a 1-inch border all around edge.

5 Cover dish with foil and bake 40 minutes. Uncover and bake 10 minutes longer or until apples are tender and crumbs on top are brown. Let stand 10 minutes before serving. Serve warm. Makes 8 servings.

Each serving: About 305 calories, 2 g protein, 48 g carbohydrate, 13 g total fat (2 g saturated), 0 mg cholesterol, 275 mg sodium.

Old-Fashioned Raspberry Ice Cream

PREP: 10 MINUTES PLUS CHILLING AND FREEZING

Top with No-Cook Berry Sauce (page 196).

4 cups raspberries
⅜ cup sugar
⅛ teaspoon salt
1 cup heavy or whipping cream
1 cup milk

1 In food processor with knife blade attached, blend raspberries until pureed. Press raspberries through medium-mesh sieve into large bowl (you should have about 1½ cups puree); discard seeds.

2 With wire whisk, beat sugar and salt into raspberry puree until sugar is dissolved. Add cream and milk and whisk until blended. Cover and refrigerate until well chilled, about 1 hour.

3 Pour chilled mixture into ice-cream can or freezer chamber of ice-cream maker. Freeze as manufacturer directs. Serve immediately or freeze to harden. Use within 2 weeks. Makes about 1 quart or 8 servings.

Each serving: About 225 calories, 2 g protein, 28 g carbohydrate, 12 g total fat (8 g saturated), 45 mg cholesterol, 60 mg sodium.

Pink Grapefruit Sorbet

PREP: 20 MINUTES PLUS FREEZING • COOK: 20 MINUTES

3 large pink or red grapefruit
1 cup sugar
¼ cup light corn syrup

1 With vegetable peeler, remove four 4-inch-long strips peel (about ¾ inch wide each) from grapefruit, then squeeze 2 cups juice. In 2-quart saucepan, heat sugar, corn syrup, peel, and *4 cups water* until sugar dissolves and syrup boils.

2 Pour sugar syrup and grapefruit juice through strainer into large bowl. Discard peel and pulp. Pour juice mixture into 9" by 9" metal baking pan; cover with foil. Freeze until partially frozen, about 4 hours, stirring occasionally.

3 In food processor with knife blade attached, blend

sorbet until smooth but still frozen. Return to pan; cover and freeze until almost firm, at least 3 hours.

4 Just before serving, return mixture to food processor and blend until smooth, above. Makes about 5 cups or 10 servings.

Each serving: About 120 calories, 0 g protein, 31 g carbohydrate, 0 g total fat, 0 mg cholesterol, 5 mg sodium.

Blackberry Semifreddo

PREP: 30 MINUTES PLUS FREEZING

True to its name—*semifreddo* means "half cold"—this creamy Italian dessert should be removed from the freezer and allowed to stand at room temperature just long enough to be only partially frozen.

2½ cups blackberries
1¼ cups raspberries
1 cup sugar
3 large egg whites
1 cup heavy or whipping cream

1 Line 9" by 5" loaf pan with plastic wrap, allowing plastic wrap to extend over sides of pan.

2 In food processor with knife blade attached, blend blackberries and raspberries until pureed. Press berries through medium-mesh sieve into large bowl; discard seeds. Set aside.

3 In 1-quart saucepan, heat sugar with ¼ *cup water* to boiling over high heat; boil 2 minutes.

4 Meanwhile, in large bowl, with mixer at high speed, beat egg whites just until soft peaks form. Beating at high speed, slowly pour hot syrup in thin stream into egg whites. Continue beating 8 to 10 minutes, until whites stand in stiff peaks.

5 In small bowl, with same beaters and at medium speed, beat cream until stiff peaks form. Fold egg whites, one-third at a time, into berry puree, then fold in whipped cream. Spoon mixture into loaf pan. Cover with plastic wrap and freeze 6 hours or overnight.

6 To serve, remove semifreddo from freezer and remove plastic wrap from top. Invert semifreddo onto platter; discard plastic wrap and let stand 15 minutes to soften slightly. Cut into ¾-inch-thick slices to serve. Makes 12 servings.

Each serving: About 160 calories, 2 g protein, 23 g carbohydrate, 8 g total fat (5 g saturated), 27 mg cholesterol, 20 mg sodium.

BERRY ABCs

A pretty presentation—whether you're scattering berries on cereal or making a shortcake—has a lot to do with how berries are selected and stored. Here are some tips:

PURCHASE POINTERS
• Choose plump, dry, firm berries that are uniformly colored. Check for withered, crushed, or moldy fruit (the mold can spread from berry to berry) and stained packages.
• Dewy, water-sprinkled berries may look picture-perfect, but they're not; moisture accelerates molding and decaying.

Strawberries
• The sweetest berries are bright red with fresh green stems attached; pale, yellowish-white strawberries are unripe and sour.
• Leave caps on until after washing so berries don't get waterlogged. Use a huller, paring knife, or even your fingers to remove caps.
Peak season: April through June
Cup for cup: 1 pint equals about 3¼ cups whole, 2¼ cups sliced.

Blueberries
• Blueberries should be deep-blue; reddish ones are unripe and best saved for jams or pies. The silver-white bloom on the surface of the blueberries is a natural protective coating—not mold.
• Common blueberries are about ½ inch in diameter; wild berries (also called lowbush blueberries), are pea-size, much tarter, and hold their shape exceptionally well during baking.
Peak season: June through August (for wild blueberries, August and September)
Cup for cup: 1 pint equals about 2½ cups.

Raspberries
• Select brightly colored berries without hulls. (When the color deepens to a dusky shade, the berries are past their prime.)
• Don't miss the sweeter, milder golden berries and moderately tart purple (black) varieties, which are becoming more widely available in farmers' markets and supermarkets.
Peak season: June, July, September, and October
Cup for cup: ½ pint equals about 1 cup.

Old-Fashioned Raspberry Ice Cream (opposite page)

Blackberries
• Buy deeply colored berries. Choose from large maroon boysenberries with a rich, tart taste; deep-red loganberries, which are big, long, and tangy; medium to large dark-purple marionberries with small seeds and intense blackberry flavor; and large, glossy black olallieberries ranging from sweet to tart.
Peak season: June through October
Cup for cup: ½ pint equals about 1 cup.

SMART STORAGE TIPS
• Because berries are more fragile and perishable than any other fruit, they can deteriorate within 24 hours of purchase. You can store them in their baskets for brief periods, but to keep for 2 to 3 days, place berries, unwashed, on a paper-towel-lined jelly-roll or baking pan, cover loosely with paper towels and plastic wrap, and refrigerate. (Blueberries are the exception: They last up to 10 days in the fridge.) For fullest flavor, let berries come to room temperature before eating.
• To freeze berries, wash and drain, then spread in a single layer on a jelly-roll pan. Once they're frozen, transfer to a freezer-weight self-sealing plastic bag and freeze for up to 1 year. When using frozen berries for baking, there's no need to thaw, just extend cooking time for pies by 10 to 15 minutes; muffins and breads, 5 to 10 minutes. (Again, blues are the exception: They should be frozen unwashed then quickly rinsed under cold water before using.)

Black & White Bread Pudding

PREP: 40 MINUTES PLUS STANDING
BAKE: 1 HOUR 20 MINUTES

For chocolate lovers everywhere–as delicious alone as with the sinfully rich custard sauce. We love the warm pudding with the cold sauce!

1 loaf (16 ounces) sliced firm white bread
4 cups milk
½ cup sugar
1 tablespoon vanilla extract
½ teaspoon salt
9 large eggs
3 ounces white chocolate, grated
3 ounces bittersweet chocolate, grated
White-Chocolate Custard Sauce (recipe follows)

1 Preheat oven to 325°F. Grease 13" by 9" glass or ceramic baking dish; set aside. Place bread slices on large cookie sheet; lightly toast in oven 20 to 30 minutes, turning once. Place bread slices in baking dish, overlapping slightly.

2 Meanwhile, in very large bowl, with wire whisk or fork, beat milk, sugar, vanilla, salt, and eggs until blended. Stir in grated chocolates. Pour milk mixture evenly over bread; let stand 30 minutes for bread to absorb most of the milk mixture, occasionally spooning mixture over bread.

3 Cover baking dish with foil; bake 1 hour. Uncover and bake 15 to 20 minutes longer until top is golden.

4 While pudding is baking, prepare White-Chocolate Custard Sauce. Serve bread pudding warm. Or, refrigerate to serve cold later. Makes 16 servings.

WHITE-CHOCOLATE CUSTARD SAUCE: Finely chop *3 ounces white chocolate;** place in large bowl. In small bowl, with wire whisk, beat *4 large egg yolks;* gradually whisk in *¼ cup sugar* until combined; set aside. In heavy 2-quart saucepan, over medium heat, heat *1 cup milk* and *¾ cup heavy or whipping cream* until small bubbles form around edge of pan. Into egg mixture, beat small amount of hot milk mixture. Slowly pour egg mixture back into milk mixture, stirring rapidly to prevent lumping. Reduce heat to low; cook, stirring constantly, until mixture thickens slightly and coats back of a spoon well, about 5 minutes. (Mixture should be about 160°F., but do not

boil or it will curdle.) Pour mixture over white chocolate, stirring to combine. Serve custard sauce warm or refrigerate to serve cold. Makes about 2½ cups.

*Or use *one 3-ounce Swiss confectionery bar* or one-half 6-ounce package white baking bar.

Each serving of bread pudding without sauce: About 240 calories, 9 g protein, 28 g carbohydrate, 11 g total fat (5 g saturated), 129 mg cholesterol, 285 mg sodium.

Each tablespoon White-Chocolate Custard Sauce: About 40 calories, 1 g protein, 3 g carbohydrate, 3 g total fat (2 g saturated), 29 mg cholesterol, 5 mg sodium.

Cherries & Cream Rice Pudding

PREP: 15 MINUTES PLUS CHILLING
COOK: 1 HOUR 15 MINUTES

½ vanilla bean or 1 tablespoon vanilla extract
6 cups milk
¾ cup sugar
¾ cup arborio rice (Italian short-grain rice) or regular long-grain rice
½ cup dried cherries or raisins
2 tablespoons dark rum (optional)
¼ teaspoon salt
½ cup heavy or whipping cream

1 With knife, cut vanilla bean lengthwise in half. Scrape out and reserve seeds from inside both halves.

2 In 4-quart saucepan, heat milk, sugar, vanilla-bean seeds, and vanilla-bean halves to boiling over medium-high heat, stirring occasionally. (If using vanilla extract, add in step 3 with rum.) Stir in rice; heat to boiling. Reduce heat to low; cover and simmer 1 hour and 15 minutes, stirring occasionally, until mixture is very creamy and slightly thickened (pudding will firm up upon chilling). Remove and discard vanilla-bean halves.

3 Spoon rice pudding into large bowl; stir in dried cherries, rum, and salt. Cool slightly, then cover and refrigerate until well chilled, at least 6 hours.

4 Up to 2 hours before serving, whip cream until stiff peaks form. Fold whipped cream, half at a time, into rice pudding. Makes 12 servings.

Each serving with rum: About 230 calories, 5 g protein, 34 g carbohydrate, 8 g total fat (5 g saturated), 30 mg cholesterol, 110 mg sodium.

◄ *Black & White Bread Pudding*

Nantucket Indian Pudding

PREP: 30 MINUTES PLUS COOLING • BAKE: 2 HOURS

A baked cornmeal and molasses pudding adapted by the early English settlers in New England and later known as "hasty pudding" by the colonists. To make this ahead, mix batter and pour into baking dish up to 2 hours before baking. Then pop it into the oven and let it bake, maintenance-free, while you cook and serve the rest of the meal.

⅔ cup yellow cornmeal
4 cups milk
½ cup light molasses
4 tablespoons margarine or butter (½ stick),
    cut up
¼ cup sugar
1 teaspoon ground ginger
1 teaspoon ground cinnamon
½ teaspoon salt
¼ teaspoon ground nutmeg
Whipped cream or vanilla ice cream

1 Preheat oven to 350°F. Grease shallow 1½-quart glass or ceramic baking dish.

2 In small bowl, combine cornmeal and 1 cup milk. In 4-quart saucepan, heat remaining 3 cups milk to boiling over high heat. Stir in cornmeal mixture; heat to boiling. Reduce heat to low and cook, stirring often to avoid lumps, 20 minutes. (Mixture will be very thick.) Remove saucepan from heat; stir in molasses, margarine or butter, sugar, ginger, cinnamon, salt, and nutmeg until blended.

3 Pour batter evenly into baking dish. Place baking dish in roasting pan; place on oven rack. Carefully pour *boiling water* into roasting pan to come halfway up side of baking dish. Cover with foil and bake pudding 1 hour. Remove foil and bake pudding 1 hour longer or until lightly browned and just set. Carefully remove baking dish from water. Cool pudding in pan on wire rack for 30 minutes. Serve pudding warm with whipped cream or vanilla ice cream if you like. Makes 8 servings.

Each serving without whipped or ice cream: About 245 calories, 5 g protein, 34 g carbohydrate, 10 g total fat (4 g saturated), 17 mg cholesterol, 275 mg sodium.

▌ FOOD EDITOR'S TIP ▐

Q. What's the secret to perfect whipped cream? Mine is either too stiff or doesn't whip at all.

A. First, be sure you're using heavy or whipping cream—light cream and half-and-half don't have enough fat to thicken. Then, thoroughly chill the cream, bowl, and beaters. Start beating cream at a low speed—using a stand mixer, handheld mixer, or old-fashioned rotary beater—and speed up as the cream thickens slightly; this helps stabilize it. Whip just until stiff peaks form when beaters are lifted; whipping too long can cause cream to break down into butter and whey.

Sweeten whipped cream with granulated or confectioners' sugar (add about 1 tablespoon per liquid cup), just when the mixture starts to thicken. When the cream is fluffy, gently fold in vanilla extract or a liqueur like Amaretto, Grand Marnier, crème de menthe, or crème de cacao (1 teaspoon per liquid cup). It's ideal to whip cream right before serving, but it will hold in the refrigerator for a few hours before it begins to "weep" (separate, with a watery layer on the bottom).

Citrus Pudding-Cake

PREP: 20 MINUTES • BAKE: 40 MINUTES

A lemon-orange pudding layer topped with its own "soufflé." Spoon it right from the baking dish while it's still steaming hot.

¾ cup sugar
¼ cup all-purpose flour
⅛ teaspoon salt
1 cup milk
3 large eggs, separated
4 tablespoons margarine or butter (½ stick),
    melted
¼ cup fresh lemon juice
¼ cup fresh orange juice
2 teaspoons grated orange peel

1 Preheat oven to 350°F. Grease 8" by 8" glass baking dish. In large bowl, combine sugar, flour, and salt. With wire whisk, beat in milk, egg yolks, melted margarine or butter, lemon juice, orange juice, and orange peel.

2 In small bowl, with mixer at high speed, beat egg whites until soft peaks form. Fold one-fourth of whites into orange mixture; gently fold in remaining whites. Pour batter into baking dish.

3 Set baking dish in roasting pan; place on oven rack. Carefully pour *boiling water* into roasting pan to come halfway up sides of baking dish. Bake 40 minutes or until top is golden and set (dessert will separate into pudding and cake layers). Cool in pan on wire rack for 10 minutes, then serve right away. Makes 6 servings.

Each serving: About 255 calories, 5 g protein, 33 g carbohydrate, 12 g total fat (3 g saturated), 112 mg cholesterol, 200 mg sodium.

Sticky Toffee Pudding

PREP: 30 MINUTES • BAKE: 30 MINUTES

The term pudding in England refers to many kinds of desserts. This pudding–all the rage in Great Britain and Australia–is a moist cake with a sticky broiled-on brown-sugar topping.

1 cup chopped pitted dates
1 teaspoon baking soda
1 cup sugar
10 tablespoons margarine or butter (1¼ sticks), softened
1 large egg
1 teaspoon vanilla extract
2 cups all-purpose flour
1 teaspoon baking powder
1 cup packed brown sugar
¼ cup heavy or whipping cream
Whipped cream (optional)

1 Grease 13" by 9" broiler-safe baking pan. In medium bowl, combine dates, baking soda, and *1½ cups boiling water*; let stand 15 minutes.

2 Preheat oven to 350°F. In large bowl, with mixer at medium speed, beat sugar and 6 tablespoons margarine or butter until creamy. Add egg and vanilla; beat until blended. At low speed, beat in flour and baking powder. Add date mixture and beat until combined (batter will be very thin). Pour batter into baking pan. Bake 30 minutes or until golden and toothpick inserted in center comes out clean.

3 Meanwhile, in 2-quart saucepan, heat brown sugar, heavy cream, and remaining 4 tablespoons margarine or butter to boiling over medium heat; boil 1 minute. Set aside.

4 Turn oven control to broil. Spread brown-sugar mixture evenly over top of hot dessert. Place pan in broiler at closest position to source of heat; broil until bubbly, about 30 seconds. Cool in pan on wire rack 15 minutes. Serve warm with whipped cream if you like. Makes 12 servings.

Each serving without whipped cream: About 340 calories, 3 g protein, 62 g carbohydrate, 10 g total fat (2 g saturated), 18 mg cholesterol, 275 mg sodium.

Brownie Pudding

PREP: 20 MINUTES • BAKE: 30 MINUTES

A "magical" dessert that separates during baking into a fudgy brownie on top of silky chocolate pudding. Serve hot, before brownie layer absorbs the pudding!

2 teaspoons instant-coffee powder or granules
1 cup all-purpose flour
½ cup sugar
2 teaspoons baking powder
¼ teaspoon salt
¾ cup unsweetened cocoa
½ cup milk
4 tablespoons margarine or butter (½ stick), melted
1 teaspoon vanilla extract
½ cup packed light brown sugar
Vanilla ice cream (optional)

1 Preheat oven to 350°F. In cup, dissolve instant coffee in *2 tablespoons hot tap water*; set aside.

2 In medium bowl, combine flour, sugar, baking powder, salt, and ½ cup cocoa. In 2-cup glass measuring cup, combine milk, melted margarine or butter, vanilla, and dissolved instant coffee. With spoon, stir liquid mixture into dry mixture just until blended. Pour batter into ungreased 8" by 8" glass baking dish.

3 In small bowl, with spoon, combine brown sugar and remaining ¼ cup cocoa; sprinkle over batter. Carefully pour *1¾ cups boiling water* over brownie mixture in baking dish; do not stir.

4 Bake 30 minutes (dessert will separate into cake and pudding layers). Cool in pan on wire rack 10 minutes, then serve right away. Top with ice cream if you like. Makes 8 servings.

Each serving without ice cream: About 235 calories, 4 g protein, 44 g carbohydrate, 7 g total fat (2 g saturated), 2 mg cholesterol, 250 mg sodium.

New York Pumpkin Crème Caramel

PREP: 30 MINUTES PLUS OVERNIGHT TO CHILL
BAKE: 55 MINUTES

A dessert even nonpumpkin-pie fans will enjoy. Prepare a day ahead to allow custard to chill and set properly. If you like, this dessert can be made up to 2 days ahead—unmold when ready to serve.

6 strips orange peel (about 3" by 1" each)
1¼ cups sugar
1 can (12 ounces) evaporated milk
1 cup heavy or whipping cream
1 cup solid-pack pumpkin (not pumpkin-pie mix)
6 large eggs
¼ cup orange-flavor liqueur
1 teaspoon vanilla extract
1 teaspoon ground cinnamon
Pinch nutmeg
Pinch salt

1 In 1-quart saucepan, heat orange peel, ¾ cup sugar, and ¼ *cup water* to boiling over high heat. Cover and cook 10 minutes. With fork, remove orange-peel strips and discard. Continue cooking sugar mixture, uncovered, until it turns amber in color, about 3 minutes longer. Pour caramel into 9" by 5" loaf pan, swirling to coat bottom. (Hold pan with pot holders to protect hands from heat of caramel.) Set aside.

2 In heavy 2-quart saucepan, heat evaporated milk, heavy cream, and remaining ½ cup sugar just to boiling over medium-high heat.

3 Meanwhile, preheat oven to 350°F. In large bowl, with wire whisk, mix pumpkin, eggs, orange liqueur, vanilla, cinnamon, nutmeg, and salt until blended.

4 Gradually whisk hot milk mixture into pumpkin mixture until blended. Pour pumpkin mixture through strainer into 8-cup glass measuring cup, then into caramel-coated loaf pan. Place loaf pan in roasting pan; place on oven rack. Pour *boiling water* into roasting pan to come three-quarters of the way up side of loaf pan. Bake 55 minutes or until knife comes out clean when inserted 1 inch from edge of custard (center will jiggle slightly).

5 Carefully remove loaf pan from water. Allow crème caramel to cool 1 hour in pan on wire rack. Refrigerate crème caramel overnight. To unmold, run small spatula around sides of loaf pan; invert crème caramel onto serving plate, allowing caramel syrup to drip down from pan (some caramel may remain in pan). Makes 12 servings.

Each serving: About 180 calories, 4 g protein, 21 g carbohydrate, 9 g total fat (5 g saturated), 106 mg cholesterol, 61 mg sodium.

Creamy Lemon-Ricotta Cheesecake

PREP: 20 MINUTES PLUS COOLING AND CHILLING
BAKE: 1 HOUR 25 MINUTES

Adding a whole pint of half-and-half to the batter gives this delicate cake a light, silky texture. We love the quick wafer crust too.

30 vanilla wafers
4 tablespoons margarine or butter (½ stick)
4 teaspoons grated lemon peel
1¼ cups sugar
¼ cup cornstarch
2 packages (8 ounces each) cream cheese, softened
1 container (15 ounces) ricotta cheese
4 large eggs
2 cups half-and-half or light cream
⅓ cup fresh lemon juice
2 teaspoons vanilla extract
Lemon-peel strips and mint sprigs for garnish

1 In food processor with knife blade attached or in blender at medium speed, blend vanilla wafers until fine crumbs form. (You should have about 1 cup crumbs.)

2 Preheat oven to 375°F. In small saucepan, melt margarine or butter over low heat; stir in 1 teaspoon lemon peel. In 9" by 3" springform pan, with fork, stir wafer crumbs and melted margarine mixture until moistened. With hand, press mixture firmly onto bottom of pan. Bake crust 10 minutes. Cool completely in pan on wire rack, about 30 minutes. Wrap outside of pan with foil.

3 Turn oven control to 325°F. In cup, combine sugar and cornstarch until blended. In large bowl, with mixer at medium speed, beat cream cheese and ricotta cheese until smooth, about 5 minutes; slowly beat in sugar mixture. At low speed, beat in eggs, half-and-half, lemon juice, vanilla, and remaining 3 teaspoons lemon peel just until blended, scraping bowl often with rubber spatula.

4 Pour cream-cheese mixture onto crust. Bake cheesecake 1 hour and 15 minutes. Turn off oven; let cheesecake remain in oven 1 hour longer. Remove cheesecake from oven. Cool completely in pan on wire rack. Cover and refrigerate cheesecake at least 6 hours or overnight until well chilled. Remove side of pan to serve. Garnish with lemon peel and mint sprigs. Makes 16 servings.

Each serving: About 315 calories, 8 g protein, 27 g carbohydrate, 22 g total fat (11 g saturated), 112 mg cholesterol, 200 mg sodium.

Our Sublime Hot Fphuge Sauce

PREP: 5 MINUTES • COOK: 10 MINUTES

Make a double batch, to pour over toasted pound cake or your favorite ice cream. It will keep in the refrigerator for up to one week; to reheat, zap the amount you need in the microwave on medium, or warm over low heat in a saucepan on the stovetop.

Our Sublime Hot Fudge Sauce

1 cup heavy or whipping cream
¾ cup sugar
4 squares (1 ounce each) unsweetened
   chocolate, chopped
2 tablespoons light corn syrup
2 tablespoons margarine or butter (¼ stick)
2 teaspoons vanilla extract

In heavy 2-quart saucepan, heat heavy or whipping cream, sugar, chocolate, and corn syrup over medium heat until mixture comes to a boil, stirring occasionally. Cook 4 to 5 minutes longer, until sauce thickens slightly (mixture should be gently boiling), stirring constantly. Remove saucepan from heat; stir in margarine or butter and vanilla until smooth and glossy. Serve immediately, or let cool completely, cover, and refrigerate. (Do not cover sauce until it is cold, or the water from condensation will make it grainy.) Makes about 1¾ cups.

Each tablespoon: About 85 calories, 1 g protein, 8 g carbohydrate, 6 g total fat (3 g saturated), 12 mg cholesterol, 15 mg sodium.

Butterscotch Sauce

PREP: 5 MINUTES • COOK: 10 MINUTES

This recipe makes a large batch of velvety sauce.

4 cups packed light brown sugar
2 cups heavy or whipping cream
1⅓ cups light corn syrup
½ cup margarine or butter (1 stick)
4 teaspoons distilled white vinegar
½ teaspoon salt
4 teaspoons vanilla extract

In 5-quart Dutch oven (do not use smaller pan because mixture bubbles up during cooking), heat brown sugar, heavy cream, corn syrup, margarine or butter, vinegar, and salt to boiling over high heat, stirring occasionally. Reduce heat to low; simmer, uncovered, 5 minutes, stirring frequently. Remove saucepan from heat; stir in vanilla. Sauce will have thin consistency when hot but will thicken when chilled. Cool sauce completely. Store in refrigerator for up to 2 weeks. Reheat to serve warm over ice cream. Makes about 6 cups.

Each tablespoon: About 75 calories, 0 g protein, 13 g carbohydrate, 3 g total fat (1 g saturated), 7 mg cholesterol, 35 mg sodium.

No-Cook Berry Sauce

Spoon this fast, fresh jewel-tone topping over ice cream, pound cake, or waffles, or stir a couple of tablespoons into a glass of lemonade for a delicious new drink. The amount of sugar needed depends on the flavor of the fruit, so sweeten to taste—the sauce should retain the natural tanginess and flavor of whichever berry you're using.

3 cups raspberries, blackberries, strawberries, or
   blueberries
½ to ⅔ cup confectioners' sugar, depending on
   berries' sweetness

1 to 2 teaspoons fresh lemon or lime juice, or to
   taste

1 In food processor with knife blade attached, blend berries until pureed. Sift ½ cup confectioners' sugar over berries; pulse until smooth. Press berry mixture through medium-mesh sieve to remove seeds. Discard seeds.

2 Stir in 1 teaspoon lemon or lime juice. Taste and adjust sugar and citrus juice. Cover and refrigerate if not serving immediately. Sauce will thicken upon standing; whisk just before serving if necessary. Keep sauce refrigerated and use within 3 days. Makes about 1½ cups.

Each tablespoon: About 15 calories, 0 g protein, 4 g carbohydrate, 0 g total fat, 0 mg cholesterol, 0 mg sodium.

CHOCOLATE TRUFFLES
THE ULTIMATE AFTER-DINNER TREAT

These bittersweet confections are easy to make. For extra flavor, you can add 2 tablespoons of your favorite liqueur, such as Amaretto, to the melted chocolate mixture.

PREP: 25 MINUTES PLUS CHILLING

8 ounces bittersweet chocolate*
½ cup heavy or whipping cream
3 tablespoons unsalted butter, softened and cut up
⅓ cup hazelnuts (filberts), toasted and finely
   chopped
3 tablespoons unsweetened cocoa

1 In food processor with knife blade attached, blend chocolate until finely ground.

2 In 1-quart saucepan, heat heavy cream over medium-high heat to boiling. Add cream to chocolate in food processor and blend until smooth. Add butter and blend well.

3 Line 9" by 5" metal loaf pan with plastic wrap. Pour chocolate mixture into pan; spread evenly. Refrigerate until cool and firm enough to handle, about 3 hours.

4 Remove chocolate mixture from pan by lifting edges of plastic wrap and inverting chocolate block onto cutting board; discard plastic wrap. Cut chocolate mixture into 32 pieces. (To cut chocolate mix-

ture easily, dip knife in hot water and wipe dry.) Quickly roll each piece into a ball. Roll half of the balls in chopped hazelnuts and roll other half of balls in cocoa. Refrigerate truffles in airtight containers for up to a week or freeze for up to a month. Remove truffles from freezer 5 minutes before serving. Makes 32 truffles.

*Or use 6 squares (1 ounce each) semisweet chocolate and 2 squares (1 ounce each) unsweetened chocolate.

*Each truffle: About 65 calories, 1 g protein,
5 g carbohydrate, 6 g total fat (3 g saturated),
8 mg cholesterol, 2 mg sodium.*

PIES & CAKES

Cheddar-Crust Vermont Apple Pie

PREP: 1 HOUR PLUS COOLING
BAKE: 1 HOUR 15 MINUTES

Your family will love this New England tradition. The dough can be prepared a day ahead if refrigerated, and up to 2 weeks ahead if frozen. You can make the entire pie up to a day in advance. Reheat, loosely covered with foil, in 350°F. oven about 20 minutes.

2½ cups all-purpose flour
3 ounces shredded extrasharp Cheddar
   cheese (¾ cup)
½ teaspoon salt
3 tablespoons shortening
½ cup plus 2 tablespoons margarine or butter
6 large Cortland apples (about 3¼ pounds)
1 tablespoon lemon juice
⅔ cup sugar
¼ teaspoon ground cinnamon

1 In medium bowl, mix 2¼ cups flour with Cheddar cheese and salt. With pastry blender or two knives used scissor-fashion, cut in shortening and ½ cup margarine or butter (1 stick) until mixture resembles coarse crumbs. Sprinkle *4 to 6 tablespoons cold water*, 1 tablespoon at a time, into flour mixture, mixing lightly with a fork after each addition until dough is just moist enough to hold together. Shape dough into 2 balls, 1 slightly larger than the other. Flatten smaller ball into a disk; cover with plastic wrap and refrigerate until ready to use.

2 On lightly floured surface, with floured rolling pin, roll larger ball of dough into a round 2 inches larger all around than inverted 9½-inch deep-dish pie plate. Gently ease dough into pie plate; trim edge leaving 1-inch overhang. Cover and refrigerate at least 30 minutes.

3 Meanwhile, peel, core, and slice apples into ⅜-inch-thick slices. Place apple slices in large bowl; toss with lemon juice. In small bowl, mix sugar and cinnamon with remaining ¼ cup flour. Add sugar mixture to apple slices; toss well to coat. Spoon apple mixture into chilled piecrust; dot with remaining 2 tablespoons margarine or butter.

4 Preheat oven to 425°F. Roll remaining dough for top crust into 11-inch round. Center round over filling in bottom crust. Trim edge, leaving 1-inch overhang. Fold overhang under; bring up over pie-plate rim and pinch to form high decorative edge. Cut

short slashes in top crust to allow steam to escape during baking.

5 Place sheet of foil underneath pie plate; crimp foil edges to form a rim to catch any drips during baking. Bake pie 1 hour and 15 minutes or until apples are tender when pierced with a knife and pie is bubbly. To prevent overbrowning, cover pie loosely with a tent of foil during last 10 minutes of baking. Cool pie on wire rack 1 hour; serve warm. Or, cool completely to serve later. Makes 10 servings.

Each serving: About 405 calories, 6 g protein, 56 g carbohydrate, 19 g total fat (5 g saturated), 9 mg cholesterol, 315 mg sodium.

Apple Crumb Pie

PREP: 40 MINUTES • BAKE: ABOUT 1 HOUR 45 MINUTES

We added a cup of sour cream to the apple mixture for a creamy-good flavor.

1½ cups all-purpose flour
½ teaspoon salt
4 tablespoons margarine or butter (½ stick)
¼ cup shortening
3 pounds Granny Smith apples (about 7 large)
⅔ cup sugar
⅓ cup dark seedless raisins
3 tablespoons cornstarch
½ teaspoon ground cinnamon
Crumb Topping (page 201)
1 container (8 ounces) sour cream
1 teaspoon vanilla extract

1 In medium bowl, mix flour and salt. With pastry blender or two knives used scissor-fashion, cut in margarine or butter with shortening until mixture resembles coarse crumbs. Sprinkle about *4 tablespoons cold water*, 1 tablespoon at a time, into flour mixture, mixing lightly with fork after each addition until dough is just moist enough to hold together. Shape dough into a disk and refrigerate 30 minutes or until firm enough to roll.

2 Meanwhile, peel, core, and cut apples into ¾-inch chunks. In large bowl, toss apples with sugar, raisins, cornstarch, and cinnamon until well combined. Set aside.

Top to bottom: Cheddar-Crust Vermont Apple Pie, ➤
Georgia Chocolate-Pecan Pie (page 206)

LET IT ROLL
5 STEPS TO A PERFECT CRUST

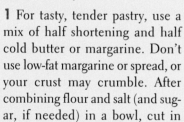

You don't have to be a food pro to create delicious crusts that won't stick to the counter in a gummy mess, come out lopsided, or fall apart en route to the pie plate. Here are simple tips from our test kitchens to try at home.

1 For tasty, tender pastry, use a mix of half shortening and half cold butter or margarine. Don't use low-fat margarine or spread, or your crust may crumble. After combining flour and salt (and sugar, if needed) in a bowl, cut in shortening and butter with pastry blender or with two knives used scissor-fashion until mixture turns into coarse, pea-sized crumbs.

2 For a flaky crust, sprinkle cold water over crumb mixture, a tablespoon at a time, mixing quickly with a fork. Stir lightly just until crumbs are moist enough to hold together under slight pressure. (Avoid vigorous mixing or the fat will oversoften and produce a sticky dough.) Gently gather dough in your hands and shape into a disk.

3 To prevent sticking, place dough on a lightly floured surface. Roll out with even strokes from center to edge in all directions; apply lighter pressure at edges so they won't crack. If bits of dough stick to rolling pin, remove immediately so they don't lead to holes. Note: When rolling out dough on a cutting board, place a damp dish cloth under the board so it won't slip, causing uneven rolling.

4 For a smooth pie-plate transfer, wrap dough loosely around the rolling pin. Then unroll it into the plate, easing dough into bottom and up side of pie plate. Pat gently with fingers to ease out air pockets underneath. Never stretch dough to fit pie plate—it will shrink while baking. If the circle is too small, keep rolling.

5 To make a picture-perfect edge, trim dough with kitchen shears, leaving amount of overhang recipe directs. Fold excess under and pinch to make stand-up rim, then create decorative edge of your choice. Shown here, rope edge: Press thumb into dough at angle, then pinch dough between thumb and index finger of same hand. Place thumb in groove left by index finger and repeat. For double-crust pie, place top crust over filling, then trim top crust even with bottom crust before making decorative edge.

3 Preheat oven to 400° F. On lightly floured surface, with floured rolling pin, roll dough into a round 2 inches larger in diameter than inverted 9½-inch deep-dish pie plate. Ease dough into pie plate; trim edge, leaving 1-inch overhang. Fold overhang under; pinch to form decorative edge. Cover and refrigerate.

4 While crust is chilling, prepare Crumb Topping.

5 Add sour cream and vanilla to apple mixture and toss well to coat evenly. Spoon apple mixture into chilled crust. Sprinkle top of apples evenly with Crumb Topping.

6 Place sheet of foil underneath pie plate; crimp foil edges to form a rim to catch any drips during baking. Bake pie for 1 hour at 400° F. Turn oven control to 350° F. and bake 35 to 45 minutes longer, until filling is bubbly and top is golden. Cover with foil if top begins to brown too quickly. Remove from oven and cool slightly on wire rack to serve warm, or cool completely to serve at room temperature later. Makes 10 servings.

CRUMB TOPPING: In medium bowl, stir ⅔ *cup all-purpose flour*, ⅓ *cup packed brown sugar*, and ¼ *teaspoon ground cinnamon*. With pastry blender or two knives used scissor-fashion, cut in 3 *tablespoons cold margarine* or butter until mixture resembles coarse crumbs.

Each serving: About 410 calories, 4 g protein, 65 g carbohydrate, 16 g total fat (5 g saturated), 10 mg cholesterol, 175 mg sodium.

Rustic Apricot Crostata

PREP: 45 MINUTES PLUS CHILLING AND COOLING
BAKE: 40 TO 45 MINUTES

Butter is essential to the texture and flavor; we don't recommend substituting margarine.

½ cup blanched almonds, toasted
3 tablespoons cornstarch
2½ cups all-purpose flour
¼ teaspoon salt
1 cup butter (2 sticks), softened
½ cup plus 2 teaspoons sugar
1 large egg plus 1 large egg yolk
2 teaspoons vanilla extract
1 jar (12 ounces) apricot preserves (about 1 cup)

1 In food processor with knife blade attached, or in blender at high speed, blend toasted almonds with cornstarch until finely ground.

2 In medium bowl, combine nut mixture, flour, and salt.

3 In large bowl, with mixer at high speed, beat butter and ½ cup sugar until creamy. Add whole egg and vanilla; beat until almost combined (mixture will look curdled). With spoon, stir in flour mixture until dough begins to form. With hands, press dough together. Divide dough into 2 pieces, 1 slightly larger than the other. Shape each piece into a disk and wrap each with plastic wrap; refrigerate 1½ to 2 hours, until dough is firm enough to roll.

4 Preheat oven to 375°F. Remove both pieces of dough from refrigerator. On lightly floured surface, roll larger piece of dough into an 11-inch round. Press dough into 11-inch tart pan with removable bottom.

5 On lightly floured waxed paper, roll remaining piece of dough into 12-inch round. With pastry wheel or knife, cut dough into twelve 1-inch-wide strips. Refrigerate 15 minutes.

6 Spread apricot preserves over dough in tart pan to ½ inch from edge. Place 5 strips, 1 inch apart, across tart, trimming ends even with side of tart pan. Repeat with 5 more strips placed diagonally across first ones, trimming ends, to make a diamond lattice pattern.

7 With hands, roll trimmings and remaining strips of dough into about ¼-inch-thick ropes. Press ropes around edge of tart to create a finished edge. (If rope pieces break, just press pieces together.)

8 In cup, beat egg yolk with 1 *tablespoon water*. Brush egg-yolk mixture over lattice and edge of tart; sprinkle with remaining 2 teaspoons sugar.

9 Bake tart 40 to 45 minutes, until crust is deep golden. If crust puffs up during baking (check occasionally during first 30 minutes of baking), stick tip of knife into tart to let air escape. Transfer tart to wire rack to cool completely. Makes 12 servings.

Each serving: About 395 calories, 5 g protein, 52 g carbohydrate, 19 g total fat (10 g saturated), 76 mg cholesterol, 210 mg sodium.

Italian Triple-Berry Tart

PREP: 40 MINUTES PLUS CHILLING AND COOLING
BAKE: 30 MINUTES

You can make the pastry cream and crust a day ahead—just fold in the whipped cream and top with berries when ready to serve.

TART SHELL:
1½ cups all-purpose flour
2 tablespoons sugar
½ teaspoon salt
¼ cup shortening
4 tablespoons cold margarine or butter (½ stick)

PASTRY CREAM:
3 large egg yolks
⅓ cup sugar
2 tablespoons cornstarch
1 cup milk
2 tablespoons margarine or butter
1 teaspoon vanilla extract
½ cup heavy or whipping cream

2 cups blueberries
2 cups raspberries
2 cups blackberries
Confectioners' sugar

1 Prepare Tart Shell: In medium bowl, with fork, stir flour, sugar, and salt. With pastry blender or two knives used scissor-fashion, cut in shortening with margarine or butter until mixture resembles coarse crumbs. Sprinkle about *4 tablespoons cold water*, 1 tablespoon at a time, into flour mixture, mixing lightly with a fork after each addition until dough is just moist enough to hold together. Shape dough into a disk; wrap with plastic wrap and refrigerate 30 minutes or until firm enough to roll.

2 Meanwhile, prepare Pastry Cream: In small bowl, with wire whisk, mix egg yolks, sugar, and cornstarch until blended. In 2-quart saucepan, heat milk to simmering over medium heat. While constantly beating with wire whisk, gradually pour about half of simmering milk into yolk mixture. Reduce heat to low. Return yolk mixture to saucepan and cook, whisking constantly, until Pastry Cream thickens and boils; boil 1 minute. Remove saucepan from heat; stir in margarine or butter and vanilla. Transfer Pastry Cream to medium bowl; cover surface directly with

plastic wrap to prevent skin from forming, and refrigerate until cold, at least 2 hours.

3 Preheat oven to 425°F. On lightly floured surface, with floured rolling pin, roll dough into a 14-inch round. Press dough onto bottom and up side of 11" by 1" tart pan with removable bottom. Fold overhang in and press against side of tart pan to form a rim ⅛ inch above edge of pan. With fork, prick dough at 1-inch intervals to prevent puffing and shrinking during baking.

4 Line tart pan with foil and fill with pie weights, dried beans, or uncooked rice. Bake tart shell 20 minutes; remove foil with weights and bake 10 minutes longer or until golden. Cool completely on wire rack.

5 Up to 2 hours before serving, in small bowl, with mixer at medium speed, beat cream just until stiff peaks form. Whisk Pastry Cream until smooth; fold in whipped cream. Fill tart shell with Pastry-Cream mixture; top with berries and sprinkle with confectioners' sugar. Makes 12 servings.

Each serving: About 285 calories, 4 g protein, 32 g carbohydrate, 16 g total fat (6 g saturated), 70 mg cholesterol, 180 mg sodium.

Raspberry-Peach Pie

PREP: 30 MINUTES PLUS COOLING
BAKE: 1 HOUR 15 MINUTES

Make this top-crust-only dessert in a shallow baking dish or deep-dish pie plate.

1¼ cups all-purpose flour
½ plus ⅛ teaspoon salt
2 tablespoons shortening
6 tablespoons cold margarine or butter (¾ stick)
1¼ cups sugar
⅓ cup cornstarch
9 ripe medium peaches (about 3 pounds)
2½ cups raspberries
1 tablespoon lemon juice

1 In medium bowl, combine flour and ½ teaspoon salt. With pastry blender or two knives used scissor-fashion, cut in shortening and 4 tablespoons margarine or butter (½ stick) until mixture resembles coarse crumbs. Sprinkle about *4 tablespoons cold*

Italian Triple-Berry Tart ➤

water, 1 tablespoon at a time, into flour mixture, mixing lightly with a fork after each addition until dough is just moist enough to hold together. Shape dough into a disk; wrap with plastic wrap and refrigerate until ready to use.

2 Preheat oven to 425°F. In large bowl, combine sugar, cornstarch, and ⅛ teaspoon salt. Peel and slice peaches; toss with sugar mixture in bowl. With rubber spatula, gently stir in raspberries and lemon juice. Spoon peach mixture into 6-cup baking dish or 9½-inch deep-dish pie plate; dot with remaining 2 tablespoons margarine or butter.

3 On lightly floured surface, with floured rolling pin, roll dough 1½ inches larger all around than top of baking dish. Center dough over filling. Trim pastry edge, leaving 1-inch overhang. Fold overhang under; pinch dough onto rim of baking dish to seal. With tip of knife, cut slits in piecrust to allow steam to escape during baking.

4 Place sheet of foil underneath baking dish; crimp foil edges to form a rim to catch any drips during baking. Bake pie 1 hour and 15 minutes or until filling begins to bubble and crust is golden, covering if necessary after 1 hour to prevent crust from overbrowning. Cool pie on wire rack 1 hour to serve warm. Or cool completely to serve later. Makes 10 servings.

Each serving: About 315 calories, 3 g protein, 56 g carbohydrate, 10 g total fat (2 g saturated), 0 mg cholesterol, 225 mg sodium.

Pear Tarte Tatin

PREP: 1 HOUR PLUS COOLING • BAKE: 25 MINUTES

Golden, caramelized Bosc pears make our version a sure winner on any table.

1½ cups all-purpose flour
½ teaspoon salt
2 tablespoons plus ¾ cup sugar
¼ cup shortening
10 tablespoons margarine or butter (1¼ sticks)
1 tablespoon fresh lemon juice
7 firm, slightly ripe Bosc pears (about 3½ pounds), peeled, cored, and each cut lengthwise in half

1 In medium bowl, with fork, stir flour, salt, and 2 tablespoons sugar. With pastry blender or two knives used scissor-fashion, cut in shortening and 4 tablespoons margarine or butter until mixture

resembles coarse crumbs. Sprinkle about *4 tablespoons cold water*, 1 tablespoon at a time, into flour mixture, mixing lightly with fork after each addition until dough is just moist enough to hold together. Shape dough into a disk; wrap with plastic wrap and refrigerate 30 minutes or until firm enough to roll.

2 Meanwhile, in heavy 12-inch skillet (preferably cast iron) with oven-safe handle, heat lemon juice, ¾ cup sugar, and 6 tablespoons margarine or butter (¾ stick) over medium-high heat until mixture boils. Place pears in skillet, cut side down. Cook 12 minutes. Carefully turn pears over; cook 10 minutes longer or until syrup is caramelized and thickened.

3 Preheat oven to 425°F. Just before pears are done, on lightly floured surface, with floured rolling pin, roll dough into a 14-inch round. Place dough on top of pears in skillet; fold edge of dough under to form a rim around pears. With knife, cut six ¼-inch slits in dough to allow steam to escape during baking. Bake tart 25 minutes or until crust is golden.

4 When tart is done, place large platter over top of tart. Quickly turn skillet upside down to invert tart onto platter. Cool tart about 1 hour to serve warm, or cool completely to serve later. Makes 12 servings.

Each serving: About 295 calories, 2 g protein, 42 g carbohydrate, 14 g total fat (3 g saturated), 0 mg cholesterol, 215 mg sodium.

Banana Cream Pie

PREP: 35 MINUTES PLUS CHILLING • BAKE: 25 MINUTES

Pouring half the filling into the pie shell, then arranging the banana slices on top keeps the crust nice and crisp.

1¼ cups all-purpose flour
1 tablespoon plus ¾ cup sugar
¾ teaspoon salt
¼ cup butter-flavor shortening or shortening
6 tablespoons margarine or butter (¾ stick)
⅓ cup cornstarch
3¾ cups milk
5 large egg yolks
1¾ teaspoons vanilla extract
3 medium, ripe bananas
¾ cup heavy or whipping cream

1 In medium bowl, mix flour, 1 tablespoon sugar, and ½ teaspoon salt. With pastry blender or two knives used scissor-fashion, cut in shortening and 4 tablespoons margarine or butter (½ stick) until mixture resembles coarse crumbs. Sprinkle 3 *to 4 tablespoons cold water*, 1 tablespoon at a time, into flour mixture, mixing lightly with a fork after each addition until dough is just moist enough to hold together. Shape dough into ball.

2 Preheat oven to 425°F. On floured surface, with floured rolling pin, roll dough into a round 1½ inches larger all around than inverted 9-inch pie plate. Ease dough into pie plate; trim edge leaving 1-inch overhang. Fold overhang under; pinch to form high edge; flute. With fork, prick bottom and side of piecrust in many places to prevent puffing during baking. Line piecrust with foil and fill with pie weights, dried beans, or uncooked rice. Bake piecrust 10 minutes; remove foil with weights and bake 10 to 15 minutes longer, until golden. If pastry puffs up during baking, gently press it to pie plate with back of spoon. Cool on wire rack.

3 In 3-quart saucepan, mix cornstarch, ¾ cup sugar, and ¼ teaspoon salt; stir in milk until smooth. Over medium heat, cook until mixture boils and thickens, stirring constantly; boil 1 minute.

4 In small bowl, beat egg yolks slightly. Into yolks, beat small amount of hot milk mixture. Slowly pour yolk mixture back into milk mixture, stirring rapidly to prevent lumping. Over low heat, cook mixture about 2 minutes, stirring constantly, until mixture is very thick.

5 Remove saucepan from heat; stir in remaining 2 tablespoons margarine or butter (¼ stick) and 1½ teaspoons vanilla. Slice 2 bananas. Pour half the filling into piecrust. Arrange sliced bananas over custard; spoon remaining filling over banana layer. Place plastic wrap directly on surface of filling and refrigerate pie about 4 hours or until filling is cold and set.

How Tarte Tatin Got Its Name

The beloved French upside-down caramelized apple tart, formally known as Tarte des demoiselles Tatin, is actually the result of a mishap. In the late 1800's, Caroline and Stephanie Tatin— sisters who ran a hotel in Sologne, France— dropped one of their famous apple pies and salvaged it by turning it upside-down to feed their hungry guests.

6 To serve, in small bowl, with mixer at medium speed, beat heavy cream and remaining ¼ teaspoon vanilla until stiff peaks form. Spread whipped cream over filling. Slice remaining banana and arrange around edge of pie. Makes 10 servings.

Each serving: About 425 calories, 7 g protein, 45 g carbohydrate, 25 g total fat (10 g saturated), 143 mg cholesterol, 310 mg sodium.

Warm Banana-Pecan Tart

PREP: 45 MINUTES PLUS CHILLING • BAKE: 30 MINUTES

To keep last-minute preparation down to a minimum, bake the crust up to 2 days ahead, and prepare and refrigerate the toasted pecan cream up to a day in advance. Assemble the tart just before serving.

1½ cups all-purpose flour
½ teaspoon salt
Sugar
¼ cup shortening
6 tablespoons margarine or butter (¾ stick)
½ cup pecans, toasted
3 large egg yolks
1 tablespoon cornstarch
¾ cup half-and-half or light cream
1 teaspoon vanilla extract
5 ripe medium bananas (about 2 pounds), thinly sliced diagonally

1 In medium bowl, with fork, stir flour, salt, and 2 tablespoons sugar. With pastry blender or two knives used scissor-fashion, cut in shortening and 4 tablespoons margarine or butter (½ stick) until mixture resembles coarse crumbs. Sprinkle about *4 tablespoons cold water*, 1 tablespoon at a time, into flour mixture, mixing lightly with fork after each addition until dough is just moist enough to hold together. Shape dough into a disk; wrap with plastic wrap and refrigerate 30 minutes or until firm enough to roll.

2 Meanwhile, prepare toasted pecan cream: In food processor with knife blade attached or in blender at medium speed, pulse pecans with ¼ cup sugar until very finely ground. In small bowl, with wire whisk, mix egg yolks, cornstarch, and ¼ cup sugar until blended. In 2-quart saucepan, heat half-and-half to simmering over medium heat. While constantly beating with wire whisk, gradually pour about half of simmering cream into bowl with yolk mixture. Reduce heat to low. Return yolk mixture to saucepan and cook until thickened, whisking constantly, 4 to 5 minutes. Stir in toasted pecan mixture, vanilla, and remaining 2 tablespoons margarine or butter (¼ stick). Transfer toasted pecan cream to medium bowl; cover surface directly with plastic wrap to prevent skin from forming and refrigerate at least 30 minutes.

3 While cream is chilling, preheat oven to 425°F. On lightly floured surface, with floured rolling pin, roll dough into a 14-inch round. Press dough onto bottom and up side of 11" by 1" round tart pan with removable bottom. Fold overhang in and press against side of tart pan to form a rim ⅛ inch above edge of pan. With fork, prick dough at 1-inch intervals to prevent puffing and shrinking during baking.

4 Line tart shell with foil and fill with pie weights, dried beans, or uncooked rice. Bake tart shell 20 minutes; remove foil with weights and bake 10 minutes longer or until golden. (If crust puffs up during baking, gently press it to tart pan with back of spoon.) Turn oven control to broil.

5 Arrange banana slices, overlapping slightly, in tart shell. Spoon toasted pecan cream evenly on top of bananas and sprinkle with 1 tablespoon sugar. Cover edge of crust with foil to prevent overbrowning. Place tart on oven rack at closest position to source of heat and broil until top is lightly caramelized, 1 to 2 minutes. Serve tart warm. Makes 12 servings.

Each serving: About 295 calories, 4 g protein, 36 g carbohydrate, 16 g total fat (4 g saturated), 58 mg cholesterol, 175 mg sodium.

Chocolate Angel Pie

PREP: 20 MINUTES PLUS COOLING • BAKE: 1 HOUR

The meringue shell cooks best in a metal pie pan.

3 large egg whites
¼ teaspoon salt
¼ teaspoon cream of tartar
2½ teaspoons vanilla extract
2¼ cups confectioners' sugar
½ cup unsweetened cocoa
1 teaspoon instant espresso-coffee powder
2 cups heavy or whipping cream
2 tablespoons milk
Chocolate curls for garnish

1 Preheat oven to 300°F. Grease and flour 9-inch metal pie pan.

2 In small bowl, with mixer at high speed, beat egg whites, salt, and cream of tartar until soft peaks form. Beating at high speed, add 1 teaspoon vanilla and sprinkle in 1 cup confectioners' sugar, 2 tablespoons at a time, beating well after each addition until sugar dissolves and whites stand in stiff, glossy peaks.

3 With metal spatula, evenly spread meringue over bottom and up side of pie pan, making an edge above pie pan rim. Bake meringue 1 hour. Turn off oven and let meringue remain in oven 1 hour to dry out. Cool meringue shell in pie pan on wire rack.

4 Meanwhile, prepare filling: Sift cocoa with remaining 1¼ cups confectioners' sugar. In cup, dissolve espresso powder in *1 teaspoon hot tap water*. In large bowl, with mixer at medium speed, beat heavy or whipping cream, dissolved espresso, and remaining 1½ teaspoons vanilla just until soft peaks form. Reduce speed to low; gradually beat in cocoa mixture until thoroughly blended and stiff peaks form (do not overbeat). Beat in milk.

5 With rubber spatula, spread chocolate cream into cooled meringue shell. If not serving pie right away, cover and refrigerate until ready to serve. Garnish with chocolate curls. Makes 10 servings.

Each serving: About 290 calories, 3 g protein, 31 g carbohydrate, 18 g total fat (11 g saturated), 66 mg cholesterol, 95 mg sodium.

Georgia Chocolate-Pecan Pie

PREP: 45 MINUTES PLUS COOLING
BAKE: 1 HOUR 10 MINUTES

Sinfully rich—this will be a favorite at any family get-together. Prepare crust through step 2 up to a day in advance—be sure to wrap well with plastic wrap or place pastry-lined pie plate in well closed plastic bag.

1¼ cups all-purpose flour
½ teaspoon salt
2 tablespoons shortening
8 tablespoons margarine or butter(1 stick)
2 squares (1 ounce each) unsweetened chocolate
1¾ cups pecan halves
¾ cup packed dark brown sugar

Chocolate Angel Pie

¾ cup dark corn syrup
1 teaspoon vanilla extract
3 large eggs

1 In medium bowl, mix flour and salt. With pastry blender or two knives used scissor-fashion, cut in shortening and 4 tablespoons margarine or butter (½ stick) until mixture resembles coarse crumbs. Sprinkle 3 *to 4 tablespoons cold water*, 1 tablespoon at a time, into flour mixture, mixing lightly with fork after each addition until dough is just moist enough to hold together. Shape dough into a disk.

2 On lightly floured surface, with floured rolling pin, roll dough into a round 1½ inches larger all around than inverted 9-inch pie plate. Gently ease dough into pie plate; trim edge, leaving 1-inch overhang. Fold overhang under; pinch to form decorative edge. With fork, prick bottom and side of piecrust in many places to prevent puffing during baking. Cover and refrigerate piecrust at least 30 minutes.

3 Meanwhile, preheat oven to 425°F. In heavy 1-quart saucepan, melt unsweetened chocolate with remaining 4 tablespoons margarine or butter over low heat, stirring frequently. Set the melted chocolate aside to cool slightly.

4 Line pie shell with foil and fill with pie weights, dry beans, or uncooked rice. Bake piecrust 10 minutes; remove foil with weights and bake 10 minutes longer or until lightly browned. If pastry puffs up during baking, gently press it to pie plate with back of spoon. Cool piecrust on wire rack at least 10 minutes. Turn oven control to 350°F.

5 Coarsely chop 1 cup pecans; reserve remaining pecan halves.

6 In large bowl, with wire whisk, mix cooled chocolate mixture, brown sugar, corn syrup, vanilla, and eggs until blended. Stir in chopped pecans and pecan halves.

7 Pour pecan mixture into cooled crust. Bake pie 45 to 50 minutes until edges of filling are set (center will jiggle slightly). Cool pie on wire rack. Makes 12 servings.

Each serving: About 395 calories, 5 g protein, 43 g carbohydrate, 24 g total fat (4 g saturated), 53 mg cholesterol, 225 mg sodium.

Alabama Sweet-Potato Meringue Pie

PREP: 1 HOUR PLUS COOLING
BAKE: 1 HOUR 30 MINUTES

A Southern favorite, the sweet-potato filling is made with a touch of molasses and cinnamon.

1¼ cups all-purpose flour
1 teaspoon salt
4 tablespoons margarine or butter (½ stick)
2 tablespoons shortening
1½ pounds sweet potatoes (about 3 large) peeled and cut into 1-inch chunks
3 large eggs, separated
¾ cup packed light brown sugar
1½ cups half-and-half or light cream
2 tablespoons light molasses
1¼ teaspoons ground cinnamon
¼ teaspoon ground nutmeg
¼ teaspoon cream of tartar
⅓ cup sugar

1 In medium bowl, mix flour and ½ teaspoon salt. With pastry blender or two knives used scissor-fashion, cut in margarine or butter, and shortening until mixture resembles coarse crumbs. Sprinkle 3 *to 4 tablespoons cold water*, 1 tablespoon at a time, into flour mixture, mixing lightly with a fork after each addition until dough is just moist enough to hold together. Shape dough into a disk.

2 On lightly floured surface, with floured rolling pin, roll dough into a round 2 inches larger all around than inverted 9½-inch deep-dish pie plate. Gently ease dough into pie plate; trim edge, leaving 1-inch overhang. Fold overhang under; pinch to form decorative edge. With fork, prick bottom and side of piecrust in many places to prevent puffing during baking. Cover and refrigerate at least 30 minutes.

3 Meanwhile, preheat oven to 425°F. In 2-quart saucepan, heat sweet potatoes and enough water to cover to boiling over high heat. Reduce heat to low; cover and simmer 10 minutes or until sweet potatoes are fork-tender. Drain and mash sweet potatoes (you should have about 2 cups).

4 Line piecrust with foil; fill with pie weights, dry beans, or uncooked rice. Bake 10 minutes; remove foil with weights and bake 10 minutes longer or until lightly browned. If pastry puffs up during baking, gently press it with back of spoon. Cool piecrust on wire rack at least 10 minutes. Turn oven control to 375°F.

5 In large bowl, with wire whisk, beat mashed sweet potatoes with egg yolks, brown sugar, half-and-half, molasses, cinnamon, nutmeg, and remaining ½ teaspoon salt until blended. Cover and refrigerate egg whites until ready to use.

6 Pour sweet-potato mixture into cooled crust. Bake pie 55 to 60 minutes, until knife inserted 1 inch from edge of pie comes out clean. Transfer pie to wire rack while preparing meringue. Turn oven control to 400°F.

7 In small bowl, with mixer at high speed, beat egg whites and cream of tartar until soft peaks form; gradually sprinkle in sugar, 2 tablespoons at a time, beating until whites stand in stiff peaks.

8 Spread meringue over hot filling to edge of crust; swirl meringue with back of spoon to make attractive top. Bake 10 minutes or until meringue is golden. Cool pie on wire rack. Makes 10 servings.

Each serving: About 355 calories, 6 g protein, 55 g carbohydrate, 13 g total fat (4 g saturated), 75 mg cholesterol, 325 mg sodium.

Fudge Pecan Pie

PREP: 30 MINUTES PLUS COOLING
BAKE: 65 TO 75 MINUTES

Joyce Koncak, 58, a mother of 3 who has long loved to bake, opened up Sweetie Pies Bakery in Austin's Travis County Farmers' Market 17 years ago and has sold countless pies, including this favorite, dreamed up 13 years ago by Sweetie Pies baker Helen Iselt.

PASTRY:
1½ cups all-purpose flour
½ teaspoon salt
4 tablespoons cold margarine or butter
¼ cup shortening

FILLING:
4 tablespoons margarine or butter
2 squares (1 ounce each) unsweetened chocolate
1 bottle (16 ounces) light corn syrup
4 large eggs
1 teaspoon vanilla extract
¼ cup all-purpose flour
¼ cup sugar
¼ teaspoon salt
1½ cups pecans

1 Prepare Pastry: In medium bowl, mix flour and salt. With a pastry blender or two knives used scissor-fashion, cut in margarine or butter, and shortening until coarse crumbs form.

2 Sprinkle about *4 tablespoons cold water*, 1 tablespoon at a time, into flour mixture, mixing lightly with fork until dough is just moist enough to hold together. Wrap dough with plastic wrap and refrigerate 30 minutes or until firm enough to roll.

3 Meanwhile, prepare Filling: In 4-quart saucepan, melt margarine or butter, and chocolate over low heat, stirring frequently. With wire whisk, beat in corn syrup, eggs, and vanilla. Gradually whisk in flour, sugar, and salt until blended.

4 Preheat oven to 350°F. On lightly floured surface, with floured rolling pin, roll dough into a round 2 inches larger in diameter than inverted 9½-inch deep-dish pie plate. Ease dough into pie plate; trim edge, leaving 1-inch overhang. Fold overhang under; pinch to form high decorative edge.

5 Chop 1 cup pecans; spread over crust. Carefully, pour filling over chopped pecans; arrange remaining ½ cup pecans on top. Bake 65 to 75 minutes, until filling is set and knife inserted 1 inch from edge comes out almost clean. Cool pie on wire rack. Makes 10 servings.

Each serving: About 520 calories, 7 g protein, 59 g carbohydrate, 30 g total fat (6 g saturated), 85 mg cholesterol, 340 mg sodium.

FOOD-PROCESSOR PIE CRUST THE RIGHT WAY

- Be sure shortening, butter or margarine, and water are well-chilled—the motor will heat them up.

- Pulse dry ingredients (flour, sugar, and salt).

- Add fat; then pulse only until mixture resembles very coarse crumbs.

- With machine running, add water gradually, stopping just before the dough forms a ball. Beware: The food processor works so quickly that it's easy to add too little liquid; be sure to use what the recipe calls for, so the dough is moist enough to roll and transfer to a dish.

Pine Nut Tart

PREP: 30 MINUTES PLUS CHILLING AND COOLING
BAKE: 50 TO 55 MINUTES

This favorite Italian dessert is filled with homemade almond paste and topped with pignoli.

1½ cups all-purpose flour
2 tablespoons plus ⅔ cup sugar
¾ teaspoon salt
¼ cup shortening
10 tablespoons margarine or butter
¾ cup slivered blanched almonds
¼ cup cornstarch
½ teaspoon baking powder
3 large eggs
2 teaspoons vanilla extract
¼ teaspoon almond extract
1 cup pine nuts (pignoli), toasted

1 In medium bowl, with fork, stir flour, 2 tablespoons sugar, and ½ teaspoon salt. With pastry blender or two knives used scissor-fashion, cut in shortening and 4 tablespoons margarine or butter (½ stick) until mixture resembles coarse crumbs. Sprinkle about *4 tablespoons cold water*, 1 tablespoon at a time, into flour mixture, mixing lightly with fork after each addition until dough is just moist enough to hold together. Shape dough into a disk; wrap with plastic wrap and refrigerate 30 minutes or until firm enough to roll.

2 Preheat oven to 425°F. On lightly floured surface, with floured rolling pin, roll dough into 14-inch round. Press dough onto bottom and up side of 11" by 1" round tart pan with removable bottom. Fold overhang in and press against side of tart pan to form a rim ⅛ inch above edge of pan. With fork, prick dough in 1-inch intervals to prevent puffing and shrinking during baking.

3 Line tart shell with foil and fill with pie weights, dried beans, or uncooked rice. Bake tart shell 20 minutes; remove foil with weights and bake 10 minutes longer or until golden. (If crust puffs up during baking, press it to pan with back of spoon.) Turn oven control to 375°F.

4 In food processor with knife blade attached, pulse almonds, cornstarch, baking powder, and remaining ¼ teaspoon salt until almonds are very finely ground.

5 In large bowl, with mixer at low speed, beat almond mixture, remaining ⅔ cup sugar, and 6 tablespoons softened margarine or butter (¾ stick) until crumbly. Increase speed to medium-high and beat until well combined, about 3 minutes, constantly scraping bowl with rubber spatula. Add eggs, 1 at a time, vanilla, and almond extract; beat until smooth.

6 Pour filling into warm tart shell. Arrange pine nuts evenly over filling. Bake tart 20 minutes or until golden and filling is firm. Cool tart in pan on wire rack. When cool, carefully remove side from pan. Makes 12 servings.

Each serving: About 360 calories, 8 g protein, 32 g carbohydrate, 24 g total fat (5 g saturated), 53 mg cholesterol, 290 mg sodium.

Tangerine Chiffon Cake

PREP: 30 MINUTES PLUS COOLING
BAKE: 1 HOUR 15 MINUTES

Make this tender cake with tangerines while they're in season, and with oranges at other times of the year.

5 tangerines or 3 large oranges
2¼ cups cake flour (not self-rising)
1 tablespoon baking powder
1 teaspoon salt
1½ cups sugar
½ cup vegetable oil
5 large egg yolks
7 large egg whites
½ teaspoon cream of tartar
Tangerine Glaze (recipe follows)

1 Preheat oven to 325°F. Grate 4 teaspoons peel and squeeze ¾ cup juice from tangerines or oranges. In large bowl, combine flour, baking powder, salt, and 1 cup sugar; whisk in oil, egg yolks, peel, and juice until smooth.

2 In another large bowl, with mixer at high speed, beat egg whites and cream of tartar to soft peaks. Beating at high speed, gradually sprinkle in ½ cup sugar until whites stand in stiff peaks. Fold one-third of whites into yolk mixture; fold in remaining whites.

3 Pour batter into ungreased 10-inch tube pan. Bake 1 hour and 15 minutes or until top springs back when touched. Invert cake in pan on bottle; cool.

4 With knife, loosen cake from side of pan and remove. Prepare Tangerine Glaze; spread over top of cake. Let stand 1 hour or until set. Makes 16 servings.

TANGERINE GLAZE: With spoon, mix *1 cup confectioners' sugar* and *1 teaspoon grated tangerine or orange peel.* Stir in *5 to 6 teaspoons tangerine or orange juice* until glaze is spreadable.

Each serving: About 250 calories, 4 g protein, 40 g carbohydrate, 9 g total fat (1 g saturated), 67 mg cholesterol, 230 mg sodium.

Lemon-Poppyseed Pound Cake

PREP: 25 MINUTES PLUS COOLING
BAKE: 1 HOUR 20 MINUTES

2 cups all-purpose flour
2 tablespoons poppyseeds
½ teaspoon baking powder
¼ teaspoon baking soda
¼ teaspoon salt
2 large lemons
¾ cup margarine or butter, softened
1½ cups plus ⅓ cup sugar
4 large eggs
1 teaspoon vanilla extract
½ cup sour cream

1 Preheat oven to 325°F. Grease and flour 9" by 5" metal loaf pan. In medium bowl, combine first 5 ingredients. Grate 1 tablespoon peel and squeeze 3 tablespoons juice from lemons.

2 In large bowl, with mixer at low speed, beat margarine or butter with 1½ cups sugar until blended. At high speed, beat until light, about 5 minutes. Add eggs, 1 at a time, beating well after each addition. Beat in lemon peel and vanilla. At low speed, alternately add flour mixture and sour cream, beginning and ending with flour mixture. Spoon batter into pan and bake 1 hour 20 minutes or until toothpick inserted in center of cake comes out clean.

3 Cool cake in pan on wire rack 10 minutes. Remove from pan. Mix lemon juice and ⅓ cup sugar; brush over top and sides of warm cake. Cool completely. Makes 16 servings.

Each serving: About 265 calories, 4 g protein, 36 g carbohydrate, 12 g total fat (3 g saturated), 56 mg cholesterol, 200 mg sodium.

Tangerine Chiffon Cake ➤

Almond Pound Cake

PREP: 20 MINUTES PLUS COOLING
BAKE: 60 TO 65 MINUTES

A moist, buttery luxury made with almond paste for extra richness; this keeps well in the freezer too.

3 cups cake flour (not self-rising)
1 tablespoon baking powder
½ teaspoon salt
1 cup milk
2 teaspoons vanilla extract
1 tube or can (7 to 8 ounces) almond paste, crumbled
1¾ cups sugar
¾ cup margarine or butter (1½ sticks), softened
4 large eggs
⅓ cup sliced natural almonds

1 Preheat oven to 350°F. Grease and flour 10-inch tube pan. On waxed paper, combine flour, baking powder, and salt. In cup, mix milk and vanilla.

2 In large bowl, with heavy-duty mixer at low speed, beat almond paste and sugar until they have a sandy consistency. (If heavy-duty mixer is unavailable, place almond paste and sugar in food processor with knife blade attached and pulse until fine crumbs form. Transfer almond-paste mixture to large bowl and proceed as directed in recipe.) Beat in margarine or butter. Increase speed to high; beat until well blended, about 5 minutes, scraping bowl often with rubber spatula. Reduce speed to low; add eggs, 1 at a time, beating well after each addition.

3 With mixer at low speed, alternately add flour mixture and milk mixture, beginning and ending with flour mixture, until batter is smooth, occasionally scraping bowl.

4 Pour batter into pan. Sprinkle almonds evenly on top. Bake 60 to 65 minutes, until toothpick inserted in center comes out clean. Cool cake in pan on wire rack 10 minutes. With metal spatula, loosen cake and remove from pan. Cool completely on wire rack. Makes 16 servings.

Each serving: About 340 calories, 6 g protein, 46 g carbohydrate, 15 g total fat (3 g saturated), 55 mg cholesterol, 275 mg sodium.

Kentucky Bourbon Brown-Sugar Pound Cake

PREP: 30 MINUTES PLUS COOLING
BAKE: 1 HOUR 20 MINUTES

In our test kitchens, we prepared this recipe on several occasions with butter and with margarine. It works both ways, but for a true taste of the South, try it with butter.

3 cups all-purpose flour
¾ teaspoon salt
½ teaspoon baking powder
½ teaspoon baking soda
¾ cup milk
2 teaspoons vanilla extract
6 tablespoons bourbon whiskey
1½ cups packed dark brown sugar
½ cup plus ⅓ cup sugar
1 cup margarine or butter (2 sticks), softened
5 large eggs
2 tablespoons orange juice
Strawberries and blueberries for garnish (optional)

1 Preheat oven to 325°F. Grease and flour 12-cup fluted tube pan. In medium bowl, combine flour, salt, baking powder, and baking soda. In 1-cup glass measuring cup, combine milk, vanilla, and 4 tablespoons bourbon.

2 In large bowl, with mixer at medium speed, beat brown sugar and ½ cup sugar until free of lumps. Add margarine or butter and beat at high speed until light and creamy, about 5 minutes. Add eggs, 1 at a time, beating well after each addition. At low speed, alternately add flour mixture and milk mixture, beginning and ending with flour mixture.

3 Pour batter into pan. Bake 1 hour and 20 minutes or until cake springs back when lightly touched with finger and toothpick inserted in center comes out clean. Cool cake in pan on wire rack for 10 minutes. Remove cake from pan.

4 In small bowl, combine orange juice, ⅓ cup sugar, and remaining 2 tablespoons bourbon; brush mixture all over warm cake. Cool cake completely. Garnish with berries if you like. Makes 24 servings.

Each serving: About 230 calories, 3 g protein, 33 g carbohydrate, 9 g total fat (5 g saturated), 66 mg cholesterol, 200 mg sodium.

Old-Fashioned Cocoa Cake

PREP: 30 MINUTES PLUS COOLING • BAKE: 40 MINUTES

A sheet cake with a thick layer of chocolate butter cream—a great bring-along for a casual party.

2½ cups all-purpose flour
1½ cups sugar
¾ cup unsweetened cocoa
1½ teaspoons baking soda
¾ teaspoon salt
1½ cups buttermilk
¾ cup mayonnaise
1 tablespoon vanilla extract
2 large eggs
Rich Chocolate Frosting (recipe follows)

1 Preheat oven to 350°F. Grease 13" by 9" metal baking pan.

2 In large bowl, combine flour, sugar, cocoa, baking soda, and salt.

3 In medium bowl, with wire whisk, mix buttermilk, mayonnaise, vanilla, and eggs until almost smooth.

4 With spoon, stir buttermilk mixture into flour mixture until batter is smooth. Spoon batter into baking pan. Bake 35 to 40 minutes, until toothpick inserted in center of cake comes out clean. Cool cake in pan on wire rack.

FOOD EDITOR'S TIP

Q. What's the difference between natural and Dutch cocoa? Is one better than the other?

A. Both are unsweetened cocoa made from roasted cocoa beans with more than three-fourths of the fat (cocoa butter) removed—and both are equally good. Dutch (also called European-style) cocoa is treated with an alkali agent that neutralizes some of cocoa's acidity and yields a richer, darker—even reddish—product. (It's named for the Dutchman Coenraad J. van Houten, who developed it in the mid-1800's.) In our *Good Housekeeping* kitchens, we use only natural cocoa because it's most readily available nationwide. As a rule, don't swap cocoas—use what the recipe recommends. If you add Dutch cocoa to a cake that calls for the natural unsweetened type—or vice versa—the result could be heavy, with a less rich color and a slightly soapy taste.

5 Prepare Rich Chocolate Frosting. When cake is cool, spread with frosting. Makes 18 servings.

RICH CHOCOLATE FROSTING: In heavy small saucepan, melt *4 squares (1 ounce each) semisweet chocolate* and *2 squares (1 ounce each) unsweetened chocolate* over low heat. Remove saucepan from heat; cool chocolate to room temperature. In large bowl, with mixer at low speed, beat *2 cups confectioners' sugar, ¾ cup margarine or butter (1½ sticks)*, softened, and *1 teaspoon vanilla extract* until almost combined. Add melted, cooled chocolate. Increase speed to high and beat about 1 minute or until light and fluffy.

Each serving: About 385 calories, 5 g protein, 52 g carbohydrate, 20 g total fat (4 g saturated), 28 mg cholesterol, 380 mg sodium.

New England Maple-Walnut Cake

PREP: 50 MINUTES PLUS COOLING
BAKE: 25 TO 30 MINUTES

Three moist cake layers flavored with maple syrup and robed in luscious homemade frosting.

⅔ cup walnuts
1 cup sugar
2¼ cups cake flour (not self-rising)
2 teaspoons baking powder
½ teaspoon salt
¼ teaspoon baking soda
¾ cup pure maple syrup or maple-flavor syrup
½ cup milk
½ teaspoon imitation maple flavor
¾ cup margarine or butter (1½ sticks), softened
3 large eggs
Maple Butter Cream (recipe follows)
Walnut halves for garnish (optional)

1 Preheat oven to 350°F. Grease three 8-inch round cake pans. Line bottoms with waxed paper; grease paper. Dust pans with flour.

2 In food processor with knife blade attached, or in blender at medium speed, blend walnuts and 2 tablespoons sugar until walnuts are finely ground.

3 In medium bowl, combine flour, baking powder, salt, and baking soda. In 2-cup measuring cup, mix maple syrup, milk, and maple flavor until blended.

4 In large bowl, with mixer at low speed, beat margarine or butter and remaining sugar until blended. Increase speed to high; beat until mixture has a sandy appearance, about 2 minutes, occasionally scraping bowl with rubber spatula. At medium-low speed, add eggs, 1 at a time, beating well after each addition.

5 Alternately add flour mixture and maple-syrup mixture, beginning and ending with flour mixture, until batter is smooth, occasionally scraping bowl with rubber spatula. Fold in ground-walnut mixture.

6 Pour batter into pans. Bake 25 to 30 minutes, until toothpick inserted in center of cake comes out clean. Cool layers in pans on wire racks for 10 minutes. Remove from pans; cool completely on wire racks.

7 Meanwhile, prepare Maple Butter Cream.

8 Place 1 cake layer on cake plate; spread with ⅔ cup butter cream. Repeat layering, ending with a cake layer. Frost side and top of cake with remaining butter cream. Garnish with walnut halves if you like. Refrigerate cake if not serving right away. Makes 16 servings.

MAPLE BUTTER CREAM: In 2-quart saucepan, with wire whisk, mix *½ cup all-purpose flour* and *⅓ cup sugar* until blended. Gradually whisk in *1 cup milk* and *⅔ cup pure maple syrup* or maple-flavor syrup until smooth. Cook over medium-high heat, stirring often, until mixture thickens and boils. Reduce heat to low and cook 2 minutes, stirring constantly. Cool completely. In large bowl, with mixer at medium speed, beat *1 cup margarine or butter (2 sticks)*, softened, until creamy. Gradually beat in cooled milk mixture. Beat in *¼ teaspoon imitation maple flavor*. Increase speed to medium-high; beat until smooth with an easy spreading consistency.

Each serving: About 440 calories, 4 g protein, 52 g carbohydrate, 25 g total fat (5 g saturated), 43 mg cholesterol, 425 mg sodium.

Brandied Bûche de Noël

PREP: 1 HOUR 30 MINUTES PLUS COOLING AND CHILLING
BAKE: 10 MINUTES

French for "Christmas log," our *bûche de Noël* is made from spiced chocolate cake and an easy butter cream.

⅓ cup all-purpose flour
¼ cup unsweetened cocoa
1 teaspoon ground cinnamon
¾ teaspoon ground ginger
Pinch ground cloves
Pinch salt
5 large eggs, separated
¼ teaspoon cream of tartar
½ cup sugar
2 tablespoons margarine or butter (¼ stick),
    melted and cooled slightly
Confectioners' sugar
Brandied Butter Cream (recipe follows)
Nontoxic greens for garnish
Meringue Mushrooms (opposite page)

1 Prepare cake roll: Preheat oven to 375°F. Grease 15½" by 10½" jelly-roll pan; line with waxed paper; grease paper and dust with flour.

2 On waxed paper, combine flour, cocoa, cinnamon, ginger, cloves, and salt.

3 In small bowl, with mixer at high speed, beat egg whites and cream of tartar until soft peaks form. Beating at high speed, gradually sprinkle in ¼ cup sugar, beating until sugar dissolves and whites stand in stiff peaks.

Brandied Bûche de Noël

4 In large bowl, using same beaters and with mixer at high speed, beat egg yolks and remaining ¼ cup sugar until very thick and lemon-colored.

5 With rubber spatula or wire whisk, gently fold beaten egg whites into beaten egg yolks, one-third at a time. With same rubber spatula or wire whisk, gently fold flour mixture into egg mixture, one-third at a time. Fold in melted margarine or butter, mixing just until combined.

6 With metal spatula, spread batter evenly in pan. Bake 10 minutes or until top of cake springs back when lightly touched with finger.

7 Sprinkle clean cloth towel with confectioners' sugar. When cake is done, immediately invert hot cake onto towel. Peel off waxed paper and discard. Starting from a long side, roll cake with towel jelly-roll fashion. Cool cake roll, seam side down, on wire rack until completely cool, about 1 hour.

8 Meanwhile, prepare Brandied Butter Cream.

9 Assemble cake: Gently unroll cooled cake. With metal spatula, spread white Brandied Butter Cream almost to edges. Starting from same long side, roll cake without towel. With sharp knife, cut 1½-inch-thick diagonal slice off each end of roll; set aside. Place rolled cake, seam side down, on long platter. Spread some chocolate Brandied Butter Cream over roll. Place 1 end piece on side of roll to resemble branch. Place remaining end piece on top of roll to resemble another branch. Spread remaining frosting over roll and branches, leaving cut side of branches unfrosted. With metal spatula, spread frosting to resemble bark of tree. Refrigerate cake at least 2 hours before serving. Garnish platter with greens and Meringue Mushrooms if you like. Makes 14 servings.

BRANDIED BUTTER CREAM: In 2-quart saucepan, combine *1 cup sugar* and *½ cup all-purpose flour*. With wire whisk, mix in *1 cup milk* until smooth. Cook over medium-high heat, stirring often, until mixture thickens and boils. Reduce heat to low and cook 2 minutes, stirring constantly. Cool completely, about 45 minutes. Meanwhile, in small saucepan, melt *1 square (1 ounce) semisweet chocolate* and *1 square (1 ounce) unsweetened chocolate* over low heat; cool slightly.

In large bowl, with mixer at medium speed, beat *1 cup margarine or butter* (2 sticks), softened, until creamy. Gradually beat in cooled flour mixture. When mixture is smooth, beat in *2 tablespoons brandy* and *1 teaspoon vanilla extract* until blended. Spoon half of white butter cream into small bowl; stir

melted chocolate into butter cream remaining in large bowl.

Each serving: About 310 calories, 4 g protein, 33 g carbohydrate, 19 g total fat (4 g saturated), 78 mg cholesterol, 240 mg sodium.

Meringue Mushrooms

PREP: 20 MINUTES PLUS COOLING • COOK: 2 HOURS

Pipe all the mushrooms the same size, or make them in a variety of sizes, as we did, for a realistic look.

2 large egg whites
⅛ teaspoon cream of tartar
⅓ cup sugar
Unsweetened cocoa
1 square (1 ounce) semisweet chocolate, melted

1 Line large cookie sheet with foil.

2 In small bowl, with mixer at high speed, beat egg whites and cream of tartar until soft peaks form; gradually beat in sugar, 2 tablespoons at a time, beating well after each addition, until sugar completely dissolves and whites stand in stiff, glossy peaks.

3 Preheat oven to 200°F. Spoon meringue into large decorating bag with large writing tip. Pipe meringue onto cookie sheet in 15 mounds, each about 1½ inches in diameter, to resemble mushroom caps. If you like, place some cocoa in small fine-meshed strainer; use to dust meringue mushroom caps. Pipe remaining meringue upright onto cookie sheet in fifteen 1¼-inch lengths to resemble mushroom stems. Bake meringues 1½ hours. Turn oven off; let meringues stand in oven 30 minutes longer to dry. Cool meringues completely on cookie sheet on wire rack.

4 With tip of paring knife, cut a small hole in center of underside of a mushroom cap. Dip pointed end of mushroom stem in melted chocolate; attach stem to mushroom cap by inserting chocolate-dipped end into hole in underside of mushroom cap. Repeat with remaining caps and stems. Let chocolate dry, about 1 hour.

5 Store mushrooms in tightly covered container up to a week. Makes 15 mushrooms.

Each mushroom: About 30 calories, 1 g protein, 6 g carbohydrate, 0 g total fat, 0 mg cholesterol, 10 mg sodium.

Seattle Cappuccino Angel Food Cake

PREP: 30 MINUTES PLUS COOLING
BAKE: 35 TO 40 MINUTES

1 cup cake flour (not self-rising)
½ cup plus 1 tablespoon confectioners' sugar
1⅔ cups egg whites (about 12 large)
4 teaspoons instant espresso-coffee powder
1½ teaspoons cream of tartar
½ teaspoon salt
½ plus ⅛ teaspoon ground cinnamon
1½ teaspoons vanilla extract
1¼ cups sugar

1 Preheat oven to 375°F. On waxed paper, mix flour and ½ cup confectioners' sugar; set aside.

2 In large bowl, with mixer at high speed, beat egg whites, instant espresso-coffee powder, cream of tartar, salt, and ½ teaspoon cinnamon until soft peaks form; beat in vanilla. Beating at high speed, sprinkle in sugar, 2 tablespoons at a time, beating mixture until sugar completely dissolves and egg whites stand in stiff, glossy peaks.

3 Sift flour mixture over egg whites, one-third at a time, folding in with rubber spatula after each addition, just until flour disappears.

4 Spoon batter into ungreased 10-inch tube pan. Bake cake 35 to 40 minutes, until top springs back when lightly touched with finger. Invert cake in pan on funnel or bottle; cool completely in pan.

5 With metal spatula, carefully loosen cake from pan; place on cake plate. In cup, mix remaining

---

WHY ANGEL FOOD COOLS UPSIDE DOWN

Angel food cake, which is leavened only with beaten egg whites, doesn't have the stability of cake leavened with baking powder or soda. Cooling it thoroughly in the pan in an upside-down position allows the cake's delicate structure to firm up. If cooled without inverting, the cake will lose volume. If removed from pan too early, it will collapse. If your pan does not have legs for support, it can be set upside down on an inverted funnel or on the neck of a sturdy bottle.

---

1 tablespoon confectioners' sugar with remaining ⅛ teaspoon cinnamon; sprinkle over cake. Makes 16 servings.

Each serving: About 120 calories, 3 g protein, 26 g carbohydrate, 0 g total fat, 0 mg cholesterol, 110 mg sodium.

Lemon-Lime Angel Cake Roll

PREP: 30 MINUTES PLUS CHILLING • BAKE: 20 MINUTES

1¼ cups granulated sugar
⅓ cup cornstarch
⅓ cup fresh lemon juice (2 large lemons)
⅓ cup fresh lime juice (3 large limes)
1 large egg yolk
1 tablespoon margarine or butter
1 package (16 ounces) angel-food cake mix
Confectioners' sugar

1 In 2-quart saucepan, with wire whisk, mix granulated sugar and cornstarch until combined. Whisk in lemon juice, lime juice, egg yolk, and *1 cup water* until blended. Heat lemon mixture to boiling over medium heat, whisking constantly; boil 1 minute, whisking. Remove saucepan from heat; stir in margarine or butter. Pour lemon mixture into medium bowl; cover surface with plastic wrap. Refrigerate until cool, about 1½ hours.

2 Meanwhile, preheat oven to 350°F. Grease bottom of 15½" by 10½" jelly-roll pan. Line pan with 18-inch-long sheet waxed paper. Do not grease paper. Prepare cake mix as label directs. Spread batter in pan. Bake 20 minutes or until cake is golden and top springs back when lightly touched with finger.

3 Evenly sprinkle top of cake with confectioners' sugar. Place clean cloth towel and wire rack over top of cake and invert cake in pan; cool completely.

4 When cake is cool, run small metal spatula around sides of cake to loosen from pan. Remove pan. Peel off waxed paper and discard. With metal spatula, spread cooled lemon-lime filling to within 2 inches of edges. Starting from a long side, roll cake without towel jelly-roll fashion. Place rolled cake, seam side down, on long platter. Sprinkle with confectioners' sugar before serving. Makes 12 servings.

Each serving: About 245 calories, 3 g protein, 56 g carbohydrate, 2 g total fat (0 g saturated), 18 mg cholesterol, 270 mg sodium.

COOKIES

Mississippi Mud Bars

PREP: 20 MINUTES PLUS COOLING • BAKE: 35 MINUTES

Bake up to 2 weeks ahead, cut, wrap, and freeze.
They're terrific straight from the freezer too!

MUD CAKE:
¾ cup margarine or butter (1½ sticks)
1¾ cups sugar
¾ cup unsweetened cocoa
4 large eggs
2 teaspoons vanilla extract
½ teaspoon salt
1½ cups all-purpose flour
½ cup pecans, chopped
½ cup flaked coconut
3 cups mini marshmallows

FUDGE TOPPING:
5 tablespoons margarine or butter
1 square (1 ounce) unsweetened chocolate
⅓ cup unsweetened cocoa
⅛ teaspoon salt
¼ cup evaporated milk or heavy or whipping
   cream
1 teaspoon vanilla extract
1 cup confectioners' sugar
½ cup pecans, coarsely broken
¼ cup flaked coconut

Mississippi Mud Bars

1 Preheat oven to 350°F. Grease and flour 13" by 9"
metal baking pan.

2 Prepare Mud Cake: In 3-quart saucepan, melt
margarine or butter over low heat, stirring occasionally. With wire whisk, beat in sugar, cocoa, then eggs,
1 at a time, vanilla, and salt until well blended.
Remove saucepan from heat. With spoon, stir in
flour just until blended. Stir in pecans and flaked
coconut. Spread batter in pan (batter will be thick).

3 Bake cake 25 minutes. Remove pan from oven.
Sprinkle marshmallows on top of cake in even layer.
Return cake to oven and bake 10 minutes longer or
until marshmallows are puffed and golden. Cool
cake completely in pan on wire rack.

4 When cake is cool, prepare Fudge Topping: In
2-quart saucepan, heat margarine or butter and
chocolate over low heat until mixture melts, stirring
constantly. With wire whisk, beat in cocoa and salt
until smooth. Then beat in undiluted evaporated
milk or cream and vanilla (mixture will be thick).
Beat in confectioners' sugar until smooth.

5 Pour hot topping over cooled cake. Cool fudge-
topped cake for 20 minutes; sprinkle with pecans and
coconut. Wrap in pan to store. (If you like, freeze up
to 2 weeks before serving.) Serve chilled or at room
temperature. To serve, cut lengthwise into 4 strips,
then cut each strip crosswise into 8 pieces. Makes
32 bars.

Each bar: About 205 calories, 3 g protein, 27 g carbohydrate, 11 g total fat (2 g saturated), 27 mg cholesierol, 140
mg sodium.

Pennsylvania-Dutch Brownies

PREP: 20 MINUTES PLUS COOLING
BAKE: 15 TO 20 MINUTES

"There are seven chocolate factories in our area, and
the heavenly aroma is often in the air. One day as I
prepared a pan of spice bars, the smell of chocolate
wafted into my consciousness and this recipe," says
Yvonne D. Kanoff of Mount Joy, Pennsylvania.

4 tablespoons margarine or butter (½ stick)
1 square (1 ounce) unsweetened chocolate
¼ cup light molasses
2 large eggs
1½ cups all-purpose flour

1 teaspoon ground ginger
½ teaspoon ground cloves
½ teaspoon baking soda
½ teaspoon salt
1 cup plus 2 teaspoons sugar
1⅛ teaspoons ground cinnamon

1 Preheat oven to 375°F. Grease 13" by 9" metal baking pan; set aside.

2 In 4-quart saucepan, melt margarine or butter with chocolate over low heat. Remove saucepan from heat. With wire whisk or fork, stir in molasses, then eggs.

3 With spoon, stir in flour, ginger, cloves, baking soda, salt, 1 cup sugar, and 1 teaspoon cinnamon just until blended. Spread batter evenly in pan. Bake 15 to 20 minutes until toothpick inserted 2 inches from edge comes out clean. Meanwhile, in cup, combine remaining 2 teaspoons sugar and ⅛ teaspoon cinnamon; set aside.

4 Remove pan from oven; immediately sprinkle brownies with cinnamon-sugar mixture. Cool brownies in pan on wire rack at least 2 hours. When cool, cut brownies lengthwise into 3 strips, then cut each strip crosswise into 5 pieces. Cut each piece diagonally in half. Makes 30 brownies.

Each brownie: About 80 calories, 1 g protein, 14 g carbohydrate, 2 g total fat (1 g saturated), 14 mg cholesterol, 80 mg sodium.

Triple-Layer Almond Shortbread Brownies

PREP: 1 HOUR PLUS COOLING • BAKE: 40 TO 50 MINUTES

Trufflelike cake nestled in a rich shortbread crust, with a semisweet chocolate glaze on top.

1 cup whole natural almonds
½ cup sliced almonds
¾ cup confectioners' sugar
1¾ cups margarine or butter (3½ sticks), softened
¼ teaspoon almond extract
2¾ cups all-purpose flour
5 squares (1 ounce each) unsweetened chocolate
3 large eggs
2 cups sugar
¼ teaspoon salt

2 teaspoons vanilla extract
6 squares (1 ounce each) semisweet chocolate
⅓ cup heavy or whipping cream

1 Preheat oven to 350°F.

2 Place whole and sliced almonds in 15½" by 10½" jelly-roll pan, keeping whole almonds separated from sliced ones. Bake 10 minutes or until toasted, stirring almonds occasionally but still keeping them separated. Cool.

3 In food processor with knife blade attached or in blender at medium speed, blend whole almonds with ¼ cup confectioners' sugar until finely ground. Reserve sliced almonds.

4 In large bowl, with mixer at low speed, beat ¾ cup margarine or butter (1½ sticks) and remaining ½ cup confectioners' sugar until blended. Increase speed to high; beat until creamy. At low speed, beat in ground-almond mixture, almond extract, and 1¾ cups flour just until blended (dough will be stiff).

5 Line 15½" by 10½" jelly-roll pan with foil, allowing foil to come up over sides. Pat dough evenly into jelly-roll pan. Bake 20 to 25 minutes, until golden. Cool in pan on wire rack.

6 Meanwhile, in heavy 2-quart saucepan, heat unsweetened chocolate and remaining 1 cup margarine or butter (2 sticks) over low heat until melted, stirring frequently. Remove saucepan from heat. Cool chocolate mixture slightly, about 10 minutes.

7 In large bowl, with mixer at high speed, beat eggs, sugar, salt, and 1 teaspoon vanilla until ribbon forms when beaters are lifted, about 5 to 10 minutes. Beat in chocolate mixture until blended. With spoon, stir in remaining 1 cup flour. Pour chocolate mixture over shortbread crust; spread evenly to edges. Bake 20 to 25 minutes longer, until toothpick inserted 1 inch from edge comes out almost clean. Cool in pan on wire rack.

8 In heavy 2-quart saucepan, heat semisweet chocolate with heavy cream over low heat until chocolate is melted, stirring frequently. Remove saucepan from heat; stir in remaining 1 teaspoon vanilla. Lift foil with brownie out of pan; peel foil from sides. With metal spatula, spread chocolate glaze over brownie. Sprinkle reserved almond slices on top. Let stand until set, about 2 hours (or refrigerate 30 minutes). Cut lengthwise into 6 strips, then cut each strip crosswise into 12 pieces. Makes 6 dozen brownies.

Each brownie: About 125 calories, 2 g protein, 13 g carbohydrate, 8 g total fat (2 g saturated), 10 mg cholesterol, 70 mg sodium.

Hazelnut Cookies

PREP: 1 HOUR PLUS COOLING
BAKE: 25 MINUTES PER BATCH

Susan Willey Spalt of Carrboro, North Carolina, got the recipe for these delectable meringuelike sandwich cookies from her mother, who learned how to make them as a new bride. "My mother died several years ago," says Spalt. "But when I'm baking these, I can hear her voice saying 'Don't be impatient. You can't hurry these cookies.'"

2 cups hazelnuts (filberts)
¾ cup sugar
5 large egg whites
⅓ cup all-purpose flour
5 tablespoons margarine or butter, melted and cooled
6 squares (1 ounce each) semisweet chocolate, melted and cooled

1 Preheat oven to 350°F. Place hazelnuts in 13" by 9" metal baking pan. Bake 10 to 15 minutes, until toasted. Wrap hot hazelnuts in clean cloth towel. With hands, roll hazelnuts back and forth to remove skins. Cool completely.

2 Turn oven control to 275°F. Grease 2 large cookie sheets. In food processor with knife blade attached, blend hazelnuts with ¼ cup sugar until finely ground.

3 In large bowl, with mixer at high speed, beat egg whites until soft peaks form. Beating at high speed, sprinkle in remaining ½ cup sugar, 1 tablespoon at a time, beating well after each addition until sugar completely dissolves and whites stand in stiff peaks. With rubber spatula, fold in ground hazelnuts, flour, and melted margarine or butter.

4 Drop mixture by rounded teaspoons, about 2 inches apart, onto cookie sheets. Bake cookies on 2 oven racks 25 minutes, rotating cookie sheets between upper and lower racks halfway through baking time, until cookies are firm and edges are golden. Remove to wire racks to cool. Repeat with remaining batter.

5 When cookies are cool, with small metal spatula, spread thin layer of melted chocolate onto flat side of half of cookies. Top with remaining cookies, flat side down, to make sandwiches. Spoon remaining chocolate into small self-sealing plastic bag; snip 1 corner of bag to make small hole. Squeeze thin lines of choco-late over cookies. Let stand until set. Makes about 4 dozen sandwich cookies.

Each sandwich cookie: About 75 calories, 1 g protein, 7 g carbohydrate, 5 g total fat (0 g saturated), 0 mg cholesterol, 25 mg sodium.

Czechoslovakian Cookies

PREP: 25 MINUTES PLUS COOLING
BAKE: 45 TO 50 MINUTES

These rich buttery bars from Barbara Karpinski of Somerset, New Jersey, are a Christmas tradition—a recipe handed down from mother-in-law to daughter-in-law.

1 cup butter (2 sticks), softened (do not use margarine)
1 cup sugar
2 large egg yolks
2 cups all-purpose flour
Pinch salt
1 cup walnuts, chopped
½ cup strawberry preserves

1 Preheat oven to 350°F. Grease 9" by 9" metal baking pan.

2 In large bowl, with mixer at low speed, beat butter and sugar until mixed, occasionally scraping bowl with rubber spatula. Increase speed to high; beat until light and fluffy.

3 With mixer at low speed, beat in egg yolks until well combined, constantly scraping bowl with rubber spatula. Add flour and salt and beat until blended, occasionally scraping bowl. With spoon, stir in chopped walnuts.

4 With lightly floured hands, pat half of dough evenly into bottom of pan. Spread strawberry preserves over dough. With lightly floured hands, pinch off ¾-inch pieces from remaining dough and drop over preserves; do not pat down.

5 Bake 45 to 50 minutes until golden. Cool completely in pan on wire rack. When cool, cut into 3 strips, then cut each strip crosswise into 10 pieces. Makes 30 bars.

Each bar: About 130 calories, 2 g protein, 11 g carbohydrate, 9 g total fat (4 g saturated), 31 mg cholesterol, 70 mg sodium.

Clockwise from left: Wooden Spoon Cookies (page 226), Czechoslovakian Cookies, Hazelnut Cookies

Peanutty Yummy Bars

PREP: 30 MINUTES • BAKE: 55 MINUTES

This rich peanut-butter bar with an oatmeal crust (from Susanne Corker of Lake Orion, Michigan) is sure to be a winner with kids 12 months of the year.

⅓ cup quick-cooking oats, uncooked
1⅔ cups all-purpose flour
⅓ cup plus 1½ cups packed light brown sugar
½ cup margarine or butter (1 stick), softened
3 tablespoons plus ⅓ cup chunky peanut butter
3 large eggs
4½ teaspoons light molasses
2 teaspoons baking powder
½ teaspoon salt
1 cup salted cocktail peanuts, chopped
1 package (6 ounces) semisweet-chocolate pieces (1 cup)
Confectioners' sugar for garnish

1 Preheat oven to 350°F. Grease 13" by 9" metal baking pan.

2 Prepare crust: In large bowl, with mixer at low speed, beat oats, 1 cup flour, ⅓ cup packed brown sugar, 4 tablespoons margarine or butter, and 3 tablespoons peanut butter until blended. Pat dough evenly into pan and bake 15 minutes.

3 Meanwhile, in large bowl, with mixer at medium speed, beat eggs, molasses, 1½ cups packed brown sugar, ⅓ cup peanut butter, and remaining 4 tablespoons margarine or butter until well combined, constantly scraping bowl with rubber spatula. Reduce speed to low; add baking powder, salt, and remaining ⅔ cup flour and beat until blended, occasionally scraping bowl. With spoon, stir in peanuts and chocolate pieces.

4 Spread mixture evenly over hot crust. Bake 40 minutes longer or until golden. Cool completely in pan on wire rack. Sprinkle with confectioners' sugar if you like. When cool, cut lengthwise into 4 strips, then cut each strip crosswise into 12 pieces. Makes 4 dozen bars.

Each bar: About 125 calories, 3 g protein, 16 g carbohydrate, 6 g total fat (1 g saturated), 13 mg cholesterol, 100 mg sodium.

Layered Date Bars

PREP: 30 MINUTES PLUS COOLING • BAKE: 40 MINUTES

These date bars come from Mary Beth Rollick of Munroe Falls, Ohio, who still has her Aunt Mary Jane's original recipe card. Her aunt used to make these date bars for a local holiday custom called "tasting the tree." During the 12 days of Christmas everyone visited all their relatives and close neighbors to sample their special homemade treats.

1 package (10 ounces) pitted dates (2 cups),
   coarsely chopped
½ cup walnuts, finely chopped
¼ cup sugar
1½ cups all-purpose flour
1½ cups old-fashioned oats, uncooked
1 cup packed brown sugar
1 teaspoon baking soda
¾ cup margarine or butter (1½ sticks), softened

1 Preheat oven to 350°F. In 2-quart saucepan, heat dates, walnuts, sugar, and 1¼ *cups water* to boiling over high heat. Reduce heat to low; simmer, uncovered, 10 to 15 minutes, until dates are soft and mixture is thick, stirring occasionally. Set aside.

2 Meanwhile, in large bowl, combine flour, oats, brown sugar, and baking soda. With hand, knead in margarine or butter until dough forms. Press half of dough evenly in bottom of 13" by 9" metal baking pan. Bake 15 minutes or until pale golden.

3 Spread date mixture evenly over hot crust. Sprinkle remaining oat mixture on top. Bake 25 minutes

---

FOOD EDITOR'S TIP

Q. Can I bake my favorite cookies in a jelly-roll pan?

A. A jelly-roll pan, with ¾-inch-high sides all around, is meant for thin sponge cakes that will be filled and rolled (its rim is designed to hold in a thin batter), but it's also great for bar cookies. It works in a pinch for slice-and-bake, drop, and rolled cookies, too, if you don't have a cookie sheet: Invert the pan and place the dough on the flip side for optimal heat distribution and even browning. But for the best cookies, stick to a good old cookie sheet; its wide, open surface, with one or more rolled edges, allows good heat distribution from every direction, for even results.

---

longer or until golden. Cool completely in pan on wire rack. When cool, cut lengthwise into 4 strips, then cut each strip crosswise into 8 pieces. Makes 32 bars.

Each bar: About 155 calories, 2 g protein, 25 g carbohydrate, 6 g total fat (1 g saturated), 0 mg cholesterol, 100 mg sodium.

Cinnamon Twists

PREP: 1 HOUR PLUS CHILLING AND COOLING
BAKE: 15 TO 17 MINUTES PER BATCH

Carrie Deegan of Glen Cove, New York, has been baking cookies for years to rave reviews. About 4 years ago, she decided to sell some of her favorites, just during the holidays. This tender cream-cheese cookie coated with walnut-and-cinnamon sugar is one of her newer creations.

1 package (8 ounces) cream cheese, softened
1 cup margarine or butter (2 sticks), softened
2½ cups all-purpose flour
¾ cup walnuts
1 cup sugar
2 teaspoons ground cinnamon
1 large egg, beaten

1 In large bowl, with mixer at low speed, beat cream cheese and margarine or butter until blended, constantly scraping bowl with rubber spatula. Increase speed to high; beat until light and creamy, about 2 minutes. With mixer at low speed, gradually add 1 cup flour and beat until blended. With spoon, stir in remaining 1½ cups flour until smooth.

2 On lightly floured sheet of plastic wrap, pat dough into a 9" by 9" square. Wrap in plastic wrap and refrigerate 2 hours or until dough is firm enough to roll.

3 Meanwhile, in food processor with knife blade attached, finely grind walnuts with ¼ cup sugar. In small bowl, stir cinnamon and remaining ¾ cup sugar into walnut mixture until well blended; set aside.

4 Preheat oven to 400°F. Grease large cookie sheet. On lightly floured sheet of waxed paper, with floured rolling pin, roll dough square into 11" by 10½" rectangle. With pastry brush, brush some beaten egg over top of dough rectangle; sprinkle with half of walnut mixture. Gently press walnut mixture into dough. Invert dough rectangle onto another sheet of lightly floured waxed paper, nut side down. Brush with beaten egg; sprinkle with remaining walnut mixture, and gently press nut mixture into dough.

5 Cut dough lengthwise into three 3½-inch-wide bars, then cut each bar crosswise into ½-inch-wide strips to make sixty-six 3½" by ½" strips in all. Twist each strip twice, then place, about 1 inch apart, on cookie sheet.

6 Bake twists 15 to 17 minutes, until lightly browned. With pancake turner, gently loosen twists from cookie sheet and remove to wire rack to cool. Repeat with remaining strips. Makes 5½ dozen cookies.

Each cookie: About 75 calories, 1 g protein, 7 g carbohydrate, 5 g total fat (1 g saturated), 7 mg cholesterol, 50 mg sodium.

Ricotta-Cheese Cookies

PREP: 30 MINUTES PLUS COOLING
BAKE: 15 MINUTES PER BATCH

Naoma R. Felt of Bradenton, Florida, bakes these soft, Italian-style cookies frequently; they're a hit with everyone. The baked cookies freeze well.

2 cups sugar
1 cup margarine or butter (2 sticks), softened
1 container (15 ounces) ricotta cheese
2 teaspoons vanilla extract
2 large eggs
4 cups all-purpose flour
2 tablespoons baking powder
1 teaspoon salt
1½ cups confectioners' sugar
3 tablespoons milk
Red and green sugar crystals

1 Preheat oven to 350°F. In large bowl, with mixer at low speed, beat sugar and margarine or butter until blended. Increase speed to high; beat until light and fluffy, about 5 minutes. At medium speed, beat in ricotta, vanilla, and eggs until well combined.

2 Reduce speed to low. Add flour, baking powder, and salt; beat until dough forms.

3 Drop dough by level tablespoons, about 2 inches apart, onto ungreased large cookie sheet. Bake about 15 minutes or until cookies are very lightly golden (they will be soft). With pancake turner, remove to rack to cool. Repeat with remaining dough.

4 When cookies are cool, prepare icing: In small bowl, stir confectioners' sugar and milk until smooth. With small metal spatula or knife, spread icing on cookies; sprinkle with red or green sugar crystals. Set cookies aside to allow icing to dry completely, about 1 hour. Makes about 6 dozen cookies.

Each cookie: About 90 calories, 1 g protein, 14 g carbohydrate, 3 g total fat (1 g saturated), 3 mg cholesterol, 100 mg sodium.

Finska Kakor

PREP: 1 HOUR PLUS COOLING
BAKE: 17 TO 20 MINUTES PER BATCH

These Scandinavian cookies (the name means Finnish cakes) are rich and shortbreadlike; Sue Larraway of Sunnyvale, California, says she can't imagine Christmas without them.

1 cup blanched almonds
2 tablespoons plus ½ cup sugar
4 cups all-purpose flour
1½ cups margarine or butter (3 sticks), softened
2 teaspoons almond extract
1 egg white, beaten

1 In food processor with knife blade attached, blend almonds with 2 tablespoons sugar until finely chopped; set aside.

2 Into large bowl, measure flour, margarine or butter, almond extract, and ½ cup sugar. With hand, knead ingredients until well blended and mixture holds together.

3 Preheat oven to 350°F. On work surface, between 2 sheets of waxed paper, roll half of dough into 12" by 8" rectangle. With pastry brush, brush dough rectangle with some egg white. Sprinkle with half of almond mixture. With rolling pin, gently press almonds into dough.

4 Cut dough rectangle lengthwise into 8 strips. Cut each strip crosswise into 4 bars. With pancake turner, place bars, about ½ inch apart, on ungreased large cookie sheet.

5 Bake bars 17 to 20 minutes, until lightly browned. Remove to wire rack to cool. Repeat with remaining dough. Makes 64 bars.

Each bar: About 85 calories, 1 g protein, 8 g carbohydrate, 5 g total fat (1 g saturated), 0 mg cholesterol, 60 mg sodium.

Jelly Centers

PREP: 45 MINUTES PLUS CHILLING AND COOLING
BAKE: 10 TO 12 MINUTES PER BATCH

This recipe from Ann Marie Reinle of Massapequa, New York, was a prized "family secret" that a friend shared with Reinle only after moving away.

1 cup margarine or butter (2 sticks), softened
1¼ cups sugar
2 large eggs, separated
2 teaspoons vanilla extract
3 cups all-purpose flour
⅛ teaspoon baking powder
⅛ teaspoon salt
About 1 cup raspberry preserves

1 In large bowl, with mixer at low speed, beat margarine or butter with 1 cup sugar until blended, occasionally scraping bowl with rubber spatula. Increase speed to high; beat until light and fluffy, about 3 minutes. At low speed, beat in egg yolks and vanilla until blended. Gradually beat in flour, baking powder, and salt. Shape dough into 2 balls; flatten each slightly. Wrap each ball in plastic wrap and refrigerate 1 hour or until firm enough to roll.

2 Preheat oven to 350°F. Between 2 sheets of floured waxed paper, roll half of dough ⅛ inch thick, keeping remaining dough refrigerated. With floured 2-inch cookie cutter (we like rounds or stars) cut out as many cookies as possible. Place cookies, about ½ inch apart, on ungreased large cookie sheet; reserve trimmings. With ½-inch round or star-shaped cookie cutter, cut out centers from half of cookies. Remove centers; add to trimmings.

3 In cup, with fork, beat egg whites slightly. With pastry brush, brush cookies with cutout centers with some egg white, then sprinkle with some of remaining ¼ cup sugar. Bake all cookies 10 to 12 minutes, until cookies are lightly browned. With pancake turner, remove cookies to wire rack to cool.

4 Repeat steps 2 and 3 with trimmings and remaining dough to make more cookies.

5 When cookies are cool, spread center of each cookie *without* cutout center with ¼ to ½ teaspoon preserves; top each with a cookie *with* a cutout center, gently pressing cookies together to form a sandwich. Makes about 4½ dozen sandwich cookies.

Each sandwich cookie: About 95 calories, 1 g protein, 14 g carbohydrate, 4 g total fat (1 g saturated), 8 mg cholesterol, 55 mg sodium.

Sand Tarts

PREP: 1 HOUR 30 MINUTES PLUS CHILLING,
COOLING, AND DECORATING
BAKE: 12 TO 15 MINUTES PER BATCH

This simple butter cookie from Vivian A. Eck of Williamsport, Pennsylvania, has been a family favorite for 5 generations. The children like to help cut out and decorate the cookies with colored sugars or frosting.

1 cup butter (2 sticks), softened (do not use margarine)
1½ cups sugar
2 large eggs
1 teaspoon vanilla extract
3 cups all-purpose flour
½ teaspoon baking powder
½ teaspoon salt
Ornamental Frosting (page 233), optional

1 In large bowl, with mixer at low speed, beat butter with sugar until blended. Increase speed to high; beat until light and creamy. At low speed, beat in eggs and vanilla until mixed, then beat in flour, baking powder, and salt until well combined, occasionally scraping bowl with rubber spatula. Shape dough into 4 balls; flatten each slightly. Wrap each in plastic wrap and freeze at least 1 hour or refrigerate overnight until dough is firm enough to roll.

2 Preheat oven to 350°F. On lightly floured surface, with floured rolling pin, roll 1 piece of dough slightly thinner than ¼ inch, keeping remaining dough refrigerated. With floured 3- to 4-inch assorted cookie cutters, cut dough into as many cookies as possible; reserve trimmings. Place cookies, about 1 inch apart, on ungreased large cookie sheet.

3 Bake cookies 12 to 15 minutes until golden around edges. With pancake turner, remove cookies to rack to cool. Repeat with remaining dough and trimmings.

4 When cookies are cool, if you like, prepare Ornamental Frosting. Use to decorate cookies as desired. Set cookies aside to allow frosting to dry completely, about 1 hour. Makes about 6 dozen cookies.

Each cookie without frosting: About 60 calories, 1 g protein, 8 g carbohydrate, 3 g total fat (2 g saturated), 13 mg cholesterol, 45 mg sodium.

Clockwise from top of plate: Great-Granny's Old-Time ➤
Spice Cookies (page 232), Sand Tarts, Jelly Centers

Wooden Spoon Cookies

PREP: 25 MINUTES PLUS COOLING
BAKE: 5 TO 7 MINUTES PER BATCH

"These are literally eaten as fast as I can make them," says Cindie David of Lawrenceville, Georgia. She got the recipe from her mother-in-law, who got it from *her* mother. After baking, each hot cookie is rolled around the handle of a wooden spoon.

¾ cup blanched almonds, ground
½ cup margarine or butter (1 stick), softened
½ cup sugar
1 tablespoon all-purpose flour
1 tablespoon heavy or whipping cream

1 Preheat oven to 350°F. Grease and flour 2 large cookie sheets. In 2-quart saucepan, combine ground almonds, margarine or butter, sugar, flour, and cream. Heat over low heat, stirring occasionally, until margarine or butter melts. Keep mixture warm over very low heat.

Top to bottom: Peanutty Yummy Bars (page 221), Sally Ann Cookies

2 Drop batter by rounded teaspoons, about 3 inches apart, onto cookie sheet. (Do not place more than 6 on cookie sheet because, after baking, cookies must be shaped quickly before hardening.)

3 Bake cookies 5 to 7 minutes, until edges are lightly browned and centers are just golden. Let cookies remain on cookie sheet 30 to 60 seconds, until edges are just set. With pancake turner or long, flexible metal spatula, flip cookies over quickly so lacy texture will be on outside after rolling. Working as quickly as possible, roll each cookie into a cylinder around handle of wooden spoon; remove to wire rack. If cookies become too hard to roll, return to oven briefly to soften. As each cookie is shaped, remove from spoon handle; cool on wire rack. Repeat until all batter is used. Makes about 3 dozen cookies.

Each cookie: About 50 calories, 1 g protein, 3 g carbohydrate, 4 g total fat (1 g saturated), 1 mg cholesterol, 35 mg sodium.

Sally Ann Cookies

PREP: 1 HOUR PLUS FREEZING AND COOLING
BAKE: 15 TO 20 MINUTES PER BATCH

This recipe for spicy molasses refrigerator cookies—from Sue Riesterer of Manitowoc, Wisconsin—originally called for lard but we adapted it to use margarine or butter. The name comes from a cookie sold in stores about 35 years ago.

1½ cups sugar
1 cup margarine or butter (2 sticks)
5½ cups all-purpose flour
1 cup light molasses
½ cup cold strong coffee
2 teaspoons baking soda
2 teaspoons ground ginger
½ teaspoon ground nutmeg
½ teaspoon salt
¼ teaspoon ground cloves
Sally Ann Frosting (recipe follows)
Holiday décors (optional)

1 In large bowl, with mixer at low speed, beat sugar with margarine or butter until blended. Increase speed to high; beat until creamy. At low speed, beat in flour and remaining ingredients except frosting and décors until well blended. Cover bowl with plastic wrap and freeze 1 hour or until firm enough to handle.

2 Divide dough into thirds. On lightly floured surface, shape each third into a 12-inch-long log. Wrap each log in plastic wrap and freeze at least 4 hours or overnight, until firm enough to slice.

3 Preheat oven to 350°F. Grease large cookie sheet. Slice 1 log into ¼-inch-thick slices. Place slices, 1½ inches apart, on cookie sheet. Bake 15 to 20 minutes, until set and lightly browned around the edges. Cool on cookie sheet 1 minute, then, with pancake turner, remove to wire rack to cool completely. Repeat with remaining dough.

4 When cookies are cool, prepare Sally Ann Frosting. With small metal spatula or knife, spread frosting on cookies. If you like, sprinkle cookies with décors. Set cookies aside to allow frosting to dry completely, about 1 hour. Makes about 12 dozen cookies.

SALLY ANN FROSTING: In 2-quart saucepan, stir *1 cup sugar* and *1 envelope unflavored gelatin* until well mixed. Stir in *1 cup cold water*; heat to boiling over high heat. Reduce heat to low; simmer, uncovered, 10 minutes. Into small bowl, measure *2 cups confectioners' sugar*. With mixer at low speed, gradually add gelatin mixture to confectioners' sugar until blended. Increase speed to high; beat until smooth and fluffy with an easy spreading consistency, about 10 minutes. Beat in *¼ teaspoon vanilla extract*. Keep bowl covered with plastic wrap to prevent frosting from drying out.

Each cookie without décors: About 55 calories, 0 g protein, 10 g carbohydrate, 1 g total fat (0 g saturated), 0 mg cholesterol, 40 mg sodium.

Honey Cookies

PREP: 40 MINUTES PLUS CHILLING AND COOLING
BAKE: 18 TO 22 MINUTES PER BATCH

Dawn Zimmerman of Couderay, Wisconsin, gives us this barely sweet, slightly salty cookie that her Czechoslovakian grandma loved to make.

1 cup margarine or butter (2 sticks), softened
¼ cup honey
2 teaspoons vanilla extract
2 cups all-purpose flour
2 cups walnuts, chopped
½ teaspoon salt

1 In large bowl, with mixer at high speed, beat margarine or butter until creamy. Add honey and vanilla; beat until well blended.

2 With mixer at low speed, beat in flour, walnuts, and salt until dough forms. Cover bowl with plastic wrap and refrigerate dough at least 1 hour.

3 Preheat oven to 325°F. With lightly floured hands, shape dough by heaping teaspoons into balls. Place balls, about 2 inches apart, on ungreased large cookie sheet. Press floured 4-tine fork across top of each ball.

4 Bake 18 to 22 minutes until golden. With pancake turner, remove cookies to rack to cool. Repeat with remaining dough. Makes about 3½ dozen cookies.

Each cookie: About 105 calories, 1 g protein, 7 g carbohydrate, 8 g total fat (1 g saturated), 0 mg cholesterol, 85 mg sodium.

Darlene's Oatmeal Cookies

PREP: 20 MINUTES PLUS COOLING
BAKE: 12 TO 15 MINUTES PER BATCH

Darlene Heitz and her husband of 48 years, Glenn, sells produce and baked goods at Iowa's Charles City Market. The recipe for these crunchy oatmeal cookies—a hand-me-down from Glenn's mother—has an unusual twist. The oatmeal and raisins are ground (we used a processor, but Heitz has always relied on a simple grinder).

2 cups old-fashioned oats, uncooked
1 cup dark seedless or golden raisins
2 cups all-purpose flour
1 teaspoon baking soda
½ teaspoon salt
1 cup margarine or butter, softened
1 cup granulated sugar
1 cup packed light brown sugar
2 large eggs
2 teaspoons vanilla extract

1 Preheat oven to 350°F. In food processor with knife blade attached, pulse oats and raisins until ground. Place in bowl; stir in flour, baking soda, and salt.

2 In large bowl, with mixer at low speed, beat margarine with both sugars until blended. Increase speed to high; beat until light and creamy. At low speed, beat in eggs and vanilla, then beat in oat mixture.

3 Drop dough by rounded tablespoons, about 2 inches apart, onto ungreased large cookie sheet. Bake 12 to 15 minutes, until cookies are browned. Cool on wire rack. Repeat with remaining dough. Makes about 3 dozen cookies.

Each cookie: About 165 calories, 3 g protein, 26 g carbohydrate, 6 g total fat (1 g saturated), 12 mg cholesterol, 140 mg sodium.

Greek Christmas Cookies

PREP: 50 MINUTES PLUS COOLING
BAKE: 15 MINUTES PER BATCH

Diane Sanchez of Auburndale, Florida, grew up in the Panama Canal Zone, and says it was always a treat at Christmastime to go to her grandmother's to help with the holiday baking. These cookies, which have been in the family for at least 40 years, were always her favorite!

1 cup margarine or butter (2 sticks)
2 cups confectioners' sugar
2 cups all-purpose flour
1 teaspoon ground cinnamon
½ teaspoon ground nutmeg
½ teaspoon ground cloves
⅛ teaspoon salt
1 large egg yolk
2 cups blanched almonds, ground
About 1 cup red candied cherries, each cut in
   half

1 Preheat oven to 350°F. In large bowl, with mixer at low speed, beat margarine or butter with confectioners' sugar until blended. Increase speed to high; beat until light and creamy. At low speed, beat in flour, cinnamon, nutmeg, cloves, salt, and egg yolk. With hand, knead in almonds.

2 Roll dough into 1-inch balls (dough will be crumbly). Place balls, about 2 inches apart, on ungreased large cookie sheet. Gently press a cherry half on top of each ball. Bake 15 minutes or until bottoms of cookies are lightly browned. With pancake

turner, remove cookies to wire rack to cool. Repeat with remaining dough and cherries. Makes about 6 dozen cookies.

Each cookie: About 75 calories, 1 g protein, 9 g carbohydrate, 4 g total fat (1 g saturated), 3 mg cholesterol, 40 mg sodium.

Greek Cinnamon Paximadia

PREP: 1 HOUR PLUS COOLING • BAKE: 50 MINUTES

From Kathryn Marie Petrofanis of San Pedro, California, a twice-baked biscottilike cookie (*paximadia* is Greek for biscuits).

½ cup margarine or butter (1 stick), softened
½ cup shortening
1½ cups sugar
3 large eggs
1 teaspoon vanilla extract
2 teaspoons baking powder
½ teaspoon baking soda
About 4 cups all-purpose flour
1½ teaspoons ground cinnamon

1 In large bowl with mixer at low speed, beat margarine or butter, shortening, and 1 cup sugar until blended. Increase speed to high; beat until light and fluffy, about 5 minutes. At low speed, add eggs, 1 at a time, and vanilla, and beat until well mixed.

2 Gradually add baking powder, baking soda, and 3 cups flour and beat until well blended. With wooden spoon, stir in remaining 1 cup flour until soft dough forms. If necessary, add additional flour (up to ½ cup) until dough is easy to handle.

3 Preheat oven to 350°F. Divide dough into 4 equal pieces. On lightly floured surface, shape each piece of dough into an 8-inch-long log. Place 2 logs, about 4 inches apart, on each of 2 ungreased large cookie sheets. Flatten each log to 2½ inches wide.

4 Place cookie sheets on 2 oven racks and bake 20 minutes or until lightly browned and toothpick inserted in center comes out clean, rotating cookie sheets between racks halfway through baking. In pie plate, mix cinnamon with remaining ½ cup sugar.

5 Remove cookie sheets from oven. Transfer hot loaves (during baking, logs will spread and become loaves) to cutting board; with serrated knife, cut diagonally into ½-inch-thick slices. Coat slices with cinnamon sugar. Return slices, cut side down, to same cookie sheets. Bake slices 15 minutes. Turn slices over and return to oven, rotating cookie sheets between upper and lower racks, and bake 15 minutes longer or until golden. Remove cookies to wire racks to cool. Makes about 4 dozen cookies.

Each cookie: About 105 calories, 1 g protein, 14 g carbohydrate, 5 g total fat (1 g saturated), 13 mg cholesterol, 60 mg sodium.

GH Gingerbread Cutouts

PREP: 45 MINUTES PLUS COOLING AND DECORATING
BAKE: 12 MINUTES PER BATCH

If you want to hang these cookies on a wreath or tree, make 1 or 2 holes in the top of each cookie *before* baking. After decorating, thread nylon fishing line or thin ribbon through hole(s) in each cookie for hanging.

½ cup sugar
½ cup light molasses
1½ teaspoons ground ginger
1 teaspoon ground allspice
1 teaspoon ground cinnamon
1 teaspoon ground cloves
2 teaspoons baking soda
½ cup margarine or butter (1 stick), cut into
    chunks
1 large egg, beaten
3½ cups all-purpose flour
Ornamental Frosting (page 233)

1 In 3-quart saucepan, heat sugar, molasses, ginger, allspice, cinnamon, and cloves to boiling over medium heat, stirring occasionally. Remove saucepan from heat; stir in baking soda (mixture will foam up in the pan). Stir in margarine or butter until melted. With fork, stir in egg, then flour.

2 On floured surface, knead dough until mixed. Divide dough in half; wrap half in plastic wrap and set aside.

3 Preheat oven to 325°F. With floured rolling pin, roll remaining half of dough slightly thinner than ¼ inch. With floured 3- to 4-inch assorted cookie cut-

ters, cut dough into cookies; reserve trimmings. Place cookies, 1 inch apart, on ungreased cookie sheet. Reroll trimmings and cut out more cookies.

4 Bake cookies 12 minutes or until edges begin to brown. Remove cookies to wire racks to cool. Repeat with remaining dough.

5 When cookies are cool, prepare Ornamental Frosting; use to decorate cookies as desired. Set cookies aside to allow frosting to dry completely, about 1 hour. If not using right away, store cookies in tightly covered container. Makes about 3 dozen cookies.

Each cookie without frosting: About 90 calories, 1 g protein, 15 g carbohydrate, 3 g total fat (1 g saturated), 6 mg cholesterol, 105 mg sodium.

FOOD EDITOR'S TIP

Q. What's the difference between sulphured and unsulphured molasses? My old cookbook has a gingerbread recipe that calls for the sulphured kind. And does it matter whether I use light or dark?

A. Old-fashioned molasses was a by-product of the sugar refining process; sulfur dioxide was used to lighten and clarify the thick brown syrup left after sugar crystals were extracted from the cane juice. Today, most molasses is unsulphured—produced from pure sugarcane juice (not sugar by-product), so sulfur-dioxide processing is not necessary. You can use either sulphured or unsulphured, whether light or dark, in gingerbread and gingerbread cookies. Light molasses is produced when sugarcane juice is boiled, then clarified and blended for uniform color, sweetness, and consistency. This mild, or "first" molasses is often poured on pancakes in the South, and used in baking where a somewhat sweeter taste is preferred. A second boiling and clarifying process yields dark, hearty, or "second" molasses, which is less sweet. It's added to gingerbread or Indian pudding for a more robust flavor. Blackstrap molasses, produced after a third boiling, is very thick, dark, and bitter. It's higher in iron, calcium, and potassium content than the other two kinds, and is sold in some grocery and health-food stores. Its strong taste makes it perfect for yeast breads and baked beans.

Mom's Pfeffernusse

PREP: 1 HOUR 30 MINUTES PLUS CHILLING AND COOLING
BAKE: 8 TO 10 MINUTES PER BATCH

"These cookies, which originated in Germany, are unlike any other pfeffernusse [pepper nuts] I've ever tasted," says Carol A. Buck of Sherman Oaks, California. "They literally melt in your mouth, and have a spicy orange flavor."

2 cups sugar
4 large eggs
3½ cups all-purpose flour
2 tablespoons grated orange peel
1 teaspoon ground cinnamon
1 teaspoon ground allspice
1 teaspoon baking powder
1 teaspoon lemon extract
½ teaspoon ground cloves

1 In large bowl, with mixer at low speed, beat sugar and eggs until blended. Increase speed to high; beat until creamy. Reduce speed to low; add flour, grated orange peel, cinnamon, allspice, baking powder, lemon extract, and cloves and beat until well combined, occasionally scraping bowl with rubber spatula. With lightly floured hands, shape dough into 4 balls; flatten each slightly. Wrap each in plastic wrap and freeze 1 hour or refrigerate overnight. (Dough will be very sticky even after chilling.)

2 Preheat oven to 400°F. Grease large cookie sheet. On well-floured surface, with floured rolling pin, roll 1 piece of dough into 10" by 6" rectangle, keeping remaining dough in refrigerator. With floured pastry wheel or sharp knife, cut dough lengthwise into 6 strips, then cut each strip crosswise into 10 pieces. Place cookies, about ½ inch apart, on cookie sheet.

3 Bake cookies for 8 to 10 minutes, until lightly browned. With pancake turner, remove cookies to wire racks to cool. Repeat with remaining dough. Makes 20 dozen cookies.

Each cookie: About 15 calories, 0 g protein, 3 g carbohydrate, 0 g total fat, 4 mg cholesterol, 5 mg sodium.

Miss Elsie's Almond Slices

PREP: 45 MINUTES PLUS FREEZING AND COOLING
BAKE: 15 MINUTES PER BATCH

This recipe from Ann Wood of Columbia, Maryland, has always been a family secret—until now! Wood's grandmother, "Miss Elsie," began baking these in Greensboro, North Carolina, during the 1930's. They were so popular that she started selling them in her neighborhood. Now they're yours to make.

1½ cups butter (3 sticks), melted (do not use margarine)
1 cup packed light brown sugar
1 cup sugar
3 large eggs
1 teaspoon vanilla extract
½ teaspoon lemon extract
1 cup slivered almonds, finely ground
5½ cups all-purpose flour
2 teaspoons ground cinnamon
1½ teaspoons baking soda
1 teaspoon salt
1 teaspoon ground nutmeg

1 In large bowl, with spoon, combine melted butter, brown sugar, and sugar. Add eggs, vanilla, lemon extract, and ground almonds; beat to combine well. Stir in flour, cinnamon, baking soda, salt, and nutmeg until dough forms. Cover bowl with plastic wrap and freeze dough 1 hour or until easy to handle.

2 Divide dough into 8 pieces. On lightly floured surface, with floured hands, shape each piece into a 6-inch-long log. Wrap each log in plastic wrap and freeze at least 4 hours or overnight, until firm enough to slice.

3 Preheat oven to 350°F. Grease large cookie sheet. Slice logs into very thin (about ³⁄₁₆-inch) slices. Place slices, 1½ inches apart, on cookie sheet. Bake 15 minutes or until cookies are browned. With pancake turner, remove cookies to wire rack to cool. Makes about 24 dozen cookies.

Each cookie: About 25 calories, 0 g protein, 3 g carbohydrate, 1 g total fat (0 g saturated), 5 mg cholesterol, 25 mg sodium.

◄ *Clockwise from top: Pennsylvania-Dutch Brownies (page 218) Miss Elsie's Almond Slices, Honey Cookies (page 227), Christmas Rocks (page 232), Mom's Pfeffernusse*

Christmas Rocks

PREP: 45 MINUTES PLUS COOLING
BAKE: 12 TO 15 MINUTES PER BATCH

When Betty Pfeifer of Bay Village, Ohio, was in high school, her cooking teacher had the class make holiday treats to take home. This cookie was such a hit with Pfeifer's mother that she requested the recipe from the teacher—and Pfeifer has been making it ever since with only a few changes (such as replacing the citron in the original with bright candied cherries and pineapple).

½ cup packed brown sugar
⅓ cup shortening
6 tablespoons margarine or butter (¾ stick), softened
2 large eggs
1½ cups all-purpose flour
1 teaspoon baking powder
1 teaspoon ground cinnamon
½ teaspoon baking soda
½ teaspoon salt
¼ teaspoon ground cloves
2 cups walnuts, coarsely chopped
2 cups dark seedless raisins
½ cup dried currants
½ cup red and/or green candied cherries, each cut in half
½ cup diced candied pineapple

1 In large bowl, with mixer at low speed, beat brown sugar, shortening, and margarine or butter until mixed, occasionally scraping bowl with rubber spatula. Increase speed to high; beat mixture until creamy, about 2 minutes.

2 With mixer at low speed, beat in eggs, then flour, baking powder, cinnamon, baking soda, salt, and cloves just until mixed. With spoon, stir in walnuts and remaining ingredients.

3 Preheat oven to 350°F. Drop dough by rounded tablespoons, about 1½ inches apart, on ungreased large cookie sheet. Bake 12 to 15 minutes until set and lightly browned. With pancake turner, remove cookies to wire rack to cool. Repeat with remaining dough. Makes about 4 dozen cookies.

Each cookie: About 120 calories, 2 g protein, 16 g carbohydrate, 6 g total fat (1 g saturated), 9 mg cholesterol, 70 mg sodium.

Great-Granny's Old-Time Spice Cookies

PREP: 1 HOUR 10 MINUTES PLUS CHILLING, COOLING, AND DECORATING • BAKE: 8 TO 10 MINUTES PER BATCH

These cookies come from Shirley A. Fisher of Bethlehem, Pennsylvania. Fisher's great-grandmother handed this recipe down in the late 1890's, and it's been in the family ever since. Early on, the cookies weren't decorated, but later some icing and colored sugars were added. Even the cookie cutters have been handed down, with new additions along the way. Fisher bakes these cookies all year—for Valentine's Day, Easter, even the Fourth of July.

5½ cups all-purpose flour
1 teaspoon ground cinnamon
1 teaspoon ground allspice
½ teaspoon ground nutmeg
½ teaspoon baking soda
½ teaspoon salt
1 cup margarine or butter (2 sticks), softened
1¼ cups packed light brown sugar
1 jar (12 ounces) dark molasses
Ornamental Frosting (opposite page), optional

1 In large bowl, combine flour, cinnamon, allspice, nutmeg, baking soda, and salt. In another large bowl, with mixer at low speed, beat margarine or butter with brown sugar until blended. Increase speed to high; beat until light and creamy. At low speed, beat in molasses until blended, then beat in 3 cups flour mixture. With spoon, stir in remaining flour mixture. Divide dough into 4 equal pieces. Wrap each piece in plastic wrap and freeze at least 1 hour or refrigerate overnight, until dough is firm enough to roll.

2 Preheat oven to 350°F. On well-floured surface, with floured rolling pin, roll 1 piece of dough ⅛ inch thick, keeping remaining dough refrigerated (dough will be soft). With floured 3- to 4-inch assorted cookie cutters, cut dough into as many cookies as possible; reserve trimmings. Place cookies, about 1 inch apart, on ungreased large cookie sheet.

3 Bake cookies 8 to 10 minutes, until just browned. Cool cookies on cookie sheet 5 minutes. With pancake turner, remove cookies to wire rack to cool completely. Repeat with remaining dough and reserved trimmings.

4 When cookies are cool, if you like, prepare Ornamental Frosting. Use to decorate cookies as desired. Set cookies aside to allow frosting to dry completely, about 1 hour. Makes about 4 dozen cookies.

Each cookie without frosting: About 120 calories, 2 g protein, 21 g carbohydrate, 4 g total fat (1 g saturated), 0 mg cholesterol, 95 mg sodium.

ORNAMENTAL FROSTING

We used this hard-drying frosting—left white or tinted with food coloring—to decorate Great-Granny's Old-Time Spice Cookies (opposite page) and Sand Tarts (page 224), and GH Gingerbread Cutouts (page 229).

PREP: 8 MINUTES

1 package (16 ounces) confectioners' sugar
3 tablespoons meringue powder*
Assorted food colorings or food color pastes (optional)

1 In bowl, with mixer at medium speed, beat confectioners' sugar, meringue powder, and *⅓ cup warm water* until blended and mixture is so stiff that knife drawn through it leaves a clean-cut path, about 5 minutes.

2 If you like, tint frosting with food colorings; keep covered with plastic wrap to prevent drying out. With small metal spatula, artists' paintbrushes, or decorating bags with small writing tips, decorate cookies with frosting. (You may need to thin frosting with a little *warm water* first.) Makes about 3 cups.

*Meringue powder is available in specialty stores wherever cake-decorating equipment is sold.

Each tablespoon: About 40 calories, 0 g protein, 10 g carbohydrate, 0 g total fat, 0 mg cholesterol, 3 mg sodium.

Noisettines

PREP: 1 HOUR PLUS CHILLING AND COOLING
BAKE: 30 MINUTES

Laurence Mancini Ilanjian of Taconic, Connecticut, created these hazelnut "tassie" cookies (*noisette* is French for hazelnut) in memory of the "Noisettine" tarts she loved buying at a local bakery in Geneva, Switzerland, when she was a student there.

1 package (3 ounces) cream cheese, softened
½ cup plus 1 tablespoon margarine or butter, softened
1 cup all-purpose flour
1⅓ cups hazelnuts (filberts)
⅔ cup packed light brown sugar
1 large egg
1 teaspoon vanilla extract

1 In large bowl, with mixer at high speed, beat cream cheese with ½ cup margarine or butter until creamy. Reduce speed to low; add flour and beat until well mixed. Cover bowl with plastic wrap and refrigerate 30 minutes.

2 Meanwhile, preheat oven to 350°F. Place hazelnuts in 9" by 9" metal baking pan. Bake 10 to 15 minutes until toasted. Wrap hot hazelnuts in clean cloth towel. With hands, roll hazelnuts back and forth to remove skins. Cool completely.

3 Reserve 24 hazelnuts for garnish. In food processor with knife blade attached, blend remaining hazelnuts with brown sugar until hazelnuts are finely ground.

4 In medium bowl, with spoon, combine hazelnut mixture with egg, vanilla, and remaining 1 tablespoon margarine or butter.

5 With floured hands, divide chilled dough into 24 equal pieces (dough will be very soft). Gently press each piece of dough evenly onto bottom and up sides of 24 ungreased miniature muffin-pan cups. Spoon filling by heaping teaspoons into each pastry cup; place 1 whole hazelnut on top of filling in each cup.

6 Bake 30 minutes or until filling is set and crust is golden. With tip of knife, loosen cookie cups from muffin-pan cups and place on wire rack to cool completely. Makes 2 dozen cookies.

Each cookie: About 135 calories, 2 g protein, 11 g carbohydrate, 10 g total fat (2 g saturated), 13 mg cholesterol, 75 mg sodium.

Aunt Tess's Anisette Cookies

PREP: 1 HOUR PLUS CHILLING AND COOLING
BAKE: 12 MINUTES PER BATCH

Ann Cullen of Wantagh, New York, offers a cookie recipe from her sister Theresa. Theresa (Tess) always baked a variety of cookies to share with her family, and this old-fashioned Italian cookie with a festive anise glaze was one of her best.

½ cup margarine or butter (1 stick), softened
½ cup sugar
3 large eggs
1 teaspoon vanilla extract
2 teaspoons anise extract or anisette (anise-
    flavor liqueur)
2½ cups all-purpose flour
1 tablespoon baking powder
¾ cup confectioners' sugar
Red and green sprinkles (optional)

1 In large bowl, with mixer at low speed, beat margarine or butter with sugar until blended. Increase speed to high; beat until creamy. At medium speed, beat in eggs, vanilla, and 1 teaspoon anise extract, constantly scraping bowl with rubber spatula. Reduce speed to low; beat in flour and baking powder, occasionally scraping bowl. Shape dough into 4 balls. Wrap each ball in plastic wrap and freeze at least 1 hour or refrigerate overnight.

2 Preheat oven to 350°F. On lightly floured surface, divide 1 ball of dough into 9 equal pieces, keeping remaining dough refrigerated. With lightly floured hands, roll each piece of dough into a 7-inch-long rope; bring ends of rope together and gently twist several times. Pinch twisted ends together to seal.

3 Place cookies, about 2 inches apart, on ungreased large cookie sheet. Bake cookies 12 minutes or until bottoms are lightly browned. With pancake turner, remove cookies to wire rack to cool. Repeat with remaining dough.

4 When cookies are cool, prepare glaze. In small bowl, mix confectioners' sugar with remaining 1 teaspoon anise extract and *2 tablespoons water*. Brush *top* of cookies with glaze; place on rack. Top with sprinkles if you like. Set cookies aside to allow glaze to dry, about 1 hour. Makes 3 dozen cookies.

Each cookie without sprinkles: About 80 calories, 1 g protein, 12 g carbohydrate, 3 g total fat (1 g saturated), 18 mg cholesterol, 70 mg sodium.

Chocolate Sambuca Cookies

PREP: 30 MINUTES PLUS CHILLING AND COOLING
BAKE: 10 TO 12 MINUTES PER BATCH

A close friend shared this recipe with Leslie R. Husted of Clinton, New York, several years ago. Her family looks forward to nibbling on these every year at holiday time, and she makes batches to give as gifts.

12 squares (1 ounce each) semisweet chocolate
4 tablespoons margarine or butter (½ stick)
3 large eggs
⅓ cup sambuca (anise-flavor liqueur)
1 cup sugar
1 cup blanched almonds, finely ground
⅔ cup all-purpose flour
¾ teaspoon baking soda
⅓ cup confectioners' sugar

1 In 2-quart saucepan, melt chocolate with margarine or butter over low heat, stirring frequently. Remove saucepan from heat; cool chocolate mixture slightly.

2 In medium bowl, with wire whisk, mix eggs, sambuca, and ½ cup sugar; blend in chocolate mixture.

3 With spoon, stir ground almonds, flour, and baking soda into chocolate mixture until combined (dough will be very soft). Cover bowl with plastic wrap and refrigerate at least 4 hours or overnight.

4 Preheat oven to 350°F. In small bowl, combine confectioners' sugar with remaining ½ cup sugar. With lightly floured hands, roll dough by rounded tablespoons into balls. Roll balls in sugar mixture to coat. Place balls, about 2 inches apart, on ungreased large cookie sheet. Bake 10 to 12 minutes, until cookies are just set and look puffed and cracked. Let cookies remain on cookie sheet 1 minute to cool slightly. With pancake turner, remove cookies to wire rack to cool completely. Repeat with remaining dough and sugar mixture. Makes about 4 dozen cookies.

Each cookie: About 85 calories, 2 g protein, 12 g carbohydrate, 4 g total fat (0 g saturated), 13 mg cholesterol, 20 mg sodium.

CONDIMENTS, SAUCES & JAMS

Tomato Chutney

PREP: 25 MINUTES • COOK: 45 TO 50 MINUTES

A tangy-sweet condiment made with ripe tomatoes, crunchy apple, vinegar, and spices—serve hot or cold with grilled meats, or spread on bread.

3 pounds ripe tomatoes (about 9 medium), peeled and cut into ½-inch pieces
2 garlic cloves, minced
1 medium Granny Smith apple, peeled and grated
1 small onion, chopped
½ cup cider vinegar
⅓ cup packed brown sugar
⅓ cup golden raisins
2 tablespoons minced, peeled fresh ginger
½ teaspoon salt
¼ teaspoon coarsely ground black pepper

In 12-inch skillet, heat all ingredients to boiling over high heat. Reduce heat to medium; cook, uncovered, 45 to 50 minutes, stirring occasionally, until mixture thickens. Spoon chutney into bowl; cover and refrigerate until well chilled. Use within 2 weeks. Makes about 3½ cups.

Each ¼ cup: About 60 calories, 1 g protein, 15 g carbohydrate, 0 g total fat, 0 mg cholesterol, 90 mg sodium.

Pear Chutney

PREP: 30 MINUTES • COOK: ABOUT 15 MINUTES

A nice accompaniment to roast pork, ham, or poultry. Or, serve with cream cheese and crackers for an impromptu hors d'oeuvre.

12 ounces dried pear halves, chopped (2 cups)
1 large red onion, finely chopped (1 cup)
2½ cups pear nectar
2 cups dark seedless and/or golden raisins
¾ cup cider vinegar
½ cup dried tart cherries
⅓ cup sugar
1 tablespoon mustard seeds
1 tablespoon grated, peeled fresh ginger
¼ teaspoon salt
1 cinnamon stick (3 inches)

1 In 4-quart saucepan, heat all ingredients and *1 cup water* to boiling over high heat, stirring occasionally. Reduce heat to low; simmer, uncovered, 15 minutes or until pears are very soft, stirring frequently.

2 Discard cinnamon stick. Spoon chutney into jars for gift giving. Store in refrigerator for up to a month. Makes about 6 cups.

Each ¼ cup: About 115 calories, 1 g protein, 30 g carbohydrate, 0 g total fat, 0 mg cholesterol, 25 mg sodium.

Red-Pepper Chutney

PREP: 25 MINUTES PLUS CHILLING • COOK: 40 MINUTES

You can prepare this sweet and spicy relish up to 2 weeks in advance. Refrigerate until ready to use.

1½ cups cider vinegar
1 cup sugar
6 large red peppers, diced
3 firm, medium pears, peeled and cut into ½-inch pieces
1 small red onion, diced
⅓ cup dark seedless raisins
1½ teaspoons mustard seeds
1 teaspoon salt
⅛ teaspoon ground allspice

1 In nonreactive 5-quart Dutch oven, heat vinegar and sugar to boiling over high heat; boil 10 minutes.

2 Add peppers, pears, onion, raisins, mustard seeds, salt, and allspice; heat to boiling. Reduce heat to medium-high and cook, uncovered, stirring occasionally, for 30 minutes or until syrupy. Cover and refrigerate until chilled, about 4 hours. Makes about 6 cups.

Each ¼ cup: About 65 calories, 1 g protein, 17 g carbohydrate, 0 g total fat, 0 mg cholesterol, 90 mg sodium.

Clockwise from top: Red-Pepper Chutney, ➤
Sweet Corn Relish (page 241), Kirby Cucumber Salad (page 147), Watermelon Pickles (page 239)

Fennel & Nectarine Salsa

PREP: 20 MINUTES

This crunchy salsa goes well with grilled or broiled fish, poultry, or pork.

1 small fennel bulb, chopped, plus 1 tablespoon minced fennel fronds, if available
1 ripe large nectarine, pitted and chopped
1 green onion, minced
2 teaspoons olive oil
2 teaspoons seasoned rice vinegar
⅛ teaspoon salt
Pinch coarsely ground black pepper
4 large fresh basil leaves, thinly sliced

In medium bowl, stir all ingredients. Cover and refrigerate if not serving right away. Makes about 1½ cups.

Each ¼ cup: About 30 calories, 0 g protein, 4 g carbohydrate, 2 g total fat (0 g saturated), 0 mg cholesterol, 100 mg sodium.

Orange-Fennel Salsa

PREP: 15 MINUTES

3 small navel oranges
1 medium fennel bulb (1½ pounds), trimmed and coarsely chopped
1 jalapeño chile, seeded and minced
¼ cup chopped fresh cilantro leaves
½ small red onion, thinly sliced
¼ teaspoon salt

Cut peel and white pith from oranges. Over medium bowl, cut on either side of membranes to remove each segment from oranges, allowing fruit and juice to drop into bowl. Add fennel, jalapeño, cilantro, red onion, and salt; stir to combine. Cover and refrigerate if not serving right away. Makes about 3 cups.

Each ¼ cup: About 35 calories, 1 g protein, 8 g carbohydrate, 0 g total fat, 0 mg cholesterol, 70 mg sodium.

Olive & Lemon Salsa

PREP: 10 MINUTES

2 lemons
2 small navel oranges
¼ cup coarsely chopped pimiento-stuffed olives
2 tablespoons chopped shallot
2 tablespoons chopped fresh parsley leaves
½ teaspoon sugar
¼ teaspoon coarsely ground black pepper

Cut peel and white pith from lemons and oranges. Cut fruit into ¼-inch slices, discarding seeds. Cut slices into ½-inch pieces. In small bowl, combine lemon and orange pieces, olives, shallot, parsley, sugar, and black pepper, stirring gently. Cover and refrigerate if not serving right away. Makes about 2 cups.

Each ¼ cup: About 130 calories, 3 g protein, 28 g carbohydrate, 3 g total fat (1 g saturated), 0 mg cholesterol, 705 mg sodium.

Chimichurri Sauce

PREP: 20 MINUTES

Spoon this Argentinian herb sauce on meat or sandwiches.

1 large garlic clove, minced
½ teaspoon salt
1½ cups loosely packed fresh Italian parsley leaves, minced
1 cup loosely packed fresh cilantro leaves, minced
¾ cup olive oil
2 tablespoons red wine vinegar
½ teaspoon crushed red pepper

1 On cutting board, with side of chef's knife, mash garlic with salt to a smooth paste.

2 In small bowl, stir garlic mixture with parsley and remaining ingredients until well blended. Makes about 1 cup.

Each tablespoon: About 90 calories, 0 g protein, 1 g carbohydrate, 10 g total fat (1 g saturated), 0 mg cholesterol, 70 mg sodium.

Jalapeño: Green, about 2 inches long, a pepper with punch: It's the most popular hot pepper, widely used in Mexican dishes. Slice raw for nachos or cook in chili.

Anaheim: Long, slender, twisted, and green or red, these are among the most common chiles in American markets. Also called California, New Mexico, Long Green, or Big Jim, they range from mild to moderately hot. Use for chiles relleños or mince to flavor sauces.

Cascabel: The Spanish word means "small bell"—like a sleigh bell—and the cascabel resembles one; its seeds rattle around inside. Moderately hot, usually sold dried, it has a tough, brownish-red skin. Best for stews.

Habanero: These look like small translucent orange lanterns, and are the hottest-tasting domestic peppers. They're green when mature, then ripen to yellow, then orange. The habanero's distinct flavor is nice in salsas.

Poblano: This dark-green, elongated bell-shaped pepper ranges from mild to hot. Fry in strips for fajitas or stuff and bake.

Serrano: These small, dark-green, torpedo-shaped peppers are extremely hot and usually eaten raw, in fiery salsas.

Pepper Pointers

1 Refrigerate fresh peppers, wrapped in paper towels, in a plastic bag for up to 1 week. Keep dried hot peppers in an airtight container at room temperature for up to 4 months.

2 Handle raw hot peppers with care: Wear rubber gloves to avoid irritating skin; don't rub eyes, nose, or mouth. When finished, wash hands and gloves in warm soapy water.

3 Remove ribs and seeds from large peppers before eating to prevent bitterness.

Watermelon Pickles

PREP: 1 HOUR PLUS STANDING AND CHILLING
COOK: ABOUT 25 MINUTES

Prepare these 2 weeks in advance and keep in the refrigerator—no need for complicated processing and canning. Better than store-bought!

12 pounds watermelon (about ½ large
   watermelon)
¾ cup salt
5 cups sugar
2½ cups distilled white vinegar
6 whole cloves
6 whole allspice
4 cinnamon sticks
1 teaspoon cracked black pepper

1 Cut watermelon into large chunks. With sharp knife, trim dark green outer skin from watermelon rind and discard. Cut off most of red flesh, leaving about ⅛-inch-thick layer. Reserve watermelon flesh for fruit salad another day. Cut watermelon rind into 1-inch cubes (you should have 12 cups).

2 In large bowl, dissolve salt in *8 cups water*. Add rind and let stand 4 to 5 hours at room temperature.

3 Drain rind; rinse with cold running water and drain again. In nonreactive 5-quart Dutch oven or heavy saucepot, heat rind with *water* to cover to boiling over high heat. Reduce heat to medium and cook, uncovered, until rind is tender-crisp, about 10 minutes. Drain.

4 In same Dutch oven, combine sugar, vinegar, cloves, allspice, cinnamon sticks, pepper, and 2½ *cups water*. Heat to boiling over high heat; boil 3 minutes. Add rind and cook until tender, about 10 minutes. Skim any foam. Remove Dutch oven from heat and cool pickles to room temperature. Cover and refrigerate up to 2 weeks. Drain before serving. Makes about 5 cups, drained.

Each ¼ cup: About 45 calories, 0 g protein, 11 g carbohydrate, 0 g total fat, 0 mg cholesterol, 220 mg sodium.

Sweet Corn Relish

PREP: 20 MINUTES PLUS CHILLING • COOK: 30 SECONDS

Tastes great whether it's made with fresh or frozen corn, and keeps well for several days in the refrigerator.

8 ears corn, husks and silk removed, or 4 cups
    frozen whole-kernel corn (one 20-ounce
    package), thawed
3 tablespoons fresh lime juice
2 tablespoons olive oil
¾ teaspoon ground cumin
¾ teaspoon ground coriander
¾ teaspoon salt
½ teaspoon chili powder
1 large red pepper, diced

1 If using fresh corn, with sharp knife, cut kernels from cobs (you should have about 4 cups). Heat large saucepot filled with *water* to boiling over high heat. Add fresh corn; heat to boiling. Boil 30 seconds. Drain corn; rinse under cold running water and drain again.

2 In medium bowl, with wire whisk or fork, mix lime juice, olive oil, cumin, coriander, salt, and chili powder. Add corn and red pepper; toss well. Cover and refrigerate until chilled, about 2 hours. Makes about 5 cups.

Each ¼ cup: About 50 calories, 1 g protein, 8 g carbohydrate, 2 g total fat (0 g saturated), 0 mg cholesterol, 85 mg sodium.

No-Cook Tomato Sauce

PREP: 15 MINUTES PLUS 15 MINUTES TO STAND

Toss all 7 cups with 1 pound hot pasta.

2 pounds ripe tomatoes (about 6 medium), cut
    into ½-inch pieces
½ pound fresh mozzarella cheese, cut into
    ½-inch pieces
1 cup packed fresh basil leaves, cut into strips

◀ *A variety of pasta sauces (clockwise from top left): Plum Tomato & Sage Sauce (page 242), Roasted Tomato Sauce, No-Cook Tomato Sauce*

2 tablespoons olive oil
1 tablespoon red wine vinegar
1 teaspoon salt
¼ teaspoon coarsely ground black pepper

In medium bowl, combine tomatoes with their juice, mozzarella, basil, olive oil, vinegar, salt, and pepper, stirring gently to mix well. Allow sauce to stand at room temperature at least 15 minutes or up to 1 hour to develop flavor. Makes about 7 cups.

Each cup: About 150 calories, 8 g protein, 8 g carbohydrate, 12 g total fat (4 g saturated), 26 mg cholesterol, 340 mg sodium.

Roasted Tomato Sauce

PREP: 10 MINUTES PLUS 20 MINUTES TO COOL
COOK: 50 TO 60 MINUTES

Makes enough for 1 pound of spaghetti or linguine.

3 pounds ripe plum tomatoes (about 16 medium),
    each cut lengthwise in half
6 garlic cloves, unpeeled
2 tablespoons olive oil
¾ teaspoon salt
¼ teaspoon coarsely ground black pepper
Grated Romano cheese (optional)

1 Preheat oven to 450°F. In 15½" by 10½" jelly-roll pan, toss tomato halves and unpeeled garlic cloves with 1 tablespoon olive oil. Arrange tomatoes, cut side down, in jelly-roll pan. Roast tomatoes and garlic 50 to 60 minutes, until tomatoes are well browned and garlic cloves are soft.

2 Let tomatoes and garlic cool in pan 20 minutes or until easy to handle.

3 Over medium bowl, carefully peel tomatoes. Place tomato pulp in bowl with any juice from jelly-roll pan. Squeeze garlic from skins into same bowl. Discard skins from tomatoes and garlic. With spoon, crush tomatoes and garlic. Stir in salt, pepper, and remaining 1 tablespoon olive oil. Serve sauce at room temperature or transfer to saucepan; heat over medium-low heat until hot. Serve with grated Romano cheese if you like. Makes about 3 cups.

Each ½ cup: About 90 calories, 2 g protein, 12 g carbohydrate, 5 g total fat (1 g saturated), 0 mg cholesterol, 290 mg sodium.

Plum Tomato & Sage Sauce

PREP: 30 MINUTES • COOK: 1¼ HOURS

Use 3 cups sauce for 1 pound of pasta. If you have a lot of tomatoes, double the recipe, and freeze in batches for fresh-tasting tomato sauce during the winter.

2 tablespoons olive oil
1 small onion, finely chopped
3 pounds ripe plum tomatoes (about 16 medium), peeled and chopped
½ cup chicken broth
⅓ cup dry white wine
2 tablespoons butter (optional)
1 tablespoon chopped fresh sage leaves
1 teaspoon salt
Shredded Parmesan cheese

1 In 10-inch skillet, heat olive oil over medium-low heat. Add onion and cook until very tender and slightly golden, about 15 minutes.

2 To onion in skillet, add chopped tomatoes with their juice, chicken broth, and white wine; heat to boiling over high heat. Reduce heat to low; cover and simmer 30 minutes, stirring and pressing tomatoes with back of slotted spoon occasionally during cooking to crush them.

3 Remove cover and simmer tomato mixture 25 to 30 minutes longer, stirring occasionally, until sauce has reduced and thickened slightly. Stir in butter, sage, and salt. Serve with shredded cheese if you like. Makes about 4 cups.

Each ½ cup: About 75 calories, 2 g protein, 9 g carbohydrate, 4 g total fat (1 g saturated), 0 mg cholesterol, 330 mg sodium.

Arrabbiata Sauce

PREP: 15 MINUTES • COOK: ABOUT 1 HOUR

Spoon into pint or quart jars; include an extra gift of dry pasta, such as fusilli or penne, along with a note that 2 cups of sauce is enough for 1 pound of pasta.

½ cup extravirgin olive oil
6 garlic cloves, crushed with side of chef's knife
4 cans (35 ounces each) Italian plum tomatoes
1 tablespoon salt
1 to 1½ teaspoons crushed red pepper

1 In 8-quart Dutch oven, heat olive oil over medium heat until hot but not smoking. Add garlic and cook, stirring, 2 minutes; do not brown. Stir in tomatoes with their juice, salt, and red pepper; heat to boiling over high heat. Reduce heat to low; simmer, uncovered, 50 minutes or until sauce thickens slightly, stirring occasionally and crushing tomatoes with back of spoon.

RIPENING DO'S & DON'TS

To withstand shipping, tomatoes are picked before they are ripe and may not be ready to eat by the time they reach your supermarket. To coax them into juicy redness:

• Store them at room temperature (refrigeration prevents ripening and kills flavor). A good spot is in your fruit bowl—where the presence of other fruit speeds up the process—or in a sealed brown paper bag, which traps ethylene gas, a natural ripening agent in all fruit.

• Don't store tomatoes stem side down, whether in a bowl or a bag. The rounded "shoulders" are the most tender part and will bruise simply from the weight of the fruit.

• Don't ripen tomatoes on a windowsill. Direct sunlight softens tomatoes, but does not help to ripen them.

• Continue to store tomatoes at room temperature once they're ripe; use within two to three days. If you must refrigerate a fully ripe tomato to prevent spoilage, let it come to room temperature before serving to bring out the best flavor.

• Freeze ripe tomatoes if you have a surplus. Rinse gently and pat completely dry. Then, freeze whole in a freezer-weight zip-tight plastic bag for up to 6 months. Use right from the freezer, in soups and stews.

2 For smooth, traditional texture, press tomato mixture through food mill into large bowl. (Or, leave sauce as is for a hearty, chunky texture.) Cool sauce slightly. Spoon into jars. Store in refrigerator for up to a week. Or spoon into freezer-proof containers and freeze for up to 2 months. Makes about 14 cups.

Each ¼ cup: About 30 calories, 1 g protein, 3 g carbohydrate, 2 g total fat (0 g saturated), 0 mg cholesterol, 230 mg sodium.

Big-Batch Tomato Sauce

PREP: 30 MINUTES • COOK: ABOUT 1 HOUR

Our recipe makes 10 cups—and when you stock your freezer with this easy sauce, dinner is always close at hand. Spoon over pasta (use 3 cups per pound) or use for our baked ziti.

3 tablespoons olive oil
3 medium carrots, finely chopped
1 large onion, finely chopped
2 garlic cloves, minced
3 cans (28 ounces each) Italian-style tomatoes in puree
1 bay leaf
¾ teaspoon salt
¼ teaspoon coarsely ground black pepper

1 In 5-quart Dutch oven or saucepot, heat olive oil over medium heat until hot. Add carrots and onion and cook, about 20 minutes, until vegetables are very tender and golden, stirring occasionally. Add garlic; cook 2 minutes, stirring.

2 Meanwhile, place tomatoes with their puree in large bowl. With hands or slotted spoon, crush tomatoes well.

3 Add tomatoes with their puree, bay leaf, salt, and pepper to Dutch oven; heat to boiling over high heat. Reduce heat to low; cover and simmer 15 minutes. Uncover Dutch oven and simmer sauce 20 minutes longer, stirring occasionally. Discard bay leaf. Makes about 10 cups.

Each ½ cup: About 25 calories, 1 g protein, 4 g carbohydrate, 1 g total fat (0 g saturated), 0 mg cholesterol, 240 mg sodium.

Cape Cod Cranberry Sauce

PREP: 5 MINUTES PLUS CHILLING • COOK: 10 MINUTES

1 bag (12 ounces) cranberries (3 cups)
1 cup packed brown sugar
½ cup golden raisins
2 tablespoons cider vinegar
1 cinnamon stick (3 inches long)
Pinch ground cloves
Pinch salt
1 large Rome Beauty apple, peeled, cored, and diced

In 3-quart saucepan, heat cranberries, brown sugar, raisins, vinegar, cinnamon stick, cloves, salt, and ¾ *cup water* to boiling over high heat. Reduce heat to medium-low and cook, uncovered, 6 minutes, stirring occasionally. Add diced apple and cook until most of cranberries pop and mixture thickens slightly, about 4 minutes longer. Discard cinnamon stick. Spoon into serving bowl; cover and refrigerate until well chilled, about 3 hours. Makes about 4 cups.

Each ¼ cup: About 85 calories, 0 g protein, 22 g carbohydrate, 0 g total fat, 0 mg cholesterol, 15 mg sodium.

Santa Fe Cranberry Sauce

PREP: 5 MINUTES PLUS CHILLING • COOK: 10 MINUTES

½ cup apple juice or apple cider
½ cup sugar
1 teaspoon cider vinegar
1 bag (12 ounces) cranberries (3 cups)
1 or 2 pickled jalapeño chiles, seeded and minced

In 2-quart saucepan, heat all ingredients to boiling over high heat. Reduce heat to medium and cook, uncovered, until most of cranberries pop and mixture thickens slightly, about 10 minutes, stirring occasionally. Spoon into serving bowl; cover and refrigerate until well chilled, about 3 hours. Makes about 2¼ cups.

Each ¼ cup: About 70 calories, 0 g protein, 18 g carbohydrate, 0 g total fat, 0 mg cholesterol, 45 mg sodium.

Left to right: Blackberry-Blueberry Skillet Jam, Three-Berry Skillet Jam, Strawberry Skillet Jam

California Apricot-Cranberry Sauce

PREP: 15 MINUTES PLUS CHILLING • COOK: 10 MINUTES

½ cup dried apricot halves, cut into ¼-inch strips
¾ cup cranberry-juice cocktail
1 bag (12 ounces) cranberries (3 cups)
⅔ cup sugar
1 tablespoon minced, peeled fresh ginger

In 2-quart saucepan, soak apricots in cranberry juice 10 minutes. Add cranberries, sugar, and ginger; heat to boiling over high heat. Reduce heat to medium and cook, uncovered, until most of cranberries pop and mixture thickens slightly, about 10 minutes, stirring occasionally. Spoon into serving bowl; cover and refrigerate until well chilled, about 3 hours. Makes about 2½ cups.

Each ¼ cup: About 90 calories, 0 g protein, 25 g carbohydrate, 0 g total fat, 0 mg cholesterol, 2 mg sodium.

Strawberry Skillet Jam

PREP: 5 MINUTES PLUS CHILLING • COOK: 10 MINUTES

2 cups sliced strawberries, crushed
1 tablespoon plus 1 teaspoon powdered fruit pectin
½ teaspoon margarine or butter
1 cup sugar

1 In 12-inch skillet, stir together strawberries, pectin, and margarine or butter. Heat over medium-high heat, stirring constantly, until mixture boils. Stir in sugar; heat to boiling. Boil 1 minute; remove skillet from heat.

2 Pour jam into two ½-pint jars with tight-fitting lids. Cover and refrigerate until jam is set, about 6 hours. Keep jam refrigerated and use within 3 weeks. Makes about 2 cups.

Each tablespoon: About 30 calories, 0 g protein, 8 g carbohydrate, 0 g total fat, 0 mg cholesterol, 2 mg sodium.

Blackberry-Blueberry Skillet Jam

PREP: 5 MINUTES PLUS CHILLING • COOK: 10 MINUTES

2 cups blackberries, crushed
2 cups blueberries, crushed
2 tablespoons powdered fruit pectin
½ teaspoon margarine or butter
¾ cup sugar

1 Into bowl, press half of crushed blackberries through medium-mesh sieve to remove seeds. Discard seeds.

2 In 12-inch skillet, stir together blueberries, sieved blackberries, remaining crushed blackberries, pectin, and margarine or butter. Heat over medium-high heat, stirring constantly, until mixture boils. Stir in sugar; heat to boiling. Boil 1 minute; remove skillet from heat.

3 Pour jam into two ½-pint jars with tight-fitting lids. Cover and refrigerate until jam is set, about 6 hours. Keep jam refrigerated and use within 3 weeks. Makes about 2 cups.

Each tablespoon: About 25 calories, 0 g protein, 6 g carbohydrate, 0 g total fat, 0 mg cholesterol, 2 mg sodium.

Three-Berry Skillet Jam

PREP: 5 MINUTES PLUS CHILLING • COOK: 10 MINUTES

1 cup blackberries, crushed
1 cup raspberries, crushed
1 cup sliced strawberries, crushed
1 tablespoon plus 1 teaspoon powdered fruit pectin
½ teaspoon margarine or butter
1 cup sugar

1 Into bowl, press half of crushed blackberries and crushed raspberries through medium-mesh sieve to remove seeds. Discard seeds.

2 In 12-inch skillet, stir together strawberries, sieved berry mixture, remaining crushed blackberries and raspberries, pectin, and margarine or butter. Heat over medium-high heat, stirring constantly, until mix-

ture boils. Stir in sugar; heat to boiling. Boil 1 minute; remove skillet from heat.

3 Pour jam into two ½-pint jars with tight-fitting lids. Cover and refrigerate until jam is set, about 6 hours. Keep jam refrigerated and use within 3 weeks. Makes about 2 cups.

Each tablespoon: About 30 calories, 0 g protein, 10 g carbohydrate, 0 g total fat, 0 mg cholesterol, 2 mg sodium.

Blushing Apple Butter

PREP: 30 MINUTES • COOK: ABOUT 1 HOUR 10 MINUTES

A flavorful cholesterol- and fat-free spread. Yummy on toast or bagels.

3¾ pounds Granny Smith apples (about 8 large), peeled, cored, and thinly sliced
1½ cups apple cider or apple juice
1 cup cranberries
3 strips (3" by 1" each) lemon peel
3 tablespoons fresh lemon juice
1½ cups sugar

1 In 5-quart Dutch oven, heat apples, cider, cranberries, lemon peel, and lemon juice to boiling over high heat. Reduce heat to low; simmer, uncovered, 10 minutes or until apples are very soft, stirring occasionally.

2 Stir in sugar; heat to boiling over high heat. Reduce heat to medium; cook, partially covered, 1 hour or until apple butter is very thick, stirring occasionally (mixture may sputter and splash, so be careful when stirring).

3 Spoon apple butter into blender in small batches and blend (with center part of blender cover removed to allow steam to escape) until smooth.

4 Spoon apple butter into jars or crocks for gift giving. Store tightly covered in refrigerator for up to 3 weeks. Makes about 4½ cups.

Each tablespoon: About 30 calories, 0 g protein, 8 g carbohydrate, 0 g total fat, 0 mg cholesterol, 0 mg sodium.

INDEX

CREDITS

Cover: Ann Stratton. Page 7: Alan Richardson. Page 8 (all): Steve Wisbauer. Page 9 (top): David Hamsley. Page 9 (bottom): Richard Mitchell. Page 10: David Hamsley. Page 11 (top): Nedjeliko Matura. Page 11 (bottom): Ann Stratton. Page 12 (top): Steven Mark Needham. Page 12 (bottom): Steve Wisbauer. Page 13: David Hamsley. Page 14 (illustration): Christine Haberstock. Page 15 (top): Ann Stratton. Page 15 (bottom): Alan Richardson. Page 16: David Hamsley. Page 17 (top): David Hamsley. Page 17 (bottom): Steve Wisbauer. Page 18: David Hamsley. Page 20: Angelo Caggiano. Page 22: Jonelle Weaver. Page 24: Ann Stratton. Pages 26 and 29: Angelo Caggiano. Pages 32 and 34: Ann Stratton. Page 37: Jonelle Weaver. Page 41: Ann Stratton. Page 42: Mark Thomas. Page 44: Ann Stratton. Page 46: Mark Thomas. Page 49: Michael Grand. Page 53: Steven Mark Needham. Pages 56 and 63: Mark Thomas. Pages 65 and 67: Ann Stratton. Page 68: Alan Richardson. Page 73: Steven Mark Needham. Pages 74 and 77: Mark Thomas. Pages 81 and 82: Steven Mark Needham. Pages 84 and 87: Ann Stratton. Page 88: Kenneth Chen. Page 91: Ann Stratton. Pages 93, 95, 96, and 98: Beatriz Da Costa. Page 101: Ann Stratton. Page 104: Jonelle Weaver. Page 108: Mark Thomas. Page 112: Alan Richardson. Page 114: Mark Thomas. Pages 119, 123, and 127: Ann Stratton. Page 131: Steven Mark Needham. Pages 133 and 134: Ann Stratton. Page 136: Angelo Caggiano. Page 141: Ann Stratton. Page 144: Alan Richardson. Page 148: Ann Stratton. Pages 151, 152, and 160: Mark Thomas. Pages 162, 167, and 168: Brian Hagiwara. Pages 172, 174, 177, and 181: Mark Thomas. Page 183 (both): Alan Richardson. Page 184: Steven Mark Needham. Page 189: Ann Stratton. Page 190: Steven Mark Needham. Page 195: Alan Richardson. Page 196: Peter Ardito. Pages 199, 200, 203, 207, and 211: Ann Stratton. Page 214: Alan Richardson. Pages 218, 221, 225, 226, 230, 233, and 237: Mark Thomas. Page 239: Deborah Denker. Pages 240 and 244: Ann Stratton.